China
and the Foreign Powers:

The Impact of
and Reaction to
Unequal Treaties

BOOKS IN ENGLISH BY WILLIAM L. TUNG

China and Some Phases of International Law (1940)

Cases and Other Readings on International Law (1940)

The Political Institutions of Modern China (1964)

International Law in an Organized World (1968)

International Organization under the United Nations System (1969)

China and the Foreign Powers (1970)

CHINA
AND
THE FOREIGN POWERS:

THE IMPACT OF
AND REACTION TO
UNEQUAL TREATIES

By

William L. Tung

Professor of Political Science
Queens College, The City University of New York

1970

Oceana Publications, Inc.
Dobbs Ferry, New York

Library of Congress Catalog Card Number: 71-127328
International Standard Book Number: 0-379-00463-1

Manufactured in the united States of America

To Men and Women Working for
Sovereign Equality
for All Nations

PREFACE

This book deals with China's foreign relations from the middle of the nineteenth century to the present time, with special emphasis on the impact of and reaction to unequal treaties. As a result of military and diplomatic setbacks since the 1840's, China's weakened position had led to the imposition of many harsh and inequitable terms by foreign powers. These included the cession and lease of territories, division of spheres of influence, stationing of foreign warships and armed forces, opening of ports and inland navigation, establishment of foreign concessions and settlements, enforcement of extraterritorial jurisdiction and uniform tariffs, as well as acquisition of railway, mining, and other economic concessions. Through the use of force and other aggressive measures, several powers not only detached China's former dependencies but also intruded into her border regions.

Although China's troubles were partly due to her own impotence, the Chinese attitude toward foreign powers in recent decades has had much to do with the national humiliation endured during the past century. This is the thesis of my present work. It begins with an analytical description of the substance of these unequal treaties, followed by a summary of China's endeavors to rectify the long-standing injustices at the Paris Peace Conference of 1919 and the Washington Conference of 1921-1922. The discussion includes popular reaction to foreign encroachments as evidenced by various student movements and mass demonstrations. Particular emphasis is laid on the efforts of the National Government to terminate the aforesaid rights and privileges unilaterally enjoyed by foreign powers in China. The last part of the book describes China's national aspirations, including recovery of lost territories, consolidation of border regions, demarcation of national boundaries, and reassertion of her influence in Asia and beyond.

To every action there is a reaction. This study attempts to explain the underlying causes of the anti-imperialistic policies of Chinese political parties and the basic reasons for the present hostility of Communist China to the Soviet Union and the United States. While relations between China and foreign powers were not established on the principle of equality and reciprocity, it has been my serious intention to treat the subject with fairness and objectivity.

The scope of this work necessitates the discussion of China's foreign relations conducted by the Manchu Court, the Peking government prior to 1928, the National Government in Canton, Wuhan, Nanking, and Taipei, as well as the Communist government in Peking after 1949. This undertaking might invite the displeasure of those whose emotional attitudes resulting from civil war would not tolerate any objective analysis of the regime in opposition. It must be emphasized, however, that, despite my own political convictions, factual description for the purpose of academic research does not imply personal approval or disapproval of their performances.

The sources of this book are largely drawn from official documents, particularly treaties with and concerning China. A special Index of Treaties is thus provided in addition to the Subject Index. For the convenience of Western readers, works in English are cited wherever available. The Bibliographical Note gives an analytical explanation of important references.

In preparing this book, I am most appreciative of the kindness and generosity of my friend and former colleague, Dr. Raymond L. Carol, Professor and Chairman of the Department of Political Science of St. John's University, New York, who has diverted much of his own research time to editing my manuscript. My special indebtedness is to Professor Chaoying Fang of Columbia University for his valuable comments and suggestions, particularly on the first chapter. I am also grateful to many of my friends and former colleagues in government and diplomatic services of China and several other countries, who have generously relayed to me many valuable experiences relating to various topics presently under discussion but choose not to be quoted.

For an intermittent period of two years, Queens College and The City University of New York made available to me the part-time services of two graduate assistants: Mrs.

Roslyn Kaplan and Mr. Sanford Balsan. I wish to express my deep appreciation to the administrators of the two institutions for this thoughtful arrangement, and to Mrs. Kaplan for her valuable editorial assistance and Mr. Balsan for his preliminary investigation of certain aspects of the subject. My gratitude to my wife, Portia, is beyond expression, for her critical review of the manuscript and painstaking check of bibliographical materials. While extending my sincere thanks to all who have contributed to the completion of this book, I am solely responsible for statements of facts and views.

W. L. T.

Jamaica Hills, New York

TABLE OF CONTENTS

Chapter 7. WESTERN RESPONSE TO CHINA'S APPEAL AT
THE WASHINGTON CONFERNECE (1921-1922)

LIST OF TABLES AND ILLUSTRATIONS

MAP OF CHINA

CHRONOLOGICAL CHART OF CHINESE HISTORY*

Hsia	c. 21st - 17th century B.C.
Shang	c. 17th – 11th century B.C.
Chou	c. 11th century – 221 B.C.
Spring and Autumn Period	770 – 475 B.C.
Warring States Period	475 – 221 B.C.
Ch'in	221 – 206 B.C.
Han	206 B.C. – A.D. 220
Western (or Former) Han	206 B.C. – A.D. 24
Eastern (or Later) Han	25 – 220
Three Kingdoms	220 – 265
Tsin	265 – 420
Southern and Northern Dynasties	420 – 589
Sui	589 – 618
T'ang	618 – 907
Five Dynasties	907 – 960
Sung	960 – 1279
Northern Sung	960 – 1127
Southern Sung	1127 – 1279
Yuan (Mongols)	1279 – 1368
Ming	1368 – 1644
Ch'ing (Manchus)	1644 – 1912
Republic	1912 –

---

*For Chinese history prior to Hsia Dynasty, see Chi-yun Chang, <u>Chinese History of Fifty Centuries</u> (Taipei, 1962), Vol. I, which covers the periods of Fu Hsi, Shen Nung, Hung Ti, Yao, and Shun.

Chapter 1
INTRODUCTION

I. CHINA'S TRADITIONAL ATTITUDE TOWARD FOREIGN
   COUNTRIES AND PEOPLES

1. Relations with Other States

China has been predominant on the Asiatic mainland due
to her vast area, immense manpower, and high civilization.
For centuries, some neighboring princes recognized the
Chinese Emperor's unique position as the Son of Heaven and
maintained a tribute-trade relationship with the Middle Kingdom for mutual benefit.[1] In return, they also received some
noble titles from the Emperor and, on certain occasions,
his protection in case of internal or external difficulties.
While such a relationship was not established on an equal
basis, the tributary system differed from modern imperialism or colonialism in that China merely claimed suzerainty
over these states without the intention of exploiting their
economic or other resources.[2]

The virtues of kindness, tolerance, fraternity, and
pacifism, as advocated by Confucius and Mencius,[3] were not
necessarily followed by the Chinese rulers, many of whom
resorted to diplomatic and forcible means to expand their
domains.[4] But, like all great empires in the world, the
Chinese dynasties were also subject to cyclical prosperity
and decline. Sometimes, the nomads from the north took
advantage of China's weakness and engaged in military adventures to threaten her national security.[5] From the time
of her first unification by Shih Huang-ti of the Ch'in dynasty
(221-206 B.C.), China had been on the defensive militarily
toward the northern nomads. As a matter of fact, the imperial army succeeded in penetrating into the steppes only

1

during three periods, under the Han emperor Wu-ti (140-87 B.C.), the founders of the Ming dynasty from 1368 to 1424, and the early Manchu emperors in the seventeenth and eighteenth centuries.[6] On several occasions, the northern nomads even occupied China for certain periods of time, but, in most cases, the captors eventually became the captured through assimilation chiefly because of the larger population and higher civilization of the Chinese.

Whereas a number of Asian states, notably Korea and Annam, had been dominated by China at one time or another, cross-fertilization of cultures with other countries also took place, especially during the T'ang dynasty (618-907). More than six hundred new Sanskrit books were then brought to Chang-an from India;[7] Buddhism had since become popular among the populace. China extended her welcome to Japanese envoys and students, and introduced Chinese culture and Buddhism to that insular nation in the Pacific.[8] In the West, the Roman Empire was highly regarded by the Chinese and was mentioned in The History of the Later Han.[9] It is clear, therefore, that China's foreign relations even at the peak of her power were not limited to the tributary system. The exorbitant claims of superiority by the Manchu authorities in recent times could be attributed to their unawareness of the advancement of science, technology, and weaponry in the Western countries.

2. Conception of Aliens in General

In comparison with other countries, China has treated aliens fairly well notwithstanding some exceptional incidents. During the T'ang dynasty, many Japanese students came to Chang-an. Nestorian missionaries were received with due consideration by Chinese officials and people, and were allowed to preach and practice the Christian religion. Foreign traders, including Arabs, Persians, and Indians prospered in Chinese ports.[10] The courtesy and generosity that the imperial court of the Yuan dynasty extended to Marco Polo has been well known in the West. The Jesuits came to China during the last decades of the Ming dynasty and were permitted to spread Christianity over the land. [11]

Much misunderstanding about the Chinese conception of aliens was caused by the translation of the Chinese character 'yi' into 'barbarians'. Actually, the character has, at least, nine meanings. In designating a non-Chinese, it signifies only the origin of the person as having come from the east.[12] In their communications, however, Manchu officials did use the word to imply less civilized peoples from foreign lands. Because the misconception of this character invited Western displeasure, the use of the character 'yi' to represent foreigners has since been dropped from official correspondence.[13]

3. Contempt for Trade and Traders

In traditional China, trade and traders commanded little respect from Chinese society. Among the four standard professions in China, trade was considered the lowest stratum. People engaging in these professions were ranked in the following order: scholars, farmers, artisans, and traders. China's historical contempt for trade had also been reflected in her attitude toward foreign traders.

Furthermore, the conduct of early traders from the West failed to give China a good impression, because "a want of regard for Chinese laws characterized the foreigners who went to China in the seventeenth and eighteenth centuries." In the opinion of a keen observer, "they were either adventurers or desperate characters, and, with the exception of a few missionaries, they were all animated by the sole desire to seek fortunes in a new land." [14] With respect to personal attitudes, Martin Kieffer commented that the Chinese "proved frequently more tolerant and broad-minded than Westerners." In analyzing the difficulty of establishing normal relationships between China and the West, he deemed that "the Westerners could indeed blame their greed and arrogance at least as much as the unreceptive mood of the Chinese who, after all, wished only to be left alone." [15]

International trade is developed as a consequence of gradual interdependence among different peoples and nations, and, under international law, should not be arbitrarily enforced without the mutual consent of the parties concerned. In the exercise of the right of sovereignty, China, like any other State, may decide to permit, encourage, restrict, or prohibit foreign trade. Although unusually severe restrictions in this regard will be resented by the state or states adversely affected, any measure of retaliation must be carried out with a due sense of proportion. Neither international law nor reason and morality can justify the use of force to acquire or promote commercial privileges. [16]

II. EARLY ATTEMPTS TO TRADE WITH CHINA

1. Arrival of Western Traders in China

In the exploration of new opportunities in remote regions of the world, Western missionaries sometimes even preceded the traders. The arrival of Christian missionaries in China has already been described.[17] Among Western traders the Portuguese came to China first; they were allowed to pursue commercial activities with the Chinese in three designated ports for almost three decades (1517-1545). Due to public indignation for various reasons, their trade was later restricted to Macao, a Chinese port south of Canton. By 1557, they were permitted to settle in Macao and conduct periodic trade with Canton.[18]

Other Europeans were equally anxious to seek fortunes in the Celestial Empire, and did not want to lag behind. Within the following decades, nationals from Spain, England, and Holland undertook business adventures in China,[19] but their trade was limited to the port of Canton under strict regulations and supervision of local officials. Much to the satisfaction of the Emperor, the Dutch emissaries sent to Peking in 1655 complied with all the required rites and ceremonies of the Manchu Court.[20]

2. Early Sino-Russian Treaties on Trade and Frontier Matters

Whereas most Western nationals came to China via sea, Russians traveled by overland routes to the Chinese border to exchange goods with local inhabitants. Formal permission to trade was, however, not granted by the Emperor in spite of the requests of several Czarist emissaries during the period 1654-1676.[21] The failure of these missions was largely due to their refusal to 'kotow', an imperial ceremony of audience in the Chinese Court requiring kneelings and prostrations, which were more complicated than the bow or curtsy as practiced in the West. Arrogance might have been the reason for China's insistence on this traditional ceremony. On the other hand, non-conformity with Chinese court protocols by Western emissaries also contributed to the delay in establishing diplomatic relations with China.

The failure of Russian missions to reach an agreement with China on trade and frontier matters was followed by a serious border conflict. The Russian advance to the Amur region during the middle of the seventeenth century eventually led to an armed confrontation at Albazin with Chinese troops in 1685-1686, but both countries desired peaceful settlement of boundary disputes and normalization of trade relations. The Treaty of Nerchinsk, concluded on August 27, 1689,[22] was the first treaty between China and a Western power. Consisting of six articles, the treaty provided for Russian evacuation of Albazin,[23] demarcation of boundaries,[24] extradition of fugitives,[25] and permission to subjects of both countries to cross the frontier for private and business reasons.[26] This treaty was negotiated on the basis of equality and reciprocity.

Normal relations between China and Russia then lasted for over a century. Treaties for further regulation of boundaries, trade, and frontier matters were concluded in 1727, 1768, and 1792.[27] As a consequence of boundary demarcation, China actually lost a sizable area of border land to Russia.[28] After the Opium War, Russia followed England and France in adopting coercive measures against China, jointly or independently, for the advancement of territorial and commercial interests.

3. Failure of Three British Missions

England traded intermittently with Amoy and Formosa (Taiwan) from 1670 to 1688. At that time, Formosa was already incorporated into China Proper under Manchu rule.

Since the second quarter of the eighteenth century, the British East Indian Company had diverted its attention to the Canton trade. The Macartney mission sent by the English government was received in Peking with courtesy and hospitality in 1793.[29] In audience with the Emperor, the ambassador was even permitted to bend on one knee in lieu of 'kotow', but his petition for more trade ports was refused.[30]

During the Anglo-American War, 1812-1814, a British warship, the H.M.S. Doris, violated Chinese neutrality by bringing captured prizes to Macao and seizing an American ship at Whampoa in April-May 1814.[31] This incident led to an immediate protest from the Chinese government and resulted in serious friction. In order to remove past grievances so as to establish normal trade relations, the British government dispatched Ambassador Amherst to China in 1816. Because of his refusal to accept some ceremonial arrangements with respect to an immediate audience after his arrival in Peking, the Amherst mission returned to Canton without accomplishing anything.[32]

In Canton, Chinese merchants maintained their interests through local guilds (co-hong). In order to avoid incurring heavy debts to foreign traders as happened in the 1780's, only thirteen guilds were designated by the government to conduct foreign trade. After the British government terminated the East Indian Company's monopoly of the China trade in 1834, Lord Napier was appointed chief superintendent for the control of English trade in Canton.[33] Because of non-compliance with the Chinese regulations on trade and residence then prevailing in Canton, Lord Napier created serious friction with local authorities[34] In September, he left for Macao in complete disappointment. [35]

III. THE INITIATION AND CONSEQUENCES OF UNEQUAL
      TREATIES

1. The War Setting the Precedent for Unequal Treaties

After the failure of the three British missions to establish normal trade relations and as a consequence of China's

strong objection to the illicit traffic of opiu.
decided to use force for a final settlement i
called Opium War was terminated by the Tr
of August 29, 1842. While the events leadin
conflict and details of the treaty will be di
following chapter, it is important at this junctu   ᵤss
briefly the relative responsibilities of the two Lᵤuntries for
the war, which set the precedent for unequal treaties in China.

8

In the Opium War, China suffered the first humiliating
defeat from a Western power.36 British public opinion on
this war was divided. The government opposition raised
strong objections to fighting for a vicious and illicit trade.
William E. Gladstone condemned it vigorously: "A war more
unjust in its origin, a war more calculated to cover this
country with permanent disgrace, I do not know and have not
read of."37 In his judgment, the war was "to protect an infamous contraband traffic."38 On the other hand, the support-
ers argued that a war would be fought anyway for the normalization of diplomatic and commercial relations as well as
for the protection of British lives and property and that the
controversy over opium smuggling constituted only an immediate cause of hostilities. Nonetheless, debate in British Parliament at that time was almost entirely concerned with the
opium traffic.39

China should also share the blame for the commencement
of this unnecessary war. Due to its contemptuous attitude
toward the West, the Manchu Court insisted on maintaining
China's isolation and refused to establish normal relations
with Western powers. Although every nation may exercise
its sovereign right to lay down trade regulations and to
prohibit the import of certain commodities, the Chinese
officials should have handled the situation with utmost civility
and tact, especially in their dealings with foreign traders.40
Weakened by inefficient and corrupt administration and unprepared for an external war against a modern power, the
Chinese government should have resorted to every peaceful
means to reach an agreement with the British authorities.
Lacking knowledge of the Western world and unwilling to
treat other states on an equal footing, the Manchu Court
brought China misfortunes with far-reaching consequences.

2. The Impact on China's Territorial Sovereignty

International treaties are concluded generally on a reciprocal basis for the execution of certain rights and obligations between contracting parties. They may appear under different titles, such as agreements, conventions, arrangements, protocols, declarations, regulations, final acts, and exchange of notes,[41] but the principle of equality is normally the guiding rule of their provisions. Contrary to standard practice, many of China's treaties with foreign powers were unequal in nature, unilaterally benefitial to the latter at the expense of the former.[42] The Sino-British treaty, signed in Nanking on August 29, 1842, for the termination of the Opium War, set the precedent for other states to impose harsh and humiliating terms on China.[43] Similar provisions were embodied in the Sino-American and Sino-Franco treaties of 1844.[44] By the application of the most-favored-nation clause, sixteen other countries also obtained unilateral rights and privileges in China.[45]

Through diplomatic pressures and the use of force, several powers forced China to disclaim her traditional positions in former dependencies, cede and lease strategic parts of her territories, and assign specific areas in Chinese ports and cities as foreign concessions and settlements. Acting individually, Great Britain, Russia, and Japan penetrated deeply into Tibet, Sinkiang, Outer Mongolia, and Manchuria. Joined by Germany and France, they simultaneously claimed different regions of China as their spheres of influence. Leaseholds were arbitrarily transferred from one power to another without previous consent of the lessor. Within a few decades, the Chinese empire was on the verge of dismemberment.[46]

In addition to territorial acquisitions, foreign powers also exacted many unilateral rights and privileges in China. These included the stationing of warships and armed forces, opening of ports and inland navigation, exercise of extraterritorial jurisdiction, enforcement of uniform tariff, operation of postal agencies and wireless stations, employment of foreign nationals in charge of maritime customs and postal administration, as well as concessions of railway construction, mining, and other enterprises. These special rights and privileges were most favorable to the foreign powers concerned, but extremely detrimental to China's national sovereignty, judicial and administrative integrity, as well as economic and industrial development.[47]   Non-reciprocal in form and substance, the aforesaid provisions were not extended to the Chinese government and people in the territories of the treaty powers. Consequently, the unequal treaties created a serious impact on the Chinese nation, psychologically and materially.

3. China's Reaction to Foreign Intrusions

The reaction of the Chinese people to foreign encroachments has been reflected in their long-standing grudges against imperialism and popular demand for modernization through reform and revolution.[48] Because of the impotence and corruption of the Manchu Court, the Ch'ing dynasty was overthrown in 1911. Notwithstanding domestic turmoil during the early republican period, the Peking government took steps to revise or abolish the unequal treaties by multilateral appeal to the powers concerned. Failing completely to achieve this end at the Paris Peace Conference of 1919, China received a sympathetic response at the Washington Conference in 1921-1922. Through British and American good offices, a Sino-Japanese agreement was signed at Washington for the restoration of the former German rights in Shantung to China; but Western powers did not forthrightly support China's request to declare null and void Japan's Twenty-one Demands of 1915. Nor were the participating powers of the Conference willing to terminate immediately extraterritorial jurisdiction and restrictive tariff in China.[49]

The anti-imperialist movement, which flared up during the May Fourth Movement of 1919, spread further among the Chinese masses after the bloody incident of May 30, 1925.[50] China's resentment against imperialist holdings was demonstrated in the forcible taking over of British concessions in Hankow and Kiukiang during the course of the Northern Expedition. In this connection, credit must be given to the realistic policies of the United States and Great Britain in response to the rapid development of Chinese nationalism. It was largely due to their cooperation that China restored the right of tariff autonomy in 1928.[51]

For the abolition of extraterrritoriality and other unilateral privileges, the National Government resorted to bilateral

rather than multilateral approaches. [52] While negotiations
were in full swing, Japan invaded Manchuria on September 18,
1931, and followed with continuous aggressions against Shanghai and North China. Sino-Japanese conflicts eventually developed into full-scale hostilities on July 7, 1937. [53] The war
delayed but did not stop China's determination to terminate
unequal treaties. On January 11, 1943, China simultaneously
concluded new treaties with the United States and Great
Britain, and with other states soon afterward, thus abolishing all their unilateral rights and privileges previously described. [54]

Unfortunately, the Yalta Agreement on the Far East, secretly agreed upon by the leaders of the Soviet Union, the United States, and Great Britain in February 1945, forced China to
grant territorial, political, and economic concessions to Moscow, without previous consultation with the Chinese government. The betrayal by these wartime allies in this particular
respect caused damaging effects on postwar China and has
been deeply resented by the Chinese.[55] The injustice done to a
close ally in violation of all the basic principles of international law and morality was unparalleled in modern history. Once
again, the Western powers inflicted new wounds to a resurgent
nation, which had just wiped out a century of humiliations.

A succession of misfortunes has befallen China again. Externally bound by the Yalta Agreement, the nation has further
suffered a prolonged civil strife between the Nationalists and
Communists after World War II. Since October 1, 1949, the
People's Republic in Peking has been challenging the legitimate
authority of the National Government which now retreated to
Taiwan. A nation unable to speak with one voice is easy prey
in the international community, and an object of contempt to
those Westerners who have long held a sense of superiority
over non-Westerners.[56] It is important to note, however, that,
despite disagreements on domestic issues, the Chinese are in
unison with respect to the recovery of Chin'a lost territories
and reassertion of her rightful position in the world.[57] Western statesmen of the 1970's, who still have a vivid memory
of the wanton destruction of imperialism in the past and are
aware of the reasons for China's strong reaction to foreign
agression, will probably refrain from repeating former mistakes by taking advantage of her current adversities.

On the other hand, the Chinese should not have forgotten that most of the troubles of their nation were caused by its own weakenesses and that Western ideas and technology had contributed much to its modernization. The external difficulties confronting China today are due partly to the legacy of imperialism and partly to the adverse effects of her internal disunity. For the fulfillment of her long-sought objectives, China must forsake her extreme attitude of enmity to all and friendship to none,[58] and should rely on pacific means to settle outstanding disputes with other states. Meanwhile, since China today is no longer a slumbering dragon, the powers concerned had better change their basic attitudes from contempt and fear to positive cooperation.[59] The following chapters will fully reveal the long-standing grievances and unfulfilled aspirations of the Chinese nation and people.

NOTES TO CHAPTER 1

1. Among the tributaries to the Chinese Empire during the Ch'ing dynasty, as officially recorded in the Ta-Ch'ing Hwei-tien, were the following: Korea, once in four years; Ryukyu (Liuchiu), twice in three years; Annam, once in two years; Laos, once in ten years; Siam, once in three years; Sulu, once in five years; and Burma, once in ten years. See also R. Montgomery Martin, China: Political, Commercial, and Social (London, 1847, 2 vols.) I, p. 264; John K. Fairbank and S.Y. Teng, "On the Ch'ing Tributary System," Harvard Journal of Asian Studies, Vol. 6 (1941), pp. 135-246; Mar Mancall, "The Ch'ing Tributary System: An Interpretation," in John K. Fairbank (ed.), The Chinese World Order: Traditional China's Foreign Relations (Cambridge, 1968), pp. 63-89.

2. For further discussion of suzerainty, see William L. Tung, International Law in an Organizing World (New York, 1968), pp. 45-46.

3. The Chou dynasty (c. 11th century-221 B.C.) produced the most distinguished philosophers of China. Besides Confucius and Mencius, there were the following: Lao Tzŭ, a contemporary of Confucius, emphasizing simplicity and primitiveness; Mo Tzŭ, advocating universal brotherhood; Hsün Tzŭ, expounding humanistic ideas of Confucius with modifications; Han Fei Tzŭ, upholding legalism; and still others who all lived during the Spring and Autumn Period (770-475 B.C.) and the Warring States period (475-221 B.C.).

4. For instance, Ch'in Shih Huang-ti, Han Wu-ti, T'ang T'ai-tsung, Ming Ch'êng-tsou, as well as K'ang-hsi and Ch'ien-lung of the Ch'ing dynasty.

5. Among the northern invaders were the Hsiung-nu during the early period of the Han dynasty; the Liao and the Chin during the Sung dynasty; the Mongols and the Manchus, who established the Yuan and the Ch'ing dynasties respectively.

6. For a summary of these military operations, see L. Carrington Goodrich, A Short History of the Chinese People (New York, 1963), pp. 37-39, 189-190; Kenneth Scott Latourette, A Short History of the Far East (New York, 3rd ed., 1957), pp. 101-102, 136, 143-144.

7. Now named Sian, Chang-an was China's capital for many centuries. Yuan Tsung, a renowned Chinese monk, went to India to collect these books, which were later translated by him into Chinese.

8. Japan's geographical location made her secure from attempted invasions by the Mongols in 1274 and 1281.

9. In that book, the Roman Empire was called Ta (great) Ch'in (the Chinese dynasty under which the country was reunified after the turmoil of the Warring States period). The use of these two Chinese characters to describe the Romans implied high respect for the country and people. See Hung-chu Wu, "China's Attitude towards Foreign Nations and Nationals Historically Considered," Chinese Social and Political Science Review, Vol 10 (1926), p. 22. While recognizing that the name Ta Ch'in was particularly used to refer to the West, Wolfgang Franke was not sure of the exact location of that country. See his China and the West (translated by R.A. Wilson; Columbia, S.C., 1967), p. 4. It seems, however, that a silk route at times did serve as a link between China and Rome.

10. See Hung-chu Wu, op. cit., p. 27.

11. In 1605, there were more than two hundred converts in Peking. As early as 1322, Friar Jordanus, the Dominican, came to China after he was compelled to leave Bombay. For the Franciscans in China, see Henry Yule, Cathay and the Way Thither (London, 1913-1916, 4 vols.), I, p. 171.

12. According to Tz'ŭ Yuan, a standard Chinese dictionary, the character 'yi' denotes the following meanings: (1) safe; (2) pleasant; (3) class; (4) hurt; (5) great; (6) extinguish; (7) exhibit; (8) normalcy; and (9) east, designating foreign countries in the east, and hence broadened to mean foreign countries, and applied to foreigners in general. See its 1915th edition, published by the Commercial Press, Shanghai, Vol. 1, Section Ch'ou, pp. 239-240.

13. Art. LI of the Sino-British Treaty of June 26, 1858 stipulated that "henceforth the character 'I' [yi] shall not be applied to the Government or subjects of Her Britannic Majesty, in any Chinese official document issued by the Chinese authorities either in the capital or in the provinces." For the text of the Treaty, see the Statistical Department of the Inspector General of the Chinese Maritime Customs, Treaties and Conventions between China and Foreign States (2nd ed., Shanghai, 1917, 2 vols.; hereafter cited as Chinese Customs, Treaties), I, pp. 404-421; Hertslet, Treaties, etc., between Great Britain and China; and between China and Foreign Powers; and Orders in Council, Rules, Regulations, Acts of Parliament, Decrees, etc., Affecting British Interests in China (edited by Edward Hertslet; 3rd ed. by Godfrey E. P. Hertslet; London, 1908, 2 vols.; hereafter cited as Hertslet, Treaties), I, pp. 18-35.

14. V. K. Wellington Koo, The Status of Aliens in Chine (new York, 1912; hereafter cited as Koo), p. 64. Koo's view was shared by several early writers on China, including John Francis Davis and S. Wells Williams.

15. Martin Kieffer's Preface to Roger Pelissier, The Awakening of China, 1793-1949 (edited and translated by Kieffer; New York, 1967), p. 14.

16. See L. Oppenheim, International Law: A Treatise (edited by H. Lauterpacht; London, 2 vols.; Vol. I, 8th ed., 1955; Vol. II, 7th ed., 1952), II, pp. 134-135; William L. Tung, International Law in an Organizing World, pp. 382-383. Due to her self-sufficiency and traditional contempt for traders, China did not consider foreign trade as important as Western free traders, who "could never understand why the Chinese government restricted its merchants' trade." John K. Fairbank, Trade and Diplomacy on the China Coast: The Opening of the Treaty Ports 1842-1854 (Cambridge, 1953, 2 vols.), I, p. 74.

17. See supra, p. 2 and note 11.

18. For early Portuguese attempts to trade with China and their settlement in Macao, see Hosea Ballou Morse, The International Relations of the Chinese Empire (New York, 1910-1918 3 vols.; hereafter cited as Morse), I, pp. 42-44; Teh-ch'ang Chang, "Maritime Trade at Canton During the Ming Dynasty," Chinese Social and Political Science Review, Vol. 17 (1933-1934), pp. 264-282. For China's first direct contact with the West during the Yuan dynasty, see Edwin O. Reischauer and John K. Fairbank, East Asia: The Great Tradition (Vol. I of A History of East Asian Civilization; Boston, 1960), pp. 284-285.

19. For further information on the early arrival of Europeans in China, see John K. Fairbank, Edwin O. Reischauer, and Albert M. Craig, East Asia: The Modern Transformation (Vol. II of A History of East Asian Civilization: Boston, 1965), pp. 15-30; L. Carrington Goodrich, op. cit., pp. 219-220; Wolfgang Franke, op cit., pp. 19-22, 27-33.

20. See S. Wells Williams, The Middle Kingdom: A Survey of the Geography, Government, Literature, Social Life, Arts, and History of the Chinese Empire and Its Inhabitants (New York, 1907, 2 vols.), II, pp. 435, 438.

21. These included the Baikoff mission in 1654, Perfilieff and Ablin in 1660, Milovanoff in 1670, and Spathary in 1676. For

details, see Vincent Chen, <u>Sino-Russian Relations in the Seven-teenth Century</u> (The Hague, 1966), pp. 48-75.

22. This treaty was written in Chinese, Russian, Latin, English, and French. For its text, see Chinese Customs, <u>Treaties</u>, I, pp. 3-13; Hertslet, <u>Treaties</u>, I, pp. 437-439. See also biographies of Sabsu and Songgotu by Chaoying Fang in A. W. Hummel (ed.), <u>Emminent Chinese of the Ch'ing Period</u> (Washington, D.C., 2 vols., 1943-1944), I, pp. 630-631, 664-665.

23. Art. III.

24. Arts. I, II.

25. Arts. IV, VI.

26. Art. V.

27. For their texts, see Chinese Customs, <u>Treaties</u>, I, pp. 14-69; Hertslet, <u>Treaties</u>, I, pp. 439-449.

28. Particularly through the Treaty of Kiakhta of October 24, 1727. See Chaoying Fang, "Tulišen," in A. W. Hummel, <u>op. cit.</u>, I, pp. 784-787; <u>infra</u>, Ch. 11, note 75.

29. See Peter Auber, <u>China: An Outline of Its Government, Laws, and Policy</u> (London, 1834), p. 200.

30. See George L. Staunton, <u>An Authentic Account of An Embassy from the King of Great Britain to the Emperor of China</u> (London, 1798, 2nd ed., 2 vols.), II, pp. 144, 214, 232. For the Mandate of Emperor Ch'ien-lung to King George III, see Harley Farnsworth MacNair, <u>Modern Chinese History, Selected Readings</u> (Shanghai, 1927), pp. 2-9.

31. See John Francis Davis, <u>The Chinese: A General Description of the Empire of China and Its Inhabitants</u> (London, 1836, 2 vols.), I, p. 88; Peter Auber, <u>op. cit.</u>, pp. 241-250.

32. Ibid., p. 256; John Francis Davis, <u>Sketches of China</u> (London, 1841, 2 vols.), I, pp. 54-56, 151-155.

33. William John Napier was appointed on December 10, 1833; he did not arrive in Canton until July 25, 1834. Robert Morrison, an outstanding Sinologue, became his Chinese secretary and interpreter, but this learned missionary died on August 1, 1834.

34. For details of Lord Napier's failure, see Morse, I, Ch. VI. Among other things, the Chinese authorities charged him "with

of the laws of the empire (and we today should add, of of nations) in introducing arms and armed forces into une factories, and in firing on the forts and forcing a passage into the river." Ibid., I, p. 137.

35. The Chinese viceroy at Canton even ordered an embargo on British trade in September 1834. Lord Napier died in Macao on October 11, 1834.

36. For China's relations with foreign nations prior to the Opium War, consult Lo-shu Fu (ed.), A Documentary Chronicle of Sino-Western Relations, 1644-1820 (Tucson, 1967, 2 vols.). Pertinent information can also be found in T'ing-i Kuo (ed.), Chronological Records of the History of Modern China (in Chinese; Taipei, 1963, 2 vols.).

37. John Morley, Life of William Ewart Gladstone (New York, 1903, 3 vols.), I, p. 226.

38. Loc. cit.

39. In this respect, John Morley, Gladstone's biographer, made the following comment: "The Chinese question was the simplest. British subjects insisted on smuggling opium into China in the teeth of Chinese law." Ibid., p. 225.

40. Because of the immense profit derived from opium traffic, foreign traders were most reluctant to comply with the Chinese law and give it up. One American missionary made the following remark to Rev. W. H. Medhurst, D.D. in this connection: "This traffic is staining the British name in China with the deepest disgrace, as some of the subjects of Great Britain continue to carry on an armed contraband trade in a destructive poison, enriching themselves by merchandising that which impoverishes and murders the poor infatuated and besotted Chinese." According to Rev. Medhurst, however, American citizens were also involved in this illicit traffic, even though there were individual exceptions among the merchants of both nations. See North China Herald, November 10, 1855. It is important to note that the American Government did not intervene in the opium question on behalf of its nationals as the British had done. For further information on the Opium War, reference may be made to Edgar Hold, The Opium Wars in China (Chester Springs, Pa., 1964); Maurice Collis, Foreign Mud (New York, 1947); Arthur Waley, The Opium War through Chinese Eyes (New York, 1958); John K. Fairbank, Trade and Diplomacy on the China Coast: The Opening of the Treaty Ports 1842-1854, I, pp. 57-151.

41. For the terminology of treaties, see William L. Tung, International Law in an Organizing World, pp. 328-330.

42. For the complexity and injustice of China's treaty commitments, see Westel W. Willoughby, Foreign Rights and Interests in China (Baltimore, 1927, 2 vols.; hereafter cited as Willoughby), I, pp. 1-8.

43. See infra, pp. 20-21.

44. See infra, pp. 21-22.

45. They were Russia, Belgium, Germany, Portugal, Denmark, the Netherlands, Spain, Italy, Austria-Hungary, Japan, Peru, Brazil, Mexico, Switzerland, Norway and Sweden. See infra, pp. 23, 29-30, 75-83.

46. For a brief review of this tragic situation, see Roger Pelissier, The Awakening of China 1739-1949, pp. 193-229; Robert C. North, Moscow and Chinese Communists (Stanford, 1953), pp. 31-41. See also infra, pp. 20, 27, 45-50, 70-74.

47. See infra, pp. 74-75, 83-127. Undoubtedly, there was a basic conflict of interests between the Chinese and the Westerners with respect to the provisions of the unequal treaties, which were "admired by the old China hands and denounced by the young Chinese patriots." John K. Fairbank, Trade and Diplomacy on the China Coast: The Opening of the Treaty Ports 1842-1854, I, p. 114.

48. See, in particular, infra, pp. 145-154, 219-230, 297-300, 305-308, 313-319, 345-357, 404-410. A summary of China's reform and revolutionary movements can be found in Chien-nung Li, The Political History of China, 1840-1928 (translated and edited by Ssu-yu Teng and Jeremy Ingalls; Princeton, 1956), pp. 144-256; Harold M. Vinacke, A History of the Far East in Modern Times (6th ed., New York, 1959), pp. 205-226. Commenting on the contributions made by thousands of Chinese intellectuals who studied abroad, C. Martin Wilbur considered that "this group of leaders was the drawing force in nearly every aspect of the multifaceted process of China's modernization — military, technological, scientific, diplomatic, financial, political, ideological, and literary." His Preface to Y.C. Wang, Chinese Intellectuals and the West, 1872-1949 (Chapel Hill, 1966), p. v.

49. See infra, pp. 205-230, 239-284. For a brief review of China's diplomatic efforts at the Paris Peace Conference and the Washington Conference, see Harold M. Vinacke, op. cit., pp. 385-388, 414-436.

50. See infra, pp. 164-166, 231-232.

51. See infra, pp. 233-234, 254-257. For a summary of the Nation-
    alist struggle for equality among nations, see Franz H. Michael
    and George E. Taylor, The Far East in the Modern World (New
    York, 1964, rev. ed.), pp. 399-401.

52. See infra, pp. 249, 254-257.

53. See infra, pp. 257-268.

54. In China in Revolution: The First Phase 1900-1913 (New
    Haven, 1968), Mary C. Wright rightly observed that the re-
    covery of sovereign rights has been the watchword of new
    China ever since the turn of the century. See, in particular,
    pp. 4-19, 63. For China's eventual achievement of this ob-
    jective, see Harold M. Vinacke, op. cit., pp. 456-461; infra,
    pp. 268-270, 308-313, 319-324.

55. For details, see infra, pp. 270-271; Stephen C. Y. Pan, "Legal
    Aspects of the Yalta Agreement," American Journal of Inter-
    national Law, Vol. 46, No. 1 (January 1952), pp. 40-59.

56. According to Wolfgang Franke, author of China and the West,
    "an educated European in the 19th century knew far less about
    China than his predecessors in the 17th and 18th centuries,"
    and even many open-minded Europeans and Americans "were
    not always able to shake off their Western feeling of super-
    iority." English edition (translated by R.A. Wilson, Columbia,
    S.C., 1967), pp. 140, 144. Unfortunately, this observation still
    holds true for many Westerners today. After the Communist
    control of the mainland, commented by Franke, "the arrogant
    and superior attitude of the West toward China has increasingly
    given way in the last ten years to one of fear and hatred."
    Ibid., p. 149.

57. See infra, pp. 300-307 and pertinent sections in Chs. 10-12.

58. For China's bitter experience of standing alone in the 1930's in
    the face of Japan's invasion, see infra, pp. 237-238.

59. After analyzing China's traditional and present foreign policies,
    John K. Fairbank concluded that "the best way to stimulate
    Chinese expansion is for us to mount an over-fearful and over-
    active preparation against it." Fairbank, "China's Foreign
    Policy in Historical Perspective," Foreign Affairs, Vol. 47, No.
    3 (April 1969), p. 463. For basic objectives of China's foreign
    Policy, see also Charles P. Fitzgerald, The Chinese View of
    Their Place in the World (London, 1964), pp. 68-72.

Chapter 2

WESTERN DEMAND FOR TRADE AND OTHER PRIVILEGES THROUGH DIPLOMACY AND COERCION

I. THE IMPOSITION OF UNEQUAL TREATIES

1. The Opium War and the Treaty of Nanking

Opium smoking for other than medical purposes was prohibited by Emperor Yung-cheng in 1729, when foreign opium was first imported to China by Portuguese traders from Goa and Damán. By his edict of 1800, Emperor Chia-ch'ing forbade both importation and domestic cultivation of opium. Smuggling was prevalent, however, and became increasingly serious when English dealers carried Indian opium to Canton on a large scale.[1] Captain Charles Elliot, who assumed the office of British chief superintendent on December 14, 1836, supported the opium trade backed by force. The Chinese objection to the opium trade was not so much due to its drain of specie, but chiefly because of its destructive effect on the health of the people.[2]

When Lin Tse-su, the Imperial High Commissioner, arrived in Canton in March 1839, he ordered foreign merchants to give up all opium to the local government. The surrendered opium was eventually destroyed on the spot by order of an imperial rescript.[3] As illicit traffic of the drug continued, the Chinese authorities were compelled to enforce strict regulations governing foreign shipping. The new restrictions resulted in still more conflicts.

Sino-British relations were further complicated by Captain Elliot's violation of Chinese jurisdiction. On July 7, 1839, there was a clash between local residents and British sailors

19

on the Kowloon side of the Hongkong anchorage. According to judicial findings, the incident was occasioned by the sailors' attempt to obtain liquor. In the judgment of the court, it was "a shameful riot attended with unmanly outrage upon men, women, and children, and the loss of innocent life."[4] A Chinese national, Lin Wei-hi, died as a result of the riot. Captain Elliot took jurisdiction over the sailors involved and made compensation to the aggrieved villagers and to the family of the deceased. "In return he received an acknowledgment that the death was due solely to accident; but the Chinese authorities naturally treated this subornation of perjury." [5]

The Chinese authorities could not recognize British jurisdiction over the sailor who had murdered Lin Wei-hi and demanded his surrender. Considering the movement of Chinese war-junks a threat to its ships near Chuenpi,[6] the British navy started the preventive war by opening fire first and forced them to retreat with heavy damage and loss.[7] Then hostilities were extended along the Chinese coast.

To the Chinese, the main issue was the prohibition of the opium trade, the case of Lin Wei-hi regarded merely as an incident. The nation neither expected, nor prepared for, a full-scale war with England. After occupying Tinghai, Chusan, Canton, Hongkong, Amoy, Ningpo, Chinkiang, and other ports, England was in the position to dictate peace terms. The Manchu Court was finally compelled to conclude the Treaty of Nanking on board H.M.S Cornwallis, on August 29, 1842.[8]

The Treaty of Nanking of 1842 was the first international instrument by which a foreign power imposed unilateral terms on China; in this respect, Great Britain led the way for other countries. The importance of this treaty can be illustrated by its essential provisions:[9] (1) cession of Hongkong;[10] (2) opening of five ports, namely, Canton, Amoy, Foochow, Ningpo, and Shanghai, to British trade and residence as well as the stationing of consular officers;[11] (3) payment of an indemnity of twenty-one million dollars, including six million for the compensation of confiscated opium;[12] (4) abolition of cohong monopoly of foreign trade;[13] (5) equality of British and Chinese officials with corresponding rank in mutual communications;[14] and (6) establishment of a uniform tariff of export and import duties and other dues.[15] Thus, as a consequence

of the Opium War, England acquired from China all the concessions and privileges previously unobtainable through
diplomacy.

As the Treaty of Nanking was chiefly for the termination
of war, several important issues were left to be decided by
a Supplementary Treaty signed between the representatives
of the two countries on October 8, 1843. Generally known as
the Treaty of Hoomun Chai (The Bogue), [16] it provided for:
(1) grant of extraterritoriality and a uniform tariff of 5% ad
valorem as incorporated in the attached General Regulations; [17] (2) application of the most-favored-nation clause; [18] (3)
extradition of fugitives; [19] (4) right of residence and traveling
of British subjects at open ports, [20] (5) stationing of one English cruiser at each of these ports, [21] and (6) prevention of
smuggling and piracy. [22] All these important terms had serious
impacts on the Chinese situation, internally and externally.

No provision was made concerning opium trade in these two
treaties. Although the Chinese government was compelled to
pay for destroyed opium, compensation alone could by no means
be interpreted as legalizing this infamous traffic. It was said
that the demand for compensating confiscated opium represent-
ted an official recognition of opium traffic by the British Government. [23] Since the Chinese government never accepted its
legitimacy, however, Sir Henry Pottinger, the British plenipotentiary, warned his countrymen that they would receive no
protection in the opium trade. [24]

2. British Pattern Followed by
the United States and France

After the signing of the Treaty of Nanking, the United
States and France were anxious to obtain similar rights and
privileges from China by the establishment of treaty relations. Despite its late start, [25] American trade with Canton
advanced rapidly and ranked second only to the English by
the time of the Opium War. For the conclusion of a commercial
treaty, the United States government appointed Caleb Cushing, a Congressman from Massachusetts, as Envoy Extraordinary and Minister Plenipotentiary. He arrived in Macao on
February 24, 1844. By persuasion and threat, Cushing first
attempted to go to Peking for an audience. [26] Evidently unable
to do so, he finally reconciled himself to open negotiations

with the Chinese plenipotentiary at Wanghia, a Chinese village near Macao, on June 21. The first Sino-American treaty was signed on July 3, 1844.[27]

Following the general lines of the Treaty of Nanking, this American treaty embodied more details on commercial relations at the Chinese ports opened for foreign trade. Most-favored-nation treatment was stipulated,[28] but diplomatic representation was not mentioned. Upon the insistence of the American envoy,[29] extraterritoriality was explicitly granted.[30] The United States agreed not to render protection to American citizens engaging in opium and clandestine trade.[31] At the instance of American missionaries, certain rights not provided in the British treaties were extended to American citizens, including the building of churches and hospitals,[32] employment of Chinese scholars, and purchase of books,[33] most of these had not been expressly permitted before. This treaty was subject to revision by mutual consent after twelve years.[34] Uniform tariff and other rights and privileges were either expressly provided for in the treaty or automatically extended to the Americans through application of the most-favored-nation clause.

As early as 1660, French ships came to Canton, but their trade volume was comparatively small throughout the eighteenth century. A French officer in the capacity of consul to supervise French traders had been intermittently functioning there since 1802.[35] Soon after the signing of the Treaty of Wanghia, a French emissary, Monsieur Théodose M.M. J. de Lagrené arrived in Macao,[36] and started negotiations for a treaty. Following closely the American model, the first Sino-Franco treaty was signed on board the French warship, Archimède, at Whampoa, on October 24, 1844.[37] M. de Lagrené also obtained for France the special right to protect Roman Catholic missions in China through an imperial rescript of December 28, 1844.[38]

3. Similar Treaties Extended to Belgium, Sweden and Norway

Belgium attempted to follow the path of England, France, and the United States, but did not obtain a treaty. Through an imperial rescript of July 25, 1845, however, Belgium was granted trade privileges under the provisions of existing treaties.[39] On March 20, 1847, the representatives of the Emperor of China and the King of Sweden and Norway signed the Treaty of Commerce at Canton,[40] similar to the American Treaty of 1844.

At that time, there was no need for China to appease small nations; trade privileges in these cases were probably granted in order to prevent monopolies by the major powers. Before long, however, unilateral provisions of these treaties aroused deep resentment by the Manchu Court and the informed people of China, especially the Cantonese.

II. CHINA'S SUBMISSION TO ANGLO-FRANCO FORCES

1. Western Demands for Further Privileges through Treaty Revisions

Because of the Opium War, the people in Canton became intensely hostile to foreigners. The antagonism of local inhabitants compelled the English to defer their right of entry into the city,[41] for they could scarcely enjoy any security or advantage by the employment of forcible means.[42] Meanwhile, the British government had more important demands in mind. As stated before, the American and French treaties of 1844 provided for their possible revision at the end of twelve years. By applying the most-favored-nation clause, the Treaty of Nanking of 1842 could be revised in 1854. Other Western powers shared the same interest in seeking new privileges.

Toward this common goal, the British government stressed the following points: (1) to extend foreign trade to other parts of China, or at least to obtain free navigation of the Yangtze River and the opening of more ports; (2) to legalize the opium trade; (3) to abolish inland transit dues; and (4) to arrange residence of foreign envoys at Peking.[43] These proposals received support and cooperation from the American and French governments, but failed to secure Chinese consent for treaty revisions.[44] By that time, the Manchu Court realized that any revision would serve only the purpose of the West.

2. Anglo-Franco Joint Expedition and the Tientsin Treaties of 1858

Unsuccessful in achieving their ends through negotiations, Great Britain and France decided to use force against China after the termination of the Crimean War. The British found a convenient casus belli in the Arrow incident. This Chinese owned but Hongkong registered lorcha, while lying off Canton, was boarded by Chinese soldiers on October 8, 1856. With the purpose of arresting a notorious pirate of Chinese nationality, Li Ming-tai, twelve Chinese sailors were removed from the Arrow for investigation. The British consul challenged Chinese jurisdiction over the crew and protested against the alleged hauling down of the British flag on the ship.

The place of registration should be the determining factor of the lorcha's nationality and jurisdiction. It was later revealed, however, that the Arrow's registration at Hongkong had expired eleven days before the incident.[45] The Chinese authorities should have notified the British consul of their intended action, even though repression of piracy and extradition of fugitives were of common concern in accordance with the Sino-British Supplementary Treaty of 1843.[46] On the other hand, this incident alone was not so serious as to develop into war without ulterior motives on the part of the British.[47]

France's commercial interest in China was very limited, but, ever since 1844, she had obtained a special position to protect Catholic churches in China. From 1850 to 1864, a major part of the Chinese Empire was overrun by the Taiping Rebellion or Revolution, resulting in disorder and devastation in hundreds of cities and villages.[48] In Silian, a remote corner of Kwangsi province, where the insurrection started, a missionary named Auguste Chapdelaine was arrested and executed in February 1856. It was claimed that the local magistrate was involved in the murder. In reply to the French demand for redress, High Commissioner Yeh Ming-chin pointed out that mission work should be limited to five open ports in accordance with treaty provisions and that many missionaries took part in the revolt. This gave France an excuse to join England for a military expedition in order to obtain a satisfactory settlement of the case and chiefly to press for treaty revisions. Conceding that a state should be responsible for the act of a minor officer,[49] the resort to war as a measure of retaliation could not be justified.

Taking advantage of China's domestic insurrection, the Anglo-Franco forces had no difficulty in winning a quick victory. After conquering Canton and capturing High Commissioner Yeh in January 1858,[50] the Allied navy moved to the North, demolished the Taku forts, and took military occupation of Tientsin. While Russia and the United States stayed out of the war, their envoys followed their British and French colleagues for the conduct of negotiations with the Chinese plenipotentiaries in Tientsin.[51]

Considerably weakened by the large-scale civil war with no end in sight, China was compelled to sign treaties in 1858 with the four powers: Russia on June 13;[52] the United States on June 18,[53] England on June 26,[54] and France on June 27.[55] Through application of the most-favored-nation clause and with minor variations, the four treaties of Tientsin incorporated the essentials of the existing treaties and conferred new privileges, including residence of foreign envoys at the Capital,[56] opening of additional ports and the Yangtze River for foreign shipping up to Hankow, inland trade and travel through passports,[57] toleration of the Christian religion, and agreement on a new tariff to be drawn up.[58] In addition, China had to pay indemnities to England and France in accordance with separate articles attached to the treaties of Tientsin. [59] Having acquired these concessions from China, Western powers were determined to enforce treaty provisions to the fullest extent.

3. Anglo-Franco Second Expedition and the Peking Conventions of 1860.

By an imperial edict of July 3, 1858, the Emperor approved of the four Tientsin treaties, and the envoys were notified to that effect.[60] In the South, however, there was deep resentment against foreign intruders. The English and French forces frequently marched into the countryside to pacify areas far away from Canton, contrary to treaty provisions and rules of international law. Fortunately, no serious incidents were created by these expeditions. The imminent problem centered around the entry of the four envoys to Peking for the exchange of ratifications of the Tientsin treaties within one year.

The Chinese government had given notice to the envoys that they should come to Peking through Peitang or by routes other than the forbidden zone of the Peiho, where Taku fortifications were located. General Ignatieff of Russia arrived in Peking by way of Kiakhta, and exchanged ratifications with China at the end of May 1860. The American envoy, J. E. Ward, reached Peking by way of Peitang on June 28.[61] But, due to his unwillingness to comply with ceremonial requirements for audience, he decided to return from Peking to Peitang, where he exchanged ratifications with the Chinese representative on August 16, 1860.[62]

On the other hand, the English and French envoys insisted on coming to Peking up the Peiho, the passage of which was forbidden by the Chinese government. Admiral Sir James Hope, Commander of the British squadron, moved his ships to the mouth of the Peiho. On June 24, he sent an ultimatum to the shore authorities and started an attack on the following day. But the British suffered such heavy losses that even the admiral himself was wounded.[63] At that time, France was engaged in military operations in Annam. The English and French envoys asked their home governments for reinforcements to continue the war, even though the Chinese regarded it only as a local incident.[64] It is difficult to understand why the two envoys would not come to Peking as their American colleague had done, according to the route designated by the Chinese government. They had neither the need nor the right to employ warships to force their way, unless they were determined to find some excuses for further military ventures.

With the arrival of strong reinforcements, the Anglo-Franco froces resumed military operations in the North in August 1860. Within a month, they landed at Peitang, demolished the Taku forts, and entered into Tientsin. While still engaging in large-scale civil war against the Taiping Rebellion, the Manchu Court offered little resistance, and soon appointed plenipotentiaries to sue for peace. Peking surrendered on October 13, the Emperor and the Imperial family fled to Jehol. On October 18, the allied forces destroyed the Inperial Summer Palace, Yuenmingyuen, which had been thoroughly looted a few days before.[65] As this luxurious palace had no military value whatsoever, its looting and destruction failed to impress the Chinese with Western civility and discipline.

Entering the Captial in state, the English and French envoys signed separately with the Chinese plenipotentiary the Conventions of Peking on October 24 and October 25 respectively. Meanwhile, ratifications of the Tientsin Treaties of 1858 were exchanged. Similar in content and coming into effect immediately, these two conventions reaffirmed the residence of foreign diplomats in the Captial, increased the indemnity to Tls. 8,000,000 for each, and expressed deep regret on the part of the Chinese for the Taku misunderstanding.[66] China also ceded to England "that portion of the township of Kowloon in the province of Kwangtung," which had been previously leased in perpetuity to the latter.[67]

Russia proved again to be more skillful in diplomacy by gaining the most without the sacrifice of one man. Through the conclusion of boundary treaties at the time of China's distress, she had already acquired an immense portion of Chinese territory. Only two years before, China was compelled by circumstances to cede to Russia the left bank of the Amur down to the Ussuri in the Treaty of Aigun of May 16, 1858.[68] While England and France used force to exact favorable terms from China, General Ignatieff remained in Peking to render good offices and mediation. In return, he succeeded in pressuring the Chinese government to sign, on November 14, 1860, an Additional Treaty of Peking, by which China ceded to Russia a tremendous area between the Amur and the Ussuri rivers and the Sea of Japan.[69] Opposition to such highhanded demands would have been futile, while the nation was disrupted within and threatened without.

III. FURTHER EXTENSION OF UNEQUAL TREATIES

1. The Problem of Treaty Revision and
the Margary Affair

Ever since the ratification of the Tientsin Treaties of 1858, foreign privileges and influence had been well established in China. The British Treaty further provided that either of the contracting parties "may demand a further revision of the tariff, and of the commercial articles of this Treaty, at the end of ten years." [70] On the basis of this provision, a Supplementary Convention to the Treaty of Tientsin was signed on October 23, 1869. [71] However, because of the strong opposition by British merchants to several articles, especially those on appointment of Chinese consular officers in Hongkong and payment of one and one half duties on foreign woolen fabrics, [72] the British government failed to ratify this Convention.

After waiting for seven years, England found another opportunity for treaty revision in the Margary affair. To explore China's Southwest, the government of British India dispatched, an expedition under Colonel Horace A. Browne in 1874, [73] with a young consular officer, Augustus Raymond Margary, as an interpreter. On February 21 of the following year, Margary and five Chinese of his party were killed by a Chinese armed band at the frontier between Burma and Manyün in Yunnan province, where there had been a rebellion for almost two decades. [74]

Pending the ascertainment of facts, the British Minister, Sir Thomas Francis Wade, presented six demands to the Chinese government on March 19. Among these were the satisfaction of audience procedures, tariff, and other claims, which had no connection with the incident. [75] In spite of China's reasonable reply and her general disapproval of his extraneous demands, [76] Mr. Wade went so far as to deliver an ultimatum that the Chinese government must give satisfactory reply by September 29, 1876. In order to reach a peaceful settlement, the Chinese government appointed Li Hung-chang to negotiate with Mr. Wade at Chefoo, resulting in the conclusion, on September 13, 1876, of the Sino-British Agreement for the Settlement of the Yunnan Case, Official Intercourse, and Trade between the Two Countries. [77]

2.   The Sino-British Chefoo Agreement of 1876

This Agreement contained three sections and a separate article; only the first section concerned the settlement of the Yunnan case: (1) opening of Yunnan frontier trade; (2)   stationing of British officers at Talifu or other suitable place for a period of five years; (3) permission for a Mission from India into Yunnan; (4) payment of Tls. 200,000, to compensate the families of those killed, claims of British merchants, and of the expenses incurred; and (5) a Chinese mission to England for the expression of regret.[78] The second Section dealt with official intercourse, including the consideration of a code of etiquette, appointment of Chinese diplomatic and consular missions abroad, and further clarification of judicial procedure.[79] Revised regulations for trading were embodied in the third Section, concerning opium trade, customs and transit duties, opening of new ports, and the complaints of Hongkong.[80] A separate article was appended to the Agreement, granting a British mission of exploration to Tibet.

The representatives of other powers in China were not only critical of Mr. Wade's conduct of the negotiations, but also of the inclusion of official intercourse and trade matters, the execution of which depended also on their assent.[81] After its approval by the Emperor on September 17, 1876 China had fulfilled all the conditions in the Agreement. On the other hand, the British government took into consideration the unfriendly attitude of the interested powers and postponed its ratification for nine years.[82] Once again, the Chinese government was compelled to accept humiliating terms, this time on account of the murder of Margary, a minor officer in a remote region of the country.

3. Treaty Relations with Other Powers

In forcing China to grant trade and other advantages, England led the way; but the benefits so obtained were shared by other powers through the application of the most-favored-nation clause. From the signing of the Convention of Peking in 1860 to the British ratification of the Chefoo Agreement in 1885, ten more nations entered into treaty relations with China: Germany,[83] Portugal,[84] Denmark,[85] the Netherlands,[86] Spain,[87] Italy,[88] Austria-Hungary,[89] Japan,[90] Peru,[91] and Brazil.[92] Including Great Britain, the United States, France, Russia, Belgium, Norway and Sweden, there were sixteen in all.

Soon afterward, Mexico signed a commercial treaty with China on December 14, 1899.[93] By the Treaty of Amity of June 13, 1918 and the attached declaration, Switzerland was also entitled to the enjoyment of extraterritoriality and other privileges.[94] This was the only unequal treaty obtained by a small nation after the establishment of the Chinese Republic for the reason that China was then most anxious to send a diplomatic mission to that neutral country for the collection of information concerning the progress of World War I and the preparation for future peace. With the division of Norway and Sweden in 1905, there were altogether nineteen countries which had entered into unequal treaties with China. It would not be an easy task to negotiate for their abolition in years to come.

NOTES TO CHAPTER 2

1. The smuggling was carried out by English boats. So. "the deliveries of opium have frequently been accomp. conflict of fire-arms between those vessels and the g   .il- ment preventive craft." Captain Elliot to Lord Palmerston, April 20, 1838. Correspondence relating to China, 1840, p. 299.

2. See also Imperial High Commissioner Lin's proclamation of March 26, 1839. Chinese Repository (monthly, May 1832 – December 1851, Canton), April 1839.

3. The destruction of 20,291 chests of surrendered opium began on June 3, 1839. Although nationals of other countries were also involved in opium trade, "the opium surrendered in 1839, whether in English, Parsee, or American hands, was entirely British owned." Morse, I, pp. 208, 226. Further infor- mation about High Commissioner Lin and events leading to the first Sino-British war can be found in Hsin-Pao Chang, Com- missioner Lin and the Opium War (Cambridge, 1964); Ch'ung- yung Lin, A Biography of Lin Tse-sü (in Chinese; Taipei, 1967).

4. Morse, I, p. 237.

5. Ibid., I, p. 238.

6. Two British ships, Volage 28 and Hyacinth 20, arrived there on November 2, 1839. British warships and transports then along the Chinese coast numbered approximately fifty, with four thousand troops, all under the supreme command of Admiral George Elliot. See John Ouchterlony, The Chinese War: An Account of All the Operations of the British Forces from the Commencement to the Treaty of Nanking (London, 1844), p. 40.

7. See Chinese Repository, November 1839; Morse, I, pp. 246- 247.

8. After protracted negotiations, the final terms of the treaty were similar to those proposed by Lord Palmerston two and one half years previously. When the instruments of ratification were exchanged at Hongkong on June 26, 1843, the Conserva- tive government came into power in Great Britain. For the text of the treaty, see Appendix A; Chinese Customs, Treaties, I, pp. 351-356; Hertslet, Treaties, I, pp. 7-12.

9. For the text of the Treaty of Nanking of 1842, see Chinese Customs, Treaties, I, pp. 351-356; Hertslet, Treaties, I, pp. 7-12.

10. Art. 3.

11. Art. 2.

12. Arts. 4-6. Also included in this amount were three million dollars of debts due to British merchants from some co-hong and twelve million dollars to cover the expenses of the war. In addition, the British government kept six million dollars received during the war for the ransom of the city of Canton.

13. Art. 5.

14. Art. 11.

15. Art. 10.

16. For its text, see Appendix B; Chinese Customs, Treaties, I, pp. 390-399.

17. For the provision of extraterritoriality, see Art 13 of the General Regulations (ibid., I, pp. 383-389). These Regulations were enforced at the five ports, and were later superseded by Art. 1 of the Sino-British Treaty of Tientsin, June 26, 1858 (ibid., I, pp. 404-421; Hertslet, Treaties, I, pp. 18-25). See also Arts. 1-2 of the Supplementary Treaty of 1843.

18. Art. 8.

19. Art. 9.

20. Art. 6.

21. Art. 10. This provision was ostensibly designed "to enforce good order and discipline among the crews of merchant shipping, and to support the necessary authority of the consul over British subjects."

22. Arts. 12, 14.

23. See Morse, I, pp. 316-317.

24. See Chinese Repository, January, August, 1843. For further information on British trade during this period, see Michael Greenberg, British Trade and the Opening of China 1800-42 (Cambridge, England, 1951). A Sino-British agreement on the regulation of opium trade was reached in 1858. See Morse, I, pp. 554-555.

25. The first American ship, Empress of China, reached Canton in 1784. Besides tea, American traders brought back silk, china-

ware, and spices, with very little export to balance the trade. However, they expected to develop a future market in this populous country for American manufactured goods.

26. In reply to the Chinese argument that Sir Henry Pottinger, the British plenipotentiary, in a similar situation, had to return from North China to Canton for the conduct of diplomatic negotiations, Cushing went so far as to make the following statement: "The rules of politeness and ceremony observed by Sir H. Pottinger were doubtless just and proper in the particular circumstances of the case; but, to render them fully applicable to the United States, it would be necessary for my government, in the first instance, to subject the people of China to all the calamities of war, and especially to take possession of some island on the coast of China, as a place of residence for its minister." Chinese Repository, August 1845, Mr. Cushing to Viceroy Cheng, March 23, 1844.

27. Its full title is the Treaty of Peace, Amity, and Commerce between the United States and the Chinese Empire, with ratifications exchanged at Canton on December 31, 1845. For its text, see Appendix C; Chinese Customs, Treaties, I, pp. 677-690. The schedule of customs duties fixed by the Treaty of Wanghia can be found in ibid., I, pp. 691-698.

28. Art. 2.

29. In connection with the death of Hsü A-man, caused by American firearms, during mob violence in Canton in the middle of June 1844, Cushing insisted on American jurisdiction over American nationals. In his letter to American consul Forbes at Canton on June 22, 1844, he emphatically stated:

> "In my opinion, the rule which obtained in favor of Europeans and Americans in the Mohammedan countries of Asia is to be applied to China. Americans are entitled to the protection and subject to the jurisdiction of the officers of their government. The right to be protected by the officers of their country over them, are inseparable facts.

> "Accordingly, I shall refuse at once all applications for the surrender of the party who killed Hsü A-man; which refusal involves the duty of instituting an examination of the facts by the agency of officers of the United States." Chinese Repository, November 1845.

30. On criminal jurisdiction, Art. 21 of the Treaty read:

> "Subjects of China who may be guilty of any crim-

inal act toward citizens of the United States shall be arrested and punished by the Chinese authorities according to the laws of China, and citizens of the United States who may commit any crime in China shall be subject to be tried and punished only by the Consul or other public functionary of the United States; and in order to the prevention of all controversy and disaffection, justice shall be equitably and impartially administered on both sides."

With respect to other disputes of American nationals among themselves or with other nationals, art. 25 provided:

"All questions in regards to rights, whether of property or person, arising between citizens of the United States in China shall be subject to the jurisdiction of and regulated by the authorities of their own government; and all controversies occurring in China between the citizens of the United States and the subjects of any other Government shall be regulated by the Treaties existing between the United States and such Governments respectively, without interference on the part of China."

In case of controversies arising between American and Chinese nationals and unable to be settled amicably, they "shall be examined and decided conformably to justice and equity by the public officers of the two nations acting in conjunction." Art. 24 of the Treaty.

It should be noted that although Congress had provided for an American consul in Canton, his functions were limited until this treaty came into effect.

31. Arts. 33.

32. Art. 17.

33. Art. 18.

34. According to Art. 34(1), negotiations for the treaty revision would be conducted at the expiration of twelve years from the date of the conclusion of this Treaty.

35. See R. Montgomery Martin, China: Political, Commercial, and Social, p. 396.

36. The date of his arrival was August 14, 1844.

37. For its text, see Hertslet, Treaties, I, pp. 258-269; Chinese Customs, Treaties, I, pp. 771-790. The schedule of customs

duties fixed by the Treaty of Whampoa can be found in ibid., I, pp. 791-813.

38. Other branches of the Christian faith were later put on the same footing as the Roman Catholic religion by a Chinese proclamation of December 22, 1845. See S. Wells Williams, The Middle Kingdom: A Survey of the Geography, Government, Literature, Social Life, Arts, and History of the Chinese Empire and Its Inhabitants, II, p. 357. For early influence of Catholic missionaries in China, see Ssu-yu Teng, John K. Fairbank, Chaoying Fang, and others, China's Response to the West: A Documentary Survey 1839-1923 (New York, 1965), pp. 12-19.

39. See Chinese Customs, Treaties, II, p. 3; Hertslet, Treaties, I, p. 223.

40. For its text, see ibid., I, pp. 527-540; Chinese Customs, Treaties, II, pp. 45-71. For the tariff annexed to the treaty, see ibid., II, pp. 72-93.

41. By an arrangement made in April 1847, this right was not waived but deferred for two more years. The hostility of the local population in Canton was partly attributed to the wrongdoings of English merchants. In connection with James Innes' case, one merchant in Canton, Mr. Inglis, gave the evidence with an astonishing statement: "We never paid any attention to any law in China that I am aware of ...." The Canton riot in 1846 was partly stirred up by another English merchant, Mr. Charles S. Compton, who wantonly kicked down the fruit-stand of a Chinese hawker and later beat him with a cane. Compton was fined by the English consul, but the sentence was reversed by the supreme court in Hongkong due to irregular proceedings. In his dispatch to Lord Palmerston on November 12, 1846, Sir J. F. Davis, Governor of Hongkong and Superintendent of Trade, complained:
> "I am not the first who has been compelled to remark that it is more difficult to deal with our own countrymen at Canton, than with the Chinese government; and I offer the best proof of this in the fact that it had cost me infinitely more trouble to make Mr. Compton pay a fine of $200 than to obtain a compensation to our merchants of $46,000 for losses which accrued partly from their own misconduct."
> Papers relating to riot, p. 74, quoted from Morse, I, p. 384.

42. See Lord Palmerston to Sir S.G. Bonham, who succeeded Sir John Davis as Governor of Hongkong, October 7, December

30, 1848. <u>Proceedings naval forces,</u> pp. 154, 158; Morse, I, p. 396.

43. See Lord Clarendon to Sir John Bowring, Governor of Hong-kong, February 13, 1854 (Morse, I, Appendix Q).

44. See John W. Foster, <u>American Diplomacy in the Orient,</u> (Boston, 1904), pp. 217-218. When Peter Parker was appointed American commissioner in China, he brought to the attention of his British and French colleagues more extreme suggestions, including reform of the Chinese court system, freedom of religion for all Chinese, and appointment of Chinese envoys to Washington, London, and Paris. See Henri Cordier, <u>L'Expédition de Chine, 1860,</u> (Paris, 1906), p. 10. Parker's views were embodied in a more restricted manner in the instructions sent to William B. Reed, who was appointed the first American minister to China in April 1859. Previously, the United States government was represented in China by a commissioner.

45. For details of the <u>Arrow</u> incident, see Morse, I, pp. 422-429.

46. Art. 14 of this Sino-British Supplementary Treaty provided that "piracy and illegal traffic will be effectively prevented." Art. 9 regulated the extradition of fugitives in the follwoing manner:

> "If lawless natives of China, having committed crimes, or offences, against their own government, shall flee to Hongkong or to the English Ship of war or English merchant ships for refuge; they shall, if discovered by the English officers, be handed over at once to the Chinese officers for trial and punishment; or if, before such discovery be made by the English officers, it should be ascertained, or suspected, by the officers of the Government of China whither such criminals and offenders have fled, a communication be made to the proper English officer, in order that the said criminals and offenders may be rigidly searched for, seized, and, on proof or admission, of their guilt, delivered up."

Similar provisions were made in the Sino-American and Sino-Franco treaties of 1844.

47. The Chinese High Commissioner at Canton later returned the twelve sailors, but not exactly in the manner demanded by the British consul, who, therefore, declined to accept them and chose the use of force to settle the dispute. In England, the Arrow War became a national issue. For details of the Parliamentary debates, see Douglas Hurd, <u>The Arrow War: An Anglo-Chinese Confusion</u> (New York, 1967).

48. See infra, p. 152.

49. For details of the incident, see Morse, I, pp. 479-485.

50. Canton was taken on December 29, 1857. The British sent Yeh to Calcutta, where he died on April 10, 1859.

51. The four envoys, Lord Elgin of England, Baron Gros of France, Count Putiatin of Russia, and William B. Reed of the United States, entered the city on May 29, 1858. After arriving at Tientsin on June 2, the two Chinese plenipotentiaries, Kwei-liang and Hwashana, opened negotiations with the four envoys immediately.

52. For its text, see Chinese Customs, Treaties, I, pp. 85-100; Hertslet, Treaties, I, pp. 455-461. On May 16, 1858, Russia succeeded in concluding with China the Treaty of Aigun, by which Russia acquired a tremendous area of territory along the Chinese border. For details, see infra, pp. 352-354.

53. For its text, see Chinese Customs, Treaties, I, pp. 713-728; Hertslet, Treaties, I, pp. 540-552.

54. Its text can be found in ibid., I, pp. 18-35; Chinese Customs, Treaties, I, pp. 404-421.

55. For its text, see ibid., I, pp. 814-839; Hertslet, Treaties, I, pp. 269-286. The French treaty could have been signed earlier, but, as a courtesy to her British ally, its conclusion was postponed until June 27. See John W. Foster, op. cit., p. 241.

56. For the establishment of foreign legations in China, see Immanuel C.Y. Hsü, China's Entrace into the Family of Nations: The Diplomatic Phase 1858-1880 (Cambridge, 1960), pp. 21-108.

57. Besides the original five ports, the following were added: Newchwang, Tenchow (later substituted by Chefoo, the port being at Yentai), Chinkiang, Taiwanfu, Tamsui, Swatow, Hankow, Kiukiang, Nanking, and Kiungchow; the opening of the last four being deferred. Tientsin was added in 1860. While not expressly sanctioned in the treaties, coasting trade by foreign ships had been carried on for years. See Morse, I, p. 568. The passports were issued by foreign consuls and counter-signed by the Chinese authorities to foreigners (not including the crews of foreign ships) traveling to the interior either for pleasure or for trade.

58. The Agreement was signed in Shanghai on November 8, 1858, and contained Rules of Trade made in pursuance of Art. 26

of the Sino-British Treaty of Tientsin of June 26, 1858. For its text, see Chinese Customs, Treaties, I, pp. 422-428; Hertslet, Treaties, I, pp. 35-47. This Agreement was also known as Trade Regulations appended to the Tariff or the Tariff Rules. According to Rule 5(1), the restrictions affecting trade in opium were relaxed. The revised tariff was generally based on a uniform rate of 5% ad valorem. Besides the reduction of tonnage dues, inland transit dues were limited to one payment not exceeding 2-1/2% or one-half of the tariff duty.

59. Tls. 4,000,000 to England; Tls. 2,000,000 to France. For comments on the treaties of Tientsin and attempts of treaty revisions, see Mary C. Wright, The Last Stand of Chinese Conservatism: The T'ung-chih Restoration, 1862-1874 (New York, 1966), pp. 253-299.

60. This form of approval, similar to that of the Treaty of Nanking of 1842, was considered satisfactory to the envoys. See Henri Cordier, L'Expédition de Chine, 1860, p. 458.

61. From Peitang, approximately ten miles above Tientsin on the Peiho, the American envoy sailed to Tungchow, and then went to Peking by cart provided by the Chinese government.

62. See W. A. T. Martin, A Cycle of Cathay: or China, North and South (New York, 1900), pp. 195 sq.

63. Admiral Hope knew beforehand that the passage of the Peiho was obstructed and that the Taku fors would resist any attack. According to Justin McCarthy, "some of the English Officers who were actually engaged in the attempt of Admiral Hope frankly repudiated the idea of any treachery on the part of the Chinese, or any surprise on their own side." See his A History of Our Own Times (London, 1899, 5 vols.), III, p. 266.

64. On June 26, 1860, Western powers were notified by the English and French governments of the existence of a state of war. See Correspondence respecting China, 1859-1860, pp. 55 sq.; Morse, I, p. 589.

65. For details, see Henri Cordier, L'Expédition de Chine, 1860, p. 353; G. J. Wolseley, The Story of a Soldier's Life (London, 1903, 2 vols.), II, p. 78; Roger Pelissier, The Awakening of China, 1793-1949, p. 145. Further information on the Anglo-Franco second expedition can be found in D. Bonner-Smith and E. W. R. Lumby, The Second China War 1856-1860 (London, 1954).

66. For texts of these Conventions, see Chinese Customs, Treaties, I, pp. 430-434 (British), 885-890 (French); Hertslet, Treaties,

I, pp. 45-53 (British), 287-291 (French). After the conclusion of these two Conventions, separate articles of 1858 concerning indemnity were annulled.

67. Art. 6 of the Sino-British Convention of Peking of 1860. See also Morse, I, p. 615.

68. For its text, see Chinese Customs, Treaties, I, pp. 81-84; Hertslet, Treaties, I, pp. 454-455.

69. The text of the Additional Treaty can be found in Chinese Customs, Treaties, I, pp. 101-120; Hertslet, Treaties, I, pp. 461-472. See also infra, pp. 352-354.

70. Art. 27 of the Sino-British Treaty of 1858.

71. For its text, see Chinese Customs, Treaties, I, pp. 478-490; Hertslet, Treaties, I, pp. 61-72.

72. See Alexander Michie, The Englishman in China (Edinburgh, 1900, 2 vols.), II, p. 221.

73. Col. Browne's expedition was the second one; the first was led by Col. E.B. Sladen in 1868.

74. See Morse, II, pp. 288-294, Émile Rocher, La Province Chinoise de Yunnan (Paris, 1879-1880, 2 vols.), I, p. 190. See also Correspondence respecting the Attack on the Indian Expedition to Western China and the Murder of Mr. Margary, China, No. 1 (1876), pp. 2,6, 50-52, 63, 74, 76; Further Correspondence respecting the Attack on the Indian Expedition to Western China and the Murder of Mr. Margary, China, No. 3 (1877), pp. 111-147.

75. See Henri Cordier, Histoire des Rélations de la Chine avec les Puissances Occidentales (Paris, 1901-1902, 3 vols.), II, pp. 45, 55, 61.

76. See, for instance, Mr. Avery to Mr. Fish, April 1, 1875. Papers relating to the Foreign Relations of the United States (Washington, D.C., 1861-; hereafter cited as U.S. For. Rel.), 1875, I, p. 310.

77. For the text, see Chinese Customs, Treaties, I, pp. 491-499; Hertslet, Treaties, I, pp. 73-80.

78. See Section I (i-vi).

ction II (i-iii).

. see Section III (i-vii).

81. See the Identic Notes of Ministers of France, Russia, the United States, Spain, and Germany to Tsungli Yamen (Ministry of Foreign Affairs of the Chinese government), October 2, 1876. Henri Cordier, Histoire des Rélations de la Chine avec les Puissances Occidentales, II, pp. 92-94. For governmental organs directing Chinese foreign relations, including Tsungli Yamen, Wai-Wu Pu, and Wai-Chiao Pu, see William L. Tung, China and Some Phases of International Law, pp. 105-110.

82. The British minister himself had a guilty conscience because of this abnormal situation. See Sir T. Wade to Lord Cranville, June 3, 1882, Correspondence respecting Chefoo Convention, 1882, p. 77; Morse, II, p. 305.

83. Treaty of Tientsin, September 2, 1861 (Chinese Customs, Treaties, II, pp. 115-138; Hertslet, Treaties, I, pp. 331-342).

84. Treaty of Tientsin, August 13, 1862, which was not ratified at the time, but was later revived by the Sino-Portuguese Treaty of Peking of December 1, 1887. For their texts, see Chinese Customs, Treaties, II, pp. 251-272, 274-279; Hertslet, Treaties, I, pp. 422, 423-433.

85. Treaty of Tientsin, July 13, 1863 (Chinese Customs, Treaties, II, pp. 313-330; Hertslet, Treaties, I, pp. 249-258.

86. Treaty of Tientsin, October 6, 1863 (Chinese Customs, Treaties, II, pp. 339-351; Hertslet, Treaties, I, pp. 407-415).

87. Treaty of Tientsin, October 10, 1864 (Chinese Customs, Treaties, II, pp. 359-377; Hertslet, Treaties, I, pp. 512-522).

88. Treaty of Peking, October 26, 1866 (Chinese Customs, Treaties, II, pp. 403-420; Hertslet, Treaties, I, pp. 354-361).

89. Treaty of Peking September 2, 1869 (Chinese Customs, Treaties, II, pp. 457-476, 495-504; Hertslet, Treaties, I, pp. 215-222.

90. Treaty of Tientsin, September 13, 1871 (Chinese Customs, Treaties, II, pp. 507-514, 572-575, 642-648). See also infra, p. 46.

91. Treaty of Tientsin, June 26, 1874 (Chinese Customs, Treaties, II, pp. 798-807; Hertslet, Treaties, I, pp. 415-420).

92. Treaty of Tientsin, October 3, 1881 (Chinese Customs, Treaties, II, pp. 813-823; Hertslet, Treaties, I, pp. 234-240).

93. Treaty of Washington, December 14, 1899 (Chinese Customs, Treaties, II, pp. 833-843; Hertslet, Treaties, I, pp. 399-407.

94. Signed at Tokyo. For its text, see John V.A. MacMurray, Treatties and Agreements with and Concerning China, 1894-1919 (new York: Oxford University Press, 1921, 2 vols.; hereafter cited as MacMurray, Treaties), II, pp. 1429-1430.

Chapter 3
IMPERIALISTIC AGGRESSION AND THE ANTI-FOREIGN MOVEMENT

I. THE SINO-JAPANESE WAR, 1894-1895

1. Struggle for Power in Korea[1]

China's close relationship with Korea began as early as the second century B.C., when Emperor Wu-ti of the Han dynasty sent an expeditionary force into the northern part of the Korean peninsula. After the invasion of the T'ang army in the middle of the seventh century, Chinese influence was frimly established in this land. In 1592, a Japanese force under Hideyoshi began military operations in Korea, but was repulsed by the troops of the Ming dynasty. With the ascendency of the Manchus, traditional relations between the two countries continued. As Chinese resident at Seoul, China appointed Yüan Shih-k'ai who had been on military duty in Korea since 1880.[2]

Among the Western powers, France, Germany, Russia, and the United States made several attempts to open up Korea during the middle of the nineteenth century. An American naval expedition in 1871 destroyed Korean coastal forts, but fell short of its purpose.[3] In turn, the King of Korea appealed to the Chinese Emperor for help. When Japan concluded a treaty of amity and commerce with Korea in 1876,[4] China persuaded the latter to establish relations with the West as an antidote against the Japanese intrusion. Through the good offices of Viceroy Li Hung-chang, the United States entered into a treaty with Korea on May 22, 1882,[5] followed by England, Germany, Italy, and Russia in the ensuing years.[6] While trading was the common purpose of the contracting powers, Russia and Japan also had political ambitions in Korea.

43

As a result of a riot in Seoul in 1884 and subsequent armed conflict between the Chinese and Japanese guards, negotiations for the settlement of the dispute were conducted at Tientsin between Count Ito Hirobumi for Japan and Viceroy Li Hung-chang for China. By the signing of a Sino-Japanese Convention on April 18, 1885, the two countries agreed to withdraw, within four months, their troops, which, it was understood, could later be dispatched there by mutual notification for the suppression of disorder.[7] According to the Convention, neither Chinese nor Japanese would be engaged in training the Korean army. Russia seized this opportunity to offer military instructors in return for the usufruct of an ice-free port. This meddling in Korean affairs by a third power with ambitious designs in the Far East not only constituted a potential threat to Japan but also endangered the traditional influence of China in that region. Upon the advice of Li Hung-chang, the King turned down the Russian overture, but Japan was determined to drive Chinese power out of Korea.

2. Outbreak of Hostilities

From March to June, 1894, there was popular unrest in Korea. With the expulsion of foreigners as their rallying point, the Society of Eastern Learning (Tonghak) launched a rebellion. For the protection of foreign lives and property, Yüan Shih-k'ai notified foreign legations in Seoul of the Chinese reinforcements, which would be withdrawn after the restoration of peace in accordance with the assurance given by Viceroy Li to the Japanese government. In June, a large number of Japanese forces arrived in Seoul, Chempulpo, Fushan, and Wonsan. However, the rebellion was suppressed by the Korean government before the advent of the Chinese and Japanese troops.

To the Japanese proposal of joint intervention in enforcing domestic reforms in Korea, China replied in the negative on June 17, 1894. Concerned with the tense situation, the envoys of Russia, England, France, and the United States sent a joint note to their Chinese and Japanese colleagues, urging simultaneous withdrawal of the rival forces.[8] While the Chinese were inclined to agree, Japan resorted to force soon afterward. On August 1, war was declared by both sides.

Statesmen in Japan had persistently advocated military conquest of Korea, and were anxious to raise her international status by winning the war with China.[9] On the other hand, the Chinese government was unprepared for the war. Outnumbered by the Japanese forces, the Chinese army gradually withdrew to Pyǒngyang. As the war developed, China was defeated in Korea, Manchuria, and Shantung on land and at sea. Unsuccessful in soliciting mediation by third powers, the Manchu Court had no alternative but to sue for peace. Li Hung-chang was appointed ambassador extraordinary with full powers to negotiate with Count Ito Hirobumi, the Japanese plenipotentiary, at Shimonoseki.[10]

The Japanese war party was strong, and insisted on maximum concessions from China. But an unprecedented incident in diplomatic history occurred on March 24, when Li, leaving the third session of the peace conference, was fired upon and wounded by a fanatic Japanese patriot. Dismayed by public indignation manifested internationally and domestically, the Japanese government softened its demands for the termination of the war.[11] On March 30, an armistice agreement was signed.[12] When the cession of Chinese territories and the amount of indemnity were finally settled, the pleinipotentiaries concluded the Peace Treaty of Shimonoseki on April 17, 1895.[13]

3. Terms for Peace

By the Treaty of Shimonoseki of 1895, China was compelled to recognize the independence of Korea,[14] which served as a preliminary step for the latter's being annexed by Japan in 1910. China was to cede to Japan Liaotung, Formosa, and the Pescadores.[15] Four more cities or ports were to be opened for foreign trade: Shashih, Chungking, Suchow, and Hangchow.[16] A new treaty of commerce and navigation between the two countries was to be negotiated.[17] In addition, China had to pay a heavy indemnity of Tls. 200,000,000.[18] In order to guarantee China's fulfillment of the above conditions, Japan took temporary military occupation of Weihaiwei in the province of Shantung.[19]

Located in the southern part of Manchuria east of the Liao river, Liaotung was considered a vital strategic area and its possession by Japan would offset the balance of power in the Far East. Alarmed at their common danger, Russia, France, and Germany took immediate action and demanded that Japan restore this important peninsula to China. Japan was not then in the position to defy the joint intervention of the three major powers, and consented to the retrocession of Liaotung by signing another convention with China on November 8, 1895,[20] in exchange for an additional indemnity of Tls. 30,000,000.[21] Although Japanese statesmen, such as Count Ito and Count Mutsu, had serious doubt about the wisdom of acquiring Chinese territory on the mainland,[22] the three-power intervention was deeply resented by them, especially in view of Russia's own ambition in Manchuria.

Japan encountered difficulty in taking possession of Formosa because of local resistance. The Chinese on the island even asked protection from England and then France. After rejection by both, the independence of the Republic of Formosa was declared on May 24, 1895. Japanese forces landed at Kelung a week later, however, and occupied the whole island before the end of the year. The Republic was short-lived,[23] but the Japanese paid a high price to crush it.[24] It was not until five decades later that Formosa and the Pescadores were restored to China as a consequence of World War II.

It should be recalled that, in the Treaty of Tientsin of September 13, 1871, Japan did not obtain the same privileges from China as other powers: the most-favored-nation clause was not stipulated and Japanese nationals were not entitled to the full extent of extraterritoriality as were Westerners.[25] By the conclusion of the new Treaty of Commerce and Navigation in Peking, on July 21, 1896,[26] the above differences were completely eradicated. Besides, the Japanese could "reside and carry on trade, industries and manufactures, or pursue any other lawful avocations in all the ports, cities and towns of China," which were or would be open to foreign trade.[27] This provision constituted a source of troubles between the Japanese residents and Chinese authorities in Manchuria and other parts of China.

II. CHINA ON THE VERGE OF DISMEMBERMENT

1. Loss of Dependencies and Territories

In the scramble for dependencies, France took the lead in 1884 and Japan concluded it a decade later. Annam had been under Chinese influence since the Han dynasty. In 1407, Emperor Yanglo of the Ming dynasty "conquered the country and annexed it for the fifth time to China";[28] twenty years later, Annam reverted to the status of a vassal state. French involvement in the area began in 1787, but it was not until the 1880's that France contested China's suzerainty over Annam.[29] While negotiations for a settlement were still going on in 1883, French forces attacked Chinese positions in Annam and the coastal cities of South China. Chinese troops were not entirely unsuccessful in this war,[30] but the Manchu Court reacting with timidity, preferred to sue for peace. By signing the Convention of Tientsin on May 11, 1884, China surrendered to France her suzerainty over Annam.[31]

Soon afterward, China was compelled to relinquish her traditional influence over other neighboring countries and dependencies or tributaries, such as Burma (Burma-Tibet Convention of Peking on July 24, 1886)[32] and Sikkim (Sikkim-Tibet Agreement of Calcutta on March 17, 1890).[33] The Liuchiu (Ryukyu) Islands had been paying tribute to China, but were virtually put under Japanese control in 1881.[34] With the detachment of Korea after the Sino-Japanese War,[35] China was stripped of the last vestige of her tributary system.

By the end of the nineteenth century, the prestige of the Celestial Empire had practically dwindled to nothing. Neighboring states, such as Nepal and Bhutan, no longer looked to China for protection.[36] Due to diplomatic blunders, portions of Kiang Hung were lost to France and England in 1895 and 1897 respectively.[37] For the same reason, Macao was ceded to Portugal in 1887.[38] Russia received the most benefit in territorial acquisitions by redemarcation of her boundaries with China at different intervals, to be discussed elsewhere.[39] Because of military defeats described above, Hongkong and a portion of Kowloon were ceded to England, and Taiwan (Formosa) and Penghu (The Pescadores), to Japan.

2. Battle of Leases and Spheres of Influence

China's weakness was fully exposed after the first Sino-Japanese War. A new mode of acquiring territory was devised by foreign powers in 1898, by leases of twenty-five to ninety-nine years. These were Kiaochow Bay leased to Germany for ninety nine years, on March 6;[40] Port Arthur and Dairen (Talien-wan or Dalny) to Russia for twenty-five years, on March 27;[41] Kuangchou-wan to France for ninety-nine years, on April 10;[42] and Kowloon to England for ninety-nine years, on June 9.[43] In her lease of Weihaiwei on July 1, England stipulated the period for so long as Port Arthur would be under Russian occupation,[44] and assured Germany that the latter's interests in Shantung would not be prejudiced.[45] It should be noted, however, that not all the powers succeeded in the struggle for territorial leases in China.[46]

The manner of the seizure of Kiaochow by Germany was deeply resented by the Chinese; one European historian deemed it a principal cause of the Boxer Uprising.[47] When two German missionaries in a village of Shantung province were murdered on November 1, 1897, the Chinese government promptly apprehended and punished those guilty of or responsible for the incident. However, the Kaiser dispatched a naval force to occupy Kiaochow and presented six demands to the Chinese government, including the lease of Kiaochow, rights of railway construction and mining in Shantung, as well as indemnities.[48] A state, under international law, is indirectly responsible for loss of lives of resident aliens in case of lack of due diligence in protecting them and amends must be made in proportion to the seriousness of the delinquency, but under no circumstances should the foreign government concerned use such an incident as a pretext for the furtherance of territorial and economic acquisitions by means of force.[49]

Russia was not without interest in Kiaochow, but the lease of this port to Germany diverted Russian attention to Port Arthur and Dairen.[50] These two ports, however, were leased exclusively to Russia in 1898 for only a short period of twenty-five years. It was most astonishing that, at the conclusion of the Russo-Japanese War in 1905, Russia transferred the lease to Japan without the previous consent of China;[51] Japan subsequently demanded an extension of the

lease to ninety-nine years.[52] Kiaochow was also changed
hands from Germany to Japan as a result of World War I
until its return to China in 1922.[53] Although leased territories remained under the sovereignty of China, the actual
exercise of Chinese authority had been severely restricted
for the duration of the lease.[54]

Foreign powers in China had insatiable desires. After
taking possession of several territories by way of lease,
they went one step further to claim spheres of influence or
interest in certain particular regions: France over Yunnan,
Kweichow, and Kwangsi provinces; England over the Yangtze
Valley; Germany over Shantung; Japan over Fukien; and Russia over Manchuria. These spheres of influence, not necessarily centering around the areas where they had leased
territories, were generally achieved through declarations of
non-alienation by, or agreements with, the Chinese government.[55] In some cases, the powers agreed among themselves
to support their respective claims or to refrain from action
in special areas.[56] Such commitments without the previous
consent of China were in flat violation of her sovereignty.
After the Russo-Japanese War, Japan claimed spheres of
influence in Southern Manchuria, while the Russians still
dominated its northern region centering around the Chinese
Eastern Railway. As in the leased territories, the powers
concerned usually obtained special railway and mining concessions in their respective spheres of influence. Such concessions were often accompanied by other privileges, including a priority to grant loans.

For the maintenance of mutual interests and balance of
power in China, the five powers claiming spheres of influence aligned themselves against the intrusion of others, as
in the case of the Agreement between Great Britain and
Japan on January 30, 1902, relating to China and Korea.[57]
This Anglo-Japanese alliance was immediately countered by
the Franco-Russian Declaration of March 16, 1902.[58] The contest of power between Russia and Japan in Manchuria and
Korea culminated in a full-scale war in these areas in 1904-
1905. In this connection, both belligerents violated rules of
international law by conducting military operations in neutral
territories.

To avoid further clashes in China, the powers realized the importance of mutually understanding their repsective interests. In the Franco-Japanese Agreement in regard to the Continent of Asia, signed in Paris, on June 10, 1907, some accommodation between them could be evidenced in their willingness "to support each other ... with a view to maintaining the respective situation and the territorial rights of the two Contracting Parties in the Continent of Asia."[59] The same intention was expressed in the Russo-Japanese Political Convention of July 30, 1907.[60] However, the ruthless execution of imperialist policies contained the inherent weakness of mutual exclusiveness, a factor which actually saved China from further disintegration at the turn of the century.

3. Effect of the Open Door Policy on the Chinese Situation

Dismayed at the deteriorating situation in China and the potential danger to American interests, the United States declared in 1899 the Open Door Policy, which advocated equal treatment within the leased territories and spheres of influence claimed by Russia, Great Britain, France, Germany, and Japan. Secretary of State John Hay made his proposals through American envoys to the above countries and Italy.[61] All of them accepted this policy in priciple, but the Russian reply was equivocal.[62] Secretary Hay chose to declare on March 20, 1900, that the powers concerned had agreed with the United States on the open door policy in China. Hay's diplomatic prestidigitation had served as a restraining influence on the imperialistic struggle for concessions, but no country had any real intention to waive vested rights and privileges.[63]

The gist of Hay's proposals was three-fold: (1) no interference with any treaty port or vested rights; (2) customs duties to be collected only by the Chinese government in accordance with the Chinese treaty tariff; and (3) no discriminatory harbor dues or railway charges. Thus the Open Door Policy did not imply that all China would be open to foreign trade; nor was it fundamentally opposed to special interests of the powers concerned in their respective leased territories and spheres of influence.[64]With characteristic ambiguity, Hay's proposals could be interpreted in different ways. For example, in the Lansing-Ishii Agreement of November 2, 1917,[65] the term open door meant "equal opportunity for commerce and industry in China."[66] However, by recognizing Japan's special interests in China because of geographical propinquity and contiguity, the United States inadvertently made a commitment in this 1917 agreement in contradiction to the letter and spirit of the Open Door Policy.[67] Since neither the American government nor the other powers intended to maintain the policy by forcible means, its effectiveness was bound to be limited.[68]

III. THE BOXER UPRISING AND THE FINAL PROTOCOL OF 1901

1. Origin and Development of the Boxers

The gross injustice done to China was unequalled in modern history. A country which long enjoyed prosperity and glory now had to suffer one humiliation after another from foreigners. Six-decades of mistreatment had accumulated such a hatred among the Manchu rulers and the populace that it could easily explode into violence once the opportunity arose. The occasion presented itself in the form of the Boxer Uprising at the end of the nineteenth century. Because much has been written about this tragic episode, a brief review of its origin and development will be sufficient for present purposes.[69]

The Boxers were members of I-ho T'uan (Righteous Harmony Band or Society), which had grown up from the secret societies prevalent in China at that time.[70] Because of heavy taxes, natural calamities,[71] and intermittent persecution, many villagers were dissatisfied with local authorities and joined secret societies essentially for self-protection. Having its own characteristic organization and practices, the I-ho T'uan "appeared in Shantung as early as May 1898."[72]

Decades of foreign aggression had tremendous impact on the attitude of the Chinese people, who could hardly find reasons to be friendly toward foreigners. In the villages, the

arrogant manners and activities of many Western missionaries and their Chinese converts were resented by the populace. Their interference in lawsuits and hostility to Con-
fucianism and native customs became increasingly intoler-
able.73 This anti-foreign sentiment was shared by some
princes and officials of the Manchu Court. However, the
Boxers were not members of the militia nor did they receive support from the government at the beginning.74 It was
only after Admiral Edward Seymour led an expeditionary
force of some 1,500 men from Tientsin to Peking on June
10, 1900, and the Allied navy subsequently bombarded the
Taku forts that the Manchu Court openly endorsed their
cause and prepared for further hostilities.75

2. The Boxer Uprising and the Allied Expedition

In May and June, 1900, there were wide-spread activities against missionaries. The Boxers finally entered Peking
on June 13, and began the attack on the legations a week
later. Their breach of diplomatic inviolability with the sanction of the Manchu Court represented their complete lack of
common sense and sheer disregard of international law. Yet
it was clear that the strongest government army under the
command of Jung Lu did not give full support to the Boxers
and Tung Fu-siang's antiforeign troops.76 Otherwise, the
legation quarter could by no means have been defended by
approximately five hundred men for almost eight weeks. The
murder of Baron von Ketteler, the German minister, and
Mr. Sugiyama, chancellor of the Japanese legation, in the
midst of mob violence was most tragic.77 The Manchu Court
could not escape responsibility for all acts of commission
or omission. Nevertheless, it was not a war by China or the
Chinese people as a whole against foreign powers. The Southern viceroys and governors maintained peace and order in
their regions and foreign lives and property were fully protected throughout the disturbances,78 regardless of the Allied
military operations in the North.

The Boxer Uprising was a desperate but ignominious act
of an infuriated multitude of the Chinese people, and the
situation was later aggravated by the encouragement and support of the reactionary elements of the Manchu Court; but
its major cause could be attributed to the never-ending ag-

gression and oppression by the imperialist powers. The destruction of Chinese villages in Shantung by German soldiers from Kiaochow and the massacre of of Chinese civilians near Port Arthur by Russian troops at the slightest provocation had hardened the determination of many Chinese to take revenge at the first opportune moment.[79] However, what the Boxers had done actually defeated their own purpose.[80] The Allied forces [81] occupied Tientsin on July 13, and entered Peking on August 14, 1900. Even though the powers were not technically at war with China, they inflicted the heaviest penalties on the defeated Chinese. Never in history had a misconceived uprising cost a nation so heavily as the Boxer episode.[82]

3. The Final Settlement in 1901

After prolonged negotiations between two Chinese plenipotentiaries, Prince Ch'ing (Yi-k'uang) and Li Hung-chang,[83] and the representatives of the Allied governments,[84] the Final Protocol for the Settlement of the Disturbances of 1900 was concluded in Peking on September 7, 1901.[85] It contained twelve articles, with nineteen annexes. Among the important terms were the following: (1) payment of an indemnity of 450,000,000 Haikwan taels by the Chinese government to the powers concerned, to be secured from the balance of the revenue from maritime customs and salt gabelle, as well as native customs (Art. VI);[86] punishment of all the princes and officials involved in the outrages as stipulated in Art. IIa and Annexes 4, 5, and 6; (3) suspension of official examinations for five years in all cities where foreigners suffered death or cruel treatment (Art. IIb); (4) prohibition against importing arms and ammunitions, as well as materials for such uses, to the Chinese territory for a period of two years and subject to successive extension to be dictated by the Allied governments (Art. V); (5) extension of the legation quarter in Peking for the exclusive use of diplomatic missions with permanent armed guards, excluding residence by the Chinese (Art. VII and Annex 14); (6) demilitarization of the strategic port of Taku and the communication route between Peking and the sea, with several points to be occupied by the Allied powers as specified in Art. IX; (7) protection of foreign nationals and properties (Annex 16), and prohibition forever, under pain of death, membership in any antiforeign society (Art. Xa and Annex 15); (8) reorganization of Tsungli Yamen into Wai-wu Pu (ministry of foreign affairs, taking precedence over any other ministries of state) and modification of court ceremonial for the reception of foreign envoys (Art. XII and Annexes 18, 19).

China was also required to dispatch a special envoy to express regrets to the German and Japanese Emperors for the assissanation of Baron von Ketteler and Mr. Sugiyama respectively during the disturbances (Arts. Ia, III). In the case of the German minister, a commemorative monument on the spot of his death was to be erected (Art. Ib). Taking advantage of China's helpless situation, the Allied powers demanded revision of treaties of commerce and navigation and other related subjects, including the works of improving the navigability of the Peiho and the Whangpu (Art. XI and Annex 17). In order to raise revenue for paying the heavy indemnity, the powers agreed to increase the Chinese customs tariff on imports to five percent in actuality (Art. VI, 3).[87] This was a painful decision on their part, because it had been their persistent policy to keep the Chinese tariff as low as possible for the benefit of their exports at the expense of China.

4. Different Attitudes of the Powers Concerned

Both during and after the Boxer disturbances, the United States took a comparatively benevolent attitude toward China. The American commander, Admiral Kempff, did not join in the bombardment of the Taku forts.[88] On July 3, 1900, Secretary Hay sent circular notes to the powers concerned, reasserting the policy of the United States government. While taking concerted action for restoring peace in China, Hay tried to "preserve Chinese territorial and administrative entity, protect all rights guaranteed to friendly powers by treaty and international law, and safeguard for the world the principle of equal and impartial trade with all parts of the Chinese Empire."[89] This was a reiteration of the Open Door Policy. It should also be noted that the United States was the first country to refund a portion of the American share of Boxer indemnity to China.

Among the European powers, Germany took the severest attitude; France played a comparatively quiet role. While Great Britain generally accommodated the wishes of the Germans, Russia did everything possible to obtain control of Manchuria. The atrocities committed by German soldiers in Peking and the Russian troops in Manchuria could not be easily forgotten by the local population.[90] Japan was the only non-European power which joined the Allied Expedition. Japanese policy was conciliatory and concentrated mainly in surveillance of the Russian military operation in Manchuria,[91] which ultimately developed into the Russo-Japanese War in 1904-1905.

Through the Final Protocol of 1901, the Allied powers achieved their desired purposes. However, the expeditionary forces failed to impress upon the local population their discipline or civility. Pillage was ruthlessly carried out by troops from several powers in the occupied areas.[92] In describing the military raids in Tientsin and Peking, Hosea B. Morse concluded: "China had broken the law of nations and defied the world, and the Western world recognized none of its own rules in its treatment of the law-breaker."[93] The Boxer Uprising represented the last resistance to the West by the Manchu dynasty,[94] which consequently lost whatever remaining prestige it had among the Chinese people and was overthrown in 1911. The establishment of the republic heralded a new chapter of international relations for China.

NOTES TO CHAPTER 3

1. Formerly called Kaoli by the Chinese, Korea was also known as Chosen.

2. Yüan was sent to Seoul at the recommendation of Viceroy Li Hung-chang, who had been put in charge of Korean affairs by the Manchu Court. As advisers to the Korean government, Li recommended, at different times, a number of Westerners who had rendered services in China. They included P.G. von Möllendorff, Henry F. Murrill, and Owen N. Denny.

3. See U. S. For. Rel., 1871, pp. 116-149.

4. This was the Treaty of Kianghwa, February 26, 1876. For its text, see William F. Mayers, Treaties between the Empire of China and Foreign Powers (London, 1877; hereafter cited as Mayers), pp. 195-197. In addition to the opening of the ports of Fusan, Jenchuan (Chemulpo), and Yuensan (Wonsan) to Japanese trade, the status of Korea as an independent state was emphasized (Art. 1). This was Japan's first step to detach Korea from Chinese domination.

5. Ratifications were exchanged at Seoul on May 19, 1883. For its text, see 64th Cong., 1st Sess., Senate Doc. No. 342. A minister plenipotentiary was appointed to represent the United States at Seoul. See U. S. For. Rel., 1883, p. 603.

6. England and Germany on November 26, 1883; Italy on June 26, 1884; Russia on June 25, 1884; France on June 4, 1886.

7. For the text of the Convention, see Chinese Customs, Treaties, II, pp. 588-589, 706-713; Hertslet, Treaties, I, pp. 361-362.

8. See U. S. For. Rel., 1894, Appendix, pp. 22-31.

9. See, for instance, the statements of Count Okuma, one of the most important Japanese leaders at that time, in North-China Herald, June 29, September 7, 1894. Like China, Turkey, Persia, and Siam, Japan also suffered from unequal treaties imposed by Western powers. After long negotiations, she succeeded in concluding a treaty with England on July 16, 1894, for the eventual abolition of extraterritoriality and gradual increase of tariff duties. On November 22 of the same year, a U.S. Japanese treaty to the same effect was signed in Washington.

10. Because of public indignation against Li's responsibility for the consequences of the war, he was removed from his posts

of viceroy and high commissioner of Peiyang by the Imperial Court on February 15, 1895. Previously, Chang Yin-hwan and Shao Yu-lien had been appointed co-envoys for the peace mission, and arrived at Kobe on January 30, 1895. But the Japanese refused to negotiate with them due to their lack of full powers. See North-China Herald, February 22, 1895; U. S. For. Rel., 1894, Appendix i, p. 99. Li was then restored with all the titles and honors for the performance of this important and difficult task. John W. Foster, an American diplomat, served as adviser to the Chinese delegation at the time.

11. See John W. Foster, American Diplomacy in the Orient, p. 135.

12. For its text, see Chinese Customs, Treaties, I, pp. 599-603, 716-719; MacMurray, Treaties, I, pp. 24-25.

13. For its text, see Chinese Customs, Treaties, II, pp. 590-596, 707-713; Hertslet, Treaties, I, pp. 362-370; MacMurray, Treaties, I, pp. 18-24. Ratifications were exchanged at Chefoo on May 8, 1895.

14. Art. I. The same article provided that "the payment of tribute and the performance of ceremonies and formalities by Korea to China, in derogation of such independence and autonomy, shall wholly cease for the future."

15. Art. II.

16. Art. VI.

17. Loc. cit.

18. Art. IV. Before the Sino-Japanese War, only a small amount of foreign loans was contracted by the Chinese government, and all had been paid off except £300,000. With the cost of the war and subsequent indemnity, China began to borrow heavily from foreign banks, such as the Hongkong and Shanghai Banking Corporation and the Deutsch-Asiatische Bank.

19. For details, see Art. VIII of the Peace Treaty and the Separate Articles (MacMurray, Treaties, I, pp. 22-23).

20. For its text, see ibid., I, pp. 50-53; Hertslet, Treaties, I, pp. 370-373.

21. Art. II of the Convention.

22. See John W. Foster, Diplomatic Memoirs, (Boston, 1910, 2 vols.), II, p. 153. For Li Hung-chang's diplomacy in re-

lation to the three-power intervention, see North-China Herald, March 22, 1895.

23. See Harry J. Lamley, "The 1895 Taiwan Republic," The Journal of Asian Studies, Vol 27 (1968), pp. 739-762.

24. The Japanese casulties in the military conquest of Formosa were less than one thousand, but malaria and other diseases inflicted over forty-six hundred deaths and incapacitated approximately twenty-seven hundred. See James W. Davidson, The Island of Formosa, Past and Present (Shanghai, 1903), p. 364.

25. See Arts. 3, 13 of the Treaty of Tientsin of 1871.

26. For its text, see Chinese Customs, Treaties, II, pp. 604-614, 720-731; Hertslet, Treaties, I, pp. 373-382; MacMurray, Treaties, I, pp. 68-74.

27. Art. IV of the Treaty of 1896.

28. See J. Macgowan, The Imperial History of China (Shanghai, 1906), p. 480; Morse, II, p. 341.

29. See the statement of Marquis Tseng on June 28, 1883, cited in Henri Cordier, Histoire des Rélations de la Chine avec les Puissances Occidentales, II, p. 341.

30. Further details can be found in Morse, II, pp. 340-367; Henri Cordier, Le Conflict entre la France et la Chine (Paris: Lépold Cerf, 1883); Lloyd E. Eastman, Throne and Mandarines: China's Search for a Policy During the Sino-French Controversy, 1880-1885 (Cambridge, 1967).

31. For the text of the Convention of Tientsin (Li-Fournier) of May 11, 1884, see Chinese Customs, Treaties, I, pp. 894-896; Hertslet, Treaties, I, pp. 293-294. The withdrawal of Chinese troops from Tonkin and respect for all future treaties between France and Annam were stipulated in Art. 2 of the Convention and reaffirmed by the Protocol of Paris of April 4, 1885, and the Treaty of Tientsin of June 9, 1885. For the text of the Protocol and the Treaty, see, respectively, Chinese Customs, Treaties, I, pp. 897-899, 901-907; Hertslet, Treaties, I, pp. 294-296, 296-300.

32. Chinese Customs, Treaties, I, pp. 506-508; Hertslet, Treaties, I, pp. 88-90. Under this Convention, China recognized British authority in Burma, whose relationship with China was limited to sending tribute to Peking once every ten years (Art. 1).

33. Chinese Customs, Treaties, I, pp. 513-515; Hertslet, Treaties, I, pp. 92-94. Under this Agreement, China recognized the British protectorate over Sikkim.

34. See Morse, II, pp. 321-322.

35. Under the Treaty of Shimonoseki of April 17, 1895 (Chinese Customs, Treaties, I, pp. 590-596; Hertslet, Treaties, I, pp. 362-370). See also the Japanese-Korean Treaty of Alliance of August 26, 1894, and Protocol of February 23, 1904. Their texts can be found in William Woodville Rockhill, Treaties and Conventions with or concerning China and Korea, 1894-1904 (Washington, D.C., 1904; hereafter cited as Rockhill), pp. 429, 441, respectively.

36. Nepal used to send tribute to the Chinese Emperor once every five years. See Morse, II, p. 341.

37. Under the Sino-Franco Convention of Peking on June 20, 1895, and the Sino-British Agreement of Peking on February 4, 1897. For their text, see, respectively, Chinese Customs, Treaties, I, pp. 942-945, 532-538; Hertslet, Treaties, I, pp. 321-323; 113-119. England originally recognized China's suzerainty over Muglem and Kiang Hung under the Sino-British Convention of March 1, 1894, giving effect to Article III of the 1886 Convention relating to Burma and Tibet (Chinese Customs, Treaties, I, pp. 520-531). After France acquired a portion of Kiang Hung in 1895, England claimed virtual control of the whole area south of the Namwan River.

38. See Sino-Portuguese Treaty of Peking, December 1, 1887 (ibid., II, pp. 274-294); Hertslet, Treaties, I, pp. 423-433). For details, see Morse, II, pp. 386-388.

39. See infra, pp. 352-357.

40. Under the Sino-German Convention for the Lease of Kiaochow (Chinese Customs, Treaties, I, pp. 208-214; MacMurray, Treaties, I, pp. 112-118). The lease was actually effected by the convention of May 27, 1898 (ibid, pp. 128-130).

41. Under the Sino-Russian Convention of Peking for the Lease of Liaotung Peninsula (Chinese Customs, Treaties, I, pp. 219-226; MacMurray, Treaties, I, pp. 119-122).

42. Under the Sino-Franco Convention relating to Kuangchou-wan (Hertslet, Treaties, I, pp. 329-331; MacMurray, Treaties, I, pp. 123-124).

43. Under the Sino-British Convention for the Extension of Hong-kong (Chinese Customs, Treaties, I, pp. 539-540; Hertslet, Treaties, I, pp. 120-122; MacMurray, Treaties, I, pp. 130-131).

44. Under the Sino-British Convention for the Lease of Weihaiwei (Chinese Customs, Treaties, I, pp. 541-542; Hertslet, Treaties, I, pp. 122-123; MacMurray, Treaties, I, pp. 152-153).

45. See Morse, III, p. 118.

46. Italy demanded, in February 1899, a naval base in Sanmen Bay in Chekiang province, but the Chinese government firmly refused to make the grant in spite of the demonstration of four Italian cruisers. For Secretary Hay's attempt to obtain a naval base at Samsah Bay in Fukien province in December 1900, see U. S. For. Rel., 1915, pp. 113-115.

47. See Henri Cordier, Historie des Rélations de la Chine avec les Puissances Occidentals, III, p. 356.

48. The Kaiser appointed his brother, Admiral Prince Heinrich of Prussia as commander of the expeditionary forces to China. In his keynote speech in honor of the Admiral's mission at a banquet in Hamburg on December 18, 1897, the Emperor said: "I am conscious that it is my duty to extend and enlarge what my predecessors have bequeathed to me.... Should any one essay to detract from our just right or to injure us, then up and at him with your mailed fist." In reply, the admiral assured the Emperor: "One thing is the aim that draws me on, it is to declare in foreign lands the gospel of your Majesty's hallowed person, to preach it to every one who will hear it, and also to those who will not hear it." London Spectator, December 26, 1897.

49. For an extensive survey of the subject, see Clyde Eagleton, The Responsibility of States in International Law (New York, 1928); E. M. Borchard, Diplomatic Protection of Citizens Abroad (New York, 1915).

50. Russia's designs in Kiaochow and interest in Port Arthur and Dairen were emboided in the Cassini Convention with China on September 8, 1896, even though its existence was denied by both countries. For its text, see MacMurray, Treaties, I, pp. 79-81.

51. Under the Russo-Japanese Peace Treaty of September 5, 1905 (Hertslet, Treaties, I, pp. 608-614; MacMurray, Treaties, I, pp. 522-526). The transfer was later formalized by the conclusion between Japan and China of the Manchurian Convention

of December 22, 1905, and its Supplementary Agreement (Chinese Customs, Treaties, I, pp. 636-641, 734-735); Hertslet, Treaties, I, pp. 391-396; MacMurray, Treaties, I, pp. 549-555). For the Soviet holding of these two ports subsequent to World War II, see infra, pp. 270-271, 320-321.

52. See Group II, Art. I of the Twenty-one Demands presented by Japan to China, February 18, 1915 (MacMurray, Treaties, II, pp. 1231-1234). For Japan's ultimatum to China on May 7, 1915, and China's reply on May 8, 1915, see ibid., II, 1234-1236.

53. See Infra, pp. 160-163, 190-192.

54. According to Art. I of the Sino-Russian Agreement for the Lease of Port Arthur and Dairen, March 27, 1898, "this lease is to be without prejudice to China's authority in that territory." However, Art. IV of the same Treaty laid down the following restrictions:

> "Within the term fixed, in the territory leased to Russia, and in the adjacent waters, all movements of forces, whether naval or military, and the appointment of high officials to govern the districts, shall be entirely left to Russian officers, one man being made responsible, but he is not to have the title of Governor-General or Governor.

> "No Chinese troops of any kind whatever are to be allowed to be stationed within this boundary. Chinese within the boundary may leave or remain at their pleasure, and are not to be driven away."

55. See, for example, Art. V of the Sino-Franco Additional Convention to the Supplementary Commercial Convention of June 26, 1887, signed at Peking on June 26, 1895 (For the text of these two Conventions, see, respectively, Chinese Customs, Treaties, I, pp. 933-936, 937-941; Hertslet, Treaties, I, pp. 311-314, 321-323; the text of the 1895 Convention can also be found in MacMurray, Treaties, I, pp. 26-27); Art V of the Sino-British Agreement relating to Burma and Tibet, February 4, 1897 (Chinese Customs, Treaties, I, pp. 532-538; Hertslet, Treaties, I, pp. 113-119; MacMurray, Treaties, I, pp. 94-98); Note sent by Tsungli Yamen to the French Minister at Peking on March 15, 1897, assuring the Non-alienation of the Island of Hainan (Hertslet, Treaties, II, p. 1148; Mac-Murray, Treaties, I, p. 98); Exchange of Notes between Great Britain and China respecting Non-alienation of the Yangtze Region, February 9 and 11 1898 (Hertslet, Treaties, I, pp. 119-120; MacMurray, Treaties, I, pp. 104-105); Exchange of

Notes between France and China concerning Non-alienation of
Chinese Territory bordering on Tongking, April 10, 1898 (Mac-
Murray, Treaties, I, pp. 123-124); Note sent by Tsungli Yamen
to the Japanese Minister at Peking on April 26, 1898, assuring
the Non-alienation of the Province of Fukien (Hertslet, Treaties,
II, p. 1154; MacMurray, Treaties, I, p. 126); the Sino-British
Convention respecting Tibet, April 27, 1906, to which was annexed the Convention between Great Britain and Tibet of September 7, 1904 (Hertslet, Treaties, I, pp. 202-208; 1904 Convention also in MacMurray, Treaties, I, pp. 576-577). The
Sino-Russian Treaty of Alliance (Li-Lobanoff Treaty), signed
at Moscow in May 1896, gave Russia predominent influence
in Manchuria, including railway construction and other facilities. Unlike the Cassini Convention cited before, this Treaty
was formally acknowledged by China at the Washington Conference, 1921-1922. For its text and observations, see Mac-
Murray, Treaties, I, pp. 81-82; H. A. Gérard, Ma Mission en
Chine (Paris, 1918), pp. 135-148. At the time of the Boxer Uprising, Russia's control of Manchuria was so extensive that
China had to sign a special convention with Russia on March 26,
1902, for the re-establishment of Chinese authority there. For its
text, see Chinese Customs, Treaties, I, pp. 239-250; Hertslet,
Treaties, I, pp. 509-512; MacMurray, Treaties, I, pp. 326-329.

56. See, for example, the Declaration with regard to the Kingdom of
     Siam and Other Matters (Advantages in Yunnan and Szechwan,
     etc.), made by France and Great Britain at London, January
     15, 1896 (Hertslet, Treaties, I, p. 583; MacMurray, Treaties,
     I, pp. 54-55); the Anglo-German Bankers' Arrangement regard-
     ing Spheres of Interest in Railway Construction, September 2,
     1898 (MacMurray, Treaties, I, pp. 266-267); Exchange of Notes
     between Great Britain and Russia (Scott-Mouravieff Agreement)
     on April 28, 1899, with regard to Railway Interests in China
     (Hertslet, Treaties, I, pp. 586-589; MacMurray, Treaties, I,
     pp. 204-205); the Anglo-German Agreement relating to China,
     October 16, 1900 (Hertslet, Treaties, I, pp. 591-596; MacMur-
     ray, Treaties, I, pp. 263-267); Arts. IV-VII of the Russo-
     Japanese Peace Treaty of September 5, 1905, cited before.

57. For its text, see Hertslet, Treaties, I, pp. 597-598; MacMurray,
     Treaties, I, pp. 324-325.

58. For its text, see ibid., I, pp. 325-326.

59. MacMurray, Treaties, I, p. 640.

60. Ibid., I, pp. 657-658.

61. The notes to American envoys in Great Britain, France,
     Germany, and Russia were sent on September 6, 1899; and to

those in Japan and Italy, on November 13 and 17 respectively. The text of Secretary Hay's instructions to American envoys and their exchange of notes with the foreign offices concerned can be found in MacMurray, Treaties, I, pp. 221-235. Great Britain originated the idea of Anglo-American joint action to maintain an open door in China in 1898, but the United States Senate was then not inclined to adopt any step in the nature of an alliance. Hay's final decision was, however, prompted by a proposal made by A. E. Hippisley, an English employee of the Chinese Inspectorate of Maritime Customs and a friend of Hay's adviser on Far Eastern Affairs, W. W. Rockhill. See George F. Kennan, American Diplomacy 1900-1950 (Chicago, 1951), pp. 27-31; A. Whitney Griswold, The Far Eastern Policy of the United States (New York, 1938), p. 64.

62. See Count Muravieff to Mr. Tower, December 18, 1899 (MacMurray, Treaties, I, pp. 234-235).

63. See Tyler Dennett, John Hay, from Poetry to Politics (New York, 1933), p. 293.

64. See Westel W. Willoughby, Foreign Rights and Interests in China (Baltimore, 1927, rev. ed., 2 vols.; hereafter cited as Willoughby), I, pp. 95-97.

65. For its text, see MacMurray, Treaties, I, pp. 1394-1396.

66. Secretary Lansing to Ambassador Ishii, November 2, 1917 (ibid., I, p. 1395, para. 2).

67. In his reply to Secretary Lansing on November 2, 1917, Ambassador Ishii emphatically stated: "The Governments of Japan and the United States recognized that territorial propinquity creates special relations between countries, and, consequently, the Government of the United States recognizes that Japan has special interests in China, particularly in the part to which her possessions are contiguous." Ibid., I, p. 1395, para. 4.

68. See George F. Kennan, op. cit., p. 35; A. Whitney Griswold, op. cit., pp. 81-82.

69. Further information about the Boxer Uprising can be found from the following works: George N. Steiger, China and the Occident: The Origin and Development of the Boxer Movement (New Haven, 1927); Chester C. Tang, The Boxer Catastrophe (New York, 1955); Arthur H. Smith, China in Convulsion (London, 1901, 2 vols.); Paul H. Clements, The Boxer Rebellion: A Political and Diplomatic Review (New York, 1915); and Roland

Allen, The Seige of the Peking Legation (London, 1901); Victor, Purcell, The Boxer Uprising: A Background Study (New York, 1963).

70. In his I Ho Chüan Chiao Mên Yüan Liu Kao (Study of the Origin of the Boxer Sect), published in 1899, Lao Nai-hsüan stated that the I Ho Chüan (Righteous Harmony Fists) was affiliated with other secret societies, such as the White Lotus Society, the Eight Diagram Sect, and the Red Fist Society (pp. 1-5). Lao, a magistrate in Chihli (later known as Hopei) province, noted that it had been in existence in many villages in that province and Shantung. Lao's statement was based on Jén Tsung Jui Huang Ti Shêng Hsün (Edicts of Emperor Chia Ch'ing in Shih Ch'ao Shêng Hsün, Book 99). The Boxers later spread to Shansi and a part of Southern Manchuria. In his study of the Boxer movement, George N. Steiger considered the I'ho T'uan a lawful body despite its later association with members of Ta-tao Hui (Big Sword Society) and other secret societies. See Steiger, op. cit., p. 129. Chester C. Tang deemed that Steiger's explanation was "not founded upon sufficient evidence." Tang, op. cit., p. 37. For further information, see ibid., pp. 44-47.

71. As a result of the Yellow River flood in 1898; food was scarce in many parts of the country.

72. Chester C. Tang, op. cit., p. 237.

73. Both Catholics and Protestants were permitted to spread their gospel in accordance with the treaties of 1858. For the Imperial decree concerning the protection of foreigners and missionaries, see Tung Hua Hsü Lu, Kuang Hsü Ch'ao, Book 152, Leaf 4a. According to the Imperial decree of March 15, 1899, bishops ranked equally to viceroys and governors, and archdeacons and deans, to the sze-tai (fantai, niehtai, taotai). Because of Protestants' objections, this decree was cancelled by another rescript of March 12, 1908. See MacMurray, Treaties, I, pp. 717-718. Further information on missionaries in China may be found in Paul A. Cohen, China and Christianity, the Missionary Movement and the Growth of Chinese Anti-Foreignism, 1860-1870 (Cambridge, 1963); Shih-ch'iang Lü, the Causes of Anti-Christian Movement among Chinese Officials and Gentry, 1860-1874 (in Chinese; Taipei, 1966); Kwang-ching Liu (ed.), American Missionaries in China (Cambridge, 1966); Paul A. Varg, Missionaries, Chinese, and Diplomats (Princeton, 1958); K. S. Latourette, A History of Christian Missions in China (New York, 1929).

74. When activities of the I-ho T'uan were discovered along the Shantung-Chihli border in May 1898, local authorities

were ordered to make an investigation. The official report by the Governor of Shantung was submitted six months before the Imperial decree for the organization of the militia. See Tang, op. cit., p. 47. For the concern of foreign envoys at Peking with the Boxers, see U. S. For. Rel., 1900, pp. 96, 102. An Imperial decree of June 6, 1900 condemned the Boxers' destruction of churches and railways and ordered the generals to exterminate those leaders who disobeyed this proclamation. See Tang, op. cit., p. 67.

75. Joined by other detachments at Yangtsun with a total force of 2,066 (915 British, 540 German, 312 Russian, 158 French, 112 American, 54 Japanese, 40 Italian, and 25 Austrian), Admiral Seymour's troops first encountered the Boxers near Langfang, midway between Tientsin and Peking. The Imperial decree ordering the defense of the Taku forts and the prevention of further advance by foreign troops was issued on June 13, 1900. Four days later, the forts were bombarded. On June 20, the Imperial Council decided to recruit the Boxers into the army. The Boxers were then formally organized at Peking under the direction of Prince Chuang and Kang I. See Edward H. Seymour, My Naval Career and Travels (London, 1911), p. 342; Tang, op. cit., pp. 71-72, 93.

76. Jung Lu was against the use of the Boxers, and took a leading part in the negotiation for early evacuation of foreign envoys to Tientsin in the middle of July 1900. Sir Robert Hart recalled the seige of the legation quarter as follows: "Had the force round us really attacked with thoroughness and determination, we could not have held out a week, perhaps not even a day. So the explanation gained credence that there was some kind of protection – that somebody, probably a wise man...intervened between the issue of the order and the execution of it." Robert Hart, These from the Land of Sinim (London, 1901), p. 39. On June 25, 1900, an Imperial decree ordered the protection of foreign envoys at all costs. For details, see Morse, III, pp. 239, 246-247.

77. Mr. Sugiyama was killed on June 11, 1900, outside the Yungtingmen gate. The next day, a Boxer flaunting along the Legation Street "was summarily attacked and chastised with a walking stick by Baron von Ketteler." Ibid., III, p. 204. The German envoy was killed on June 20, when he started for the Tsungli Yamen, disregarding the protest and warning of other envoys. For details, see ibid., III, pp. 222-223.

78. The most prominent viceroys who had preserved a major part of China from war were Chang Chih-tung at Wuchang, Liu Kun-j at Nanking, and Li Hung-chang at Canton. Credit should also

be given to Shêng Hsüan-huai, Director of Telegraphs. They ignored the Imperial edict of the declaration of war on June 21, 1900. Yüan Shih-k'ai, Governor of Shantung, took the same attitude as the Southern viceroys.

79. See Chester C. Tang, op. cit., p. 35.

80. The Empress Dowager and the Emperor fled from Peking to Sian in the early morning of August 14, 1900, and remained there for almost a year. They did not return to Peking until January 7, 1902.

81. They were composed of 8,000 Japanese, 3,000 British, 4,500 Russians, 2,500 Americans, and 800 French. German troops remained in Kiaochow to stabilize the situation there.

82. After analyzing the respective responsibilities of the foreign and Chinese governments and condemning the atrocities of the Boxers, George N. Steiger commented in the follwoing words: "The concession-hunting governments of the West and the diplomatic representatives at Peking must share, with the people and officials of China, the responsibility for the atroc- ities of Boxer year – even for those atrocities which were act- ually commited by the Chinese." Steiger, op. cit., pp. 281- 282. Paul H. Clements shared the same view. Clements, op. cit., pp. 19, 26, 36. But he went further by stating that "from the day of the German seizure of Kiaochow, the Boxer Rebel- lion was a foregone conclusion, and apology and blame for succeeding events should primarily be laid at Europe's door, not at China's." p. 76.

83. By an Imperial decree of July 9, 1900, Li was again appointed Viceroy of Chihli, chiefly for convenience in his negotiations with the Allied powers in the North.

84, They were Austria-Hungary, Belgium, France, Germany, Great Britain, Italy, Japan, the Netherlands, Russia, Spain, and the United States.

85. For the text, see Chinese Customs, Treaties, II, pp. 303-341; MacMurray, Treaties, I, pp. 278-308. It took one year and twenty-four days to negotiate for peace after the seige of the legation quarter was relieved.

86. The total amount of indemnities was so enormous that it re- quired the assignment of all these important sources of revenue as security.

87. The customs duties in 1899 were actually equal to 3.18 percent of the value of all imports. As a result of the increased rate, it

was estimated that the revenue could be raised from 2,320,276 to 3,900,311 taels. See Chester C. Tang, op. cit., p. 230.

88. Admiral Kempff's opposition was based "on the ground that there had been no declaration of war against China, and that the attack would be tantamount to such declaration." Clements, op. cit., p. 129.

89. Secretary Hay's Circular concerning the Boxer Crisis, July 3, 1900 (U. S. For. Rel., 1900, p. 299; MacMurray, Treaties, I, p. 308).

90. Field Marshal von Waldersee, Commander-in-Chief of the Allied forces, arrived in Peking on October 17, 1900, and appropriated the Palace of the Empress Dowager as his residence. For the violence of German troops in Peking, see Chester C. Tang, op. cit., p. 145. German troops alone made thirty-five expeditions in North China. For John Hay's comments on German action in China, see William Roscoe Thayer, Life and Letters of John Hay (Boston, 1915, 2 vols.), II, p. 246. The massacres of Chinese in Blagovestchensk on the Amur by Russian soldiers was fully revealed in George Alexander Lensen's The Russo-Chinese War (Tallahassee, Florida, 1967), which described the events in Manchuria during the period of the Boxer Rebellion, chiefly from Russian sources. For the Russian slaughter of "many thousand Chinese men, women, and Children, whose bodies floated down the Amur," see Morse, III, p. 243. See also Arthur H. Smith, op. cit., II, p. 607. German disregard of rules of warfare could be further illustrated by quoting a part of the Kaiser's speech to the German troops at the time of their departure from Bremerhaven for China, on July 27, 1900. He declared that, in meeting the foe, "no quarter will be given, no prisoner will be taken." Morse, III, p. 309.

91. With territorial designs in Manchuria, Russia did not evacuate her troops from the occupied areas in Manchuria as promised on April 8, 1902. Czarist ambition was fully exposed in the Russo-Chinese Treaty regarding Manchuria, which was secretly handed by Count Lamdorff, Russian Foreign Minister, to Yang Ju, Chinese plenipotentiary, on February 16, 1901 (MacMurray, Treaties, I, p. 330). But the latter refused to sign it. For diplomatic negotiations for the settlement of the Manchurian situation, see also Chester C. Tang, op. cit., pp. 168, 171, 177-214.

92. See Morse, III, pp. 246, 286; Arthur H. Smith, op. cit., II, p. 583.

93. Morse, III, p. 246.

94. Because of the controlversial nature of the Boxer Uprising, facts presented and views expressed differ in some respects even in official sources. For comparison, consult U. S. For. Rel. and Consular Reports, vols. for 1895-1902; British Parliamentary Papers, China, Nos. 1-3 (1898), Nos. 1-2 (1899), Nos. 1-5 (1900), Nos. 1-7 (1901), No. 2 (1902); Documents Diplomatiques, Chine, vols. for 1894-1901.

Chapter 4

EXTENT OF FOREIGN INTRUSIONS ON CHINA'S NATIONAL SOVEREIGNTY AND TERRITORIAL INTEGRITY

Having considered the historical events leading to the conclusion of unequal treaties between China and foreign powers at different stages, it is now appropriate to appraise the extent of foreign intrusions on China's national sovereignty and territorial integrity. The scope of this undertaking is so vast as to require another chapter specifically dealing with administrative, judicial, and economic encroachments, which, in effect, also violated China's national sovereignty as political infringements. While many commitments have multiple implications, the present topical classification under these two chapters is largely for the convenience of discussion.

I. INFRINGEMENTS ON CHINA'S TERRITORIAL JURISDICTION

Under international law, a state has exclusive jurisdiction over its territorial doman with the exception of certain exemptions and immunities granted on a reciprocal basis. The exercise of territorial jurisdiction by China over foreign leaseholds, concessions and settlements, and the Legation Quarter in Peking was strictly restricted, if not completely denied, by unequal treaties. The circumstances under which such servitudes were imposed and the lack of mutuality in every respect were fatal to the establishment of cordial or even normal relations between China and the powers concerned.

1. Foreign Leaseholds

The leased territories acquired by foreign powers through force or duress as described before should legally have remained under Chinese sovereignty.[1] In actual practice, however, each one of the foreign leaseholds created a virtual imperium in imperio in China. For the duration of the tenancy, local administration was taken over by the lessee and Chinese authority was strictly limited.[2] Although the leases were inalienable according to the original aggreements,[3] Japan took over Kiaochow from Germany by force during World War I and Russia transferred Port Arthur and Dairen to Japan in 1905 without the previous consent of China. In both cases, the belligerents even conducted war in the leased territories in sheer violation of Chinese neutrality.[4]

2. Foreign Concessions and Settlements

Unlike leased territories, foreign concessions[5] and settlements were urban areas in treaty ports,[6] assigned by the Chinese authorities as residential quarters for foreigners "for the purpose of carrying on their mercantile pursuits."[7] First provided for in the Sino-British Treaty of 1842, this right was granted to British subjects in five treaty ports, and was later extended to nationals of other countries through the application of the most-favored-nation clause,[8] and to other places gradually opened to foreign trade as shown in Table I.[9] The areas so assigned were still under Chinese sovereignty, which was not only insisted upon by China but also recognized by the foreign powers concerned.[10] In practice, however, China's authority in such areas was denied in many respects, including the passage of Chinese police and armed forces and the right of plenary jurisdiction over her own nationals residing therein.[11] Administratively, the municipal councils or like organs in the concessions and settlements were controlled by foreigners, even though residents were predominantly Chinese.[12]

Concessions and settlements both meant 'areas set apart for foreign residence' or 'foreign residential areas', and have often been used synonymously. Strictly speaking, these two terms applied to two different types of areas for foreign

TABLE I

FOREIGN CONCESSIONS AND SETTLEMENTS IN CHINA
(As of 1925)

South China

CANTON:

British Concession	(1861, known locally
French Concession	as Shameen)

AMOY:

British Concession	(1851–52)
Japanese Concession	(1900)
American Concession	(a continuation of the British Concession and known by this name untill 1899)
Kulangsu International Settlement	(proclaimed by the Chinese authorities on May 1, 1902)

FOOCHOW   (1842, no defined area)

Central China

SHANGHAI:

The International Settlement	(1843)
The French Concession	(1849)
Woosung	(open to foreign trade and residence in 1898, not by treaty but at China's initiative)

NINGPO   (1842, no defined area)

HANKOW:

British Concession	(1861; Extension, 1898)
French Concession	(1886; Extension, 1902)
German Concession	

TABLE I (Continued)

Central China (Continued)

HANKOW (continued)

    Russian Concession
    Japanese Concession   (1898; Extension, 1906)

CHANGSHA   (General Foreign Settle-
                                ment, 1904)

CHUNGKING   (Japanese Settlement, 1901)

KIUKIANG   (British Concession, 1861)

WUHU   (General Foreign Settle-
                                ment, 1901; originally
                                marked out in 1877 for
                                a British Concession
                                but never taken up)

NANKING   (General Foreign Settle-
                                ment)

CHINKIANG   (British Concession, 1861)

HANGCHOW:

    Japanese Concession   (1895)
    General Foreign Settlement

SOOCHOW:

    Japanese Concession   (1895)
    General Foreign Settlement

North China

TIENTSIN:

    British Concession   (1861; Extension, 1897;
                                extramural area added
                                in 1903)
    French Concession   (1861)

TABLE I (Contiued)

North China (Continued)

TIENTSIN (continued)

Austrian Concession
German Concession
Japanese Concession
Russian Concession
Belgian Concession
Italian Concession

TSINANFU   (General Foreign Settle-
                                   ment, 1916)

HARBIN   (Russian Concession)

NEWCHWANG:

British Concession   (1861)
Foreign Settlement   (1900)

residence. Concessions designated foreign residential areas leased in perpetuity by the Chinese government to certain foreign powers, which sub-leased divided lots to foreign residents.[13] In many concessions, including those in Canton, Hankow, Kiukiang, and Tientsin, the consuls of the concession-holding countries were usually the officials in charge of their administration, assisted by certain agencies represented by foreign taxpayers. The International and French Settlements in Shanghai did not lease the land, the deeds of which were directly issued by the Chinese local authorities to interested foreigners, who organized themselves into municipal councils for administrative and legislative purposes.[14]

In addition to the above-mentioned concessions and settlements, there existed the so-called 'settlement by sufferance' as in the case of the port of Chefoo,[15] where the Chinese government did not formally grant a concession or settlement but gave implied consent to the acquisition of land by foreign residents.[16] Then a fourth class, 'voluntary settlement', emerged in several places, including Yochow and Changsha, where the Chinese government expropriated land for foreign residence and the local authorities took charge of the administration.[17] The last two types could not, however, be construed as concessions and settlements in the regular sense. [18]

It was in the concessions and settlements of the first two classes that the interested powers and their local agents made repeated efforts to expand their boundaries and authorities. Because of a lack of Chinese plenary jurisdiction over Chinese nationals in these enclaves, many undesirable elements took refuge therein under the protection of foreign authorities, who were generally lenient toward gambling, illicit trade, and other abusive practices. While peace and order was maintained in such areas due to their special status during the period of Chinese civil war, foreign concessions and settlements had long become symbols of foreign aggression and increasingly generated nationalistic sentiment among the Chinese residents.

3. The Legation Quarter at Peking

The Legation Quarter at Peking was the area set apart specially for diplomatic missions to China and was under their exclusive control. It was also made defensible. Chinese nationals could not reside inside the Quarter, and those employed by the Legations wore a special uniform outside the jurisdiction of the local government. This unique arrangement was one of the consequences of the Boxer Uprising. In order to guarantee the future safety of diplomatic missions and personnel, the Allied Powers demanded this right in their joint note of January 16, 1901,[19] and it was agreed upon by China in the Final Protocol of September 7 of the same year.[20] Detailed regulations for the administration of the Legation Quarter were drawn up by the Diplomatic Body at Peking, and formalized by the Protocol of June 13, 1914. [21]

It should be understood that, under international law, diplomatic inviolability and immunity apply only to persons with diplomatic status, diplomatic archives, and premises

used by diplomatic missions and their representatives.[22]
There was no precedent in international practice for such
an arrangement as the Legation Quarter at Peking.[23] Although the reasons for its creation were understandable, the
deprivation of Chinese authority over a portion of its own
territory deepened national resentment against foreign domination.

II.   PENETRATIONS INTO CHINA'S BORDER REGIONS

In discussing territorial ambitions of foreign powers, it
has been revealed how they detached China's dependencies,
acquired leased territories, and divided spheres of influence.
Some attention must now be given to their penetrations into
China's border regions, which included Manchuria, Tibet,
Sinkiang, and Outer Mongolia. Except Tibet, Russia had territorial designs in all these areas. Great Britain became
entangled in Tibet and Japan predominated Manchuria. Acting
either separately or jointly, their ultimate aim was to gain
control over certain portions of China's border regions contiguous to their own territories or possessions. With the
exception of Outer Mongolia, which has been made independent in 1946, each of the three powers succeeded, to a certain
extent, in their interested spheres, but all of them eventually
failed. During the period 1931-1945, Japan did achieve her
main objective of controlling all Manchuria and adjacent
Eastern Inner Mongolia, even though her military conquest
was short-lived. In this section, a brief description will be
made of the aggressive measures of the three powers in
these regions and the treaties concluded for the furtherance
of their objectives. Developments subsequent to the present
discussion will be covered under pertinent sections in the
following chapters.

1. Manchuria under the Domination of
Russia and Japan

Since the latter part of the nineteenth century, Russia
and Japan had confronted each other in Manchuria (the Three
Eastern Provinces of China). Notwithstanding conflict in
their national interests, the two powers managed to divide

their respective spheres of influence after the war of 1904-1905, and sometimes joined together against the interference of a third party. This complicated Russo-Japanese relationship in Manchuria was briefly mentioned before. In their struggle for political and economic concessions in this mutually coveted region, they offered no quid prop quo to China. Almost all the treaties these two powers concluded with China and between themselves, concerning Manchuria, were detrimental to China's sovereignty. Exclusive in substance, such treaties actually violated the letter and spirit of the Open Door Policy. [24]

In 1896, one year after the first Sino-Japanese War, Russia persuaded China to conclude the Li-Lobanoff Treaty, which binded the two countries into an alliance directed against any potential aggression by Japan. [25] Among other important matters, this Treaty gave Russia the right to extend the Trans-Siberian Railway to Manchuria, where it was commonly known as the Chinese Eastern Railway (CER). [26] Nominally under Sino-Russian joint supervision, CER was actually controlled by Russia for the advancement of her political and economic interests in Manchuria. The lease of Port Arthur and Dairen in 1898 further revealed Russia's aggressive policy,[27] which reached its climax at the time of the Boxer Uprising. [28]

The Anglo-Japanese alliance concluded in 1902[29] had strengthened the position of Japan in the Far East. As a consequence of the Russo-Japanese Peace Treaty of 1905, [30] Russia transferred to Japan the lease of Port Arthur and Dairen and railway rights in Southern Manchuria. Under pressure of circumstances, China was compelled to give consent to the transfer by signing the Sino-Japanese Convention and its Supplementary Agreement on December 22, 1905.[31] This Agreement and its attached secret protocols of the same date [32] furthered Japan's rights of railway construction and mining interests in Manchuria, to be discussed later. [33]

In 1907, Japan concluded separate agreements with France and Russia for mutual support in Asia and Manchuria respectively. [34] By an Exchange of Notes between Secretary of State Elihu Root and Ambassador Kogoro Takahira on November 30, 1908, Japan reached an understanding with the

United States to maintain the status quo in the Pacific region.[35] It should be recalled that the Anglo-Japanese alliance was renewed in 1905, and again in 1911 for a period of ten years.[36] Then World War I gave Japan a rare opportunity to penetrate deeper into China. Of the Twenty-one Demands presented to China in May 1915,[37] Group II was concerned particularly with Manchuria and Eastern Inner Mongolia, where Japan would obtain exclusive rights of railway construction and mining interests, as well as freedom of immigration, travel, and residence for Japanese subjects. The lease of Port Arthur and Dairen would be extended to ninety-nine years.

For mutual support of their respective spheres of influence, Japan and Russia signed the Convention in regard to Cooperation in the Far East on July 3, 1916. Different from the Political Convention of July 30, 1907, and another Convention of July 4, 1910, this one had a secret treaty of alliance attached to it so as to render military aid to each other whenever necessary.[38] Since both countries intended to extend their control in Manchuria, the temporary division of the northern and southern parts of Manchuria under Russian and Japanese influence respectively, could not last long. The Mukden Incident on September 18, 1931 broke the uneasy equilibrium envisaged by the above-mentioned treaties. [39]

2. British Schemes in Tibet

To the Chinese, Tibet has long been considered a part of China. After analyzing their relationships from historical sources, W. W. Willoughby, one of the highest authorities on China, concluded: "Tibet came under the suzerainty of China in the seventeenth century; this Chinese control was strengthened during the late years of the Manchu dynasty."[40] At any rate, Tibet never belonged to any country other than China. Thus in the Cheffo Agreement of September 13, 1876, Great Britain had to obtain permission from China to send a mission of exploration to Tibet. [41]

Following the Sino-British Convention relating to Sikkim and Tibet of March 17, 1890, [42] China recognized the British protectorate over Sikkim and was expected to restrain Tibet from violating the frontier of Sikkim. Appended to this Convention were Regulations regarding Trade, Communications, and Pasturage, and for Opening Yatung to Trade, signed by China and Great Britain on December 5, 1893.[43] The latter provision formally authorized trade between British India and Yatung of Tibet. Dissatisfied with China's inability to enforce these regulations and probably because of Russia's ambition in Tibet, Great Britain dispatched troops to Lhasa in 1904, the year of the outbreak of the Russo-Japanese War, and forced Tibet to sign a convention on September 7, 1904.[44] Tibet was compelled to establish trade relations with Great Britain, raze all forts and fortifications, remove all armaments between the frontier of British India and Gyantze and Lhasa of Tibet, and pay an indemnity for the expenses of the British expedition. [45]

By the use of force against Tibet and the conclusion of a treaty directly with the local government in Lhasa, Great Britain committed a serious violation of China's territorial rights over the region. The Convention revealed fully that Great Britain wanted nothing less than putting Tibet under her absolute control. Tibet was forbidden, without British consent, to undertake the following with any foreign power: cession, sale, lease, mortgage, or any other form of occupation of any portion of Tibetan territory; any interference in Tibetan affairs; admittance of foreign representatives; concessions for railways, roads, telegraphs, mining or other rights; and pledge or assignment of Tibetan revenues. [46] Furthermore, British troops would occupy Chumbi for a period of at least three years until the completion of payment of indemnity and effective opening of trade marts as specified in the Convention. [47]

Further negotiations between China and Great Britain resulted in the conclusion of the Convention respecting Tibet on April 27, 1906, [48] by which the Chinese government succeeded in modifying certain terms of the 1904 Convention. In return for a British promise not to annex the territory or interfere in the administration of Tibet, China undertook not to permit any foreign power to do likewise. While denying concessions for railways and other interests as listed in the 1904 Convention to other foreign powers, China would allow Great Britain to lay down telegraph lines between the trade marts in Tibet and India. The Sino-British Convention of 1890 and Regulations of 1893 would remain in force.[49] Negotiating these terms at a time when China Proper was subjected to the danger of dismemberment, the Manchu Court tried to restore whatever Chinese rights in Tibet it could under the circumstances.

Russian interest in Tibet and its adjacent areas was renewed in 1907, as evidenced in the conclusion of the Anglo-Russian Convention relating to Persia, Afghanistan and Tibet, on August 31 of that year. Recognizing China's suzerainty over Tibet, the two countries agreed not to undertake any negotiations with Tibet without the intermediary of the Chinese government, with the exception of British commercial relations as provided for in the 1904 Convention. Although both would respect the territorial integrity of Tibet and abstain from all interference in its internal administration, Great Britain reserved the right to occupy the Chumbi valley for so long a period and under the same conditions as stated before. [50] Following the Anglo-Russian Convention, Great Britain and China concluded the Regulations respecting Trade in Tibet on April 20, 1908, which amended those of December 5, 1893. Chinese authority over Tibet was expressly recognized in these Regulations. [51]

In 1908-1909, disturbances in Tibet necessitated China's military expeditions to Lhasa; the Dalai Lama took refuge in India and remained there until the overthrow of the Manchu dynasty in 1911. Then the Chinese government arranged with Tibet the withdrawal of Chinese troops in the following year, with the exception of a small escort of the Chinese representative at Lhasa. In the view of the British government, however, China's military operations in Tibet were in conflict with the Sino-British Convention of 1906.

For the normalization of Sino-British relations with respect to Tibet, representatives of the two countries and of Tibet met at Simla on October 13, 1913. A draft agreement was initiated on April 27 of the following year. On account of the erroneous inclusion of certain districts in the attempt to demarcate Outer Tibet and Inner Tibet and other important reasons, the Chinese government repudiated the action of its representative in initiating the draft and instructed him not to sign the final convention. Disregarding the Chinese position, Great Britain went ahead and signed the convention with Tibet on July 3, 1914. Nothing could be more contradictory than the

British recognition of Tibet as a part of Chinese territory
and under the suzerainty of China in the 1914 convention and
yet its final conclusion without the participation and consent
of the Chinese government, which, under international law,
was not bound by any of its provision.[52] The development of
the Tibetan situation in subsequent years and its legal implications will be discussed later in this work. [53]

3. Russian Intrigues in Sinkiang

China's penetration into Sinkiang[54] dates back to the Han
dynasty (202 B.C. − A.D. 220). Over the past two thousand
years, however, local leaders frequently broke away from
the central government when it could not exercise firm control over the region. Beginning with 1723, a series of re-
bellions occurred in several cities. Tso Tsung-tang, one of
the ablest generals of the Manchu dynasty, was charged with
restoring order in 1867, and his expedition proved quite
successful. Throughout the years, Russia watched the developing situation closely and finally decided to act. Russian troops
marched into Kuldja and occupied Ili in 1871. This unwarranted invasion took place on the ground that local disturbances had endangered the trade route to Kuldja, for which a
treaty of commerce had been signed between the two countries on July 25, 1851.[55] This was a weak argument for such
a strong action. Russia did give assurance that her troops
would be withdrawn when the area was pacified.

When General Tso's army approached near Ili in July
1878, China dispatched Ch'ung Hou to St. Petersburg, seeking
a peaceful settlement of the situation. According to the Treaty
of Livadia negotiated by Ch'ung Hou with the Russina government on September 3/15, 1879, Russia would gain a large
part of Ili and other exclusive privileges. [56] These terms
could not be accepted by the Manchu Court. Thus Ch'ung
Hou was recalled and substituted by Marquis Tseng Ki-tse,
one of the most distinguished diplomats of China at the time.
Tseng succeeded in concluding, on February 12/23, 1881,
the Treaty of St. Petersburg,[57] under which China recovered
most of the territory of Ili, but had to pay an indemnity of
nine million metallic roubles. [58] This Treaty had, however,
by no means ended Russia's ambitions in Sinkiang.

After the Ili incident, China remained impotent to govern Sinkiang. Taking advantage of the tumultous situation, Russia intermittently succeeded in dominating the area through her conspiracy with provincial authorities or rebel leaders whenever circumstances would permit. An immense area with sparce population but rich resources, on the border of a strong neighbor, Sinkiang could never be secure from outside interference if the central government of China were not in the position to exercise effective control. This unfortunate situation continued througout the latter part of the Manchu dynasty and the Republican period.[59]

4. Outer Mongolia in Dilemma

The Mongols founded the Yuan dynasty in 1279. After its overthrow by Emperor Chu Yüan-chang, founder of the Ming dynasty, in 1368, they were forced to retreat to the steppe. In the early seventeenth century, they came under the control of the Manchus, who eventually established the Ch'ing dynasty in 1644. Geographically, Outer Mongolia lies beyond the Gobi Desert, bordering Russia on the north and Inner Mongolia on the south; the latter has long been incorporated into Chinese provinces.[60] While Japan exerted efforts to dominate South Manchuria and Eastern Inner Mongolia,[61] Russia extended her influence in North Manchuria, Sinkiang, and particularly Outer Mongolia.

The fact that Outer Mongolia was a part of Chinese territory had never been questioned before November 3, 1912, when Russia capitalized on China's revolutionary turmoil and concluded with the Mongolian representatives an agreement governing general relations and a protocol on trade.[62] Under the agreement, Russia would "assist Mongolia to maintain the autonomous regime which she has established, as also the right to have her national army, and to admit neither the presence of Chinese troops on her territory nor the colonization of her land by the Chinese."[63] The so-called autonomous regime was undoubtedly instigated by the Russians. If the terms of that agreement were completely carried out, Mongolia would be entirely dominated by Russia and would consider China merely as one of the foreign powers.[64]

With Siberia not yet developed, Russia probably wanted to create a buffer state between herself and China, a populous and potentially powerful neighbor. On the other hand, China would not recognize Outer Mongolia as being formally under Russian control. Negotiations between the two countries led to the signing of a Sino-Russian Declaration and an Exchange of Notes on November 5, 1913, [65] by which they agreed that Outer Mongolia, while under the suzerainty of China, would be autonomous in internal administration, as well as commercial and industrial relations.[66] Without losing time, Russia concluded, in the following year, two agreements with Outer Mongolia, obtaining the right of consultation with regard to railway construction and concessions in the territory of the latter and the building of a telegraph line from Monda to Uliassutai. [67] Thus, in spite of her right of suzerainty, China became far less influential in Outer Mongolia than Russia.

Though Russia recognized that "the territory of Outer Mongolia forms a part of the territory of China" in her Note of November 5, 1913, [68] she wanted Outer Mongolia to be a party to a Tripartite Agreement of June 7, 1915.[69] Under this Agreement, Outer Mongolia accepted the terms embodied in the 1913 Declaration and Exchanges of Notes. Autonomous in internal administration, Outer Mongolia could not conclude international treaties on political and territorial questions, which would be a matter of concern to the three contracting parties. [70] Actually all these arrangements were initiated by Russia, because Outer Mongolia had become powerless to decide its own destiny.

After the Bolshevik Revolution, the opportunity arose for the Mongols to be emancipated from the Russian yoke. In November 1919, Outer Mongolia decided to terminate its autonomous status and petitioned the Chinese government to admit it as an integral part of China; this petition was readily granted by the President of the Chinese Republic.[71] The happy reunion was, nonetheless, short-lived. After the Bolsheviks consolidated their position in Russia, they resumed the traditional expansionist schemes. While repudiating the Czarist policy toward Mongolia, a Soviet-Mongolian Agreement for Establishing Friendly Relations, secretly concluded in Moscow, on November 5, 1921, recognized the People's Government of Mongolia as the only legal government of Mongolia. [72]

Against this disregard of China's sovereignty or suzerainty over Outer Mongolia and the presence of Soviet troops on its territory, the Chinese government vigorously protested. [73]

As a result of protracted negotiations, the two countries signed the Agreement of May 31, 1924.[74] The Soviet Union reaffirmed her recognition of Outer Mongolia as an integral part of the Chinese Republic, and agree to respect China's sovereignty therein. [75] The withdarawal of Soviet troops would, however, be subject to future consultation, and Russian influence penetrated even deeper into the region after the outbreak of the Sino-Japanese War in 1937.[76] The Yalta Agreement concerning Outer Mongolia and its subsequent independence from China in January 1946 will be discussed elsewhere. [77]

III. INFRACTIONS OF CHINA'S NATIONAL SOVEREIGNTY

Any acts committed by foreign powers adversely affecting the political independence or territorial integrity of a state violate the national sovereignty of that state. These may include the above-mentioned infringements on territorial jurisdiction and penetrations into border regions, as well as administrative, judicial, and economic encroachments to be considered in the following chapter. For convenience of discussion, however, the present section will treat the subject in a narrow sense and only deal with the stationing of foreign armed forces and warships, compulsory opening of ports and inland navigation, and arbitrary operation of foreign post offices and wireless stations. All these rights were secured by foreign powers either through unequal treaties or without the express consent of China, and none of them could be reciprocally applied for the actual benefit of China.

1. Stationing of Foreign Armed
Forces and Warships

No armed forces or warships of one state can enter the territory, including national waters, of another without special permission. In China, foreign powers acquired this unusual right by the conclusion of unequal treaties or the application of the most-favored-nation clause. The Final Protocol of September 7, 1901, for the settlement of the Boxer Uprising, compelled China to demilitarize the Taku fortifications and the communication route between Peking and the sea, with several strategic points to be occupied by Allied troops. [78] For further protection of the diplomatic missions at the Capital, the Legation Quarter was allowed to keep armed guards. [79] Later on, the powers concerned abused this right by interfering in the domestic affairs of China. During the Chinese revolutionary period 1911-1912, American, British, French, German, Italian, and Japanese troops occupied the Peking-Mukden Railroad from Peking to Shanhaikwan. [80] In the ensuing years, foreign troops and warships sometimes fired at the Chinese with little provocation, and not infrequently took sides in civil wars. [81] Of a different nature but even more seriuous, was the conduct of warfare by Japanese armed forces against Russia in Manchuria in 1904-1905 and against Germany in Tsingtao and other places along the Shantung Railway in 1914. On both occasions, Japan violated not only China's sovereignty but also the law of neutrality. In the former case, Russia was equally guilty of breaches of international law.

The Japanese and Russian justification for maintaining railway guards in Manchuria was seriously challenged by the Chinese government. The Peace Treaty of Portsmouth of September 5, 1905, [82] concluding the Russo-Japanese War, provided that the two contracting parties would "reserve to themselves the right to maintain guards to protect their respective railway lines in Manchuria." [83] China, of course, could not be bound by an agreement concluded between third parties. Japan argued that China's consent to this right was obtained through the Sino-Japanese Manchurian Convention of December 22, 1905 and its Supplementary Agreement. [84] Actually, in the Additional Agreement, China expressed her earnest desire for the earliest withdrawal of Japanese and Russian troops and railway guards from Manchuria. [85] The troops of the two belligerents were to be evacuated from Manchuria completely and simultaneously. [86] It should be mentioned that Japanese railway guards were also maintained along the Shantung Railway in addition to the South Manchurian Railway system.

In other cases, the stationing of foreign troops and police agents had no treaty basis whatsoever. Again, Japan has to be singled out for illustration. After the outbreak of the Chinese Revolution in Wuchang in 1911, several powers, including Great Britain, Russia, Germany, and Japan, dispatched troops to Hankow on the grounds of protecting the lives and property of their nationals. When peace was restored in that area, Japan alone refused to withdraw her army. The same attitude was taken by the Japanese government in keeping troops along the Chinese Eastern Railway on the pretext of establishing communications between the Japanese expeditionary forces in Siberia and South Manchuria, in pursuance of the Inter-Allied Agreement of 1919.[87] The presence of Japanese consular police in Manchuria for the alleged reason of protecting and controlling Japanese subjects created constant friction with the Chinese authorities. Of a different nature was the municipal police in foreign concessions and settlements in China's treaty ports for the maintenance of local order under the permission of the Chinese government.

Controversy arose between China and the treaty powers with respect to the right of foreign warships to enter her national waterways and inland ports. The Sino-British Treaty of June 26, 1858[88] was claimed as the legal basis of this right, because it provided that ''British ships of war coming for no hostile purpose, or being engaged in the pursuit of pirates, shall be at liberty to visit all ports within the dominions of the Emperor of China.''[89] Through the application of the most-favored-nation clause, the United States government upheld the right of the Villalobos, an American gunboat, to navigate up the Yangtze River in 1903. [90] In the view of the Chinese government, however, the right of navigation of foreign warships was limited to treaty ports and should not include non-treaty ports.[91] It was also contended by the diplomatic body at Peking that foreign warships could freely make surveys and soundings in China's closed ports, [92] even though such a practice would not be permitted by other powers. It should be noted that treaties or practices involving international servitudes or limitations of sovereignty of one state for the benefit of the other should be construed strictly. This is a general rule of international law, broad interpretations by the treaty powers notwithstanding.

2. Compulsory Opening of Ports and Inland Navigation

A state has exclusive jurisdiction over its national waters, in which no foreign ships may regularly navigate without its express consent by laws or treaties. The Sino-British Treaty of Nanking of 1842 opened Canton, Amoy, Foochowfoo, Ningpo, and Shanghai to foreign trade.[93] Consequent to other treaties concluded between China and foreign powers in ensuing years,[94] treaty ports had been increased to approximately seventy in number.[95] Since the interested powers were entitled to establish concessions or settlements in these ports accompanied with the exercise of consular jurisdiction, repeated attempts were made to extend their limits and privileges. Foreign diplomats at Peking interpreted the Chinese characters for treaty ports, 't'ung shang k'ou ngan' as comprising the port, the city of the port, and any road or waterway connecting these two. The Chinese government disagreed with this broad definition, and wanted to confine the limit to the port itself.[96]

Besides the treaty ports, there were twenty-two others voluntarily opened for foreign trade by the Chinese government.[97] While both types could be classified under the general term 'open ports', there was a basic difference in that local authorities retained control over municipal administration and police in voluntarily opened ports. As to whether stipulations for treaty ports could apply to voluntarily opened ports, foreign powers again differed with the Chinese position. In 1899, diplomatic envoys at Peking contested China's decision to levy wharfage dues in addition to treaty tariffs in Santuao, a voluntarily opened port in Fukien province. In their view, restrictions not to levy more than treaty tariffs in the treaty ports should be applied in this case.[98] The challenge of China's sovereignty over matters within her own jurisdiction discouraged the Chinese government from opening more ports for foreign trade.

The ports of call belonged to another category, where foreign ships were permitted to carry on a limited traffic. In accordance with the Sino-British Treaty of Chefoo, September 13, 1876,[99] certain places on the shore of the Yangtze River were designated as ports of call, where "foreign merchants are not legally authorized to land or ship goods."

In the case of foreign ships, they "shall be allowed to touch for the purpose of landing or shipping passengers or goods, but in all instances by means of native boats only, and subject to the regulations in force affecting native trade." [100] Different from open ports and ports of call were non-open ports, which foreign ships were prohibited from visiting on pain of confiscation of both ships and cargo.[101] Sometimes, foreign merchants conducted business in non-open ports without permission from the Chinese government.[102]

The opening of ports for foreign trade led to further agreement on the subject of inland navigation. The Yangtze River was opened first for that purpose by the Sino-British Treaty of June 26, 1858,[103] followed by other waterways under different treaties.[104] Through the application of the most-favored-nation clause, all treaty powers acquired the same privileges, subject to the rules and regulations agreed upon with the Chinese government.[105] The Regulations relative to Inland Steam Navigation, promulgated by the Tsungli Yamen on July 28, 1898,[106] applied to ships of all treaty powers navigating in Chinese inland waterways, subject to necessary changes.[107] Detailed rules governing navigation of foreign ships in different inland waterways were also enacted.[108] In conclusion, it was not so much the presence of foreign ships in Chinese ports and waterways but the circumstances which forced the opening of ports and inland navigation with its consequent implications that aggravated anti-foreign feeling among the Chinese public.

With respect to the right of cabotage, or coastal trade from one open port to another, it is generally reserved by a state for its own nationals. In China, however, nationals of all treaty powers could carry on such trade without reciprocity. The Sino-Mexican Treaty of December 14, 1899 was an exception among the early treaties.[109] In her later commitments China reserved inland and coastwise navigation to her own nationals.[110] Of course, China would not object to granting these privileges to foreign powers on reciprocal basis.

3. Arbitrary Operation of Foreign Post Offices and Wireless Stations

The operation of foreign post offices in China without any treaty basis violated her national sovereignty. In 1834, Great Britain opened the first post office in Hongkong, then a Chinese territory; branches in other Chinese ports soon followed. Other powers followed the British example. By 1906, there were altogether fifty-nine foreign post offices.[111] The original purpose of operating post offices in China was for the convenience of foreign representatives and residents in transmitting their mail between China and other countries, because the Chinese traditional services of 'ichan' and 'letter hongs' could not meet their needs. [112]

When foreign diplomats established residence in Peking in the 1860's, government couriers were directed to transmit their official dispatches. The Chinese Customs Inspectorate was later put in charge of the matter to a limited extent, and was then ordered to supervise a national postal service, which was created by an Imperial decree of March 20, 1896.[113] After a few years of successful experiment, China established an independent postal system under the Minister of Posts and Communications on May 28, 1911, and joined the Universal Postal Union three years later. As the Chinese postal service proved efficient and expanded rapidly, foreign post offices, illegally operated from the very beginning, no longer had any justification for their continued existence. Instead, their number was surprisingly increased to one hundred fifty by 1921. [114]

The notorious evasion of foreign parcels from customs examination encouraged the smuggling of contraband and narcotics. With their own postage stamps, foreign post offices had deprived China of that part of her revenue and hindered the development of the Chinese postal system.[115] In addition, the abnormal operation of maintaining post offices in the territory of its member states is not recognized by the Universal Postal Union.

Chinese land telegraph lines have been under government administration since 1908.[116] Several foreign companies operated cables in China.[117] The most complicated of the electrical means of communication was the wireless stations, which were established by foreign powers, without China's express consent, in Legation grounds, concessions and settlements, leased territories, railway zones and other places.[118] The continuing existence of such illegal wireless stations definitely infringed on China's national sovereignty. Because of her earnest desire for their removal, the matter was seriously discussed at the Washington Conference in 1921-1922.[119]

NOTES TO CHAPTER 4

1. The sovereign right of China over the leased territories was recognized in all the treaties effecting the leases. For instance, on the lease of Port Arthur and Dairen, Art I of the Sino-Russian Convention of March 27, 1898 (Chinese Customs, Treaties, I, pp. 219-226; MacMurray, Treaties, I, pp. 119-122) provided that "this act of lease, however, in no way violated the sovereign rights of H.M. the Emperor of China to the above-mentioned territory."

2. This restriction can be well illustrated by Art IV of the same Sino-Russian Convention of 1898:

> "During the above-specified period, on the territory leased by the Russian Government and its adjacent water area, the entire military command of the land and naval forces and equally the supreme civil administration will be entirely given over to the Russian authorities and will be concentrated in the hands of one person who however shall not have the title of Governor or Governor-General. No Chinese military land forces whatsoever will be allowed on the territory specified."

In the opinion of the United States Solicitor for the Department of State on the subject in question, "the reservation of sovereignty is merely intended to cut off possible future claim of the lessee that the sovereignty of the territory is permanently vested in them." "The intention and effect of these leases," according to him, "to have been the relinquishment by China, during the term of the lease, and the conferring upon the foreign power in each case of all jurisdiction over the territory." see U. S. For. Rel., 1900, p. 389. For the memorandum of the Solicitor and Secretary Hay's covering letter to the American Minister in Peking, see ibid., pp. 386-389.

3. See, for instance, the following provision under Art. V of the Sino-German Convention for the Lease of Kiaochow, March 6, 1898 (Chinese Customs, Treaties, I, pp. 208-214; MacMurray, Treaties, I, pp. 112-118):

> "Germany engages at no time to sublet the territory leased from China to another Power."

4. It should be noted that China maintained neutrality througout the Russo-Japanese War in 1904-1905, and had not yet entered into war against Germany at the time of Japan's attack on Kiaochow; but military operations by belligerents were extended to other areas within Chinese territory as well. See also Min-Ch'ien T. Z. Tyau, The Legal Obligations Arising out of Treaty Relations between China and Other States (Shanghai:

Commercial Press, 1917; hereafter cited as Tyau), pp. 74-86; Morse, III, pp. 427-433.

5. Here the word 'concessions' applies to foreign residential areas only, not to special rights and privileges granted by the Chinese government to foreign powers and their nationals, such as railway construction and mining interests.

6. Treaty ports were ports opened to foreign trade by treaties. Those opened by the Chinese government voluntarily were called open ports, where the whole area was available to foreign trade and residence, but no lease of land by foreigners could extend for more than thirty years.

7. Art. II of the Sino-British Treaty of August 29, 1842 (Chinese Customs, Treaties, I, pp. 351-356; Hertslet, Treaties, I, pp. 7-12).

8. See, for example, the Sino-German Convention for a Concession at Hankow, October 3, 1895 (MacMurray, Treaties, I, pp. 42-46); the Sino-German Convention for a Concession at Tientsin, October 30, 1895 (ibid. , I, pp. 46-50); the Sino-Japanese Protocol in Regard to Japanese Settlements at Open Ports of China, October 19, 1896 (Chinese Customs, Treaties, II, pp. 615-616, 732-733; MacMurray, Treaties, I, pp. 91-94). The rights of the foreigners in treaty ports were expressly stipulated in the Sino-American Treaty for the Extension of Commercial Relations, October 8, 1903 (Chinese Customs, Treaties, II, pp. 745-763; Hertslet, Treaties, I, pp. 566-578; MacMurray, Treaties, I, pp. 423-450). Art. III of the Treaty reads:

> "Citizens of the United States may frequent, reside and carry on trade, industries and manufactures, or pursue any lawful avocation, in all the ports or localities of China which are now open or may hereafter be opened to foreign residence and trade; and, within the suitable localities at those places which have been or may be set apart for the use and occupation of foreigners, they may rent or purchase houses, places of business, and other buildings, and rent or lease in perpetuity land and building thereon."

9. See The China Year Book, 1925, pp. 907-908. For the status and development of the settlements in Shanghai, see Tsien, p. 57; Tyau, pp. 58-59. A provision was made in Art. X of the Sino-Japanese Supplementary Treaty of Commerce and Navigation of October 8, 1903 (Chinese Customs, Treaties, II,

pp. 617-636; MacMurray, Treaties, I, pp. 411-422), to open Peking to international residence and trade after the withdrawal of foreign troops in Chihli province and the Legation guards, but neither materialized.

10. See, for example, Art. I of the Additional Articles to the Treaty of Commerce between the United States and China of June 18, 1858, signed at Washington, on July 28, 1868 (Chinese customs, Treaties, I, pp. 729-735; Hertslet, Treaties, I, pp. 554-557). In his instructions to Sir Frederic Bruce, British Minister to China, on April 8, 1863, Earl Russell, British Secretary for Foreign Affairs, stated that "the lands situated within the limits of the British Settlement are without doubt Chinese territory." Chinese Social and Political Science Review, Vol. 5a (1920), Nos. 1-2, p. 148.

11. For details, see William L. Tung, Imperialism and China (Shanghai: Kwaimin Press, 1930, in Chinese), Pt. II, pp. 42-43.

12. There were a few Chinese representatives on the municipal councils of the International Settlement in Shanghai and the Kulangsu International Settlement in Amoy, but they had little voice in the final decisions.

13. It was a general practice for Chinese nationals to purchase land in the concessions under the name of foreigners, who gave their consent for a financial consideration. For different reasons, similar cases existed in the International Settlement at Shanghai, where a large part of land was directly held by the Chinese.

14. For details, see Hosea B. Morse, The Trade and Administration of China (London: Longmans, Green & Co., 2nd ed., 1912), pp. 346-355.

15. See Tyau, p. 59.

16. See Hosea B. Morse, op. cit., p. 221.

17. See ibid., p. 231.

18. For different kinds of concessions and settlements, see also Willoughby, I, pp. 504-505.

19. For its text, see MacMurray, Treaties, I, pp. 309-310.

20. Art. VII of the Final Protocol of 1901 (ibid., I, pp. 278-308; Chinese Customs, Treaties, II, pp. 303-341).

21. For its text, see MacMurray, Treaties, I, pp. 315-316.

22. For details, see William L. Tung, International Law in an Organizing World, pp. 261-279.

23. For the location of foreign diplomatic missions to China and their surroundings, see the map in Chinese Customs, Treaties, II, MacMurray, Treaties, I; or Morse, III.

24. See supra, pp. 50-51.

25. See Art. I of the Li-Lobanoff Treaty of 1896 (MacMurray, Treaties, I, pp. 81-82).

26. See Art. IV of the Li-Lobanoff Treaty. For further details, see the Sino-Russian (Russo-China Bank) Contract for the Construction and Operation of the Chinese Eastern Railway, September 8, 1896 (ibid., I, pp. 74-79); the Sino-Russian Agreement regarding Supervision of Siberian Railway System, January 9, 1919 (ibid., I, pp. 82-84); the Statutes of the Chinese Eastern Railway Company, December 4/16, 1896 (ibid., I, pp. 84-88); the Russian Imperial Ukaz regarding Jurisdiction in Chinese Eastern Railway Zone, August 2, 1901 (ibid., I, pp. 88-90). See also infra, pp. 220-224, 270.

27. See the Convention of Peking for the Lease of the Liaotung Pennisula, March 27, 1898 (Chinese Customs, Treaties, I, pp. 219-226; MacMurray, Treaties, I, pp. 119-122).

28. At that time, Russian control of Manchuria was so extensive that, after the Boxer Uprising, it was necessary to conclude a special convention for the reestablishment of Chinese authority in Manchuria on April 8, 1902 (Chinese Customs, Treaties, I, pp. 239-250; Hertslet, Treaties, I, pp. 509-512; MacMurray, Treaties, I, pp. 326-329).

29. For details, see the Anglo-Japanese Agreement relative to China and Korea, January 30, 1902 (ibid., I, pp. 324-325).

30. See Arts. V, VI of the Treaty of Portsmouth of 1905 (Hertslet, Treaties, I, pp. 608-614; MacMurray, Treaties, I, pp. 522-526).

31. For the text, see Chinese Customs, Treaties, I, pp. 636-641, 734-735; Hertslet, Treaties, I, pp. 391-396; MacMurray, Treaties, I, pp. 549-553.

32. A summary of the Protocols can be found in ibid., I, pp. 554-555.

33. See infra, pp. 121-123, 156-157, 258.

34. See supra, p. 50.

35. For the text, see MacMurray, Treaties, I, pp. 770-771.

36. See the Anglo-Japanese Agreement respecting Integrity of China, etc., August 12, 1905 (ibid., I, pp. 516-519); the Anglo-Japanese Agreement respecting the Integrity of China, the General Peace of Eastern Asia and India, and the Territorial Rights and Special Interests of the Parties in Those Regions, July 13, 1911 (ibid., I, pp. 900-901). For details, consult Ian H. Nish, The Anglo-Japanese Alliance: The Diplomacy of Two Island Empires, 1894-1907 (London, 1966). The Anglo-Japanese alliance was eventually terminated upon ratification of the Four-Power Treaty, concluded in Washington, by Great Britain, Japan, France, and the United States, on December 13, 1921. For the text, see Carnegie Endowment for International Peace, Treaties and Agreements with and concerning China, 1919-1929 (Washington, D.C., 1929; hereafter cited as Carnegie, Treaties), pp. 58-61.

37. The text of the Twenty-one Demands can be found in MacMurray, Treaties, II, pp. 1231-1234.

38. For the text of the 1907, 1910, and 1916 Conventions between Japan and Russia, see, respectively, MacMurray, Treaties, I, pp. 549-555; I, pp. 803-804; II, pp. 1327-1328.

39. See infra, pp. 257-259.

40. Willoughby, I, p. 462.

41. This was provided in a separate article appended to the Chefoo Agreement, which can be found in Chinese Customs, Treaties, I, pp. 491-499; Hertslet, Treaties, I, pp. 73-80.

42. For its text, see Chinese Customs, Treaties, I, pp. 513-515; Hertslet, Treaties, I, pp. 92-94.

43. For its text, see Chinese Customs, Treaties, I, pp. 516-519; Hertslet, Treaties, I, pp. 96-98.

44. This Convention of 1904 was later annexed to the Sino-British Convention respecting Tibet of April 24, 1906. The text of both conventions can be found in Chinese Customs, Treaties, I, pp. 652-654; 655-660; Hertslet, Treaties, I, pp. 202-208; MacMurray, Treaties, I, pp. 576-577, 577-581.

45. See Arts. II, VI, VIII of the Convention of 1904.

46. Art. IX of the 1904 Convention.

47. See the Declaration of the Viceroy and Governor-General of India, which was appended to the ratified Convention of September 7, 1904 (MacMurray, Treaties, I, p. 581).

48. For the sources of its text, see supra, Ch. 4, note 47.

49. See Arts. I-IV of the 1906 Convention.

50. See Arts. I, II of the Anglo-Russian Convention of 1907 (MacMurray, Treaties, I, pp. 674-678; Hertslet, Treaties, I, pp. 620-622, for the provision on Tibet only). Arts. III-V dealt with the denial to both governments of sending represntatives to Lhasa, seeking concessions, and pledging or assigning Tibetan revenues. See also the Annex to the Convention (MacMurray, Treaties, I, p. 678).

51. The 1908 Regulations were signed at Calcutta between the British Commissioner and the Chinese Commissioner, who was assisted by a Tibetan delegate. Ratifications were exchanged at Peking on October 14, 1908. For the text, see British Treaty Series, 1908, No. 35; Chinese Customs, Treaties, I, pp. 661-668; MacMurray, Treaties, I, pp. 582-585. For the 1893 Regulations, see supra, p. 78, note 43.

52. For details, see Alastair Lamb, The McMahon Line: A Study in the Relations between India, China and Tibet, 1904 to 1914 (London & Toronto, 1966, 2 vols.), II, pp. 459-529; Statesman's Year Book, 1916, p. 805; MacMurray, Treaties, I, pp. 581-582.

53. See infra, pp. 316-319.

54. Formerly known as Chinese Turkestan, Sinkiang, bordering Russia on the west and northwest and Kashmir on the southwest, had long been the caravan link of China with Central Asia and the Near East. In his Ancient Khotan (Oxford, 1905), Sir M. Aured Stein produced documentary records of Chinese occupation and administration in that strategically important region. Under Communist rule, it is now called Sinkiang-Uighur Autonomous Region. See William L. Tung, The Political Institutions of Modern China (The Hague, 1964), pp. 306-308.

55. For its text, see Chinese Customs, Treaties, I, pp. 70-80; Hertslet, Treaties, I, pp. 449-454.

56. See Morse, II, p. 332.

57. For its text, see Chinese Customs, Treaties, I, pp. 168-187; Hertslet, Treaties, I, pp. 483-499.

58. For details of the Ili incident, see Morse, II, pp. 328-339; William L. Tung, Imperialism and China, Pt. II, pp. 23-25; Immanuel C. Y. Hsu, The Ili Crisis: A Study of Sino-Russian Diplomacy, 1878-1881 (London, 1965); En-han Li, Tseng Chi-tse Ti Wai-chiao (The Diplomacy of Tseng Chi-tse, Taipei, 1966, in Chinese).

59. Among the instances were the Soviet support of Sheng Shih-tsai as Governor of Sinkiang and subsequent instigation of up-risings in the area west of Urumchi. For details, see Chiang Chung-cheng, Soviet Russia in China (New York, 1957), pp. 99-103. For recent development, see infra., pp. 314-315.

60. For further information on Mongolia, see The China Year Book, 1925, pp. 422-428; Robert A. Rupen, Mongols of the Twentieth Century (Bloomington, 1964, 2 vols.).

61. See Group II of Japan's Twenty-one Demands of 1915 (Mac-Murray, Treaties, II, pp. 1231-1234).

62. For the text of the Agreement and the Protocol, see ibid., II, pp. 992-996.

63. Art. 1.

64. This was clearly the intention of Russia as shown in Art. 3 of the Agreement:

> "If the Mongolian Government finds it necessary to conclude a separate treaty with China or another foreign Power, the new treaty shall in no case either infringe the clauses of the present agreement and of the protocol annexed thereto, or modify them without the consent of the Imperial Russian Government."

65. For their text, see MacMurray, Treaties, II, pp. 1066-1067.

66. Arts. I-III.

67. See the Agreement concerning Railroads to Mongolia, September 30, 1914 (MacMurray, Treaties, II, pp. 1178-1179); the Agreement to Grant to the Russian Central Postal and Telegraph Department the Concession for the Construction of a Telegraph Line from Monda to Uliassutai, September 30, 1914 (ibid., II, pp. 1179-1180).

68. Art. 1 of the Note of the Russian Minister at Peking to the Chinese Minister for Foreign Affairs (ibid., II, pp. 1066-1067).

69. For its text, see ibid., II, pp. 1239-1244. Another Tripartite Agreement was concluded concerning Outer Mongolian Telegraph Line on January 24, 1916 (ibid., II, pp. 1259-1266).

70. Art. I-III.

71. For the excerpts of the Mongolian petition and the President's mandate, see Willoughby, I, pp. 457-458; quoted from Millard's Review, December 6, 1919.

72. See Art. 1 of the Agreement of 1921 (Carnegie, Treaties, pp. 53-56). It should be noted that, during a short period 1920-1921, Outer Mongolia was virtually under the occupation of Baron Ungernsternberg, a white Russian general, whose eventual defeat by the Red army established Soviet control of the region.

73. The following is an extract from the Chinese protest: ''It must be observed that Mongolia is a part of Chinese territory and, as such, has long been recognized by all countries. In secretly concluding a treaty with Mongolia, the Soviet Government has not only broken faith with its previous declarations but also violates all principles of justice.'' The China Year Book, 1923, p. 680. For the Sino-Russian relations respecting Outer Mongolia during the period 1917-1919, Yü-shu Li's two works in Chinese are important references: Chung-O Kuanhsi Shih-liao (Sources of Sino-Russian Relations), Vol. I, Wai Meng-ku (Outer Mongolia), Taipei, 1959; Wai Meng-ku Ch'e-chih Wen-t'i (The Problem of Outer Mongolia's Relinquishment of Autonomy), Taipei, 1961.

74. See The China Year Book, 1924, p. 880; Carnegie, Treaties, pp. 133-140.

75. Art. V. For the Soviet-Mongolian Railway Agreement of September 1925, see The China Year Book, 1926-1927, p. 800.

76. For the Soviet instigation of setting up a Communist regime in Outer Mongolia and the incorporation of the latter's Tannu Tuva into Soviet territory on October 13, 1941, see Chiang Chung-cheng, op. cit., pp. 98-99. See also W. A. Douglas Jackson, Russo-Chinese Borderlands (Princeton, 1962), pp. 50, 66, 111.

77. The preservation of the status quo in Outer Mongolia as one of the terms of the Yalta Agreement meant the maintenance of the Mongolian People's Republic. Thus the plebiscite for its independence held at the end of 1945 was merely a matter of formality, because the Soviet Union had complete control of the territory. See infra, pp. 270, 373, 360-362.

78. See Arts. VIII, IX of the Final Protocol of 1901 (Chinese Customs, Treaties, II, pp. 303-341; MacMurray, Treaties, I, pp. 278-308). Spain was the only signatory state of the 1901 Protocol that did not station troops in the designated strategic points: Huang-tsun, Lang-fang, Yang-tsun, Tientsin, Chun-liang Ch'eng, Tang-ku, Lun-tai, Tang-shan, Lan-chou, Chang-li, Ch'in-wang Tao, and Shan-hai Kuan.

79. See Art. VII and Annex 14 of the Final Protocol of 1901. In Art. VII of the Sino-British Convention of March 1, 1894, a demilitarized zone along the common frontier between the territorial possession of the two countries was provided. This kind of demilitarization was different from that prescribed in the 1901 Protocol. For the text of the Sino-British Convention, see Chinese Customs, Treaties, I, pp. 513-515; Hertslet, Treaties, I, pp. 92-94.

80. See the Resolutions of the Diplomatic Body regarding Military Occupation of the Railway from Peking to Shanhaikwan, January 26, 1912 (MacMurray, Treaties, I, pp. 318-319). The number of foreign troops stationed at various strategic points along the railroad varied at different times, approximately nine thousand before World War I. See "Questions for Readjustment Submitted by China to the Peace Conference," Chinese Social and Political Science Review, Vol. 52 (1920), pp. 120-121. When free communications between Peking and the sea were interrupted in 1926 as a result of the Chinese civil war, the American Minister to China, on behalf of the Diplomatic Body at Peking, sent a note to the Chinese Foreign Minister, reminding him of China's obligations under the Final Protocol of 1901. It is questionable whether the above provisions would be applicable to a situation without endangering the lives and property of foreign nationals and the Legation Quarter at Peking.

81. For instance, the Fan-hsien incident by the British warships on September 5, 197; the Tsinan incident by the Japanese troops on May 1-3, 1927. For details, see William L. Tung, Imperialism and China, Pt. II, pp. 52-68. For Japan's intervention in the armed conflicts in 1925-1926, between Marshall Chang Tso-lin and his subordinate, General Kuo Sung-lin, see The China Weekly Review, August 21, 1926, p. 289.

82. For its text, see Hertslet, Treaties, I, pp. 608-614; MacMurray, Treaties, I, pp. 522-526.

83. Additional Articles, I-III (ibid., I, p. 526). The maintenance of railway guards along the Chinese Eastern Railway was arbitrarily decided by the Russian government in its Statute

of the Chinese Eastern Railway Company, December 4/16, 1896 (ibid., I, p. 86).

84. For the text, see Chinese Customs, Treaties, I, pp. 636-641, 735-745; Hertslet, Treaties, I, pp. 391-396; MacMurray, Treaties, I, pp. 549-555.

85. Art. II of the Additional Agreement reads:

> "In view of the earnest desire expressed by the Imperial Chinese Government to have the Japanese and Russian troops and railway guards in Manchuria withdrawn as soon as possible, and in order to meet this desire, the Imperial Japanese Government, in the event of Russia agreeing to the withdrawal of her railway guards, or in case other proper measures are agreed to between China and Russia, consent to take similar steps accordingly. When tranquillity shall have been reestablished in Manchuria and China shall have become herself capable of affording full protection to the lives and property of foreigners, Japan will withdraw her railway guards simultaneously with Russia."

86. Art. III (1) of the Peace Treaty of Portsmouth of 1905.

87. Concluded at Vladivostock, the original purpose of the Agreement was to keep open the Siberian Railway for the movement of Czechoslovak troops. Japanese troops remained, while those of other Allied powers had long been withdrawn. See Willoughby, II, pp. 867-868. For the text of the Agreement, see MacMurray, Treaties, I, pp. 82-84.

88. For its text, see Chinese Customs, Treaties, I, pp. 404-421; Hertslet, Treaties, I, pp. 18-35.

89. Art. 52 of the Sino-British Treaty of 1858, which was unilateral in nature. Similar provisions can be found in Art. 29 of the Sino-Franco Treaty of June 27, 1858 (Chinese Customs, Treaties, I, pp. 814-839; Hertslet, Treaties, I, pp. 269-286). The right of anchoring British cruisers within the five treaty ports was provided in Art. 14 of the General Regulations for the British Trade at the Five Ports of Canton, Amoy, Foochowfoo, Ningpo, and Shanghai, July 22, 1843 (Chinese Customs, Treaties, I, pp. 383-389; Hertslet, Treaties, I, pp. 13-14). This article was amended by Art. 52 of the Sino-British Treaty of 1858 as cited. Reciprocal treatment was provided for in Art. X of the Sino-Peruvian Treaty of June 26, 1874 (Chinese Customs, Treaties, I, pp. 798-807; Hertslet,

Treaties, I, pp. 415-420). See also Art. IX of the Sino-Mexican Treaty of December 14, 1899 (Chinese Customs, Treaties, II, pp. 833-843; Hertslet, Treaties, I, pp. 399-407). Previous notice before the entering of warships was required in Art. VIII of the Sino-Swedish Treaty of July 2, 1908 (Chinese Customs, Treaties, II, pp. 97-112; MacMurray, Treaties, I, pp. 740-747).

90. For details of the incident and the correspondence between the Secretary of State and the Secretary of the Navy, see U. S. For. Rel., 1903, pp. 85-90.

91. See ibid., 1903, p. 86.

92. When a French warship conducted hydrographic investigations of a Chinese closed port, Colonel Denby, American Minister at Peking, supported this right on the basis of the Sino-American Treaty of June 18, 1858 (Chinese Customs, Treaties, I, pp. 713-728; Hertslet, Treaties, I, pp. 540-542). The pertinent provision of the Treaty is Art. 9, which reads:

> "Whenever national vessels of the United States of America, in cruising along the coast and among the ports opened for trade for the protection of the commerce of their country, or for the advancement of science, shall arrive at or near any of the ports of China, the commanders of said ships and the superior local authorities of government shall, if it be necessary, hold intercourse on terms of equality and courtesy in token of the friendly relations of their respective nations;..."

It seems that this provision was very vague and not necessarily applicable to the subject in question, but the American government approved of Colonel Denby's argument. See U. S. For. Rel., 1890, pp. 193-196.

93. Art. II of the Treaty of 1842 (Chinese Customs, Treaties, I, pp. 351-356; Hertslet, Treaties, I, pp. 7-12).

94. Among these were the Sino-British Treaty of June 26, 1858 (Chinese Customs, Treaties, I, pp. 404-421; Hertslet, Treaties, I, pp. 18-35); the Sino-Franco Treaty of June 27, 1858 (Chinese Customs, Treaties, I, pp. 814-839; Hertslet, Treaties, I, pp. 269-286); the Sino-Franco Treaty of October 25, 1860 (Chinese Customs, Treaties, I, pp. 885-890; Hertslet, Treaties, I, pp. 287-291); the Sino-Japanese Treaty of April 17, 1895 (Chinese Customs, Treaties, II, pp. 590-596, 707-713; Hertslet, Treaties, I, pp. 362-370; MacMurray, Treaties, I, pp. 18-24); the Sino-American Treaty of October 8,

1903 (Chinese Customs, Treaties, I, pp. 745-763; Hertslet, Treaties, I, pp. 566-578; MacMurray, Treaties, I, pp. 423-450).

95. See Tsien Tai, The Origin and Abolition of Unequal Treaties in China (Taipei, 1961, in Chinese; hereafter cited as Tsien), p. 60; Willoughby, II, p. 736. For the historical development of treaty ports in China, see En-sai Tai, Treaty Ports in China (New York, 1918).

96. See U. S. For. Rel., 1908, pp. 143-145; Koo, pp. 249-250. For further details, see Hosea B. Morse, Trade and Administration of China, p. 208; Tyau, pp. 96-105.

97. See Tsien, p. 60. For instance, by a Presidential mandate of January 8, 1914, the following ports were voluntarily opened for foreign trade: Kuei Hua Ch'eng, Kalgan, Dolonor, Ch'ih Feng, T'ao Nan, Lung K'ou (a port in Huang Hsien, Shantung), and Hu Lu Tao. The mandate emphasized that "this voluntary opening should be distinguished from opening by treaty." For its text, see MacMurray, Treaties, II, pp. 1097-1098.

98. See British Parliamentary Papers, China, No. 1 (1900), pp. 251, 276, 406; Koo, pp. 250-252.

99 For its text, see Chinese Customs, Treaties, I, pp. 491-499; Hertslet, Treaties, I, pp. 73-80.

100. Section III of the Sino-British Treaty of 1876. By the same Treaty, the following places were opened as ports of call: Ta-t'ung and Ngan-ching in Anhui; Hu-k'ou in Kiangsi; Wu-süeh, Lu-chi-k'ou, and Sha-shih in Hu-kuang. For regulations on transit duty certificates and the collection of likin, an inland transit tax, see Art. I of the same Treaty.

101. Art. V of the Sino-Japanese Treaty of July 21, 1896 reads, in part, as follows:

> "If any vessel should unlawfully enter ports other than open ports and ports of call in China or carry on clandestine trade along the coast or rivers, the vessel with her cargo shall be subject to confiscation by the Chinese government."

For the text of the Treaty, see Chinese Customs, Treaties, II, pp. 604-614, 720-731; Hertslet, Treaties, I, pp. 373-382; MacMurray, Treaties, I, pp. 68-74. It should be understood that ships of any nation under force majeure may temporarily enter ports of other nations for refuge.

102. A most notable instance was Peking, which would be opened
for foreign trade after the withdrawal of foreign troops between the sea and the Capital, in accordance with Art. 10 of
the Sino-Japanese Treaty of October 8, 1903 (Chinese Customs, Treaties, II, pp. 617-637; Hertslet, Treaties, I, pp.
383-391; MacMurray, Treaties, I, pp. 411-422). Though foreign troops remained in the designated places, yet foreign
merchants carried out their business in that non-open city.

103. Art. X of the Sino-British Treaty of 1858 reads:

> "British merchant ships shall have authority to
> trade upon the Great River [Yangtze]. The Upper
> and Lower Valley of the river being, however, dis-
> turbed by outlaws, no port shall be for the present
> open to trade, with the exception of Chinkiang, which
> shall be opened in a year from the date of the sign-
> ing of this Treaty.

> "So soon as peace shall have been restored, British
> vessels shall also be admitted to trade at such ports
> as far as Hankow, not exceeding 3 in number, as the
> British Minister, after consultation with the Chinese
> Secretary of State, may determine shall be ports of
> entry and discharge."

It should be noted that the expressions of 'hiring persons'
and 'hiring vessels' in the same Treaty meant native coolies
and cartmen and boats. This interpretation was supported by
the American government and acquiesced in by other treaty
powers, contention to the contrary by the Shanghai General
Chamber of Commerce in 1866 notwithstanding. See U. S.
Diplomatic Correspondence, 1866-1867, I, pp. 513, 536. In
practice, however, most of the pilots employed by foreign
ships in treaty ports were foreigners. See also Regulations
regarding Pilotage, November 3, 1868 (Hertslet, Treaties,
II, pp. 658-662).

104. For details of inland navigation in Chinese waterways by
foreign ships, including treaties, laws, and regulations, see
P. M. Ogilvie, International Waterways (New York, 1920),
pp. 354-375.

105. Art. VI of the Sino-Swedish Treaty of July 2, 1908 (Chinese
Customs, Treaties, II, pp. 97-110; MacMurray, Treaties, I,
pp. 740-747) reads, in part, as follows:

> "Swedish merchant vessels may proceed to all the
> treaty ports of China already opened or which may
> hereafter be opened, for the transportation of mer-
> chandise and for purposes of trade. They may also

proceed to the inland waters in China which foreign merchant vessels are at liberty to navigate,
and to the ports of call along the rivers for the
purpose of landing and shipping passengers and
goods. In all these matters they shall be subject
to the Rules and Regulations concluded by China
with other foreign powers."

106. For the text of the Regulations, see Hertslet, Treaties,
II, pp. 721-722; MacMurray, Treaties, I, pp. 159-161. Supplementary Rules can be found in ibid., I, pp. 161-163.

107. For instance, Art. XII of the Sino-American Treaty of October 8, 1903 (Chinese Customs, Treaties, I, pp. 745-763;
Hertslet, Treaties, I, pp. 566-578; MacMurray, Treaties, I,
pp. 423-450) reads, in part, as follows:

"In case either Party hereto considers it advantageous at any time that the Rules and Regulations then
in existence for such commerce be altered or amended, the Chinese Government agrees to consider amicably and to adopt such modifications thereof as are
found necessary for trade and for the benefit of
China."

In the Sino-British Treaty of September 5, 1902 (Chinese
Customs, Treaties, I, pp. 543-568; Hertslet, Treaties, I, pp.
171-188; MacMurray, Treaties, I, pp. 342-355), the two contracting parties agreed, in Article X, to supplement the
1898 Regulations by ten additional rules (Annex C). The
same rules were also annexed to the Sino-Japanese Treaty of
October 8, 1903 (Chinese Customs, Treaties, I, pp. 617-
636; Hertslet, Treaties, I, pp. 383-391; MacMurray, Treaties,
I, pp. 411-422).

108. See, for instance, the Regulations governing Trade on the
Yantsze Kiang [Yangtze River], August 1898 (Hertslet,
Treaties, II, pp. 723-726); the West River Regulations,
July 30, 1904 (MacMurray, Treaties, I, pp. 484-488); the
Sino-Russian Memorandum of Agreement concerning the
Provisional Sungari River Trade Regulations, etc., August
8, 1910 (ibid., I, pp. 805-806); the Agreement and Regulations for the Liao River and Bar Conservancy Board, July
9, 1914 (ibid., II, pp. 1125-1129). Among the Chinese inland
waterways, the most important is the Yangtze River. For its
revised Regulations, see The Collected Laws of the Chinese Republic (Shanghai, 1936, in Chinese), II, pp. 1275-1277.
A brief description of the Yangtze navigation can be found in
A. J. Toynbee, Survey of International Affairs, 1926, pp. 303-
307.

109. Art. XI of the Treaty (Chinese Customs, Treaties, II, pp. 833-834; Hertslet, Treaties, I, pp. 399-407; MacMurray, Treaties, I, pp. 214-220) reads:

> "The merchant vessels of each of the Contracting Parties shall be at liberty to frequent the ports of the other open to foreign commerce or that they hereinafter be opened.
>
> "It is, however, agreed that this concession does not extend to the coasting trade, granted only to the national vessels in the territory of each of the Contracting Parties. But, if one of them should permit it wholly or in part to any nation or nations, the other Party shall have the right to claim the same concessions or favors for its citizens or subjects, provided said Contracting Party is willing, on its part, to grant reciprocity in all its claims on this point."

110. See, for instance, Art. XIV of the Sino-Polish Treaty of September 18, 1929 (League of Nations, Treaty Series, Vol. 120 (1932), pp. 360-367); Art. XV of the Sino-Czechoslovak Treaty of February 12, 1930 (ibid., Vol. 110 (1931), pp. 286-306).

111. The breakdown was as follows: Great Britain, 16; France, 13; Germany, 14; Russia, 5; the United States, 1; and Japan, 16. The above figures do not include those in Manchuria. See Morse, III, p. 60.

112. The 'ichan', a courier service operated by the Chinese government since the Chow dynasty to maintain communications between the Emperor and local officials, was performed by couriers from border to border of various districts. 'Letter hongs' were business firms transmitting their own correspondence and also others at a reasonable rate. Neither of these services operated between China and other countries. See Morse, III, pp. 58-60.

113. For details, see ibid., III, pp. 62-65.

114. Great Britain, 12; France, 13; the United States, 1; and Japan, 124. Germany and Russia after World War I had none, but Japan expanded the post offices in Manchuria to a considerable extent. See Minister Sze's Statement at the Sixth Committee of the Washington Conference. Willoughby, II, p. 883.

115. In his correspondence to Secretary Hay, Minister Conger wrote in Peking:

> "They are not established with the consent of China, but in spite of her.... Their establishment materially interferes with and embarrasses the development of the Chinese postal service, and is an interference with Chinese sovereignty."

He pointed out that the underlying reasons for the opening of foreign post offices were "principally for political reasons, either in view of their future designs upon the Empire, to strengthen their own footing, or because jealous of that of others." See U. S. For. Rel., 1902, p. 225.

116. Chinese land telegraph lines were first installed on December 24, 1881. For details, see The China Year Book 1925, p. 412.

117. They included the Great Northern Telegraph Co., Ltd. (a Dannish corporation but largely owned by the British); the Eastern Extension, Australasia and China Telegraph Co., Ltd. (British); and the Commercial Pacific Cable Co. (an American company but largely owned by foreign cable interests). See MacMurray, Treaties, I, p. 67; British and Foreign State Papers, Vol. 107, p. 726.

118. By France at the French Settlement in Shanghai, in Kwang-chow-wan, Yunnanfu, and Tientsin; by Great Britain at Kowloon and Kashgar; by the United States at the American Legation in Peking, in Tientsin and Tangshan; and by Japan at the Japanese Legation in Peking, in Chinwantao, Tientsin, Dairen, Tsinan, Tsiangtao, Hankow, and several places in Manchuria. This information was based on the list submitted by the Chinese Delegation to the Washington Conference of 1921-1922.

119. See infra, pp. 195-196.

Chapter 5
ADMINISTRATIVE, JUDICIAL, AND ECONOMIC ENCROACHMENTS

I. ADMINISTRATIVE INTERFERENCE

Ever since the middle of the nineteenth century, foreign powers had maliciously interfered with the domestic affairs of China by means of political pressure and the application of unequal treaties. Instances are too numerous to be recounted. The obligation to employ foreigners in charge of China's customs, post, and salt administrations undoubtedly infringed on her administrative integrity. Uniform tariffs at extremely low rates not only caused considerable loss of China's revenue and the delay of industrial development, but also fundamentally violated China's political and administrative independence. Because of their far-reaching consequences, the origin and implications of both subjects will now be reviewed.

1. Foreign Supervision of China's Customs, Post, and Salt Administrations

The collection of customs duties in Shanghai by foreign agents originated from practical necessity in 1854, when the walled city of Shanghai was occupied by the Taiping rebels. Since the Chinese local official, the Taotai, took refuge in the English settlement, he was not in the position to collect customs revenues. Upon the suggestion of the British consul, the Chinese Taotai agreed, on June 29, to appoint three Inspectors of Customs at the port of Shanghai, one each to be nominated by the British, French, and American consuls. Acting collectively as a board, this initial experiment proved satisfactory to all parties concerned at the time.[1]

Encouraged by the favorable response and acting in concert with the American and French representatives, the British envoy, Lord Elgin, took further steps to formalize and expand this practice. On November 8, 1858, he concluded with China the Agreement containing Rules of Trade made in Pursuance of Article XXVI of the Treaty of June 26, 1858.[2] With one uniform system at every port in mind, Rule X of the Agreement provided that "the High Officer appointed by the Chinese government to superintend foreign trade...will be at liberty, of his own choice and independently of the suggestion or nomination of any [British] authority, to select any [British] subject he may see fit to aid him in the administration of the customs revenue."[3] Horatio N. Lay, credited with extending the customs system to other treaty ports in the following years, was appointed Inspector General of Customs in 1861, with broad authority of "general supervision over all things pertaining to the customs revenue and to foreign trade."[4] Subsequent to the conclusion of the 1901 Protocol for the settlement of the Boxer Uprising,[5] the native customs bordering on, or adjacent to the open ports, were also put under the supervision of the Inspector General of Customs.[6]

During the period of Lay's sick leave, Robert Hart took charge of the customs and eventually succeeded Lay in 1863. Prudent and tactful, Hart rendered distinguished services to the Chinese government. Upon Hart's death in 1911, Francis A. Aglen became Inspector General of Customs.[7] Due to the preponderance of British trade with China, the two governments agreed, through an exchange of notes in February 1898, that "the Inspector-General of Maritime Customs should in the future, as in the past, be of British nationality."[8] In the leased territories, however, the commissioners of the customs offices were restricted to nationals of the lessee, as in Tsingtao and Dairen under Germany and Japan respectively.[9] Prior to the appointment of a new commissioner of these offices, the Inspector General of Customs had to come to an understanding with the German or Japanese envoy whichever the case might be. The Chinese government was compelled by circumstances to comply with these abnormal arrangements detrimental to its administrative integrity. It should also be noted that, until 1907, no Chinese had ever been appointed even to a full assistantship in the Maritime Customs Administration.

The Chinese postal service was, for the period 1896-1911, operated by the Maritime Customs, which had been headed by a Britisher as stated before. Less than two months after the Sino-British exchange of notes concerning the nationality of the Inspector General of Customs, the French Chargé d'Affaires, M. Dubail, addressed the Tsungli Yamen on April 9, 1898, with three demands. The third of these urged the Chinese government to place a high functionary at the head of an independent postal service with the help of foreign officers. In selecting its foreign staff, the Chinese government was requested to take account of the recommendations of the French government.[10] In its reply the next day, the Tsungli Yamen acquiesced in the French demand.[11] It was through this diplomatic maneuver that a Frenchman became codirector general of the Chinese postal administration.

The appointment of foreigners as overseers of the Chinese salt administration originated with the Reorganization Gold Loan Agreement between China and the Five-Power Consortium on April 26, 1913.[12] The Chinese government agreed to take immediate steps for the reorganization, with the assistance of foreigners, of the system of collecting the Chinese salt tax or gabelle, which was assigned as security for this loan. The Central Salt Administration under the Ministry of Finance would be headed by a Chinese Chief Inspectorate of Salt Revenues and a foreign Associate Chief Inspectorate of Salt Revenues and a foreign Associate Chief Inspector. In each branch office, there would be one Chinese and one foreign District Inspector. All decisions concerning salt revenues and personnel would be made jointly by the Chinese and foreign officials.[13] The first Associate Chief Inspector, Richard Dane, was a Britisher. Up to February 1942, there was always a foreigner appointed to that post.

Most of the foreign nationals in responsible positions of the Chinese customs, post, and salt administrations were experienced and capable. These services were benefited by their contributions, but not all of them cooperated fully with the Chinese government. The refusal of Francis Aglen to execute the new tariff policy of the Chinese government in

1927 gave the latter no choice but to replace him.[14] In retrospect, the recruitment of experienced persons, Chinese or foreign, to set up high standards in the newly installed services was extremely desirable. It was actually not the nationality of the appointees but the forced conditions that had long irritated the feelings of the Chinese.

2. Tariff Restrictions

Every sovereign state has the right to fix its own tariff, which may also be regulated, at its own free will, by treaties with other countries on the basis of equality and reciprocity. Any unilateral restriction of customs duties on one state for the benefit of others under forced circumstances is detrimental to the national sovereignty and administrative integrity of that state. Contrary to the principle of equity and justice, foreign powers had imposed on China a low-rate uniform tariff for almost a century.

In pursuance of the provision of the Sino-British Treaty of 1842 that a fair and regular tariff be fixed,[15] a Supplementary Treaty was signed between the two countries incorporating the General Regulations for Trade on October 8, 1843.[16] A tariff schedule of 5% ad valorem with certain exceptions was included in the Regulations.[17] On the ground of declining prices in the following years, these General Regulations were amended and embodied in the Sino-British Treaty of June 26, 1858.[18] The new tariff schedule reduced the prices of certain items, expanded the free list, and adopted a strict uniform tariff of 5% ad valorem. Similar provisions of the so-called 'Tariff Rules' were incorporated in the treaties of Tientsin with other countries in 1858. Non-signatories of these treaties were entitled to the same treatment through the application of the most-favored-nation clause.

With the mounting price of commodities in the following decades, the duties actually raised only corresponded to 3.18%. No revision was, however, made until 1902, when the Boxer indemnity necessitated the increase of revenues. The powers agreed, in the Final Protocol of 1901, to increase the Chinese customs tariff on imports to 5% effective.[19] In actuality, the revised schedule did not raise the duties to 5%, because the calculation was based not on the current 1902 prices but on the lower prices of 1897-1899, in accordance with the Tariff Agreement relating to the Revised Import Tariff of 1902.[20] Nor did the 1918 revision improve the situation.[21] In fact, the Chinese tariff only yielded 3-1/2% by the 1920's, according to prevailing prices of commodities. Furthermore, the powers concerned had not observed the provisions of the treaties of Tientsin of 1858 that the tariff schedule be revised every ten years.

On the other hand, foreign merchants strongly objected to the Chinese system of levying different forms of inland taxation, generally known as likin, and other dues on commodities at the place of production, in transit, and at destination. In the Sino-British Commercial Treaty of September 5, 1902, the Chinese government recognized the disruptive aspects of this inland taxation and promised to take steps to discard it if the loss of revenues could be compensated for by an increase of customs duties. In return, the British government indicated its willingness to agree on a surtax so as to increase the import duties up to 12-1/2% and export duties up to 7-1/2%.[22] However desirable these conditions might be, tariff revision would not be possible without the consent of other treaty powers concerned to enter into the same engagements.[23]

The restrictions of the Chinese Tariff had created serious consequences. First, China was deprived of a substantial portion of revenues otherwise obtainable through a higher rate of customs duties.[24] Second, the uniform tariff made it impossible for the Chinese government to encourage or discourage the import or export of various commodities by charging differential rates of customs duties. Thirdly, the treaty powers could use this tariff policy to suffocate the industrial development and political independence of China. Fourthly, the tariff provisions were entirely unilateral and no reciprocity had been extended to China by the treaty powers. Fifthly, customs revenues were pledged for the payment of certain foreign debts and could not be made available to the Chinese government until these obligations were met. For this last reason, the Chinese government had to raise the customs duties in order to meet its expenditures.

II. EXTRATERRITORIALITY OR CONSULAR JURISDICTION

1. The Origin

The scope of extraterritoriality includes, but is not limited to, consular jurisdiction, even though these two terms have often been used interchangeably. On principle, aliens residing in a foreign state are subject to the jurisdiction of that state unless international conventions and bilateral treaties provide otherwise. There are certain exceptions, including those who are entitled to diplomatic immunities and privileges. Extraterritorial or consular jurisdiction was originally imposed by Western powers on several countries in Asia and Africa on the ground of their fundamental differences of legal and judicial systems.[25] The practice was entirely unilateral in nature, because the West never had the intention to reciprocate the same privileges to nationals of the granting states. As much has been written on this subject, a brief review of its application in China through treaty provisions will be sufficient for the present purpose.

Early treaties between China and Russia had stipulations on reciprocal extradition of fugitives, but made no provision for extraterritorial rights. Consular jurisdiction was first expressed in Art. XIII of the General Regulations for the British Trade at the Five Ports, supplemental to the Treaty of Nanking of 1842,[26] and more explicitly stated in the Sino-American Treaty of July 3, 1844.[27] Similar privileges were granted to France in the Treaty of Whampoa of 1844,[28] and to Sweden and Norway in the Treaty of Canton of 1847.[29] As it developed, the exercise of extraterritorial jurisdiction was no longer limited to consuls. Up to 1894, Japanese nationals committing offenses in China remained under Chinese jurisdiction,[30] but the situation was changed after the conclusion of the Treaty of Shimonoseki the following year.[31] Through the application of the most-favored-nation clause, extraterritoriality had been extended to other treaty powers, namely, Austria-Hungary, Belgium, Brazil, Denmark, Germany, Italy, Mexico, the Netherlands, Peru, Portugal, Russia, Spain, and Switzerland. Austria, Hungary, and Germany lost the privilege after World War I.[32] In the case of Russia, it was virtually terminated after the Bolshevik Revolution and formally relinquished by the Sino-Soviet Agreement of May 31, 1924.[33]

2. The Application

Extraterritorial jurisdiction was generally exercised by consuls of the treaty powers, but Great Britain and the United States also established the British Supreme Court in China and the United States Court for China.[34] Although extraterritorial cases would be generally adjudicated by the functionaries of the defendant's state in accordance with the law of that state, the procedures for actual application were quite complicated. Disputes between nationals of one treaty power enjoying extraterritoriality were under the jurisdiction of the consul or the court of that power. China had no jurisdiction over controversies between nationals of different treaty powers enjoying extraterritoriality; such cases would be under the competence of the consul whose national was a defendant. If the defendant were a national of a state not enjoying extraterritoriality, the case would come to the Chinese court.

Litigation involving nationals of China and treaty powers enjoying extraterritoriality would be adjudicated by the functionaries of the state whose nationals were defendants; but, if circumstances made it difficult to reach amicable arrangement, they could together examine the merits of the case and decide it equitably, in accordance with Article XVII of the Sino-British Treaty of Tientsin of 1858.[35] In criminal cases, the Sino-British Treaty of Chefoo of 1876 went further by providing that the official of the plaintiff's nationality or the 'assessor' could watch the trial and protest unfair proceedings.[36] Due to practical difficulties, the above stipulated right was exercised only by officials of the treaty powers concerned.

From the perspective of justice or law, China should have had sole jurisdiction over disputes between Chinese nationals or nationals of states not enjoying extraterritoriality in territories under Chinese sovereignty. This was, however, not always the case in Shanghai, Amoy, and Hankow, where there existed the so-called mixed courts. Taking the Mixed Court of the International Settlement in Shanghai as an example, its origin dated from 1864 for the trial of cases involving Chinese residents and between foreign nationals and Chinese residents as defendants, in accordance with its 1869 Rules.[37] Foreign assessors could attend the sessions if their nationals were plaintiffs in disputes involving Chinese nationals as defendants, but the decisions were still made by the Chinese magistrate appointed by the Taotai. When the Chinese authorities could not function in the native city of Shanghai for a short period after the outbreak of Revolution in 1911, the Consular Body took over control of the Mixed Court on November 10 of the same year, and even interfered with matters solely involving Chinese residents in the International Settlement. Only after repeated protests, the Shanghai Consular Body reached an agreement with the Kiangsu Provincial Government for the rendition of the Mixed Court in 1926. Less important but similar in nature were the mixed courts in the French Settlement in Shanghai,38 and also in Amoy and Hankow.39

With respect to the illegal extension of extraterritorial privileges, no country went further than Japan. In connection with the Japanese consulates in Fukien province and in Manchuria, the Japanese government maintained police stations, jails, and houses of detention on the pretext of supervising its nationals. No treaty provision could be found to justify the Japanese action, which greatly undermined the national sovereignty of China. Another unique feature relative to extraterritoriality was the special status of Koreans who took up residence in the agricultural land of Chienta, a Chinese territory north of the Tumen River. By the Sino-Japanese Agreement of September 4, 1909,40 China had jurisdiction over Koreans in civil and criminal cases, but a Japanese consular official could attend the court proceedings. In any case involving capital punishment, notification had to be made to the Japanese consul. A rehearing by another Chinese official would be demanded if the consular official should find irregularities in the proceedings. In this respect, the Japanese consul became, in effect, the final arbiter of Chinese court decisions.

3. The Shortcomings

As extraterrritoriality was granted on a unilateral basis to the detriment of China's national sovereignty and judicial integrity, its continued existence after vital change of circumstances inevitably created bitterness among the Chinese people. The system intself had inherent weaknesses. The unusual complexity of laws and procedures applied by consuls or courts of the treaty powers set up different standards in similar cases. Sometimes no appropriate foreign laws could be applied to particular offences committed in China. Because of a lack of authority or competence, punishment of plaintiffs or witnesses of foreign nationalities for contempt or perjury in the course of proceedings and consideration of set-offs were hardly possible. Nor were procedures for appeal easy. Few consuls had sufficient training or impartial mind to handle suits requiring legal knowledge and experience or involving the interests of their own nationals. Another difficulty was to produce evidence and witnesses for the trial of offences committed by foreigners in the interior, whereas consuls or courts of their own countries were only available in the treaty ports.

In addition to the inherent weaknesses described above, many abuses arose out of misuse of privileges by authorities of treaty powers. The most notorious was the practice by certain powers enjoying extraterritoriality of claiming persons not entitled to extraterritoriality as their own nationals. As defendants, these persons were thus not subject to the jurisdiction of Chinese courts; as plaintiffs, they could be assisted by 'assessors' during the course of proceedings. China vigorously objected to the illegal protection of the so-called 'protégés'. On this matter, the United States and Great Britain supported the Chinese position.[41]

Foreigners in China tended to evade taxation by the Chinese government on the false ground that extraterritoriality would exempt them from obedience to Chinese revenue laws. This interpretation could not possibly be accepted by the Chinese government.[42] It should also be noted that foreign corporations in China were entitled to extraterritoriality as natural persons and were generally not bound by Chinese laws. Their extensive activities in commercial and industrial fields further complicated the economic situation in China.

Foreigners enjoying extraterritoriality sometime rendered undue protection to Chinese nationals in their employ from apprehension by Chinese authroities.[43] Chinese residents in the International Settlement could not be directly arrested without going through foreign police employed by the municipal administration; it was also necessary to produce warrants countersigned by the senior consul in that settlement. Still they could not be taken away before the Mixed Court located therein conducted a preliminary hearing of the case.[44]

The diversified laws and cumbersome procedures involved in extraterritoriality made its application increasingly untenable. The abuses incidental to the system were intollerable. Above all, the judicial integrity of China was violated. These were among the reasons why the Chinese government continuously exerted maximum efforts to work for its abolition, which will be fully discussed later.[45]

III. ECONOMIC AND OTHER INTERESTS

1. Railway and Mining Concessions

The construction of railroads for facilitating transportation and communications was accepted by China with great reluctance.[46] On the other hand, foreign powers were keenly interested in acquiring railway and mining concessions in China for the furtherance of their political and economic influence. With a few exceptions,[47] Chinese railways were built mostly through foreign loans granted by groups of banks or industrial organizations, backed by their own governments.[48] Without consultation with the Chinese government, several foreign powers arbitrarily divided their spheres of interest in railway construction, notably between Japan and Russia in Manchuria and between Great Britain and Germany in the Yangtze Valley and Shantung respectively.[49] Although many of the projects were controlled by foreign private concessionaires, they usually spoke in one voice with their government leaders. Thus even commercial or industrial enterprises operated by foreigners in China were tinged with political motives. Such characteristics were also evidenced in various railway agreements, some of which are listed in Table II.

What most adversely affected China's sovereignty, however, were those railways owned and operated by foreign governments. These railway concessions were usually accompanied by mining interests.[50] This groups included the Chinese Eastern Railway (CER), the Shantung Railway from Tsingtao to Tsinan, the Yunnan-French Indo-China Railway, and the South Manchurian Railway. All these railways were strategically located in the respective spheres of influence of Russia, Germany, France, and Japan. A brief examination of each will show that its importance far transcended economic and commercial ends.

TABLE II
FOREIGN INTERESTS IN CHINA'S RAILWAYS AND
LOAN AGREEMENTS

(This Table does not include the Chinese Eastern Railway, the South Manchurian Railway, the Shantung Railway, and the Tonking–Yunnan Railway systems, which are discussed separately in this chapter. Railway loans and agreements contained in this Table only illustrate typical examples of railway imperialism and are by no means exhaustive.)

PEKING-MUKDEN RAILWAY – British (British & Chinese Corp. Ltd.).

Agreement for Shanhaikwan-Newchwang Railway Loan, October 10, 1898 (MacMurray, Treaties, I, pp. 173-181).

SHANGHAI-NANKING RAILWAY – British (British & Chinese Corp. Ltd.).

Agreement for Shanghai-Nanking Railway Loan, July 9, 1903, superseding that of May 3, 1898 (ibid., I, pp. 387-409).

PEKING-HANKOW RAILWAY – Belgian, French, and Russian interests through a Belgian Co., the Société d'Etudes de Chemins de Fer en Chine.

Provisional Contract for Lukouchiao (Peking)-Hankow Railway, May 27, 1897 (ibid., I, pp. 145-147); Additional Protocol to the above Contract, July 27, 1897 (ibid., I, pp. 148-151).

Redeemed by two loans: (1) Banque de l'Indo-Chine (France) and Hongkong & Shanghai Banking Corp. – Agreement for a Loan of £ 5,000,000 to the Board of Posts and Communications, October 8, 1908 (ibid., I, 747-751); (2) The Peking-Hankow Railway Redemption Loan – Prospectus of the 7% Peking-Hankow Railway Redemption Loan for $10,000,000, approved by the Chinese Imperial Government on October 8, 1908 (ibid., I, pp. 752-759).

TABLE II (Continued)

CHENGTIN-TAIYUAN RAILWAY — Russian (Russo-Chinese Bank). Loan Contract, and Operating Contract, for the Chengtingfu-Taiyuanfu Railway, October 15, 1902 (ibid., I, pp. 356-369).

PIENLO RAILWAY—Belgian (Compagnie Générale de Chemins de Fer et de Tramways en Chine).

Loan Contract, and Operating Contract, for the Kaifengfu-Honanfu Railway, November 12, 1903 (ibid., I, pp. 462-476).

CANTON-KOWLOON RAILWAY — British (British & Chinese Corp., Ltd.).

Agreement for the Issue and Regulation of a Loan for the Construction of the Canton-Kowloon Railway, March 7, 1907 (ibid., I, pp. 615-626).

TIENTSIN–PUKOW RAILWAY — British (Chinese Central Railways, Ltd.) and German (Deutsch-Asiatische Bank).

Preliminary Agreement for Tientsin-Chinkiang Railway May 18, 1899 (ibid., I, pp. 694-697), superseded by the Agreement for the Imperial Chinese Government 5% Tientsin-Pukow Railway Loan, January 13, 1908 (ibid., I, pp. 684-693).

SHANGHAI-HANGCHOW-NINGPO RAILWAY — British (British & Chinese Corp., Ltd.).

Agreement for the Imperial Chinese Government 5% Shanghai-Hangchow-Ningpo Railway Loan, March 6, 1908 (ibid., I, pp. 702-716).

CANTON-HANKOW RAILWAY — American (American China Development Co.) — the Sino-American Agreement of April 14, 1898 and a Supplementary Agreement of July 13, 1900.

Redeemed by the Chinese government — Agreement on the Redemption of the Canton-Hankow Railway, August 29, 1905 (ibid., I, pp. 519-522).

TABLE II (Continued)

CANTON-HANKOW RAILWAY (Continued)

Redemption Loan from Great Britain (Government of Hongkong) — Agreement of September 9, 1905 (ibid., I, pp. 528-530).

TAO-CHING RAILWAY — British (Pekin Syndicate, Ltd., originally with Italian interests).

Regulations for Mining Purposes, Iron Works, and Trans- porting Mine Products of All Kinds in the Province of Honan, June 21, 1898 (ibid., I, pp. 131-134).

TAOKOW-CHINGHUA RAILWAY — British (Pekin Syndicate, Ltd.)

Agreement for the Taokow-Chinghua Railway, July 3, 1905 (ibid., I, pp. 506-516).

SHASI-SHINGYI (Sha-Shing) RAILWAY — British (Pauling Co., Ltd.).

Agreement providing for the Financing and Construction of a Railway from a Point on the Yangtze River Opposite Shasi, via Changteh, Yuanchow and Kweiyang, to Shingyi, in the Province of Kweichow, with a Branch Line connec- ting Changteh with Changsha, July 25, 1914 (ibid., II, pp. 1130-1145).

One year after the first Sino-Japanese War, Russia and China concluded a Treaty of Alliance in May 1896.[51] On the ground of facilitating the movement of Russian troops to areas menaced by Japan, Russia obtained the right to build a railway line, later known as the Chinese Eastern Railway, across the Chinese provinces of Heilungkiang and of Kirin in the direction of Vladivostok. The construction and exploitation of this railway were accorded to the Russian controlled Russo-Chinese Bank.[52] The general supervision of the railway system would be under a joint board with a Russian as its chairman.[53] Actually, the Russian government controlled every aspect of CER,[54] and acquired mining and timber concessions in the two provinces of Manchuria,[55] where more land could be expropriated for railway purposes.[56]

In order to extend Russian influence in South Manchuria, Russia leased Port Arthur and Dairen in the Liaotung Peninsula by the Convention of Peking on March 27, 1898,[57] as described before.[58] According to this Convention, the construction of a branch line of CER to Darien[59] was also granted to Russia under the same terms as the Contract for CER of August 27, 1896.[60] To safeguard CER system, China was compelled to give Russia an assurance that the future construction of any railway from Peking to the north or to the northeast toward the Russian border would be undertaken either by Chinese capital and under Chinese supervision or, in case of the need for foreign capital, by approaching the Russian government first.[61] Shortly before, Russia had reached an understanding with Great Britain regarding their respective interests in Manchuria and the Yangtze Valley, which was duly communicated to the Chinese government.[62] With these diplomatic maneuvers, Russia penetrated deeper into her sphere of influence until it was seriously challenged by Japan in 1904.

By the same Convention for the Lease of Kiaochow of March 6, 1898,[63] Germany obtained the right to build a railway system from Kiaochow to Tsinan in Shantung province. The Chino-German Company, organized for the construction of the road, was conferred with all the advantages and benefits extended to similar companies operating in China. In addition, German nationals could hold and develop mining property for a distance of thirty li (approximately ten miles) from each side of the railway lines.[64] The development of the German leased territory Kiaochow and the Shantung Railway during World War I and its aftermath will be discussed elsewhere.[65]

At the time of her lease of Kuangchou-wan in 1898,[66] France acquired the right to build a railway from the frontier of Tongking to Yunnanfu. Unlike CER system, this railway was entirely financed and operated by the French. While not entitled to its profit or administration, China retained the right to police and protect the railway line without foreign interference.[67] When the contract for the construction of the railway was signed by the two countries on October 29, 1903,[68] the French government designated as its agent the Compagnie Française des Chemins de fer de l'Indo-Chine et du Yunnan, constituted by the most important financial establishments in France. The same contract stipulated that the transportation of Chinese troops and munitions, or provisions would have the right of way over all others at half rate.[69] In these respects, this French line was different from the railway systems under Russian, German, or Japanese control.[70]

In pursuance of the Peace Treaty of Portsmouth of September 5, 1905,[71] Russia transferred to Japan "the railway between Changchun (Kuan-cheng-tzu) and Port Arthur and all its branches, together with all rights, privileges and properties appertaining thereto in that region, as well as all coal mines in the said region belonging to or worked for the benefit of the railway."[72] This transfer was consented to by the Chinese government under the Sino-Japanese Convention of December 22, 1905,[73] with alleged secret Protocols concerning Japanese financing of one-half of the capital for the construction of the railway between Changchun and Kirin, the sale of Japanese constructed military railway between Mukden and Hsinmintun to the Chinese government, and the commitment by China not to construct any main line in the neighborhood of and parallel to the South Manchurian Railway.[74] Under the Supplementary Agreement to the 1905 Convention, China conferred on Japan "the right to maintain and work the military railway line constructed between Antung and Mukden," which would be improved so as to be fit for regular transportation purposes.[75]

To construct, maintain, and operate the above lines, the South Manchurian Railway Joint Stock Company was established under the direction and supervision of the Japanese government in accordance with the Japanese Imperial Ordinance of June 7, 1906.[76] The railways put under its jurisdiction were as follows:[77] Dairen-Changchun Railway, Nankuanling-Port Arthur Railway, Tafangshen-Liushutun Railway, Tashichiao-Yingkow Railway, Yentai-Yentai Coal Mine Railway, Sukiatun-Fushun Railway, and Mukden-Antunghsien Railway.[78] The Company also engaged in mining, especially the coal mines at Fushun and Yentai. Other transactions included land and buildings attached to the railways, electrical enterprises, and commodities conveyed by the railways. The South Manchurian Railway Company exercised, under the supervision of the Governor-General of Kwantung, broad jurisdiction over an area, in Which China's sovereignty had been constantly challenged. In comparison with CER, the South Manchurian Railway system as a tool of imperialistic exploitation was even more aggressive.

Both Japan and Russia agreed, in the Treaty of Portsmouth of 1905, "not to obstruct any general measures common to all countries, which China may make for the development of the commerce and industry of Manchuria." [79] This commitment contradicted Japan's later demand, under the alleged secret Protocols attached to the Sino-Japanese Agreement of December 22, 1905, that the Chinese government should refrain from building any main line in the neighborhood of and parallel to the South Manchurian Railway.[80] On the basis of this alleged understanding in the secret Protocols, Japan objected to the construction of the Hsinmintun-Fakumen Railway by a British concern, which later joined an American Banking Group to secure from China the construction of a railway from Chinchou to Aigun.[81] Taking into consideration this particular project and the keen competition among foreign powers to build railways in Manchuria, Secretary of State Philander C. Knox contemplated a neutralization plan for all railways in that region.

The gist of the Knox Plan was for the powers concerned to lend China sufficient funds to redeem all railways in Manchuria, and then to administer the Chinese-owned railways through an international commission.[82] On the force of the Open Door Policy, Secretary Knox expected the cooperation of Japan and Russia, both of which had predominent interests in Manchuria. China approved the neutralization plan. Great Britain was favorably inclined to this idea, but wanted to postpone its consideration pending negotiations for the Hukuang loan. Russia and Japan turned down the plan and urged the Chinese government to disapprove the Chinchow-Aigun project. France did not give support to the American proposal either. Thus the last attempt at saving Manchuria from railway imperialism failed. [83] On October 5,

1913, Japan secured consent from China for the construction of four more railways with Japanese financing.[84] After the outbreak of World War I, the European powers temporarily withdrew from the struggle for power in China. Japan seized this opportunity to present the so-called Twenty-One Demands to the Chinese government, including railway concessions, which will be examined together with other terms in the chapter below.

2. Foreign Loans

In addition to railway loans mentioned in the previous section, China raised many public loans after the first Sino-Japanese War for the payment of indemnities and administrative expenditures as well as other specific purposes. [85] As stated before, even loans borrowed from private concerns had political implications because of the express or implicit support from the grantors' governments. The important lending powers were Great Britain, France, Russia, Japan, Belgium, and the United States, whose governments or banking firms[86] usually exercised a certain degree of control over the implementation of the terms of the loans through various means of guarantee and supervision.

For the payment of the heavy indemnity to victorious Japan, China borrowed from a Franco-Russian syndicate 400,000,000 francs at 4%, guaranteed by duties levied from Chinese maritime customs. For further safeguard of the loan, Russia signed with China another contract and a protocol of exchange of declarations on July 6, 1895.[87] This Franco-Russian loan was soon followed by two Anglo-German loans from the Hongkong and Shanghai Banking Corporation and the Deutsch-Asiatische Bank: the 1896 loan of £ 16,000,000 at 5%, guaranteed by revenues from the maritime customs;[88] and the 1898 loan of £ 16,000,000 at 4-1/2%, constituting a charge on the maritime customs, the general likin tax of Soochow, Sung Hu, Kiukiang, and Eastern Chekiang, and also on the salt tax of Ichang, Hupeh, and Anhui.[89] One of the important terms for the settlement of the Boxer Uprising was the payment to the powers concerned of an indemnity of 450,000,000 Haikwan tales (£ 67,500,000), which was secured from the balance of the revenues from Chinese maritime customs and salt geballe, and also from native customs.[90]

These war indemnities and subsequent foreign loans for their payment sapped China's sources of economic strength.

Administrative reorganization loans were intended to effect currency reform and other measures of government reorganization. On April 15, 1911, China signed the first Agreement for Currency Reform and Industrial Development Loan with American, French, and German banking interests. This loan of £ 10,000,000 at 5% was made a first charge on China's revenues from taxes on consumption, production, tobacco and spirits in the Three Northeastern Provinces, as well on a salt surtax throughout China. Due to the outbreak of the Chinese Revolution in October 1911, however, only a small sum of £ 400,000 was actually paid for plague relief and industrial expenses in Manchuria.[91] After the establishment of the Republic in the following year, the Chinese government signed the Crisp Loan of £ 10,000,000 at 5%, with salt revenues as security, while negotiations for a larger amount with an international consortium were going on. The latter banking group, composed of American, British, French, and German banks, eventually pressed upon China to cancel the contract with the British firm, C. Birch Crisp & Co., which had already issued £ 5,000,000.[92]

The above-mentioned quadruple group was soon joined by the Japanese and Russian interests to constitute the so-called Six-Power Consortium. Because of the objection raised by the Wilson Administration to the terms of the loan under negotiation,[93] the American banks decided to withdraw from the Consortium. But the banking interests of the remaining five powers still went ahead and concluded with the Chinese government the Reorganization Gold Loan Agreement on April 26, 1913.[94] The amount of the loan was £ 25,000,000 at 5%, secured by a charge upon the entire revenues of the Chinese Salt Administration, which would be reorganized with a foreign adviser.[95] Meanwhile, the same banking groups would be entitled to options upon future loans.[96] Detrimental to China's national sovereignty and administrative integrity, as rightly pointed out by President Wison, this reorganization loan was never approved by the Chinese Parliament.

The Five-Power Consortium had a short life, because German interests ceased to take part in it after the outbreak of World War I as did the Russian group after the overthrow of the Czarist government. At this juncture, it is convenient to mention the new Four-Power Consortium. Proposed by the American government in June 1918, for cooperative action in procuring for the Chinese government necessary capital for economic reconstruction, this Consortium was established by an agreement of October 15, 1920, and represented by American, British, French, and Japanese banks.[97] Japan joined the Consortium on the condition that certain railways in Manchuria and Mongolia should not be under its scope of consideration.[98] Having learned from past experience, however, the Chinese government had serious doubts as to whether the consortium operations could do any good for China, involving the monopoly of banking interests, pledges of more revenues as security, and further interference with Chinese administration and domestic politics.

In addition to those described above, foreign loans in a variety of amounts were periodically negotiated by China for the defrayal of administrative reorganization,[99] current expenditures,[100] as well as commercial and industrial development,[101] including railway loans,[102] telegraph, telephone, and wireless loans.[103] The so-called Nishihara loans secured by the Peking government from Japan during the period 1917-1920 were purported to conduct military campaigns against the Southern Provinces.[104] These Japanese loans were motivated by a desire to interfere with China's domestic politics, and therefore have never been forgiven by the Chinese people. Equally notorious was the war participation loan of 20,000,000 yen, extended by Japan to China in 1918, ostensibly for organizing and equipping the Chinese army consequent to China's entrace into World War I against Germany.[105] Actually the loan was diverted by the Peking government to suppress political dissidents in the country. While not all foreign loans have been analyzed,[106] this treatment is sufficient to show how some foreign powers attempted to use loans for the perpetuation and advancement of their political and economic influence in China.

3. Other Rights and Privileges under the Most-Favored-Nation Treatment

After the conclusion of the Treaty of Nanking in 1842, the right of foreign merchants to trade was well established. [107] They were permitted to travel to the interior under special regulations and to reside in treaty ports, [108] where concessions and settlements were later created. Business could be conducted in China either on an individual basis or through corporations. [109] The Chinese government endeavored to extend due protection to foreign trademarks, for which several laws and regulations were issued. [110] Missionaries could carry out their activities in the interiror. [111] Land-holding was permissible under stipulated conditions. [112] The enjoyment of extraterritoriality by foreign nationals and corporations in China has already been described. In many respects, foreigners obtained more rights and privileges in China than in their own countries, without the necessity of of performing comparable duties.

Through the application of the most-favored-nation clause, many rights and privileges provided for in different treaties were accorded to the governments and nationals of other treaty powers. The provision of this clause first appeared in the Sino-British Supplementary Treaty of October 8, 1843.[113] There were, however, some exceptions, including special rates for frontier trade between China and neighboring countries. Nor could the most-favored-nation clause be applied to political grants or specific concessions. The Chinese government insisted that "if one country desires to participate in the privileges conceded to another country, it must consent to be bound by the conditions attached to them, and accepted by another." [114] Stipulations to that effect can be found in many later treaties. [115] In some treaties, however, the wording of the most-favored-nation clause was constructed in very broad terms, as in the case of the Sino-American Treaty of June 18, 1858, [116] and of the Sino-Japanese Treaty of October 8, 1903. [117] Certain powers even demanded the extension of the most-favored-nation treatment to railway loan agreements. [118]

In conclusion, many rights and privileges acquired by foreigners in China were legitimate. Nor were the general provisions of the most-favored-nation clause unreasonable. [119] Complaints by the Chinese were, however, centered on the lack of reciptocity. If the judicial system and legal codes were so different from those of Western countries as to require the special privilege of extraterritoriality for their nationals, why did these powers concerned not grant the same to Chinese nationals residing in their domains? Has any major power ever permitted the alienation of its territorial and administrative integrity to the extent that it was imposed on China? Even in a few treaties which provided for some elementary rights on reciprocal basis, such as immigration, residence, and pursuit of livelihood, the Chinese nationals residing in the territories of those contracting parties suffered discrimination in may respects and violence on various occasions. [120] Evidently, it was not equity and justice but power and self-interest that governed the policies of most of the foreign powers toward China throughout the nineteenth century. Although new treaties later concluded by China with other powers adhered to the principles of equality and reciprocity, [121] it took almost a century for the Chinese people to abolish the inequitable terms of early treaties, which accorded, in turn, the least favored nation treatment to them.

NOTES TO CHAPTER 5

1. The inspectors were Arthur Smith (French), Lewis Carr (American), and Francis Wade (British). Wade was succeeded by Horatio Nelson Lay a year later. The Taiping rebels actually took the walled city of Shanghai on September 7, 1853.

2. For its text, see Chinese Customs, Treaties, I, pp. 422-428; Hertslet, Treaties, I, pp. 35-47. Often called 'Trade Regulations Appended to the Tariff' or the 'Tariff Rules', this Agreement was later replaced by the Revised Tariff Agreement on August 29, 1902 (Chinese Customs, Treaties, pp. 569-642; Hertslet, Treaties, I, pp. 171-188.

3. Under the same Rule, the Customs Inspectorate was empowered to aid the Chinese government "in the prevention of smuggling; in the definition of port boundaries; or in discharging the duties of harbor-master; also in the distribution of lights, buoys, beacons, and the like, the maintenance of which shall be provided for out of the tonnage dues."

4. See the Dispatch from Prince Kung to Lay, January 21, 1861 (North China Herald, March 9, 1861).

5. Art. VI of the 1901 Protocol (Chinese Customs, Treaties, II, pp. 303-341; MacMurray, Treaties, I, pp. 278-308).

6. The term 'maritime customs' was often used to denote customs levied on foreign trade, while 'native customs' meant jurisdiction over the charges on domestic trade.

7. Hart took his final leave in the spring of 1908, and died on September 20, 1911. While officiating Inspector General of Customs from April 1909, Aglen was definitely appointed to the office on October 1, 1911. For Hart's contributions to the Chinese maritime customs, reference may be made to Stanley F. Wright, Hart and the Chinese Customs (Belfast, 1950).

8. The Tsungli Yamen's Note of February 13, 1898, in reply to the British Note of February 3, 1898 (MacMurray, Treaties, I, pp. 104-105).

9. In accordance with the Sino-German Agreement concerning the Establishment of a Maritime Customs House at Tsingtao, April 17, 1899, (ibid., I, pp. 189-203); the Sino-Japanese Agreement regarding Establishment of Maritime Customs Office at Dairen, and for Inland Waters Steam Navigation, May 30, 1907 (ibid., I, pp. 634-639).

10. For the text of the French Note, see MacMurray, Treaties, I, p. 124.

11. See ibid., I, p. 125.

12. The Five-Power Consortium consisted of France (Banque de l'Indo-Chine), Germany (Deutsch-Asiatische Bank), Great Britain (Hongkong & Shanghai Banking Corporation), Japan (Yokohama Specie Bank), and Russia (Russo-Asiatic Bank). The United States under the Taft administration was originally interested in joining the Consortium, but President Wilson deemed that the conditions of the loan would affect the administrative independence of China and reversed the American attitude. Further information on the subject can be found in Frederick V. Field, American Participation in the China Consortiums (Chicago, 1931). For the text of the Agreement, see MacMurray, Treaties, II, pp. 1007-1037. For the excerpt of President Wilson's statement, see infra, Ch. 5, notes 93.

13. Art. V of the Agreement.

14. After the removal of Aglen, A. H. F. Edwards was appointed to that post. For details, see Tsien, p. 80.

15. Art. X of the Sino-British Treaty of 1842 (Chinese Customs, Treaties, I, pp. 351-356; Hertslet, Treaties, I, pp. 7-12).

16. The General Regulations were enacted on July 22, 1843 (Chinese Customs, Treaties, I, pp. 383-389), and later attached to the Sino-British Supplementary Treaty of 1843 (ibid., I, pp. 390-399).

17. Certain items, such as tea and spices, were subject to 10% ad valorem.

18. For the text of the 1858 Treaty and the Tariff Rules, see Chinese Customs, Treaties, I, pp. 402-428; Hertslet, Treaties, I, pp. 18-47.

19. Art. VI (3) of the Final Protocol of 1901 (Chinese Customs, Treaties, II, pp. 304-341; MacMurray, Treaties, I, pp. 278-308).

20. This Agreement was concluded between China and fifteen powers. The dates of signing this Agreement and of its coming into effect are, respectively, indicated in parentheses after each signatory state: Austria-Hungary (8/29/1902; 10/31/1902); Belgium (8/29/1902; 10/31/1902); Denmark 3/23/1904; 5/5/1904); France (3/30/1904; 3/30/1904); Ger-

many (8/29/1902; 10/31/1902); Great Britain (8/29/1902; 10/31/1902); Italy (3/28/1903; 4/27/1903); Japan (8/29/1902; 10/31/1902); the Netherlands (8/29/1902; 10/31/1902); Norway (3/30/1904; 3/30/1904); Portugal 11/11/1904; 11/11/1904); Russia (3/29/1903; 4/27/1903); Spain (8/29/1902; 10/31/1902); Sweden (3/30/1904; 3/30/1904); the United States (8/29/1902; 10/31/1902). For the text of the Agreement, see Chinese Customs, Treaties, II, pp. 593-642, 953-956; MacMurray, Treaties, I, pp. 339-340. See also the Sino-British Commercial Treaty of September 5, 1902 (Chinese Customs, Treaties, I, pp. 543-568; MacMurray Treaties, I, pp. 339-342); the Sino-American Commercial Treaty of October 8, 1903 (Chinese Customs, Treaties, I, pp. 745-763; MacMurray, Treaties, I, pp. 423-450); the Sino-Japanese Commercial Treaty of October 8, 1903 (Chinese Customs, Treaties, II, pp. 617-636; MacMurray, Treaties, I, pp. 411-422).

21. Another attempt to raise the tariff in 1912 failed, because unanimous consent could not be secured from the treaty powers. The 1918 revision occurred after China joined the war on the Allied side against Germany. For the text of the Revised Import Tariff and Rules, December 19, 1918, see ibid., II, pp. 1456-1484.

22. Art. VIII, Sections 1, 2, 7 of the Sino-British Commercial Treaty of September 5, 1902, also known as the Mackay Treaty (Chinese Customs, Treaties, I, pp. 543-568; Hertslet, Treaties, I, pp. 171-188; MacMurray, Treaties, I, pp. 342-356).

23. See Art. VIII, Sections 14, 15 of the same treaty.

24. The Chinese tariff revenue from land trade was even in a worse state. In the Sino-Russian Convention on the Land Trade of 1862 (Chinese Customs, Treaties, I, pp. 127-131, 135-139) and that of 1881 (ibid., I, pp. 188-207; Hertslet, Treaties, I, pp. 483-499), Russia demanded either total exemption of customs duties or a one-third reduction. Following the Russian example, other countries with territories bordering on China also obtained a reduced rate from regular customs duties. See, for instance, Art. III of the Sino-Franco Supplementary Commercial Convention of June 26, 1887 (Chinese Customs, Treaties, I, pp. 933-936; Hertslet, Treaties, I, pp. 311-314); Art. IX of the Sino-British Convention of March 1, 1894 (Chinese Customs, Treaties, I, pp. 513-515; Hertslet, Treaties, I, pp. 92-94).

25. Also known as 'capitulations', extraterritorial jurisdiction was first granted by the Ottoman Empire in the sixteenth century.

For one time or another, Western powers had obtained the same privileges in China, Japan, Thailand, Iran, Egypt, and Morocco.

26. The appointment of British superintendents or consular officers was provided for in Art. II of the Sino-British Treaty of August 29, 1842 (Chinese Customs, Treaties, I, pp. 351-356; Hertslet, Treaties, I, pp. 7-12). It was, however, Art. XIII of the General Regulations (Chinese Customs, Treaties, I, p. 388) that first provided the treaty basis for extraterritoriality in China:

> "Whenever a British subject has reason to complain of a Chinese he must first proceed to the Consulate and state his grievance. The Consul will thereupon inquire into the merits of the case, and do his utmost to arrange it amicably. In like manner, if a Chinese has reason to complain of a British subject, he shall no less listen to his complaint and endeavor to settle it in a friendly manner.... If, unfortunately, any disputes take place of such a nature that the Consul cannot arrange them amicably, then he shall request the assistance of a Chinese officer, that they may together examine into the merits of the case, and decide it equitably. Regarding the punishment of English criminals, the English Government will enact the laws necessary to attain that end, and the Consul will be empowered to put them in force; and regarding the punishment of Chinese criminals, these will be tried and punished by their own laws, in the way provided for by the correspondence which took place at Nanking, after the concluding of the peace."

This provision was later amended by Arts. XV-XVII and XXI-XXIII of the Sino-British Treaty of June 26, 1858 (Chinese Customs, Treaties, I, pp. 404-421; Hertslet, Treaties, I, pp. 18-35).

27. Provisions for extraterritoriality can be found in Arts. XVI, XIX, XXI, XXIV, XXV of the Treaty of Wang-hia, July 3, 1844 (Chinese Customs, Treaties, I, pp. 677-690). Art. XXI solely dealt with criminal matters:

> "Subjects of China who may be guilty of any criminal act towards citizens of the United States shall be arrested and punished by the Chinese authorities according to the laws of China, and citizens of the United States who may commit any crime in China shall be subject to be tried and punished only by the

the Consul or other public functionary of the United
States thereto authorized according to the laws of
the United States; and in order to secure the prevention of all controversy and disaffection, justice shall
be equitably and impartially administered on both
sides.''

Arts. XXIV and XXVI were concerned with the settlement of
disputes and collection of debts respectively. Art. XXV prescribed procedures on civil matters:

"All questions in regard to rights, whether of property or person, arising between citizens of the United
States in China, shall be subject to the jurisdiction
of, and regulated by the authorities of their own
Government. And all controversies occurring in
China between citizens of the United States and sub-
subjects of any other Government shall be regulated
by the treaties existing between the United States and
such Governments, respectively, without interference on the part of China.''

28. For its text, see Chinese Customs, Treaties, I, pp. 771-790;
    Hertslet, Treaties, I, pp. 258-269.

29. For its text, see Chinese Customs, Treaties, I, pp. 45-71;
    Hertslet, Treaties, II, pp. 527-540.

30. See Arts. VIII and XIII of the Sino-Japanese Treaty of September
    13, 1871 (Chinese Customs, Treaties, II, pp. 507-514, 572-575,
    642-648).

31. See Art. VI of the Sino-Japanese Treaty of Peace of April 17,
    1895 (Chinese Customs, Treaties, II, pp. 590-596, 707-713;
    Hertslet, Treaties, I, pp. 362-370; MacMurray, Treaties, I,
    pp. 18-24); also Arts. XXI-XXII of the Sino-Japanese Treaty
    of Commerce and Navigation of July 21, 1896 (Chinese Cus-
    toms, Treaties, II, pp. 604-614, 720-731; Hertslet, Treaties,
    I, pp. 373-382; MacMurray, Treaties, I, pp. 68-74).

32. When China entered into World War I on the Allied side in
    1917, she declared the termination of all her treaties with
    Austria-Hungary and Germany. The abrogation of extrater-
    ritoriality in China was acquiesced in by these countries in
    the peace treaties of Versailles, St. Germain, and Trianon.
    For the text of the Chinese Declaration, see The China Year
    Book, 1921-1922, p. 698.

33. For its text, see Carnegie, Treaties, pp. 133-140. For a gen-
    eral survey of the extraterritorial system, see Shih-shun Liu,

Extraterritoriality, Its Rise and Its Decline (New York, 1925), pp. 81-99, 117-125, 217-228.

34. For details, see Willoughby, II, Ch. XXIII.

35. Art. XVII of the Sino-British Treaty of June 26, 1858 (Chinese Customs, Treaties, I, pp. 404-421; Hertslet, Treaties, I, pp. 18-35) was almost identical to Art. XIII of the General Regulations for Trade. See supra, Ch. 5, note 26.

36. Section II (iii) of the Sino-British Treaty of September 13, 1876 (Chinese Customs, Treaties, I, pp. 491–499; Hertslet, Treaties, I, pp. 73-80). Similar provisions can be found in the Sino-American Treaty of November 17, 1880 (Chinese Customs, Treaties, I, pp. 736-739; Hertslet, Treaties, I, pp. 558-560).

37. Art. 1 of the Rules governing the Mixed Court in Shanghai (ibid., II, pp. 662-664).

38. For differences between the Mixed Court in the French Settlement and that in the International Settlement in Shanghai, see the Provisional Rules governing Jurisdiction of the Mixed Courts in Shanghai, June 10, 1902 (ibid., II, pp. 802-803).

39. For details, see Willoughby, I, Ch. XXI; II, Ch. XXV; Tsien, pp. 66-68.

40. For its text, see MacMurray, Treaties, I, pp. 796-798.

41. See Koo, pp. 205,207; U.S. For. Rel., 1873, I, p. 139.

42. For details, see ibid., 1880-1881, p. 177.

43. See Willoughby, II, pp. 574-576.

44. See ibid., II, pp. 576-577; also U.S. For. Rel., 1906, Pt. I, p. 384, in conjunction with Art. 5 of the 1869 Rules governing the Mixed Court in Shanghai, on criminals escaping to the foreign settlements.

45. See infra, pp. .160, 193-194, 250-257, 271-272, 322.

46. It is interesting to note the fate of the ten-mile Shanghai-Woosung Line, the first railroad in China. Originally, a foreign concern obtained permission to build a tramway, but, instead, a railway was being constructed. After its operation for only a few weeks on the half-completed railway in 1876, the Chinese local government decided to buy out that concern and tear up the track. See Morse, III, pp. 75-76.

47. For instance, the Peking-Suiyuan Railway and the Lung-Hai Railway.

48. The stipulation in the Chinese Railway Regulations of 1904 that foreign interests in a railway company could not exceed 50% of its total capital was not carried out. For its text, see Kuang-hsü New Laws and Ordinances (Shanghai, 1909, in Chinese), p. 8 sq. Nor were the provisions of the Chinese Mining Regulations of 1907 strictly put into practice. See ibid., p. 92 sq.

49. See the Anglo-German Bankers' Arrangement regarding Spheres of Interest in Railway Construction, September 2, 1898 (MacMurray, Treaties, I, pp. 266-267).

50. Among the Chinese mines with foreign investments were the Hanyehping in Central China (Japanese), the Fushun in Manchuria (Japanese), and the Kailand in North China (British). Many mines were along the railway concessions. Much information can be found in two monographs in Chinese: (1) Hsi Wang, Chung-ying K'ai-p'ing K'uang-ch'uan Chiao-she (Sino-British Negotiations on the Kai-ping Mining Rights, Taipei, 1963); En-han Li, Wan-Ch'ing Ti Shou-hui K'uang-ch'uan Yün-tung (The Late Ch'ing Movement for the Restoration of Mining Rights, Taipei, 1967).

51. For the text of the Li-Lobanoff Treaty of 1896, see MacMurray, Treaties, I, pp. 81-82.

52. For the text of the Contract for the Construction and Working of the Chinese Eastern Railway, signed at Berlin on August 27/September 8, 1896, see Chinese Customs, Treaties, I, pp. 208-218.

53. See the Sino-Russian Agreement regarding Inter-Allied Supervision of Siberian Railway System, January 9, 1919 (MacMurray, Treaties, I, pp. 82-83).

54. In the Statutes of the Chinese Eastern Railway Company, submitted by the Russian Minister of Finance and confirmed by the Russian government on December 4/16, 1896 (ibid., I, pp. 84-88), provision was made that, in the event of a difference of opinion, CER should submit to the decision of the Russian Minister of Finance. See also the Russian Imperial Ukaz regarding Jurisdiction in Chinese Eastern Railway Zone, August 2, 1901 (ibid., I, pp. 88-90). In separate notes sent by the British, French, the Netherlands, and several other governments in 1914-1915, they informed the Russian government that their nationals were instructed to observe the Russian

municipal regulations and to pay the municipal taxes in the towns situated in the Chinese Eastern Railway Zone (ibid., II, pp. 1181-1187). But the United States persistently refused to do the same. See U.S. For. Rel., 1910, p. 219. In spite of her preliminary agreement with Russia on this matter in 1909, China declared that she never surrendered her sovereignty over the Chinese Eastern Railway Zone. See ibid., 1910, p. 222.

55. Agreements for mining and timber concessions were concluded on August 30, 1907 (MacMurray, Treaties, I, pp. 658-662, 671-674) and April 8, 1908 (ibid., 1, pp. 721-724).

56. For the text of the Agreements on the Expropriation of Lands, see ibid., I, pp. 663-671.

57. For its text, see Chinese Customs, Treaties, I, pp. 219-226; MacMurray, Treaties, I, pp. 119-122.

58. See supra, p. 48.

59. Art. VIII of the Sino-Russian Convention of March 27, 1898.

60. See supra, Ch. 5, note 54.

61. See the Note of the Tsungli Yamen to the Russian Minister at Peking in Regard to the Construction of Railways Northward and Northeastward from Peking, June 1, 1899 (MacMurray, Treaties, I, pp. 207-208).

62. See the following provisions of the Anglo-Russian Exchange of Notes regarding Railway Interests in China, April 28, 1899 (ibid., I, pp. 204-205):

> "1.   Great Britain engages not to seek for her own account, or on behalf of British subjects or of others, any railway concessions to the north of the Great Wall of China, and to obstruct, directly or indirectly, applications for railway concessions in that region supported by the Russian Government.
>
> "Russia, on her part, engages not to seek for her own account, or on behalf of Russian subjects or of others, any railway concessions in the basin of the Yangtze, and not to obstruct, directly or indirectly, applications for railway concessions in that region supported by the British Government."

63. For its text, see Chinese Customs, Treaties, I, pp. 208-214; MacMurray, Treaties, I, pp. 112-118.

64. See Arts. I, III, IV of Section II of the Sino-German Convention of March 6, 1898.

65. See infra, pp. 160-163, 190-192.

66. For the Convention and Exchange of Notes relationg to Kuangchou-wan and the Construction of a Railway from Tongking to Yunnanfu, April 9/10, 1898 (the lease being actually effected by the Convention of May 27, 1898), see Hertslet, Treaties, I, pp. 329-331; MacMurray, Treaties, I, pp. 123-125, 128-130).

67. Art. VII of the Convention.

68. For its text, see MacMurray, Treaties, I, pp. 453-462.

69. Art. XXIII of the Contract.

70. For the Memorandum on the French railway and mining concessions in China, see Rockhill, Treaties, p. 402; Documents Diplomatiques, Chine, 1894-1898, p. 23.

71. For its text, see Hertslet, Treaties, I, pp. 608-614; MacMurray, Treaties, I, pp. 522-526.

72. Art. VI of the Treaty.

73. For the text of the Convention of December 22, 1905, and its Supplementary Agreement, see Chinese Customs, Treaties, I, pp. 636-641, 735-745; Hertslet, Treaties, I, pp. 391-396; MacMurray, Treaties, I, pp. 549-555.

74. For a summary of the alleged secret Protocols to the Sino-Japanese Treaty of December 22, 1905, see ibid., I, pp. 554-555.

75. Art. VI.

76. For its text, see MacMurray, Treaties, I, pp. 555-556.

77. In accordance with the Japanese Government Order of August 1, 1906 (ibid., I, pp. 557-558).

78. Art. I of the Japanese Government Order of August 1, 1906; Art. 4 of the Articles of Incorporation of the South Manchurian Railway Joint Stock Company (ibid., I, 559-563). New railways were planned or incorporated into the South Manchurian Railway system, including the Toananfu-Anganshi Railway from Toananfu near the border of Eastern Inner Mongolia to Anganshi.

79. Art. IV.

80. See supra, p. 121.

81. For the Preliminary Agreement between Great Britain (Pauling & Co.), the United States (American Banking Group), and China, Providing for the Financing, Construction and Operation of the Railway from Chinchou to Aigun, October 2, 1919, see MacMurray, Treaties, I, pp. 800-802.

82. See Secretary Knox's Memorandum of November 9, 1909, addressed to the American Ambassador to London for transmital to the British Foreign Office. U. S. For. Rel., 1909, p. 211.

83. For details, see ibid., 1910, pp. 235, 240, 251, 261, 265, 269.

84. According to the Sino-Japanese Exchange of Notes in Regard to the Construction of Certain Railways in Manchuria, October 5, 1913 (MacMurray, Treaties, II pp. 1054-1055), the railways to be constructed were as follows: (1) from Taonanfu to Jehol, (2) from Changchun to Taonanfu, (3) from Kirin to Kaiyuen via Hailung, and (4) from a point on the Taonanfu-Jehol railway to a seaport.

85. For instance, the Plague Prevention Loan by the Agreement of January 18, 1918, between China and France (Banque de l'Indo-Chine), Great Britain (Hongkong & Shanghai Banking Corporation), Japan (Yokohama Specie Bank), and Russia(Russo-Asiatic Bank). For its text, see MacMurray, Treaties, II, pp. 1405-1406.

86. These included the Hongkong and Shanghai Banking Corporation (British); Jardine, Matheson & Co. (British); the British and Chinese Corporation (British); the Yokohama Specie Bank (Japan); the Bank of Taiwan (Japan); the Bank of Chosen (Japan); the Industrial Bank of Japan (Japan); the Banque Russo-Chinoise (Russia; later known as the Banque Russo-Asiqtique); the Deutsch-Asiatische Bank (Germany); the Banque de l'Indo-Chine (France); the Comptoir National d'Escompte de Paris (France); the Crédit Lyonnais (France); the Société Belge d'Etudes de Chemius Fer en Chine (Belgium); J.P. Morgan & Co. (the United States); Loeb & Co. (the United States); the First National Bank of New York (the United States); the International Banking Corporation (the United States; constituted by a number of American banks); Lee, Higginson & Co. (the United States).

87. For the text of the contracts and protocol, see MacMurray, Treaties, I, pp. 35-43.

88. See the Agreement between Germany, Great Britain, and China, March 23, 1896 (ibid,, I, pp. 55-59).

89. See the Agreement between Germany, Great Britain, and China, March 1, 1898 (ibid., I, pp. 107-112).

90. Art. VI of the Final Protocol of 1901 (Chinese Customs, Treaties, II, pp. 303-341; MacMurray, Treaties, I, pp. 278-308.) As the amount of indemnities distributed to the powers concerned far exceeded their actual losses, several of them later decided to remit the balance of their shares. See the Protocol regarding Apportionment of the Boxer Indemnity, June 14, 1902 (ibid., I, p. 311); Willoughby, II, Ch. XL, for the remission of the Boxer indemnities.

91. For the text of the Agreement and related documents, see MacMurray, Treaties, I, pp. 841-855.

92. For the text of the Contract of August 30, 1912, see ibid., II, pp. 967-973. The Agreement for the cancellation of the Crisp loan was signed on December 23, 1912.

93. In the statement of the American government in regard to support requested by the American banking group on March 18, 1913, President Wilson severely criticized the nature of the loan:

> "The conditions of the loan seem to us to touch very nearly the administrative independence of China itself, and this Administration does not feel that it ought even by implication, to be a party to those conditions. The responsibility on its part which would be implied in requesting the bankers to undertake the loan might conceivably go the length in some unhappy contingency of forcible interference in the financial, and even the political, affairs of that great Oriental State, just now awakening to a consciousness of its power and of its obligations to its people. The conditions include not only the pledging of particular taxes, some of them antiquated and burdensome, to secure the loan but also the administration of those taxes by foreign agents. The responsibility on the part of our Government implied in the encouragement of a loan thus secured and administered is plain enough and is obnoxious to the principles upon which the Government of our people rests."

MacMurray, Treaties, II, p. 1025.

94. For the text of the Agreement and related documents, see ibid., II, pp. 1007-1037.

95. To effect the reorganization of salt revenues, the Chinese government enacted new regulations governing the Central Salt Administration, the appointment of a foreign adviser, and the district inspectorates. See ibid., II, pp. 1026-1029.

96. For details, see Art. XVII of the Reorganization Loan Agreement of 1913.

97. The parties to the Four-Power Consortium were the British Hongkong and Shanghai Banking Corporation, the French Banque l'Indo-Chine, the Japanese Yokohama Specie Bank, and an American group of banks. For the text of the Agreement, see Carnegie, Treaties, pp. 32-36,

98. It should be noted that, during the period 1917-1918, Japan, through the Yokohama Specie Bank and others, advanced 30,000,000 yen to the Chinese government, known as the Supplementary or Second Reorganization Loan. For the text of the Agreements of September 28, 1917, and of January 6, 1918, see MacMurray, Treaties, II, pp. 1387-1388, 1400-1404.

99. For instance, the Belgian Loan of £ 1,000,000 at 5%, from the Banque Sino-Belge, through an agreement of March 14, 1912, for the consolidation of the central and local governments of China(ibid., II, pp. 947-950).

100. The agreements between China and Austria-Hungary (Arnold Karberg & Co.) on April 10, 1913, for loans of £ 2,000,000 and of £ 1,200,000 were puportedly for the purchase of torpedo boat destroyers, but were largely used to defray the current expenses of the government. For the text, see ibid., II, pp. 1004-1007.

101. Under this category were the industrial gold loan of 150,000,000 francs by an agreement between China and France (Banque Industrielle de Chine) on October 9, 1913, with supplementary contract and annexes (ibid., II, pp. 1055-1066); the loan of U.S. gold $5,000,000 as provided for in an agreement between China and the United States (Continental and Commercial Trust and Savings Bank) on November 16, 1916 (ibid., II, pp. 1337-1345); the loan of 30,000,000 yen for gold mining and forestry in the Provinces of Heilungkiang and Kirin by an agreement between China and Japan (Exchange Bank of China, in association with the Japanese Banking Syndicate consisting of the Industrial Bank of Japan, the Bank of Chosen, and the Bank of Taiwan) on August 2, 1918 (ibid., II, pp. 1434-1440).

102. See supra, Ch. 5, Section III (1); Willoughby, II, Ch. XLII.

103. See ibid., II, Ch. XXXVIII.

104. These loans negotiated through Mr. Nishihara were ostensibly for the building of railways, exploitation of mining and forestry, and other constructive purposes.

105. For the text of this loan contract of September 28, 1918, between China and Japan (Bank of Chosen, representing a syndicate consisting of the Bank of Chosen, the Industrial Bank of Japan, and the Bank of Taiwan), see MacMurray, Treaties, II, pp. 1446-1447). On the same date, Japan also signed with China two preliminary loan agreemetnts: (1) for railways in Manchuria and Mongolia (ibid., II, pp. 1448-1450), and (2) for Tsinanfu-Shuntefu and Kaomi-Hsuchow Extensions of Shantung Railway (ibid., II, pp. 1450-1452).

106. Further details of China's foreign debts can be found in The China Year Book, 1924-1925, pp. 756-758, 760-766, 809-813; 1925-1926, pp. 735-737, 739-745, 781-782.

107. See Art. II of the Sino-British Treaty of August 29, 1842 (Chinese Customs, Treaties, I, pp. 351-356; Hertslet, Treaties, I, pp. 7-12).

108. See Art. VI of the Sino-British Supplementary Treaty of Hoomum Chai, October 8, 1843 (Chinese Customs, Treaties, I, pp. 390-399). Provisions were also made in the treaties, of Tientsin and many others. The Chinese words, 'nei ti' or 'inland' applied to 'places on the sea coasts and river shores, as to places in the interior not open to foreign trade,' in accordance with Art. 4 of Section III of the Sino-British Treaty of September 13, 1876 (Chinese Customs, Treaties, I, pp. 491-499; Hertslet, Treaties, I, pp. 73-80). A passport was generally required for traveling purposes under conditions stipulated in treaties.

109. Foreign corporations enjoyed almost equal treatment as domestic ones under the Chinese corporation law except in the field of mining. The Chinese government did not levy income tax on individuals or corporations, but it reserved the right to do so on foreign corporations conducting business in China, according to Art. IV of the Sino-American Treaty of October 8, 1903 (Chinese Customs, Treaties, I, pp. 745-763; Hertslet, Treaties, I, pp. 566-578; MacMurray, Treaties, I, pp. 423-450).

110. Art. VII of the Sino-British Treaty of September 5, 1902 (Chinese Customs, Treaties, I, pp. 543-568; Hertslet, Treaties, I, pp. 171-188; MacMurray, Treaties, I, pp. 342-355) provided that "the Chinese government undertakes to afford protection to British trade-marks against infringement, imitation or colorable imitation by Chinese subjects." Foreign powers were, however, dissatisfied with the Chinese laws and regulations and their enforcement for the protection of foreign trade-marks.

111. Toleration of religion was emphatically stipulated in the treaties of 1858 and of 1860. Art. XXI of the Sino-American Treaty of June 18, 1858 (Chinese Customs, Treaties, I, pp. 713-728; Hertslet, Treaties, I, pp. 540-552) provided that "any persons, whether citizens of the United States or Chinese converts, who, according to these tenets, teach and practice the principles of Christianity, shall in no case be interferred with or molested. In Art. VI of the Sino-Franco Treaty of October 25, 1860 (Chinese Customs, Treaties, I, pp. 885-890; Hertslet, Treaties, I, pp. 287-291), French missionaries were permitted "to rent and purchase land in all the Provinces, and to erect buildings thereon at pleasure." For comments on the authenticity of this provision and its confirmation by the Sino-Franco Bertemy Convention of 1865, see Koo, p. 316; Archives Diplomatiques, LXVI, p. 305. For the text of the Convention, see Henri Cordier, Histoire Rélations de la Chine avec les Puissances Occidentales, I, p. 75. In its reply to an American note concerning the right of taking residence in the interior and acquiring land, the Chinese government stated that "while the treaties between the United States and China do not provide for this, still the American missionaries shall be treated in this matter the same as French missionaries." U. S. For. Rel., 1897, p. 62.

It should be noted that the rights and privileges of Christian missionaries were not extended to other missionaries, such as Buddhists, as demanded by Japan in 1905. See Koo, p. 288. For the Chinese attitude toward Western missionaries, see supra, p. 52.

112. The right of land-holding by missionaries was, for example, expressly provided for in Art. XIV of the Sino-American Treaty of October 8, 1903 (Chinese Customs, Treaties, I, pp. 745-763; Hertslet, Treaties, I, pp. 566-578; MacMurray, Treaties, I, pp. 423-450):

> "Missionary societies of the United States shall be permitted to rent and to lease in perpetuity, as the property of such societies, buildings or lands in all parts of the Empire for missionary purposes and, after the title deeds have been found in order and duly stamped by the local authorities, to erect such suitable buildings as may be required for carrying on their good work."

The right of land-holding by foreign merchants was restricted to the areas in open ports. Whether the land-holder was a missionary or a merchant, the legal title to the tenure was the same, a lease in perpetuity. See Tyau, p. 150. For a summary of the Chinese Rules of 1911 governing

.procedures for holding property by foreigners, see Koo, pp. 333-334.

113. Art. VIII of this Sino-British Treaty of 1843 (Chinese Customs, Treaties, pp. 390-399) provided that "should the Emperor hereafter, from any cause whatever, be pleased to grant additional privileges or immunities to any of the subjects or citizens of such foreign countries, the same privileges and immunities will be extended to and enjoyed by British subjects."

114. The Circular sent by the Tsungli Yamen to Chinese diplomatic missions abroad in 1878 (U. S. For. Rel., 1880, p. 177).

115. For instance, Art. I of the Sino-German Treaty of March 31, 1880 (Chinese Customs, Treaties, I, pp. 194-200; Hertslet, Treaties, I, pp. 342-349) provided that "should German subjects on the strength of this Article claim privileges, immunities, or advantages, which the Chinese government may further concede to another power, or the subjects of such power, they will also submit to the regulations which have been agreed upon in connection with such concession."

Art. VI of the Sino-Mexican Treaty of December 14, 1899 (Chinese Customs, Treaties, II, pp. 833-843; Hertslet, Treaties, I, pp. 399-407; MacMurray, Treaties, I, pp. 214-220) required the conditions for the application of the most-favored-nation clause in the following manner:

"It is to be understood that, in case either of the High Contracting Parties should hereafter grant, of its own accord, to any other nation, advantages subject to special conditions, the other Contracting Party shall enjoy said advantages, only provided it complies with the conditions imposed therein or their equivalent, to be mutually agreed upon."

Similar provisions appeared in other treaties, including the Sino-British Treaty of October 23, 1869 (Chinese Customs, Treaties, I, pp. 478-490; Hertslet, Treaties, I, pp. 61-72), which was not ratified; the Sino-Portuguese Treaty of Peking, December 1, 1887 (Chinese Customs, Treaties, II, pp. 274-294; Hertslet, Treaties, I, pp. 423-433).

116. A very comprehensive provision of the most-favored-nation clause can be found in Art. XXX of the Sino-American Treaty of 1858 (Chinese Customs, Treaties, I, pp. 713-728; Hertslet, Treaties, I, pp. 540-552):

"The contracting parties hereby agree that should, at any time, the Ta-Tsing Empire the⌈Ch'ing

dynasty of China] grant to any nation, or the merchants or citizens of any nation, any right, privilege,
or favor connected either with navigation, commerce, political or other intercourse which is not
conferred by this treaty, such right, privilege, and
favor shall at once freely enure to the benefit of the
United States, its public officers, merchants, and
citizens."

117. In like manner, Art IX of the Sino-Japanese Treaty of 1903
(Chinese Customs, Treaties, II, pp. 617-636; Hertslet,
Treaties, I, pp. 383-391; MacMurray, Treaties, I, pp. 411-
422) provided that "the Japanese Government, officers, subjects, commerce, navigation, shipping, industries, and property of all kinds shall be allowed free and full participation
in all privileges, immunities, and advantages which have been
or may be hereafter be granted by His Majesty, the Emperor
of China, or by the Chinese Government, or by the Provincial
or Local Administration of China to the Government, officers,
subjects, commerce, navigation, shipping, industries, or property of any other nation." It is noteworthy that this Treaty
expressly included grants by the Chinese local authorities.

118. This unreasonable demand was embodied in Art. 3(e) of the
Sino-German Exchange of Notes on December 31, 1913
(MacMurray, Treaties, II, pp. 1094-1097):

"The Chinese Government declares again to the
German Government that if hereafter Railway Loan
Agreements are made between the Chinese Government and any other country wherein the terms and
conditions concerning the construction and traffic
management are more favorable than the terms and
conditions mentioned in the foregoing, the same
privileges will be accorded to these two railways."

Japan attempted to exact similar treatment in Art. VII of the
Sino-Japanese Treaty of May 25, 1915, respecting South Manchuria and Eastern Inner Mongolia under the Twenty-One
Demands, which will be discussed in the next chapter. For
the text of that treaty, see MacMurray, Treaties, II, pp.
1220-1229.

119. For the common practice of the most-favored-nation clause,
its classification into conditional and unconditional forms, and
pertinent court decisions, see William L. Tung, International
Law in an Organizing World, pp. 332, 351.

120. See Tyau, pp. 10, 11, 179, 189; William L. Tung, China and
Some Phases of International Law, pp. 64-68.

121. See, for example, the provision of Art. XVI of the Sino-
Peruvian   Treaty   of   June   26, 1874 (Chinese   Customs,
Treaties, II, pp. 798-807; Hertslet, Treaties, I, pp. 415-420):

> "The contracting parties agree that the government,
> public officers, and citizens of the Republic of Peru,
> shall fully and equally participate in all privileges,
> rights, immunities, jurisdictions, and advantages
> that may have been, or may be hereafter, granted by
> His Majesty the Emperor of China, to the govern-
> ment, public officers, citizens or subjects of any
> other nation. In like manner, the government, public
> officers, and subjects of the Empire of China, shall
> enjoy in Peru all the rights, privileges, immunities,
> and advantages of every kind which in Peru are en-
> joyed by the government, public officers, citizens, or
> subjects of the most favored nation."

Chapter 6
CHINA AWAKENED BUT FRUSTRATED UNDER INTERNATIONAL PRESSURES

In a world where might is right, national dignity and prestige cannot be long sustained without national power. Since the middle of the nineteenth century, China's weakness had been fully exposed in political, economic, and military fields. In order to forestall further foreign intrusions on her national sovereignty and territorial integrity, China slowly but finally realized the necessity of introducing domestic reforms and reshaping her diplomatic agencies. Efforts in these directions had been undertaken in many respects, but belated and insufficient acievements failed to turn the tide.

Moderate reforms through the constitutional process first met strong resistance from reactionary circles; lukewarm endorsement by the Imperial Court in later days could no longer save the Throne. Dormant under Manchu suppression, Chinese nationalism was revived by the Taiping Rebellion and reinvigorated by Sun Yat-sen, leading to the overthrow of the Ch'ing dynasty. Unfortunately, the republic founded by Sun got off to a bad start, and was soon tarnished by Yüan Shih-k'ai's monarchic schemes. Instead of moving toward the abolition of unequal treaties previously concluded, Yüan was compelled to accept even harsher terms from Japan in the notorious Twenty-one Demands.

After the outbreak of World War I, Kiaochow and other German rights in Shantung were forcibly taken over by Japan. Bound by secret agreements, the major European powers submitted entirely to Japan's wishes when the Shantung question was discussed at the Paris Peace Conference. It was due to big-power pressures that the Conference completely ignored China's demands for the return of her Shantung rights and readjustment of other legitimate con-

145

siderations. Awakened but frustrated, the Chinese people were now at the parting of the ways as the events unfolded below will reveal.

I. RESHAPING OF THE DIPLOMATIC FRONT

1. Reorganization of Government Agencies in Charge of Foreign Affairs

China's traditional reluctance to promote diplomatic intercourse with foreign states caused the delay in setting up a central organ in charge of foreign affairs. Prior to 1861, diplomatic relations were conducted by several agencies, including the Board of Rites, the Superintendency of Dependencies, the Governor of Lia-kua provinces, and later Governors of other coastal provinces.[1] Due to practical necessity, however, the Chinese government instituted, by an imperial edict of January 19, 1861, the Tsung-li Ko-kuo Shih-wu Yamen (Office of Foreign Affairs), generally known as Tsungli Yamen.[2] This took place quite late in comparison with most advanced nations in Europe, where there existed corresponding organs in the fifteenth and sixteenth centuries.[3]

The Tsungli Yamen was not under the direction of a single Minister. Instead, its functions were supervised by a number of Ministers, who were appointed by the Throne from Princes, Grand Councillors, Grand Secretaries, and Ministers of various departments. Because of its diffusive responsibility, rudimentary organization, and the participation of the Nanyang and Peiyang High Commissioners in international negotiations,[4] the efficiency of the Yamen was undermined, and consequently caused inconveniences to foreign powers in their dealings with the Chinese government. In the Final Protocol of 1901, the reorganization of the Tsungli Yamen was demanded.[5] By an imperial edict of July 24, 1901, the Wai-wu Pu (Ministry of Foreign Affairs) was created, taking rank before the Six Ministries.[6]

Consisting of four bureaus, the Wai-wu Pu was overburdened, at the beginning, with many functions other than foreign relations, such as the supervision of maritime customs, postal, telegraph, and railway services, and even naval affairs. These extra responsibilities were gradually relieved after the establishment of several new ministries and agencies in charge of these matters. It was not, however, till 1912, that the Wai-wu Pu was remodeled along Western lines under the name of Wai-chiao Pu. The Ministry of Foreign Affairs should be the nerve center of a state in the administration of diplomatic relations, but it took China more than half a century to make efficient use of this important agency. In the establishment of permanent missions abroad, the Chinese government had also fallen far behind.

2. Special Envoys on Temporary Missions

The accreditation of Chinese envoys to foreign governments was not only urged by Western powers,[7] but also suggested by Wên Hsiang, Ch'ung Hou, and other Chinese statesmen.[8] In order to gain a better understanding of the West for the formulation of intelligent foreign policies, the Chinese government decided to send temporary missions abroad as a first step. In 1866, the Tsungli Yamen dispatched Pin Ch'un as a special envoy to investigate conditions in Europe. The mission left Peking on March 7, 1865, and visited nine European countries; two foreigners from the Imperial Maritime Customs service accompanied Pin Ch'un as his retinue.[9] The success of the mission contributed to many favorable responses from high officials to a secret Imperial decree of 1867, on the advisability of appointing permanent envoys.[10]

One year later, the Chinese government appointed Anson Burlingame, a former American Minister to Peking, to lead a mission to Europe and the United States. Highly respected in Chinese official circles, Burlingame was entrusted with the task of negotiating favorable terms for the impending treaty revision. With two Chinese officials, Chin Kang and Sun Chia-ku, as co-envoys,[11] the mission secured reasonable assurance of sympathetic consideration from Great Britain, Prussia, and the United States.[12] Thereafter, temporary envoys were also dispatched to foreign governments on various missions. These included the Ch'ung Hou mission to France in 1871 and the Kuo Sung-t'ao mission to England in 1877, both of which were undertaken to express regret for local incidents involving the loss of lives of their respective nationals. [13]

3. Establishment of Chinese Legations and Consulates

As previously described, it was only after considerable pressure from Western powers that China grudgingly gave consent to the stationing of foreign representatives in Peking;[14] it took still a longer time for her to decide on the establishment of legations and consulates abroad. When the French President, M. Thiers, received Ch'ung Hou at Versailles on November 23, 1871, he expressed the wish that China set up a permanent legation in Paris. [15] Then, in 1875, the Tsungli Yamen urged the Throne to send permanent representatives to the United States, Peru, and Spain.[16] China's first legation was, however, established in London, when Kuo Sung-t'ao was appointed permanent envoy to England after the completion of his temporary mission in 1877. Halliday Macartney, superintendent of the Chinese government arsenal at Nanking, 1865-1875, was appointed English secretary of the Legation.[17]

The year 1877 was the turning point of Chinese diplomatic history with respect to the appointment of permanent envoys: Ho Ju-chang and Liu Hsi-hung presented credentials to the Emperors of Japan and Germany respectively.[18] In the following year, Kuo Sung-t'ao became concurrently Chinese Minister to France,[19] and Ch'ung Hou was assigned as Chinese envoy to St. Petersburg.[20] In response to the 1875 memorial of the Tsungli Yamen, the Emperor appointed Ch'en Lan-pin and Yung Wing as Imperial Commissioners to the governments of the United States, Spain, and Peru, which cordially received their credentials in September 1878, May 1879, and April 1880, respectively.[21] China's decision to send permanent envoys abroad during the period 1871-1880 was important, because it indicated a definite change of attitude by the Imperial Court from flat rejection to gradual approval.

With regard to the exchange of consuls, foreign powers emphasized this right from the very beginning. The stationing of British consuls at Chinese treaty ports was provided for in the Treaty of Nanking of August 29, 1842,[22] in the treaties with the United States and France in 1844,[23] and many others in the following years.[24] The first provision for this right reciprocal to China appeared in the Burlingame Treaty of July 28, 1868, officially known as the Additional Articles to the Treaty of Commerce between the United States and China of June 18, 1858. Article III provided that "China shall have the right to appoint Consuls at ports of the United States, who shall enjoy the same privileges and immunities as those which are enjoyed by public law and Treaty in the United States by the Consuls of Great Britain and Russia, or either of them." [25] The stipulation of this article enabled China to send officials to the United States for the protection of thousands of Chinese workers in California.[26] Similar rights were provided for in later treaties. [27]

China's interest in sending consuls abroad was evidenced in the conversations between Wên Hsiang and William H. Seward, former Secretary of State, at Peking, in 1870.[28] A year later, both Ts'êng Kuo-fan and Li Hung-chang, two great statesman during the latter part of the Ch'ing dynasty, advocated the advantages of having diplomatic and consular representatives in other countries.[29] After an investigation of the conditions of Chinese laborers in Peru and Cuba in 1873,[30] the Chinese government finally reached the decision to send consuls abroad to protect the interests of the Chinese overseas.[31]

There were still obstinate officials in the Court raising objections to the maintenance of intimate contacts with foreign powers. Nontheless, the general trend and practical necessity prevailed at last. China could have benefited more if the legations and consulates had been established earlier. Lack of listening posts abroad also contributed to the nation's inadequate knowledge of the international situation and conditions in various countries. After the turn of the century, China has come to appreciate many valuable contributions made by her experienced envoys in the diplomatic front under most difficult circumstances.

II. WESTERN IMPACT ON CHINA'S DOMESTIC DEVELOP-MENT

1. Reforms through Constitutional Process

After suffering repeated humiliations in war and diplo-macy, the Imperial Court became gradually receptive to Western ideas and ideals, which had been introduced to China by foreign representatives, merchants, and mission-aries. Information brought back by Chinese envoys and students concerning political and economic progress in Japan, Europe, and the United States also served as an important guideline for various domestic programs.[32] The Chinese in-telligentsia were most impressed by the constitutional form of government and democratic institutions of other nations. Many of them gave credit for Japan's victory over Russia in 1904-1905 to the Meiji reforms, especially to the change from absolute to constitutional monarchy.

The reform movement in China gained momentum in 1898. It was led by K'ang Yu-wei and Liang Ch'i-ch'ao, who first introduced new measures in the administrative and edu-cational fields. These initial reforms commanded the confi-dence of Emperor Kuang Hsü, but antagonized the Empress Dowager. Surrounded by reactionaries, she decided to resume control of state affairs and relentlessly purged the Chinese 'New Dealers'. It was under these unfortunate circumstances that the so-called 'Hundred Days' Reform' came to an end. [33] On the other hand, the trend toward democracy was almost irresistible. In order to alleviate popular dissatisfaction with the regime, the Manchu rulers had to install some kind of constitutional institutions.

In 1905, the Imperial Court appointed five commissioners to investigate political and constitutional systems of Japan, England, France, Belgium, Germany, Italy, Austria, and the United States.[34] Upon their return to Peking a year later, they recommended constitutional monarchy for China. In their opinion, the power and wealth of many countries had much to do with constitutional systems, which were also considered an effective means of preventing revolution.[35] In pursuance of the Imperial Edict for Constitutional Prepara-tion of September 1, 1906,[36] the Principle of Constitution and other laws for the establishment of Parliament were promulgated in 1908. Then the Legislative Council (Tse-cheng Yuan) and provincial assemblies (Tse-i Chu) were set up. When the country became extremely restless in 1911, the Manchu Court made a last effort to save the Throne by adopting the more democratic Nineteen Articles as a national Constitution to be observed by both the ruler and the ruled. [37]

Some of the reforms deserved praise, but these belated acts did not go far enough to meet the demands of the people. Thus constitutional monarchy could no longer appease the nation, which was ready for a drastic revolution led by Sun Yat-sen. Because the last decade of the Ch'ing dynasty was devoted to internal readjustment and the foreign powers simply stood by observing the development, there was no material change in China's international relations one way or the other.

2. Factors Underlying Sun Yat-sen's Nationalist Revolution

The acceptance of humiliating terms from France in 1885 for the termination of the Sino-Franco War fully exposed the weakness of Manchu officialdom.[38] At that time, Sun Yat-sen made up his mind to overthrow the Ch'ing dynasty. Three important factors affected his decision for revolution: first, the corruption and inefficiency of the Manchu Court; second, foreign intrusions; and third, his peasant parentage and early association with members of secret societies and ex-Taiping soldiers. Since previous chapters have already revealed the importance of the first and second factors to China's destiny, some attention should now be given to the third factor.

Because of his peasant parentage, Sun was in a position to know more intimately of the sufferings and sentiments of the common people. Many members of the secret societies, such as the Triad or the Hung Society, originally had the political objective of restoring the Ming dynasty, which was over-thrown by the Manchus in 1644. It was, therefore, natural for them to join the common cause of revolution against the Ch'ing dynasty.[39] In order to understand the influence of the Taiping Rebellion and of his association with ex-Taiping soldiers on Sun's revolutionary ideas, a brief analysis of the events relative to foreign intervention is appropriate.

The Taiping Rebellion or Revolution broke out in 1850, with the main objective of overthrowing Manchu rule. Many members of the secret societies in the Southern provinces joined the revolt because of their common political goal, even though they did not necessarily accept the religious doctrines of the Taipings.40 For twelve years, Nanking was in the hands of the rebels, whose military conquests once extended to a dozen provinces. Manchu generalship was for a long time not equal to the task. The Taiping leaders "advised the Europenas to adopt the principle of non-intervention, and to keep apart from a contest in which they have no interest at stake."41 In spite of the warning, foreign army officers organized the well-known 'Ever Victorious Army', which saved the situation for the Manchus at a critical moment.42 The rebellion was, however, not subdued until 1864.

Although foreign intervention was not the determining factor in the failure of the Taipings, it was definitely one of the significant causes.43 The powers concerned should have prohibited their nationals from taking an active part in the Chinese civil war, to which their governments remained officially neutral. While the Taiping soldiers resented the unwarranted intervention of foreign officers, the Chinese people in general despised Manchu rulers more than ever before. A regime which could not effectively resist foreign aggression, yet was willing to accept external assistance to conduct civil strife, would inevitably be hated by the populace. There is no doubt that the Taiping events had a tremendous impact on Sun's thoughts and activities.

With the overthrow of Manchu rule and the establishment of a republic as his immediate objectives, Sun's ultimate goal was to transform China into a modern nation and emancipate her from the imperialistic yoke.44 Thus his writings manifested strong nationalism and anti-imperialism.45 It should be noted, however, that Sun was comparatively moderate in his internal and external programs. While the Chinese revolution aimed at abolishing all the unequal treaties, his basic foreign policy was to maintain friendly relations with foeign powers on equal and reciprocal terms. Pending the termination of unequal treaties through future negotiation, Sun intended to respect China's commitments made in the past. This conciliatory policy, first enunciated in the 'Manifesto to the World' in 1905 by his revolutionary society, T'ung-meng Hui, was formally declared by the new Republic on January 5, 1912. [46]

3. Political Instability During the Early Republican Period

The Wuchang Revolution on October 10, 1911 not only overthrew the Ch'ing dynasty but also brought to an end China's historical system of absolute monarchy. As the leader of the revolution, Sun Yat-sen was elected Provisional President of the Republic. On January 1, 1912, Sun began his term of office in Nanking. According to the Provisional Constitution of March 11, 1912,[47] the form of government was to be the cabinet system. During the peace negotiations between the revolutionary government and Yüan Shih-k'ai, the last premier of the Imperial government, Sun expressed his intention to resign from the Presidency in favor of Yüan with the hope of facilitating the unification of the country. Yüan coveted the Presidency, but disliked the cabinet system. Thus serious disagreement soon developed between Yüan and Sun's Nationalist Party (Kuomintang).

In 1913, the Nationalist Party had a controlling voice in the Parliament and would elect its leading member, Sung Chiao-jen, to be the Prime Minister. At Yüan's instigation, Sung was assassinated on March 20, 1913, at the railway station in Shanghai. Then the Nationalist leaders in the Southeastern provinces raised the so-called 'Second Revolution' against Yüan, but they suffered military defeat owing to a combination of factors.[48] Subsequent developments were best described by Sun himself:

> "The first blow came at the assassination of Sung Chiao-jen. Then he [Yüan] was encouraged by the obtaining of a loan from the Five-Power Consortium without Parliament's approval. The anti-Yüan coalition in the Southeast was too slow in its military action and its defeat resulted in the extinction of revolutionary forces established during the 1911 Revolution. When finally Parliament was dissolved and the Provisional Constitution abandoned, his betrayal of the Republic and Monarchian ambition were fully revealed."[49]

Despite widespread dissention in the country after the 'Second Revolution', Yuan continued to strengthen his dictatorial power. After the promulgation of the Constitutional Compact on May 1, 1914,[50] an extreme form of the presidential system was adopted, with all major powers centered in the President; the legislature was reduced to a subsidiary organ. In the ensuing year, preparation for his monarchical scheme was in full swing. A divided nation headed by a President with boundless ambition for personal glorification would be easy prey for an imperialistic neighbor. Japan did not fail to seize the opportunity to expand her influence in China.

III. JAPAN'S TWENTY-ONE DEMANDS

1. President Yüan's Acceptance under Duress

China's adversity has often been Japan's opportunity. Under the Presidency of Yüan Shih-k'ai, China was divided as just described. When World War I broke out, the Japanese government took immediate steps to dominate the Asiatic continent beyond South Manchuria. With European nations embattled in the West, there was no fear of third-power intervention as imposed by Russia, France, and Germany in their joint demand for the retrocession of the Liaotung Peninsula to China in 1895.[51] Japan's first stroke was the attack on the German leased territory of Kiaochow and the acquisition of other German rights in Shantung, in complete disregard of China's status of neutrality at that time. It was soon revealed, however, that the occupation of Kiaochow was merely a prelude to Japan's vast expansion schemes and that her ultimate aim was far beyond Shantung.

On January 18, 1915, Hioki Eki, the Japanese Minister at Peking, secretly presented the notorious Twenty-one Demands to President Yüan Shih-k'ai. These Demands, especially Group V, if accepted, would virtually put China under Japanese control.[52] As China's Resident in Korea at the time of the first Sino-Japanese War of 1894-1895, Yüan should have known well Japan's militant policy and ruthless manipulations.[53] While secret negotiations dragged on, Yüan and his government purposely leaked the news to the Chinese and foreign press to solicit the support of public opinion. Concerned with the Chinese delaying tactics and popular indignation, the Japanese government decided to act. On May 7, 1915, the Japanese Minister at Peking delivered an ultimatum to the Chinese Foreign Minister. After clarifying the various Demands as modified in the course of negotiations, the ultimatum concluded:

> "The Imperial Government therefore advise the Chinese Government that they will, in appreciation of the good will of the Imperial Government, accept without amendment all items, included in Groups I, II, III, and IV, together with the item in Group V relating to Fukien, as embodied in the Japanese amended project of April 26th.

> "In case the Imperial Government fail to receive from the Chinese Government, before 6 P.M. of May 9th, a satisfactory response to their advice they will take such independent action as they deem necessary to meet the situation." 54

When the ultimatum was delivered, the Japanese Minister also handed to the Chinese Foreign Minister an Explanatory Note. 55 Militarily, China was not in the position to defy Japan; diplomatically, the balance of power in the Far East could no longer be maintained and no country would lend a helping hand; domestically, Yüan was deeply involved in his monarchical scheme and could not afford to antagonize Japan. 56 Because of these combined factors, Yüan accepted, on May 9, all the terms of the ultimatum. 57 The Japanese demands were subsequently formalized in the Treaty respecting South Manchuria and Eastern Mongolia, and a series of exchanges of notes on matters including Hanyehping and the Fukien Question,58 none of which had, however, received the approval of the Chinese Parliament.

2. Essentials of Japan's Final Demands

The Twenty-one Demands were originally presented under five groups. Group I as finally embodied in the Treaty and Exchange of Notes respecting the Province of Shantung contained the following terms: (1) full assent to whatever agreement to be reached in the future between Japan and Germany relating to the disposition of German rights, interests, and concessions in Shantung; (2) priority of Japanese capital in building the Chefoo-Weihsien railway;[59] (3) opening of more places in Shantung for foreign residence and trade; and (4) non-alienation to any foreign power of any territory or island within Shantung or along its coast. [60] In a Note of the same date, Japan promised to restore the leased territory of Kiaochow to China after the termination of the war under the following conditions: (1) opening of the whole of Kiaochow Bay as a commercial port; (2) a concession under the exclusive jurisdiction of Japan; (3) an international concession if desired by the foreign powers; and (4) mutual agreement between China and Japan regarding the disposal of the buildings and properties of Germany. The restoration of Kiaochow would, however, take place only after Japan acquired the right of its free disposal. In other words, Kiaochow would pass to Japan first. In its Note of Reply, the Chinese government acquiesced in all these conditions. [61]

The Demands under Group II were incorporated in the Treaty and Exchange of Notes respecting South Manchuria and Eastern Inner Mongolia, consisting of the following terms: (1) extension of the lease of Port Arthur and Dairen and of the terms of the South Manchuria Railway and the Antung-Mukden Railway to ninety-nine years; (2) right of Japanese subjects to reside, travel, and lease land in South Manchuria to erect buildings for trade and manufacture or for prosecuting agricultural enterprises; (3) permission for joint undertaking of agricultural and industrial enterprises by the Chinese and Japanese; (4) exercise of consular jurisdiction over Japanese subjects pending the reform of the Chinese judicial system, with the understanding, however, that Japanese subjects should submit to Chinese police and revenue laws; [62] (5) opening for foreign trade and residence suitable places in Eastern Inner Mongolia; (6) speedy revision of the Kirin-Changchun Railway Loan Agreement in favor of Japan. [63] By separate notes, Japan obtained consent from China for: (1) right of mining by Japanese subjects in selected areas in South Manchuria; [64] (2) priority of Japanese subjects in granting loans for building necessary railways in South Manchuria and Eastern Inner Mongolia; and (3) priority of Japanese subjects to be employed as foreign advisers or instructors on political, financial, military or police matters in South Manchuria. If these terms were carried out, Japan would completely control South Manchuria and penetrate further into Eastern Inner Mongolia.

Also in the form of Exchange of Notes was Group III, dealing with the Hanyehping Company, a major arms manufacturer in Central China. The Chinese government had to approve its cooperation with Japanese capitalists, whose prior consent would be necessary for government expropriation, conversion into a state enterprise, or negotiations for foreign capital other than Japanese. [65] Group IV demanded that China not cede or lease to a third power any harbor, bay, or island along the coast of China. Under Article 6 of Group V, the Japanese government originally demanded prior consultation when the Chinese government should need foreign capital in connection with railways, mines, and harbor works in Fukien province. In the final Exchange of Notes on May 25, 1915, the Chinese government committed itself not to permit foreign nations to construct, on the coast of Fukien province, dock-yards, coaling stations for military establishments, nor to borrow foreign capital for the above purposes. [66]

From the above-mentioned terms embodied in the Treaties and Exchanges of Notes on May 25, 1915, Japan would have established strongholds from the Northeast to South China, and dominated many areas of China. What Japan demanded but did not obtain were the first five articles of Group V, which exposed the ruthlessness of Japanese imperialism. Even unfilfilled, Group V of the Twenty-one Demands had immensely antagonized the Chinese people for decades to come.

3. Japan's Unfulfilled Demands

While the first four groups dealt with specific matters and particular regions, Group V was intended to reduce China to a vassal state of Japan. Except for Article 6 on the Fukien question already described, the demands under Group V may be summarized as follows: (1) employment of influential Japanese as advisers in political, financial, and military affairs; (2) right of owning land by Japanese hospitals, churches, and schools in the interior of China; (3) joint administration of police departments in important places by employing numerous Japanese with a view to improving the Chinese police service; (4) purchase of a large quantity of

Japanese arms and establishment of an arsenal in China under joint Japanese and Chinese management to be supplied with Japanese experts and materials; and (5) right of Japan to construct a railway connecting Wuchang with Kiukiang and Nanchang, one line between Nanchang and Hangchow, and still another between Nanchang and Chaochou. [67]

It is quite evident that these demands were designed to control China's national destiny in every respect: political, economic, military, administrative, and others. The supervision of the Chinese police and colonization of the Japanese people had especially far-reaching consequences for China's future. In effect, the Chinese people would inevitably lose their national independence under the bondage of these demands. Because of China's strong objections and worldwide apprehension, the Japanese government yielded temporarily, and agreed to let these demands be "postponed for later negotiations." [68]

4. International and National Reaction to the Twenty-one Demands

It is needless to say that President Yüan Shih-k'ai found it most painful to accept the terms of the Japanese ultimatum and was fully aware of China's international obligations. In its official statement, the Chinese government disclaimed "any desire to associate themselves with any revision, which may be thus effected, of the various conventions and agreements concluded between other Powers in respect of the maintenance of China's territorial independence and integrity, the preservation of the status quo, and the principle of equal opportunity for the commerce and industry of all nations in China." [69]

During the course of the Sino-Japanese negotaitions, the United States closely watched the developments. On May 13, 1915, the American government sent identical notes to the two countries and emphatically stated that "it cannot recognize any agreement or undertaking which has been entered into or which may be entered into between the Governments of China and Japan impairing the treaty rights of the United States and its citizens in China, the political or territorial integrity of the Republic of China, or the international policy relative to China commonly known as the Open Door Policy."[70] These Notes, sent after China's acceptance of the Japanese ultimatum, were essentially for future record rather than effective protest.[71] No intervention could be expected from the European powers, since they themselves were deeply entrenched in World War I.

In China, national indignation against Japanese aggression manifested itself everywhere. Various organizations were established for the cause of national salvation and the boycott of Japanese goods.[72] Political leaders of different parties and factions expressed their solidarity behind the government against the common enemy of the Chinese nation.[73] People from every profession joined the patriotic movement, and contributed generously to the national salvation fund. The slogan, 'Don't Forget the National Humiliation', could be heard throughout the country. Signs with various expressions of anti-Japanese sentiment were seen on walls, posts, leaflets, and stationery.[74] Never before had Japan been so hated by the Chinese populace, who were united together under the banner of nationalism in 1915.[75]

IV. CHINA AT THE PARIS PEACE CONFERENCE

1. Presentation of 'Questions for Readjustment'

On August 14, 1917, China declared war against Germany and Austria-Hungary,[76] and duly informed the diplomatic representatives of the Allied Powers at Peking. In an identical note acknowledging the Chinese communication, each of the Legations concerned expressed to the Chinese government "the assurance of its solidarity of its friendship and of its support...and the regards due to a great country."[77] Despite this assurance, the morale of the Chinese people was then at a low ebb because of Japan's military intrusions on Shantung in 1914 and imposition of the Twenty-One Demands in 1915. While the Western powers concentrated their war efforts in Europe, Japan could indeed take free action in the Far East. Despondent for a long period of fear and uncertainty, the Chinese people suddenly saw a hopeful light in President Wilson's Fourteen Points put forth in his address to Congress on January 8, 1918. Most impressive of all were those advocating open diplomacy and mutual guarantee of political independence and territorial integrity. [78]

The war to end all wars was concluded in November 1918, and the first plenary meeting of the Paris Peace Conference was convened on January 18, 1919. Encouraged by President Wilson's inspiring Points, China, as an ally of the victorious powers, deemed it opportune to present to the Paris Peace Conference her legitimate grievances and request their redress. In the form of desiderata, the questions for readjustment included spheres of influence, the presence of foreign armed forces and police, foreign post offices and wireless stations, leased territories, foreign concessions and settlements, extraterritoriality, and uniform tariff. [79]

While recognizing the importance of these questions, the Council of Four (Great Britain, France, the United States, and Italy) was not receptive to the Chinese request. On May 14, Georges Clemenceau, on behalf of the Council, wrote to the Chinese delegation stating that its proposal did not "fall within the province of the Peace Conference" but "should be brought to the attention of the Council of the League of Nations as soon as that body is able to function." [80] Thus China's fervent hope that the Paris Peace Conference would right the wrongs inflicted by foreign powers since the 1840's was dashed by this one stroke. Yet the major powers were going to pour still more salt on her wounds by the arbitrary decision of the Conference on the Shantung question.

2. Japan's Claims to Former German
Rights in Shantung

The Shantung problem arose as a consequence of Japan's declaration of war against Germany on August 23, 1914. [81] Without the consent of China, then a neutral country, Japan conducted military operations in Chinese territorial waters, the German leasehold of Kiaochow and adjacent areas, as well as the whole line of the Shantung Railway between Kiaochow and Tsianan. Disregarding Chinese protests[82] and in spite of the surrender of German forces on November 7, 1914, Japanese troops took possession of the former German leasehold and other concessions. [83] As described before, Group I of the Twenty-one Demands of 1915 purported to force China to accept as a _fait accompli_ Japan's rights in Shantung. [84] Further attempts were made to advance her position there through the exchange of a series of notes [85] and the conclusion of a railway loan agreement with China in 1917. [86] It should be noted that neither the Twenty-one Demands nor the arrangements embodied in the exchange of notes were approved by the Chinese Parliament.

At the Paris Peace Conference, major decisions were mostly made through constant consultations among the 'big three', namely, Wilson of the United States, Lloyd George of Great Britain, and Clemenceau of France. Japan and Italy also had an important voice in matters concerning their own interests. In the discussion of the Shantung question, the Chinese delegation [87] had the opportunity to present its views on only three occasions: twice at the meetings of the Council of Ten on January 27 and 28, and once at the Council of Four on April 22, 1919. [88] The Council of Ten consised of two representatives each from the above-mentioned five powers, while the Council of Four was limited to the leaders of Great Britain, France, the United States, and Italy. After the departure of Italian Premier Orlando from Paris because of his displeasure at the Conference's disposal of the Fiume problem, the Council of Four was practically changed into the Council of Three. It was at these councils that the Shantung problem was discussed.

Japan firmly claimed former German rights in Shantung, with a vague promise to return such rights to China in the future except for economic privileges. The Chinese delegation refuted the Japanese claim on several grounds: first, the Sino-German treaties concerning the German leased territory of Kiaochow and other rights and concessions in Shantung were automatically terminated after the declaration of war between the two countries; second, the German leasehold was non-transferrable according to the Sino-German Convention of March 6, 1896; [89] third, the Twenty-one Demands were signed under duress and the 1918 agreements were provisional pending the final disposition at the Paris Peace Conference. The Chinese delegation also argued that self-determination and territorial integrity had already been accepted as guiding principles of the Conference.[90]

The United States was sympathetic to the Chinese cause. President Wilson, Secretary of State Robert Lansing, and other representatives of the American delegation went to the Paris Peace Conference unanimously opposed to the Japanese claim to former German rights in Shantung.[91] The Chinese delegation was much encouraged by the American attitude and advocated the Shantung case eloquently despite Japan's strong pressure on the Peking government.[92] On the other hand, Great Britain, France, and Italy entered into secret agreements with Japan in 1917, in which they had given assurances of supporting Japan's succession to German rights in Shantung.[93] Under the circumstances, President Wilson attempted to arrange a compromise by placing the former German leased territory of Kiaochow temporarily under the trustee of the five powers pending the modification of the existing Sino-Japanese treaties. Japan, however, rejected the proposal.[94]

3. Final Disposition of the Shantung Question

Although the accession of the major European powers to Japan's claim was a foregone conclusion, there remained the problem of legal procedure. At the meeting of the Council of Four on April 22, 1919, Lloyd George of Great Britain, an ally of Japan since 1902, asked the Chinese delegation to choose whether Japan's rights in Shantung would be inherited from Germany or granted by China through treaties. The Chinese reply was negative to both alternatives. President Wilson, eager to gain support from the major powers for the establishment of the League of Nations, decided to accommodate their wishes, and even spoke about the sacredness of treaties in spite of injustice. Great Britain and France reasserted their obligation to fulfill their secret assurances.[95] Threatened by Japan's withdrawal from the Peace Conference as the Italian delegation had done, the Council of Three finally edorsed Japan's position on April 30, 1919.[96]

The final disposition of the Shantung question as later stipulated in Articles 156-158 of the Treaty of Versailles [97] made no mention of the eventual restoration of Kiaochow and other German rights in Shantung to China. The Chinese delegation protested the decision of the Council of Three on May 4, and filed a reservation at the plenary session of the Conference on May 6. As a further concession, it notified the President of the Peace Conference on May 26 that China would sign the Treaty of Versailles subject to the reservation made on May 6. Unexpectedly, the Conference not only deemed this inadmissible, but also objected to other proposed forms of reservation either in an annex or even in a separate communication to its President.

Despite these setbacks, the Chinese delegation was still prepared to sign the Treaty if it was permitted to issue a written declaration prior to the signing that the Shantung question would not thereby be precluded from future reconsideration. [98] When this last proposal was ruled out, [99] the Chinese delegation issued a statement on June 28, 1919 that "the Peace Conference having denied China justice in the settlement of the Shantung question and having today in effect prevented them from signing the treaty without sacrificing their sense of right, justice and patriotic duty, the Chinese delegation submit their case to the impartial judgment of the world." [100] Thus Japan acquired former German rights in Shantung by the Treaty of Versailles, to which China was not a signatory. [101]

The failure of the Paris Peace Conference to restore the Shantung rights to China further revealed the limitations of diplomacy, extent of power politics and lack of justice in international relations. The Chinese people were not only indignant at Japan's imperialism but also in opposition to pro-Japanese leaders in the Peking government. [102] The Paris Peace Conference was a warning to Chinese intellectuals that they should undertake the task of national salvation by themselves and give up any remaining hope of Western support. The May Fourth Movement described below testified to the spontaneous reaction of the Chinese students to diplomatic frustrations encountered at the Paris Peace Conference.

V. THE MAY FOURTH MOVEMENT

1. The Nature of the Movement

In China, student protests against government misconduct has a long tradition. [103] The demonstration in Peking on May 4, 1919 manifested the deep concern of Chinese intellectuals with the continuing impotence of their own government in its dealings with Japan. The shocking decision of the Council of Three of the Paris Peace Conference to reject China's claim on the Shantung rights further incensed their anger at Japanese imperialism, which culminated in the Twenty-one Demands of 1915. While those who directly participated in the demonstration were students from Peking University and other institutions, Chinese scholars returning from Japan, Europe, and the United States exercised considerable influence on the movement through their teaching, publications, and other activities in many new orgainzations. [104]

Due to government mishandling of the situation and the resultant arrest of many students, an unfortunate incident occurred on May 4. Throughout the movement, students continuously received encouragement and support from their enlightened administration and faculty,[105] as well as from the awakened merchants and workers in different parts of the country. The following description will be limited to the origin of the incident and its expansion into a national movement.

2. The Incident of May 4, 1919

The immediate cause of the May 4th demonstration was a mass expression of student patriotism in the face of diplomatic setbacks endured under an untrustworthy government. For the commemoration of the fourth anniversary of the day Japan delivered the ultimatum on the Twenty-one Demands, [106] the students in Peking originally resolved to hold a mass meeting on May 7. Then the alarming news reached Peking that the Council of Three in Paris had already adopted a resolution to recognize Japan's succession to former German rights in Shantung as a consequence of her secret agreements with major European powers. [107] In view of the impending decision by the Paris Peace Conference, the students changed the date of the mass meeting to May 4, in protest against the unjust disposal of the Shantung question and the treacherous officials in the government responsible for China's 1918 commitments to Japan.

At the mass meeting in the early afternoon of May 4, approximately three thousand students representing thirteen colleges and universities in Peking gathered at Tien-an Gate. They issued a manifesto, urging people from all professions throughout the country to strive for the return of the Shantung rights and to punish three pro-Japanese officials, namely Ts'ao Ju-lin, Lu Tsung-yü, and Chang Tsung-hsiang. [108] When the procession was refused passage through the Legation Quarter, they appointed representatives to deliver memorandums to the diplomatic missions of the United States, Great Britain, France, and Italy. These four powers constituted the Council of Four, which was later reduced to the Council of Three after the departure of the Italian delegation from Paris, which nonetheless played a dominant role in the decision-making of the Peace Conference. [109] The parade was orderly until it reached Ts'ao's private residence, heavily guarded by police and gendarmes. A small number of students managed to force their way into the house, where they found Chang Tsung-hsiang, one of the condemned traitors. [110] Immediately losing control of their temper, the students beat Chang to the ground and set the house on fire. Several students and policemen were wounded during the fight. Finally the local authorities regained command of the situation and arrested thirty-two students. [111]

3. Development from Incident to Movement

The patriotism of the students received immediate sympathy and support from people in other cities, and what began as a local incident in Peking soon developed into a nationwide movement. Public opinion was entirely on the side of students: the administration and faculty of the colleges and universities protested against the oppressive action of the government; the chamber of commerce in Peking resolved to boycott Japanese goods; Sun Yat-sen led his government colleagues and Parliamentary members in Canton in condemning the traitors. [112] Although the arrested-students were set free on May 7, the movement against Japanese imperialism and traitorous officials continued. A national student union was established in Shanghai, and their patriotic activities spread throughout the country and abroad. [113] Among the demands submitted to President Hsü Shih-ch'ang of the Peking government, the student union urged the government not to sign the Treaty of Versailles and to punish the three pro-Japanese officials. [114] Motivated by their common cause of patriotism and nationalism, students, educators, workers, merchants, industrialists, and leaders of other professions joined together to form a united front.

The Japanese reaction in the latter part of May was a series of protests to the Peking government and a show of force by Japanese troops and warships stationed in several treaty ports of China. Completely disregarding public opinion, the Peking government under the control of the pro-Japanese Anfu clique issued mandates to commend the three condemned officials and resorted to mass arrests of students at the beginning of June. [115] In protest, the workers and merchants of Shanghai decided on the June 5th strikes and intensified the boycott campaign. Similar actions were taken in other locations and the whole nation was in an uproar. Compelled by circumstances, the government finally released the arrested students, accepted the resignation of the Premier, dismissed the three pro-Japanese officials,[116] and instructed the Chinese delegation in Paris not to sign the Treaty of Versailles. [117]

In retrospect, the students not only won a victory on this direct issue, but also stimulated the interest of intellectuals, businessmen, and workers in the domestic and foreign affairs of the country.[118] The eventual settlement of the Shantung question at Washington in 1922 was partly due to the rising patriotism and nationalism manifested by the Chinese people in 1919.[119] Furthermore, the May 4th incident brought about a new cultural movement, [120] which created a great impact on the political development of China. It is also important to note that many activists of that period have become party and government leaders in the ensuing decades.

NOTES TO CHAPTER 6

1. See Tsou-min Chu, "A Study of the Chinese Governmental Organ Directing Foreign Affairs," Review of Foreign Affairs (in Chinese), Vol. 4 (1935), No. 5, pp. 73-75. Further information on the subject can be found in two articles by Tsun-fai Chang: "The Governmental Organ and Its Process of Directing Foreign Affairs during the Ch'ing Dynasty before the Opium War," Foreign Affairs (in Chinese), Vol. 2 (1933), No. 2, pp. 1-7; "The Governmental Organ and Its Process of Directing Foreign Affairs during the Ch'ing Dynasty since the Opium War to the War between China and the Allied Powers of Great Britain and France," ibid., Vol. 2 (1933), No. 5, pp. 43-51.

2. See Ch'ou Pan Yi Wu Shih Mo (a collection of official documents relating to China's foreign relations, 1836-1874, in Chinese, 130 vols; published by the Palace Museum, Peiping, in 1929-1931), Vol. 71; Tsun-fai Chang, "The Factors Prompting the Organization of the Tsung-li Ko-kuo Shih-wu Yamen," Foreign Affairs (in Chinese), Vol. 3 (1933), No. 1, pp. 1-11; Masataka Banno, China and the West 1858-1861: The Origins of the Tsungli Yamen (Cambridge, 1964), pp. 93-126; Mary C. Wright, The Last Stand of Chinese Conservatism: The T'ung-chih Restoration, 1862-1874, pp. 224-228. Further information can found in S. M. Meng, The Tsungli Yamen: Its Organization and Functions (Cambridge, 1962).

3. See Ernest Satow, A Guide to Diplomatic Practice (London, 1957, 4th ed.), pp. 21-23.

4. These two High Commissioners governed the coastal provinces in the South and the North of China. The Tsungli Yamen underwent reorganization in 1864, but its administration still proved unsatisfactory. See Yu-chuan Chang, "The Organization of the Waichiaopu," Chinese Social and Political Science Review, Vol. 1 (1916), No. 1, p. 32.

5. This demand was embodied in Art. XII of the Protocol of 1901 (Chinese Customs, Treaties, II, pp. 303-341; MacMurray, Treaties, I, pp. 278-308):

> "An Imperial Edict of the 24th of July, 1901 (Annex No. 18), reformed the Office of foreign affairs (Tsungli Yamen), on the lines indicated by the Powers, that is to say, transformed it into a Ministry of foreign affairs (Wai-wu Pu), which takes precedence over the six other Ministries of State. The same edict appointed the principal members of this Ministry."

6. In this edict, the Imperial Court recognized the primary importance of international affairs and admitted the deficiency of the Tsungli Yamen. For its text, see MacMurray, Treaties, I, pp. 306-307. For Wai-wu Pu, see Weiching W. Yen, "How China Administers Her Foreign Affairs," American Journal of International Law, Vol. 3 (1909), No. 3, pp. 537-546.

7. See Correspondence Respecting Affairs in China, 1859-1860 (British Parliamentary Papers), pp. 255, 273; 'Secret Letter' of the Tsungli Yamen, October 12, 1867, Ch'ou Pan Yi Wu Shih Mo, T'ung Chih section, L. 32a.

8. See Knight Biggerstaff, "The Establishment of Permanent Chinese Diplomatic Missions Abroad," Chinese Social and Political Science Review, Vol. 20 (1936-1937), No. 1, p. 4

9. Also included in Pin Ch'un's suite were his son and three students of the T'ung Wen Kuan, a school established in Peking in 1862 by the Tsungli Yamen to teach foreign languages and Western sciences. For details, see Ch'ou Pan Yi Wu Shih Mo, XXXIX, 1a-2b; XLVI, 17b-18a; L, 28. It is interesting to note that, in November 1863, Anson Burlingame and W. A. P. Martin introduced to the Tsungli Yamen H. Wheaton's Elements of International Law, a standard work on modern rules governing relations among states. See Immanuel C. Y. Hsü, China's Entrance into the Family of Nations: The Diplomatic Phase 1858-1880, pp. 121-145; Ssu-yu Tneg, John K. Fairbank, Chaoying Fang, and others, China's Response to the West: A Documentary Survey 1839-1923. pp. 97-99

10. See Ch'ou Pan Yi Wu Shih Mo, L, 32a-32b; LI, 21a-21b; LII, 19b-20a, 26a-27a, 32b-33b; LIII, 4b-5a; LIV, 3a-3b, 8a-8b, 13a, 17b-18b; LV, 2b-3a, 12a-13a, 27a-27b, 34a, 39a-39b; LVI, 11a-11b.

11. See ibid., LI, 26b-28b; LII, 2a-2b.

12. The Burlingame mission departed from China early in 1868 and returned to Peking in November 1870. In Washington, Burlingame negotiated with Secretary Seward the Additional Articles to the Treaty of Commerce between the United States and China of June 18, 1858. These Articles were signed in Washington on July 28, 1868, also known as the Burlingame Treaty (Chinese Customs, Treaties, I, pp. 729-735; Hertslet, Treaties, I, pp. 554-557). Burlingame died in St. Petersburg during the mission's visit to Russia. For details of the mission's activities, see Morse, II, pp. 193-200. Frederick Wells Williams, Anson Burlingame and the First Chinese Mission (New York, 1912).

13. In June 1870, there was a riot in Tientsin, resulting in the loss of several French lives and the insult of the French Flag. See Morse, II, pp. 239-261. For details of the mission, see Knight Biggerstaff, "The Ch'ung Hou Mission to France, 1870-1871," Nankai Social and Economic Quarterly, Vol. 8 (1935-1936), No. 4, pp. 633-647. For the settlement of the Margary Affair, Kuo and Hsü Ch'ien-shên presented the letter of appology to Queen Victoria on February 7, 1877. For a full account of the Margary Affair, see supra, pp. 28-29.

14. See supra, pp. 5-6, 21, 23, 25, 27, 53.

15. See Henri Cordier, Histoire des Rélations de la Chine avec les Puissances Occidentales, pp. 403 sq.

16. See U. S. For. Rel., 1875, I, p. 381; Shou-p'êng Chu, Kuang Hsü Tung Hua Hsü Lu (a chronological history of the Kuang Hsü Period, 1875-1909, compiled from the official records of the State Historiographer's Office or Kuo-shih Kuan and from other sources, in Chinese, 220 chüan or volumes; Shanghai, T'u-shi-chi-ch'êng Co., 1909), III, 15a-15b; IV, 7a-7b; Ch'ou Pan Yi Wu Shih Mo., II, 17b-18a; IV, 17b-19a. The sending of permanent envoys was also prompted by the Formosa incident, which involved the murder of several ship-wrecked Japanese and Liuchiuan sailors in December 1871, by the aboriginal tribes in the mountainous region of Formosa. War between China and Japan was imminent; but, through British good offices, the incident was finally settled, requiring the Chinese government to pay an indemnity of half a million taels to Japan.

17. This first Chinese legation had a staff of two secretaries, two interpreters, and eleven attachés. For details, see Tê-i Chang, Sui Shih Jih Chi, in Hsi-ch'i Wang, Hsiao Fang Hu Chai Yü Ti Ts'ung Ch'ao, Bk. XI, 210a.

18. On January 15, 1877, Chang Szu-kuei was appointed assistant envoy, while Ho was chief envoy. See Shou-p'êng Chu, op. cit., XIII, 13a, 21a. Originally as assistant envoy to England, Liu was promoted to be Chinese envoy to Germany on April 30, 1877. He presented his credentials to the Kaiser in November of that year. See ibid., XV, 6b, 11b.

19. See Tê-i Chang, op. cit., 273b, 276a, 277a, 277b.

20. See Ch'ou Pan Yi Wu Shih Mo. XIII, 28b; Tê-i Chang, Shih Ê Jih Chi, in Hsi-ch'i Wang, op. cit., Bk. III, 303-304. Ch'ung Hou was a Junior Guardian of the Heir Apparent, a Minister of Tsungli Yamen, a Senior Vice-President of the Board of Civil Office, and then acted as Tartar-General in Shênching, the

capital of Manchuria. He was also a special envoy on a temporary mission to France in 1871.

21. See Ch'ou Pan Yi Wu Shih Mo., IV, 19a, XV, 36b-37a; XXI, 1a-2a. Ch'en and Yung had travelled through the United States, Peru, and Cuba before, and were well acquainted with conditions in these countries. See also Ch'en Lan-pin, Shih Mei Chi Lüeh, in Hsi-ch'i Wang, op. cit., Bk. XII, 57a, 67a, 75b, 76a-76b. For the establishment of Chinese legations abroad, see also Immanuel C. Y. Hsü, op. cit., pp. 149-210.

22. Art. II of the Sino-British Treaty of 1842 (Chinese Customs, Treaties, I, pp. 351-356; Hertslet, Treaties, I, pp. 7-12) reads, in part, as follows:
"And Her Majesty the Queen of Great Britain, &c., will appoint Superintendents, or Consular Officers, to reside at each of the above named cities or towns [Canton, Amoy, Foochowfoo, Ningpo, and Shanghai], to be the medium of communication between the Chinese authorities and the said merchants, and to see that the just duties and other dues of the Chinese government, as hereafter provided for, are duly discharged by Her Britanic Majesty's subjects."

23. See Art. XXIII of the Sino-American Treaty of July 3, 1844 (Chinese Customs, Treaties, I, pp. 677-690); Art. XXIII of the Sino-Franco Treaty of October 24, 1844 (Chinese Customs, Treaties, I, pp. 771-790; Hertslet, Treaties, I, pp. 258-269).

24. See, for instance Art. V of the Sino-Russian Treaty of July 25, 1851 (Chinese Customs, Treaties, I, pp. 70-80; Hertslet, Treaties, I, pp. 449-454); Art. VII of the Sino-British Treaty of June 26, 1858 (Chinese Customs, Treaties, I, pp. 404-421; Hertslet, Treaties, I, pp. 18-35); Art. X of the Sino-American Treaty of June 18, 1858 (Chinese Customs, Treaties, I, pp. 713-728; Hertslet, Treaties, I, pp. 540-552); Art. IV of the Sino-German Treaty of September 2, 1861 (Chinese Customs, Treaties, II, pp. 115-138; Hertslet, Treaties, I, pp. 331-342); Art VII of the Sino-Danish Treaty of July 13, 1863 (Chinese Customs, Treaties, II, pp. 313-330; Hertslet, Treaties, I, pp. 249-258); Art. I of the Sino-Dutch Treaty of October 10, 1863 (Chinese Customs, Treaties, II, pp. 339-351; Hertslet, Treaties, I, pp. 407-415); Art. IV of the Sino-Spanish Treaty of October 10, 1864 (Chinese Customs, Treaties, II, pp. 359-377; Hertslet, Treaties, I, pp. 512-522); Art. IV of the Sino-Peruvian Treaty of June 26, 1874 (Chinese Customs, Treaties, II, pp. 798-807; Hertslet, Treaties, I, pp. 415-420); Art. IX of the Sino-Portuguese Treaty of December 1, 1887 (Chinese Customs, Treaties, II, pp. 274-294; Hertslet, Treaties, I, pp. 423-433); Art. III of the Sino-Japanese

Treaty of July 21, 1896 (Chinese Customs, Treaties, II, pp. 604-614, 720-731; Hertstlet, Treaties, I, pp. 373-382; MacMurray, Treaties, I, pp. 68-74); Art. XIII of the Sino-British Agreement of Peking, February 4, 1897 (Chinese Customs, Treaties, I, pp. 532-538; Hertslet, Treaties, I, pp. 113-119; MacMurray, Treaties, I, pp. 94-98); Art. III of the Sino-Mexican Treaty of December 14, 1899 (Chinese Customs, Treaties, II, pp. 833-843; Hertslet, Treaties, I, pp. 399-407; MacMurray, Treaties, I, pp. 214-220); Art. II of the Sino-American Treaty of October 8, 1903 (Chinese Customs, Treaties, I, pp. 745-763; Hertslet Treaties, I, pp. 566-578; MacMurray Treaties, I, pp. 423-450); Art. III of the Sino-Swedish Treaty of July 2, 1908 (Chinese Customs, Treaties, II, pp. 97-112; MacMurray, Treaties, I, pp. 740-747).

25. For the text of the Additional Articles of 1868, see Chinese Customs, Treaties, I, pp. 729-735; Hertslet, Treaties, I, pp. 554-557.

26. See I Hou, Ch'u Shih T'ai Hsi Chi (chih Kang's diary), in Hsi-Chi'i Wang, op. cit., Bk. Xi, 110b.

27. See, for instance, Art. II of the Sino-British Supplementary Convention to the Treaty of Tientsin, October 23, 1869 (Chinese Customs, Treaties, I, pp. 478-490; Hertslet, Treaties, I, pp. 61-72); the Sino-Japanese Treaty of September 13, 1871 (Chinese Customs, Treaties, II, pp. 507-514, 572-575, 642-648).

28. The following excerpt was from the statement made by Wên Hsiang in reply to Seward's suggestion of sending Chinese consuls abroad:

> "That the Emperor had this in view, and the only difficulty in the way had been the want of men properly qualified to perform consular and diplomatic duties; but they were taking measures to educate youths to act as interpreters, and hoped soon to have men ready; they had sent one embassy abroad, whose chief was a foreigner, in order to prove to the Treaty Powers their friendly feelings, and represent to them the progress it was possible, in their view, to make; but they did not intend to send another, until fully qualified natives could take the charge of it."

Legation Archives, China, U.S. State Department No. 235, 144b. Here the word 'embassy', designating the Burlingame mission, was somewhat misused.

29. See Ch'ou Pan Yi Wu Shih Mo, LXXIX, 48a-48b; LXXX, 11a-11b.

30. See ibid., XCI, 27b-29b; (1875-1911), IV, 17b. Yung Wing and Ch'en Lan-pin were assigned to make this investigation.

31. In 1874, several important memorials for the establishment of consulates were submitted to the Throne by Li Hung-chang,

Wang K'ai-t'ai (Governor of Fukien province), and Li Tsung-hsi (Governor-General of the Lian Chiang provinces and Superintendent of Trade for the Southern ports. See Ch'ou Pan Yi Wu Shih Mo, XCIX, 32a-34b, 48b-50a; C, 9b-10b.

32. China also learned much of modern technology and weaponry from the West. Pertinent information can be found from, among others, the following works: Albert Feuerwerker, China's Early Industrialization: Sheng Hsuan-huai, 1844-1916 (Cambridge, 1958); Erh-min Wang, Rise of the Armaments Industry at the Close of the Ch'ing Period (Ch'ing-chi Ping Kung'yeh Ti Hsing-chi'i, in Chinese, Taipei, 1963); John L. Rawlinson, China's Struggle for Naval Development, 1839-1895 (Cambridge, 1967); Ssu-yu Teng and others, China's Response to the West, Chs. VI, XIII.

33. K'ang and Liang fled to Japan; six of the constitutional reformists were executed. Much has been written on the reform movement led by K'ang and Liang. A summary and related documents can be found in Tung-kai K'ang, K'ang Yu-wei and the 1898 Reforms (Hongkong, 1959, in Chinese), pp. 37-132. For the reactionary policy of the Manchu Court and the occurrence of the Boxer Uprising, see supra, pp. 51-52; Meribeth E. Cameron, The Reform Movement in China 1898-1912 (Stanford, 1931), pp. 23-55.

34. The five commissioners were all high-ranking officials: Tai Tse, Tuan Fang, Tai Hung-tse, Hsü Shih-ch'ang, and Shao Ying. Immediately before their departure from Peking, Tai Tse and Shao Ying were wounded by a bomb thrown by a revolutionist. They were replaced by Shang Chi-hun and Li Seng-to.

35. K'ang and Liang were then in exile overseas, but they still abhorred revolution and continuously advocated consitutional monarchy.

36. For the text, see William L. Tung, The Government of China (Shanghai, 1942, 2 vols., in Chinese), I, pp. 18-19.

37. For the English text of the Principles of Constitution (Hsien-fa Ta-kang) of September 22, 1908 and the Nineteen Articles (Shih-chiu Hsin-t'iao) of November 3, 1911, see William L. Tung, The Political Institutions of Modern China, pp. 318-321. Other documents relating to the establishment of Parliament, Provincial Assembly, and local self-government during that period can be found in his The Government of China, I, pp. 19-103. See also Meribeth E. Cameron, op. cit., pp. 100-135.

38. See supra, p. 47.

39. See Leang-li T'ang, The Inner History of the Chinese Revolution (London, 1930), pp. 4-9.

40. See Franz Michael and Chung-li Chang, The Taiping Rebellion: History and Documents (Seattle, 1966, 3 vols), I, p. 59.

41. J. M. Callery and Melchoir Yvan, History of the Insurrection in China (New York, 1853), p. 233, quoted from an official circular of the Taipings. For the contacts made by foreign official missions and private individuals with the Taiping regime in Nanking, see Franz Michael and Chung-li Chang, op. cit., I, pp. 105-106.

42. See J. C. Cheng, Chinese Sources for the Taiping Rebellion 1850-1864 (New York, 1963), pp. 99, 104, 108-109, 111, 129-137. For a history of the Chinese campaign under Lt. Col. Charles George Gordon for the suppression of the Taiping Rebellion, see Andrew Wilson, The "Ever Victorious Army" (Edinburgh, 1868). Gordon succeeded Frederick Townsend Ward and Henry Andrea Burgevine to command this army.

43. See Ssǔ-yü Têng, New Light on the History of the Taiping Rebellion (Cambridge, 1950), p. 70. The final phase of the Manchu victory was largely due to the leadership of Ts'êng Kuo-fan and his associates in the training of a new formidable army. One of the treatises on the subject is W.J. Hail, Tseng Kuo-fan and the Taiping Rebellion (New Haven, 1927). A chronological table of the major events of the Taiping Rebellion can be found in Flavia Anderson, The Rebel Emperor (Garden City, N.Y., 1959).

44. When the first Sino-Japanese War broke out in 1894, Sun prepared a letter to Li Hung-chang, then Pei-yang Minister, recommending a four-point plan: (1) the full contribution of individual abilities, (2) the full exploitation of the land, (3) the full utilization of resources, and (4) the facilitation of the distribution of goods. For the text of the letter, see The Collected Works of Sun Yat-sen (Shanghai: San-ming Book Co., 1937), IV, 'Correspondence and Telegrams', pp. 1-17. In 1895, he founded his first revolutionary society, Hsing-chung Hui (Society for the Regeneration of China). His revolutionary programs took shape at the time of the establishment of the second revolutionary society, T'ung-meng Hui (The Alliance), which expounded four major objectives: (1) the overthrow of the Manchus, (2) the rule of the country by all the people of China, (3) the establishment of a republican form of government, and (4) the equalization of land ownership. See William L. Tung, The Constitutional and Political System of Prewar China (Taipei, 1968, in Chinese), pp. 2-3, 75-76.

45. For an analysis of Sun Yat-sen's writings, including his revolutionary programs, see William L. Tung, The Political Institutions of Modern China, pp. 95-105. Sun's major work, The Three People's Principles (San Min Chu I) was translated into English by Frank W. Price under the title, San Min Chu I: The Three Principles of the People (Shanghai, 1927).

46. The Republican Manifesto was substantially identical to the Manifesto of the T'ung-meng Hui, which listed the following principles toward foreign powers:

"1. All past treaties entered into by the Manchu Government with other countries will remain in force.

"2. All indemnities and foreign loans will be acknowledged without any alteration of terms and will be paid in full by the customs in various provinces.

"3. All privileges now enjoyed by foreigners will be respected.

"4. Foreign property in cities under the jurisdiction of the military government will be protected.

"5. All treaties entered into, all concessions granted and all loans incurred by the Manchu Government after the promulgation of this Manifesto will not be acknowledged.

"6. All foreigners rendering assistance to the Manchu Government to the detriment of the interests of the National Military Government will be regarded as enemies.

"7. All materials supplied by foreigners to the Manchu Government which may be used for war will be confiscated."

Complete Works of Sun Yat-sen (in Chinese, edited by Chi-lu Huang), I, pp. 16-17; English translation from Sheng Hu, Imperialism and Chinese Politics (Peking, 1955), p. 179.

47. For the text of the 1912 Constitution, see William L. Tung, The Political Institutions of Modern China, pp. 322-325.

48. For details, see ibid., pp. 47-51.

49. The Collected Works of Sun Yat-sen (San-ming ed., 1937), IV, "A History of the Chinese Revolution," p. 13. For the loan from the Five-Power Consortium, see supra, p. 124.

50. For the text, see William L. Tung, The Political Institutions of Modern China, pp. 326-331.

51. See supra, pp. 45-46.

52. The English versions of these Demands as subsequently published by the Japanese and Chinese governments are given in

parallel columns in MacMurray, Treaties, II, pp. 1231-1234.

53. Yüan once observed to the American Minister at Peking that "Japan is going to take advantage of this war to get control of China." Paul S. Reinsch, American Diplomat in China (New York, 1922), p. 129.

54. MacMurray, Treaties, II, p. 1235.

55. For the full text of the Ultimatum and the Explanatory Note, see ibid., II, pp. 1234-1235.

56. According to the revised Presidential Election Law of December 28, 1914, Yüan could even found a system of hereditary Presidency. Soon afterward, Yüan's ambition went beyond the Presidency. For details, see William L. Tung, The Constitutional and Political Systems of Prewar China. pp. 39-46.

57. For the text of the Chinese Reply to the Japanese Ultimatum on May 8, 1915, see MacMurray, Treaties, II, p. 1236.

58. The text of the Treaties and Exchange of Notes can be found in ibid., II, pp. 1216-1230.

59. This line was a part of the railway to be built by China herself from Chefoo to Lungkow to connect with the Kiaochow-Tsinanfu Railway.

60. The first three were stipulated in the Treaty, and the last was embodied in an Exchange of Notes.

61. For the text of the Exchange of Notes respecting the Restoration of the Leased Territory of Kiaochow Bay, see MacMurray, Treaties, II, pp. 1218-1219. For Japan's military occupation of Kiaochow, reference may be made to Jefferson Jones, The Fall of Tsingtau (Boston, 1915).

62. By a separate note, the Chinese government complied with the Japanese demand that police and revenue laws involving Japanese subjects in South Manchuria and Eastern Inner Mongolia could be enforced only after consultation with Japanese concular officers. See MacMurray, Treaties, II, p. 1227. Japan's intention to extend her territorial acquisitions in South Manchuria was revealed as early as 1913 by Count Kato Takaaki, Foreign Minister of the Okuma cabinet. See Tatsuji Takeuchi, War and Diplomacy in the Japanese Empire (Chicago, 1935), pp. 183-185.

63. For the revised Agreement for Kirin-Changchun Railway Loan between China and Japan (South Manchuria Railway Company), October 12, 1917, see MacMurray, Treaties, II, pp. 1390-1394.

64. For the list of coal and iron mines selected by the Japanese in South Manchuria, see ibid., II, p. 1224.

65. For the text of the Exchange of Notes, see ibid., II, pp. 1229-1230.

66. See ibid., II, p. 1230. Japan's concern with foreign involvement arose out of a rumor that the Bethlehem Steel Company, an American corporation, signed a contract with the Chinese government on March 9, 1914, for the construction of a naval base in Fukien. Facts proved that there was no such contract.

67. Arts. 1-5 of Group V. The English versions as published by the two governments are slightly different. For comparison, see MacMurray, Treaties, II, p. 1233.

68. The Chinese Reply to the Japanese Ultimatum, May 8, 1915. Ibid., II, p. 1236.

69. Loc. cit.

70. U. S. For. Rel., 1915, p. 146.

71. This moral support by the American government was considerably weakened after the conclusion of the Lansing-Ishii Agreement on November 2, 1917. See supra, p. 51; Ch. 3, note 67. Actually, the United States government long realized the special position enjoyed by Japan in relation to her neighboring areas because of geographical contiguity. For Secretary William J. Bryan's observation on this subject, see Thomas E. LaFargue, China and the World War (Stanford, 1937), pp. 64-65.

72. See Charles F. Remer and W. B. Palmer, A Study of Chinese Boycotts, with Special Reference to Their Economic Effectiveness (London, 1933), pp. 46-54.

73. See Marius B. Jansen, The Japanese and Sun Yat-sen (Cambridge, 1954), pp. 175-212.

74. See Min-ch'ien T. Z. Tyau, China Awakened (New York, 1922), pp. 119, 141.

75. See Scott Nearing Whither China? An Economic Interpretation of Recent Events in the Far East (New York, 1927), p. 48.

76. For the Presidential Proclamation, see Government Gazette (Peking, in Chinese), August 14, 1917.

77. For the text of the Chinese communication and the identical note by the Legations at Peking, see MacMurray, Treaties, II, p. 1363.

78. The Chinese people were particularly interested in the first and last Points as reproduced below:

"I. Open covenants of peace, openly arrived at, after which there shall be no private international understandings of any kind but diplomacy shall proceed always frankly and in the public view."

"XIV. A general association of nations must be formed under specific covenants for the purpose of affording mutual guarantees of political independence and territorial integrity to great and small states alike."

For the text of the Fourteen Points, see Cong. Record, 65th Cong., 2nd Sess., pp. 680-681.

79. For details, see 'Questions for Readjustment' submitted by China to the Paris Peace Conference of 1919, in Chinese Social and Political Science Review, Vol. 5a (1919-1920), pp. 115-170.

80. U. S. For. Rel., Paris Peace Conference (13 vols.), Vol. 5, p. 621.

81. For the text of the Japanese Imperial Rescript Making a Declaration of War against Germany on August 23, 1914, see MacMurray, Treaties, II, p. 1153. Translation from the London Times (weekly edition) of August 28, 1914, from the official Japanese text.

82. For the Notes of Protest from the Chinese Ministry of Foreign Affairs, see MacMurray, Treaties, II, pp. 1154-1157.

83. It should be noted that Great Britain also participated in the military operations against German forces in Kiaochow, but Japan alone made territorial and economic claims in Shantung.

84. See supra, pp. 155-156.

85. The notes were exchanged between Baron Goto, the Japanese Foreign Minister, and the Chinese Minister at Tokyo on September 24, 1918, concerning the stationing of Japanese troops in Tsingtao and the organization of a Chinese police force with Japanese advisers to guard the Shantung (Kiaochow-Tsinan) Railway. For the text, see MacMurray, Treaties, II,

pp. 1445-1446; translation from the Japanese official text as printed in the Tokyo Chugai Shogyo, April 10, 1919. For an exchange of notes regarding extensions of the Shantung Railway of the same date and the subsequent agreement of September 28, 1918, see MacMurray, Treaties, II, p. 1452. After an unsuccessful attempt to prevent China from joining World War I, Japan granted a so-called 'War Participation' loan to China on September 28, 1918. For details, see supra, p. 125; Ch. 5, note 105. Japan also tried to persuade China to settle their issues bilaterally by giving vague promises, including the abolition of extraterritoriality. See U. S. For. Rel., Paris Peace Conference, Vol. 1, pp. 242; Vol. 2, p. 519; Vol. 11, pp. 149-150.

86. See the Preliminary Agreement for a Loan for the Tsinanfu-Shuntefu and Kaomi-Hsuchow Extensions of the Shantung Railway between China and Japan (Industrial Bank of Japan, representing a syndicate consisting of the Industrial Bank of Japan, the Bank of Chosen, and the Bank of Taiwan), September 28, 1918. For the text, see MacMurray, Treaties, II, pp. 1450-1452.

87. The Chinese delegation was headed by Lou Tseng-tsiang, Minister of Foreign Affairs, and four other members: Chengting Thomas Wang, V. K. Wellington Koo, Sao-ke Alfred Sze, and Suntchou Wei. Wang, representing the revolutionary government in Canton, was invited to join the delegation by the Peking government as an evidence of national unity. The major powers, while allotting five delegates for each of them, restricted the Chinese delegation to two. Thus only two out of a panel of five could attend any session of the Conference. Koo was practically the spokesman of the Chinese delegation on the Shantung question. Others attended the meetings at different times.

88. With regard to the meeting of January 27, 1919, the Chinese delegation was notified only a few hours before the discussion of the Shantung question. For details, see V. K. Wellington Koo, "Recollections of the Paris Peace Conference," Biographical Literature (Taipei, in Chinese), Vol. 7, No. 6 (December 1965), pp. 6-9.

89. Art. V of the Convention (MacMurray, Treaties, I, pp. 128-130). See also supra, p. 48.

90. For details, see Wunsz King, China at the Paris Peace Conference (New York, 1961), pp. 6-14. For Baron Mikino's statement on Japan's war efforts to dislodge German forces from Shantung and the validity of the 1915 and 1918 treaties,

see U.S. For. Rel., Paris Peace Conference, Vol. 5, p. 125. See also Russel H. Fifield, "Japanese Policy toward the Shantung Question at the Paris Peace Conference," Journal of Modern History, Vol. 23 (1951), pp. 265-272.

91. For details, see U. S. For. Rel., 1918, pp. 495, 516-517; 1919, I, p. 282; Robert Lansing, The Peace Negotiations – A Personal Narrative (Boston, 1921), p. 253.

92. Japan attempted to induce the Peking government to repudiate the position of the Chinese delegation at Paris. See H. W. V. Temperley, A History of the Peace Conference of Paris (London, 1924, 6 vols.), VI, pp. 378-379.

93. For the text of these understandings, see MacMurray, Treaties, II, pp. 1167-1169. For a summary, see Willoughby, I, pp. 269-271. According to his statement made in reply to Senator Borah's question on August 19, 1919, President Wilson knew of these secret understandings only after his arrival at Paris. See Hearings...on the Treaty of Peace with Germany, etc., Senate Doc. No. 106, 66th Cong., 1st Sess. (Washington: Government Printing Office, 1919).

94. See U. S. For. Rel., Paris Peace Conference, Vol. 5, p. 140.

95. See ibid., Vol. 5, pp. 142, 145-147.

96. In acquiring former German rights in Shantung, Japan promised their eventual return to China with the exception of railway, mining, and other economic concessions. Lansing, White, and Bliss of the American delegation addressed President Wilson, expressing their disagreement with his final decision. They pointed out that "it cannot be right to do wrong even to make peace." With respect to Japan's position, they commented in the same letter: "If it be right for a policeman, who recovers your purse, to keep the contents and claim that he has fulfilled his duty in returning the empty purse, then Japan's conduct may be tolerated." Robert Lansing, op. cit., pp. 257-261. According to Secretary Lansing's testimony at the Committee on Foreign Relations of the Senate on August 6, 1919, Japan would not withdraw from the Paris Peace Conference even if the Shantung decision were against her wishes. See, however, Russel H. Fifield, Woodrow Wilson and the Far East: the Diplomacy of the Shantung Question (New York, 1952) p. 243. For the influence of the major powers on the Paris Peace Conference, much information can be found in Robert Lansing, The Big Four and Others of the Peace Conference (Boston, 1921).

97. The Shantung question was stipulated under Section VIII of
     the Treaty of Versailles as follows:

> "Article 156. – Germany renounces, in favor of
> Japan, all her rights, title and privileges –particu-
> larly those concerning the territory of Kiaochow,
> railways, mines and submarine calbes – which she
> acquired in virtue of the Treaty concluded by her
> with China on March 6, 1898, and of all other ar-
> rangements relative to the Province of Shantung.

> "All German rights in the Tsingtao-Tsinanfu Rail-
> way, including its branch lines, together with its
> subsidiary property of all kinds, stations, shops,
> fixed and rolling stock, mines, plant and material
> for the exploitation of the mines, are and remain
> acquired by Japan, together with all rights and
> privileges attaching thereto.

> "The German State submarine cables from Tsingtao
> to Shanghai and from Tsingtao to Chefoo, with all
> the rights, privileges and properties attaching there-
> to, are similarly acquired by Japan, free and clear
> of all charges and encumbrances.

> "Article 157. – The movable and immovable prop-
> erty owned by the German State in the territory of
> Kiaochow, as well as all the rights which Germany
> might claim in consequence of the works or im-
> provements made or of the expenses incurred by
> her, directly or indirectly, in connection with this
> territory, are and remain acquired by Japan, free
> and clear of all charges and encumbrances.

> "Article 158. – Germany shall hand over to Japan
> within three months from the coming into force of
> the present Treaty the archives, registers, plans,
> title-deeds and documents of every kind, wherever
> they may be, relating to the administration, whether
> civil, military, financial, judicial or other, of the
> territory of Kiaochow.

> "Within the same period Germany shall give partic-
> ulars to Japan of all treaties, arrangements or
> agreements relating to the rights, title or privileges
> referred to in the two preceding Articles."

German rights and interests in China other than Shantung
were embodied in Arts. 118, 129-134, 260. For the text of
these articles, see MacMurray, Treaties, II, pp. 1486-1489.

98. See ibid., II, pp. 1497-1498.

99. Clemenceau's ruling that no reservation of any kind could be admitted either in the Treaty of Versailles or in a separate declaration before its signing was conveyed to V. K. Wellington Koo by the French Foreign Minister, Stephen Pichon, on June 27, 1919. See Russell H. Fifield, Woodrow Wilson and the Far East: the Diplomacy of the Shantung Question, p. 330.

100. MacMurray, Treaties, II, p. 1498. For the text of the Chinese, Japanese, and American Statements concerning the Shantung question, see ibid., II, pp. 1494-1500, 1504. For the Japanese promise to restore the Shantung rights to China, see the statement of Viscount Uchida, Japanese Foreign Minister, on August 2, 1919, and President Wilson's statement to correct Viscount Uchida's version of the question (ibid., II, pp. 1498-1500). At his conference with members of the Committee on Foreign Relations of the Senate on August 19, 1919, President Wilson stated that the return of the Shantung rights to China "was left undecided, but we were assured at the time that it would be as soon as possible." Cong. Record, August 20, 1919. For a brief analysis of the Shantung question, see W. L. Godshall, The International Aspects of the Shantung Question (Phildelphia, 1923).

101. China terminated her war with Germany by a Presidential mandate on September 15, 1919 (MacMurray, Treaties, II, p. 1381). The two countries resumed normal relations by signing, on May 20, 1921, a Declaration, an Agreement, and Exchange of Notes (Carnegie, Treaties, pp. 47-53). China signed the Treaty of St. Germain with Austria on September 10, 1919, and became a member of the League of Nations. China was also a signatory to the Treaty of Neuilly with Bulgaria and the Treaty of Trianon with Hungary.

102. At that time, the Peking government still looked to Japan for financial assistance to defray administrative expenses. See U. S. For. Rel., 1919, I, pp. 280-281.

103. The first student protest involved thirty thousand from the Imperial Academy, a government institution of the Han dynasty. Many more took place during the Sung and Ming dynasties. While details of these activities were recorded in all editions of the History of the Late Han Dynasty, History of the Sung Dynasty, and History of the Ming Dynasty, a concise description can be found in Tse-tsung Chow, The May Fourth Movement (Cambridge, 1964), p. 11; Tsun-p'eng Pao, History of the Youth Movement in China (in Chinese, Taipei, 1954), pp. 1-97.

104. Among the returned students connected with Peking University were: Ts'ai Yüan-p'ei (President), Hu Shih (Professor), and Ch'en Tu-hsiu (Dean of the School of Letters) who resigned in March 1919 as a result of government pressure. See Yüan-p'ei Ts'ai, "My Experience at Peking University," The Eastern Miscellany (in Chinese), Vol. 31, No. 1 (January 1934), p. 11. After the failure of the 'Second Revolution' against Yüan Shih-k'ai, many leaders of the Nationalist Party took refuge in Japan and other places, where they sparked nationalism among Chinese students. For the new spirit of Chinese intellectuals, see Bertrand Russell, The Conquest of Happiness (New York, 1930), Pt. II, p. 88.

105. For the sympathetic attitude of President Ts'ai of Peking University, see Tsun-p'eng Pao, op. cit., p. 26; Autobiography of Ts'ai Yüan-1'ei (in Chinese, Taipei, 1967), pp. 28-29.

106. See supra, pp. 154-155.

107. See supra, pp. 160-162. For the students' disappointment with the Paris Peace Conference, see also Wen-han Kiang, The Chinese Student Movement (New York, 1948), Ch. I.

108. During the negotiations on the Twenty-one Demands, Ts'ao served as Yüan Shih-k'ai's Vice-Minister of Foreign Affairs, and Lu was Chinese Minister at Tokyo. Chang held several important posts in Yüan's government. In 1918, both Ts'ao and Lu participated in the conclusion of the Nishihara loans. See supra, p. 125. At the time of the May 4th incident, they held the following positions: Ts'ao, Minister of Communications; Lu, Director-General of the Currency Reform Bureau and Chinese Director of the Chinese-Japanese Exchange Bank; Chang, Chinese Minister to Japan. It was Chang who used the words, 'gladly agree' in his exchange of notes with the Japanese government in 1918. See supra, Ch. 6, note 85; MacMurray, Treaties, II, p. 1445.

109. The disappointment of the Chinese people with the disposal of the Shantung question by the Council of Three was shared by the American and British residents in China. See Paul S. Reinsch, An American Diplomat in China (Garden City, N.Y., 1922), pp. 361-362.

110. It was said that Chang and Ts'ao held discussions at the time, but Ts'ao managed to escape from his house in disguise. Further information about student agitation during that brief period can be found in North China Herald, May 10, 1919; Tuan-Chih Ch'en, An Historical Evaluation of the May Fourth Movement (in Chinese, Shanghai, 1935), Ch. XIII. John Dewey

wrote from Peking, praising the behavior of the students very highly. See John and Alice C. Dewey, Letters from China and Japan (New York, 1920), pp. 246-247.

111. One of the wounded students from Peking University, Kuo Ch'in-kuang, died on May 7. For the number of the arrested students from different institutions in Peking, see Tuan-chih Ch'en, op. cit., p. 236.

112. Sun was then in Shanghai, after his resignation from the office of the Generalissimo of the Military Government in the Southwest. But he remained one of the members constituting the Directorate of that government. The tele-gram of protest to the Peking government was initiated by him. For the Chinese political alignment during that period, see William L. Tung, The Political Institutions of Modern China, pp. 72-78. In 1919, representatives of the govern-ments in Peking and Canton conducted negotiations in Shanghai for a peaceful settlement of their long-standing disputes, but broke up after the May 4th incident. See Chien-nung Li, The Political History of China 1840-1928 (translated and edited by Ssu-yu Teng and Jeremy Ingalls; Princeton, 1956), pp. 390-391.

113. In Tokyo, Chinese students held a mass meeting on May 7, in commemoration of the fourth anniversary of the day of national humiliation. Thirty-nine were arrested by the Japan-ese police; many of them were wounded; seven received sentences of imprisonment, which were, however, suspended in order to ease anti-Japanese sentiment. Chinese students in Japan advocated open rupture of diplomatic relations be-tween the two countries on account of the Shantung question. See North China Herald, May 10, 1919.

114. See Tse-tsung Chow, op. cit., pp. 140-141.

115. See John and Alice C. Dewey, op. cit., pp. 209-211.

116. For the government order of their dismissal, see The Eastern Miscellany (in Chinese), Vol. XVI, July 15, 1919, "Laws and Orders, " p. 233. After their dismissal, the strike in Shanghai was called off, but the boycott campaign against Japanese goods continued. See U.S. For. Rel., 1919, I, pp. 709-710.

117. For the original decision of the Peking government to sign the Treaty of Versailles, see Tsun-fai Chang, A Diplomatic History of the Republic of China (in Chinese; Chungking, 1943), I, pp. 277-278. See also Tseng-tsiang Lou [Dom Pierre-

célestin_], Ways of Confucious and of Christ (translated into English by Michael Derrich; London, 1948), p. 42. As Chinese Minister of Foreign Affairs, Lou headed the Chinese Delegation to the Paris Peace Conference.

118. See Chiang Kai-shek, China's Destiny (translated into English by Chung-hui Wang; New York, 1947), pp. 51-52; Mao Tse-tung, Selected Works of Mao Tse-tung (Peking, 1961), II, pp. 237-239, 371-373; Collected Works of Tseng Ch'i (in Chinese; Taipei, 1954), pp. 136-140. For a time, Japan suspected that the United States encouraged the Chinese student movement. See U. S. For. Rel., 1919, I, p. 702.

119. See infra, pp. 190-192. For student activities between 1919 and 1921, see Sheng Hu, Imperialism and Chinese Politics (Peking, 1955), pp. 247-257.

120. For details, see Tse-tsung Chow, op. cit., Chs. IX-XIII. See also Y. C. Wang, Chinese Intellectuals and the West, 1872-1949 (Chapel Hill, 1966), pp. 306-361.

Chapter 7
WESTERN RESPONSE TO CHINA'S APPEAL AT THE WASHINGTON CONFERENCE (1921-1922)

I. PURPOSE OF THE CONFERENCE AND QUESTIONS RELATING TO CHINA

1. Scope of the Present Examination

The immediate and vehement reaction of the Chinese people to the humiliations at the Paris Peace Conference could not escape the attention of Western statesmen, who gradually realized the urgency of responding to China's just cause in view of the increasing threat of Japanese expansion in the Far East. Although the Conference on the Limitation of Armament in Washington (1921-1922) was convened essentially for the discussion of naval disarmament, the participating powers found it equally important to search for a common course of action with respect to questions relating to China.

Sponsored by the United States,[1] the Conference was held from November 12, 1921 to February 6, 1922. It discussed two groups of questions: the limitation of naval armament by the First Committee,[2] and the situation in the Pacific and the Far East by the Second Committee. Participants of the First Committee were Great Britain, France, Italy, Japan, and the United States; these five powers, joined by China, Belgium, the Netherlands, and Portugal, constituted the Second Committee. With the exception of Eastern Siberia[3] and the Pacific Islands,[4] the Second Committee dealt exclusively with questions relating to China.

While decisions adopted by the Conference on the limitation of naval armament and other questions are equally significant, the present chapter will examine only those relating to China. For convenience of discussion, a general survey of China's proposals will be made first, followed by an analysis of the Nine-Power Treaty and the termination of the Anglo-Japanese alliance consequent to the conclusion of the Four-

Power Treaty. Next will be the Shantung question, which differred from other questions in being settled through the good offices of the United States and Great Britain collaterally with the Washington Conference. Then will come a review of the resolutions on customs tariff and extraterritorial jurisdiction. Other questions brought before the Conference will be treated under a special section, followed by another solely on treaty commitments relating to China. In conclusion, there will be an evaluation of the Washington Conference and its aftermath.

2. China's Presentation of Ten Points

At the first meeting of the Committee of the Whole on Pacific and Far Eastern Questions on November 16, 1921, Sao-ke Alfred Sze, on behalf of the Chinese delegation,[5] presented ten points or principles for its consideration. These points may be summarized as follows:

(1) observance of China's territorial integrity and political and administrative independence;

(2) adherence to the principle of the open door and equal opportunity for commerce and industry;

(3) avoidance of concluding any treaty directly affecting China or the general peace in the Pacific and the Far East without China's prior knowledge and opportunity to participate;

(4) requirement of open declaration of all treaty or contractual commitments between China and foreign powers, and re-examination of their scope and validity;

(5) removal of existing limitations upon China's political, jurisdictional, and administrative freedom of action at the earliest moment;

(6) consideration of definite terms of duration to be attached to those Chinese commitments originally concluded without time limits;

(7) strict interpretation of treaties in favor of the grantors;

(8) respect for China's right of neutrality in future wars;

(9) provision for pacific settlement of international disputes in the Pacific and the Far East; and

(10) periodic conferences by interested powers for the discussion of questions relating to the Pacific and the Far East as a basis for common policies. [6]

All the above-mentioned points were important to China's destiny, and constituted subjects of discussion at the Washington Conference.

3. The Root Resolution

After a preliminary exchange of views among the delegates, Elihu Root of the United States[7] was asked to incorporate the Chinese proposals into a single resolution for further consideration.[8] The four clauses, introduced by Root at the third meeting of the Second Committee on November 21, were finally adopted by the Conference at its fourth plenary session on December 10, 1921. In this resolution, the nine powers affirmed their intention:

"(1) To respect the sovereignty, the independence, and the territorial and administrative integrity of China;

"(2) To provide the fullest and most unembarrassed opportunity to China to develop and maintain for herself an effective and stable Government;

"(3) To use their influence for the purpose of effectually establishing and maintaining the principle of equal opportunity for the commerce and industry of all nations throughout the territory of China;

"(4) To refrain from taking advantage of the present conditions in order to seek special rights or privileges which would abridge the rights of the subjects or citizens of friendly States and from countenancing action inimical to the security of such States." [9]

While the first three clauses were based upon the Chinese proposals, the fourth clause evidently purported to reaffirm the established rights and special positions of the powers concerned.[10] It can be seen from this resolution that the Western attitude toward China had changed considerably, from contemptuous indifference at Paris to sympathetic response at Washington. Yet they were not ready to give up all vested rights and privileges.

II.   THE NINE-POWER TREATY AND THE TERMINATION OF THE ANGLO-JAPANESE ALLIANCE

1.   The Nine-Power Treaty of February 6, 1922

Taking into consideration the Chinese proposals and the Root Resolution, the nine powers concluded, on February 6, 1922, the Treaty regarding Principles and Policies to be Followed in Matters concerning China, generally known as the Nine-Power Treaty.[11] The four clauses of the Root Resolution, embodied in Article I, were to be observed by the signatories in their future engagements with any power or powers (Art. II). They agreed to adhere to the principle of the Open Door Policy (Art. III), and not to create spheres of influence (Art. IV) or practice discrimination of any kind (Art. V). Respect for China's right of neutrality at time of war was emphasized (Art. VI). Provision was also made for full and frank communications among the signatories involving the application of the Treaty (Art. VII).[12]

The shortcoming of the Nine-Power Treaty was the lack of a provision for effective means of sanctions. When Japan carried out full-scale war in China in July 1937, the Nine-Power Conference held in Brussels in November of that year failed to uphold the terms of the Treaty. The difficulty of forcing the signatories to comply with their committed obligations is the common weakenss of many international conventions, but the breach of treaty commitments by one state, even if unpunished, does not render the treaty invalid. On the whole, the Nine-Power Treaty incorporated several fundamental principles vitally important to China as an independent nation, especially respect for territorial and administrative integrity, as well as the right of neutrality. This was the first time that the Open Door Policy was reaffirmed in treaty form prohibiting any kind of discrimination. Above all, the traditional practice of the powers to establish spheres of influence in China was unequivocally repudiated.[13] The conclusion of this Treaty showed the good will of the powers concerned and vindicated China's cause to a large extent.

2. The Termination of the Anglo-Japanese Alliance

Indirectly related, but not without significance to China, was the Four-Power Treaty of December 13, 1921.[14] The Anglo-Japanese Alliance was renewed in 1911 for a period of ten years. Since the original source of danger from Russia had been removed, its continuance would not only invite suspicions in the United States [15] but also raise objections in Great Britain and Canada.[16] On the other hand, the American government was not inclined to join any peacetime alliance; Great Britain did not want to offend Japan by forthright termination of the alliance without a substitute; Australia and New Zealand expected to have some kind of mutual defense for security reasons. Inasmuch as France also had tremendous interest in the Far East, the easy way out of the Anglo-Japanese Alliance would be the conclusion of a pact among Great Britain, Japan, France, and the United States. It was under these circumstances that they signed the Four-Power Treaty of December 13, 1921, agreeing upon mutual respect for their respective rights in relation to their insular possessions and insular dominions in the region of the Pacific Ocean. [17]

Japan had taken full advantage of her alliance with Great Britain to strengthen her position in China. Substitution of that alliance by a vague provision in the Four-Power Treaty would make her more restrained at least for the time being. In this respect, China welcomed this decision of the Conference. It should also be noted that the Lansing-Ishii Agreement of November 2, 1917 was cancelled through an Exchanges of Notes between the United States and Japan on April 14, 1923. [18]

III. SETTLEMENT OF THE SHANTUNG QUESTION COL-
LATERALLY WITH THE WASHINGTON CONFERENCE

1. Sino-Japanese Discussions through American-
British Good Offices

After the failure to recover former German rights in Shantung at the Paris Peace Conference,[19] China persistently resisted all Japanese overtures for direct negotiations. Secretary of State Hughes and Arthur J. Balfour, heads of the American and British delegations respectively, realized that, if the Shantung question were brought up at the Conference by China, Japan would refuse to discuss it and thus might impair an amicable solution of that vital problem.[20] Therefore they offered good offices to bring about bilateral talks between the Chinese and Japanese delegates on November 25, 1921, with a view to assisting "a just and permanent resolution of the question."[21] The two disputing parties soon agreed to begin informal discussions collaterally with the Conference, in the presence of American and British observers.[22]

Direct conversations at the capital of a third country, in a less formal manner, had definite advantages over formal debates at an international conference. Thirty-six meetings were held from December 1, 1921 to January 31, 1922, primarily concerned with the purchase and management of the Tsingtao-Tsinanfu Railway (Kiaochow-Tsinan Railway).[23] On February 4, 1922, the long-standing dispute between China and Japan over the Shantung rights was finally settled by the conclusion of the Treaty for the Settlement of Outstanding Questions relative to Shantung, with Annex and Agreed Terms of Understanding.[24]

2. Terms of the Settlement

Since the Shantung question constituted a serious problem of Sino-Japanese relations, its amicable settlement was considered an important event in the Far East. Detailed and complicated, the provisions of the Treaty are summarized below.

(1) restoration of former German leased territory of Kiaochow to China (Art. I), and speedy transfer of its administration and public property located therein (Arts. III,V–VIII);

(2) withdrawal of Japanese troops from Kiaochow and also of the railway gendarmes (Arts. IX–XI); [25]

(3) transfer to China of the Tsingtao-Tsinanfu Railway, its branches, and all other properties appurtenant thereto, to be reimbursed with the sum of 53,406,141 gold marks, by Chinese government treasury notes, secured on the properties and railway revenues, running for a period of fifteen years, but redeemable at the end of five years (Arts. XIV–XVIII);

(4) appointment by the Chinese government, pending the redemption of the treasury notes, of a Japanese traffic manager and a Japanese chief accountant to perform coordinate functions jointly with the Chinese chief accountant (Art. XIX);

(5) international financing of the extensions of the Tsingtao-Tsinanfu Railway on terms agreeable to China (Art. XXI);

(6) joint operation of mines in Shantung formerly granted by China to Germany (Art. XXII);

(7) opening of Kiaochow to foreign trade and residence, and the establishment of an exclusive Japanese settlement or of an international settlement (Arts. XXIII–XXIV);

(8) fair compensation to Japanese companies and nationals engaged in the salt industry along the coast of Kiaochow Bay, and permission to export such salt to Japan on reasonable terms (Art. XXV);

(9) transfer to China of submarine cables between Tsingtao and Chefoo and between Tsingtao and Shanghai, with the exception of a specified portion already utilized by the Japanese government for other purposes (Art. XXVI); and

(10) transfer to China of the Japanese wireless stations at Tsingtao and Tsinanfu with fair compensation (XXVII).

All detailed arrangements were subsequently made by the two countries through the conclusion of an agreement, with annex and exchange of memoranda of December 1, 1922, [26] and an agreement relating to the Tsingtao-Tsinanfu Railway of December 5, 1922.[27] In helping the settlement of the Shantung question, Great Britain closely cooperated with the United States. To show British good will, Arthur J. Balfour announced to the plenary session of the Conference, on the same day the Shantung settlement was reported, that Great Britain was ready to return to China her leased territory of Weihaiwei in the same province of Shantung.[28]

IV. WESTERN RELUCTANCE TO RELINQUISH TARIFF AND EXTRATERRITORIAL PRIVILEGES

1. Considerations for the Revision of the Customs Tariff

Much has been said about the inequitable restrictions on China's customs tariffs.[29] The Chinese delegation raised the question at the fifth meeting of the Committee on the Pacific and the Far East on November 23, 1921.[30] After long discussion, the Treaty relating to the Revision of the Chinese Customs Tariff was concluded by the nine powers on February 6, 1922.[31] It was agreed that the Chinese customs tariff was to be revised to an effective 5% ad valorem; according to prevailing prices of commodities in the 1920's, it only yielded 3-1/2% in actuality. A Revision Commission consisting of representatives of the powers concerned was to undertake this task and to complete the revision within four months; further revisions were to be made after four years and then every seven years.[32]

The charge for transit duties would be fixed at the rate of 2-1/2% ad valorem until the conditions of abolishing likin and levying surtaxes could be fulfilled in accordance with previous treaty provisions.[33] A Special Conference was to be held in China, for the purpose of discussing various tariff problems, including the levying of a surtax on dutiable imports from 2-1/2% to 5%.[34] The principles of uniformity in the rates at all land and maritime frontiers and of equal treatment and opportunity for all contracting parties were stressed.[35]

The inability of the Washington Conference to satisfy China's desire for tariff autonomy was largely due to the self-interest of foreign powers,[36] but the Peking government could not be completely absolved from responsibility. In view of the disunity of the country and the large number of military forces causing a severe drain on public revenues, delegates of several powers voiced serious doubt about the advisability of "placing large funds at the disposal of a weak administration."[37] The Conference even adopted a resolution on February 1, 1922, expressing its earnest hope that the Chinese government take immediate and effective steps to reduce military forces and expenditures.[38] In order to alleviate foreign concern with the disposal of customs revenues, the Chinese government went so far as to declare that it had no intention to effect any change in the administration of the Chinese Maritime Customs.[39] Notwithstanding this assurance, China could obtain only such concessions from the powers as stipulated in the Treaty of February 6, 1922.[40]

2. Conditions for the Abolition of Extraterritorial Rights

The origin, application, and abuses of extraterritoriality have been discussed before.[41] China had seized every opportunity to negotiate for its early abolition. In the Sino-British Treaty of September 5, 1902,[42] the Sino-American Treaty of October 8, 1903,[43] and the Sino-Japanese Treaty of October 8, 1903,[44] the powers agreed to render every assistance to China's efforts for judicial reform with a view to relinquishing their extraterritorial rights. The Chinese delegation at the Washington Conference brought up the subject again on November 16, 1921, with the hope that "immediately, or as soon as circumstances will permit, existing jurisdictional and administrative freedom of action are to be removed."[45]

In response to the Chinese request, the Conference adopted a resolution on December 10, 1921,[46] to set up a commission to investigate the practice of extraterritoriality in China and also Chinese laws and judicial administration. The commission was to be composed of one member from each of the signatories and of other powers which enjoyed extraterritorial rights in China and acceded to this resolution. These powers would be individually free to accept or reject any portion of its recommendations, but should not exact concessions from China as conditions of their acceptance. China was expected to afford to the commission every facility for the performance of its functions, but had no obligation to accept its recommendations either. [47] It is, therefore, clear that the powers at the Washington Conference were sympathetic to China's proposition, but not yet ready to give up their vested right of extraterritoriality.

V. EVASIVE RESOLUTIONS ON CHINA'S OTHER QUESTIONS

1. Withdrawal of Foreign Armed Forces

Many other questions relating to China were discussed at the Washington Conference, but not all of them yielded successful results. With respect to the withdrawal of foreign armed forces and railway guards,[48] the Conference adopted a vague resolution on on February 1, 1922.[49] The powers expressed their intention to comply with China's wishes at such a time as she could be deemed capable to protect the lives and property of foreigners. An inquiry into the pertinent conditions was to be made by the representatives of China and their diplomatic envoys in Peking[50] In view of intermittent civil strife in China, the powers were understandably most reluctant to relinquish their right to station troops and warships in Chinese territory at the time of the Washington Conference.

2. Unification of Railways in China

Railway imperialism had done much harm to China.[51] As a consequence of an exchange of views with the powers at the Washington Conference, the Chinese delegation issued a statement on January 19, 1922, endorsing the idea of unifying existing and future railways in China "under the control and operation of the Chinese government with such foreign financial and technical assistance as may be needed."[52] The Conference expressed the same hope in its resolution of February 1, 1922. [53]

The Chinese people had a vivid memory of the methods employed by foreign powers to establish political and economic influence in China by railway construction and loans. No matter how attractive international cooperation in the proposed project might appear, they could not refrain from suspecting the implications of foreign financing. Meanwhile, the powers concerned did not work out a feasible plan either: thus the unification plan was never carried out.

3. Removal of Foreign Postal Agencies and Wireless stations

The Washington Conference recognized the justice of China's desire for the abolition of foreign postal agencies and wireless stations on her territory.[54] In a resolution of February 1, 1922, France, Great Britain, Japan, and the United States agreed to abandon their postal agencies in China, except those in leased territories, on the following conditions: maintenance of efficient Chinese postal service; assurance of maintaining existing postal administration with respect to the Status of the foreign Co-Director General.[55] Consequent to the above exceptions and conditions, the only immediate concession from the powers was to afford facilities to the Chinese customs authorities to examine, in foreign postal agencies, those articles which might contain dutiable or contraband goods.[56]

Concerning the maintenance of foreign wireless stations in China, the Conference adopted a complicated resolution on February 1, 1922.[57] The stations were classified under the following categories: First, those on the grounds of foreign legations should limit their use to sending and receiving government messages; unofficial messages could be conveyed only when all other telegraphic communications were interrupted. Second, those operated by foreign governments and nationals within Chinese territory under treaties or concessions should limit their use in accordance with the agreed terms. Third, unauthorized stations should be transferred to the Chinese government upon appropriate compensation. Fourth, those in the leased territories, the South Manchurian Railway Zone or the French Concession at Shanghai would be a subject for further discussion between China and the powers concerned. The Chinese government made it clear by a declaration that it did "not recognize or concede the right of any foreign Power or of the nationals thereof to install or operate, without its express consent, radio stations in legation grounds, settlements, concessions, leased territories, railway areas or other similar areas."[58]

4. Foreign Leased Territories in China

Foreign leased territories in China on the eve of the Washington Conference were Kiaochow under Germany, Weihaiwei and Kowloon under Great Britain, Kuangchou-wan under France, and Port Arthur and Dairen under Japan.[59] Inasmuch as these leased territories constituted an imperium in imperio,[60] the Chinese delegation was prepared to demand their restitution at the Conference from the powers concerned. Early on November 22, 1921, China declared that she was ready "to give an understanding not to alienate or lease any portion of her territory or littoral to any Power."[61] Then, on December 3 of the same year, V.K. Wellington Koo pleaded this case before the Committee on the Pacific and Far Eastern Questions.[62]

During the course of discussions, France expressed her willingness to give up Kuangchou-wan if the other powers would do the same. Japan insisted on keeping her leased territories. Great Britain stressed the importance of maintaining Kowloon for the security of Hongkong, but promised to resore Weihaiwei when Japan returned the Shantung rights to China.[63] Consequently, China recovered only Kiaochow through bilateral negotiations with Japan. The rendition of Weihaiwei did not take place until 1930.[64]

VI. TREATY COMMITMENTS OF OR WITH RESPECT TO CHINA

1. Nature and Scope of Commitments

China had been victimized not only by unequal treaties but also by many commitments not formally concluded or ratified by the Chinese Parliament. There were also many inter-power agreements, which affected the rights and interests of China without her previous knowledge and consent. Bypassing regular channels, foreign governments and nationals sometimes secured informal commitments from local authorities.[65] Among many others not ratified by the Chinese Parliament were the Reorganization Gold Loan Agreement of April 26, 1913,[66] the Treaties and Exchanges of Notes concerning Japan's Twenty-one Demands of 1915,[67] and several Sino-Japanese agreements concluded in 1918 and 1919, relating to military and railway matters.[68] According to the provisions of the Chinese Constitution prevailing during that period, approval of the Parliament was necessary for raising public loans, signing contracts involving the national treasury, declaring war, negotiating for peace, and concluding treaties.[69] Legally, China should not have been held responsible for commitments under treaties and agreements concluded by her government officials without the approval of the Chinese Parliament.

The inter-power agreements were concluded either for mutual abstention from certain actions in specified areas or for mutual support for certain general interests in China. Most of these were entered into by the powers during the period of their struggle for spheres of influence in China. The following list is by no means exhaustive:

1. Anglo-Franco Declaration with regard to Siam and Other Matters (Advantages of Yunnan and Szechwan, etc.), January 15, 1896.[70]

2. Anglo-German Arrangement regarding Spheres of Interest in Railway Construction, September 2, 1898.[71]

3. Anglo-Russian Exchange of Notes (Scott-Mouravieff Agreement) with regard to Railway Interests in China, April 28, 1899.[72]

4. Anglo-German Agreement relating to China, October 10, 1900.[73]

5. Russo-Japanese Peace Treaty of September 5, 1905.[74]

6. Franco-Japanese Agreement in regard to the Continent of Asia, June 10, 1907.[75]

7. Russo-Japanese Political Convention of July 30, 1907.[76]

8. Anglo-Russian Convention relating to Persia, Afghanistan and Tibet, August 31, 1907.[77]

9. American-Japanese Exchange of Notes (Root-Takahira Agreement), November 30, 1908.[78]

10. Russo-Japanese Convention in regard to Manchuria, July 4, 1910. [79]

11. Russo-Japanese Convention in regard to Cooperation in the Far East, July 3, 1916. [80]

12. American-Japanese Exchange of Notes on China (Lansing-Ishii Agreement), November 2, 1917. [81]

13. Four-Power (France, Great Britain, Japan, and the United States) Agreement for the Establishment of the Financial Consortium in China, October 15, 1920. [82]

The impact of these inter-power agreements on China has been described before. [83]

The three Anglo-Japanese Agreements (Treaties of Alliance) concluded in 1902, 1905, and 1911 had far-reaching consequences in the Far East and particularly in China. [84] Russia and Japan signed secret conventions relating to China during the period of 1907-1912.[85] Japan entered into secret understandings in 1917 with Russia, [86] Great Britain, [87] France,[88] and Italy,[89] regarding the ultimate disposal of former German rights in Shantung, which made the Paris Peace Conference sacrifice justice for peace in this particular respect.[90] Although several of the above-mentioned inter-power agreements were terminated, they had already inflicted damages to China and created serious repercussions on her relations with the powers concerned.

2. Conference's Resolution Subsequent
to China's Proposals

Unlike China's own commitments through formal treaties, inter-power agreements affecting China were beyond her control. At the Washington Conference, however, China found an opportunity to call on the powers "not to conclude between themselves any treaty or agreement directly affecting China or the general peace in these regions without previously

notifying China and giving her an opportunity to participate."[91] In further consideration of the complexity of China's
treaty commitments, the Chinese delegation submitted the
following proposal to the Conference at the first meeting
of its Committee on Pacific and Far Eastern Questions on
November 16, 1921:

> "All special rights, privileges, immunities
> or commitments, whatever their character or con-
> tractual basis, claimed by any of the Powers in or
> relating to China are to be declared, and all such
> or future claims not so made known are to be
> deemed null and void. The rights, privileges, im-
> munities and commitments, not known or to be
> declared are to be examined with a view to determ-
> ining their scope and validity and, if valid, to
> harmonizing them with one another and with the
> principles declared by this Conference." [92]

Speaking on behalf of the Chinese delegation at the Committee's twenty-first meeting, V.K. Wellington Koo emphas-
sized the importance of publicity and registration as required
by the Covenant of the League of Nations.[93] With respect to
China's engagements, the Li-Lobanoff Treaty of 1896 was the
only one not officially published; Koo promised to supply its
authentic text to the Conference.[94] In response to the Chinese appeal, the Committee finally reached a decision on the
publicity and listing of commitments. At its fifth plenary
session on February 1, 1922, the Conference adopted the
Resolution regarding Existing Commitments of China or with
Respect to China.[95]

According to the Resolution, the powers concerned were to
supply a list of existing treaties under whatever designation
with China or in relation to China to the Secretary-General
of the Conference, and also a list of existing contracts between
their nationals with the central government, administrative
agencies or local authorities of China. Thereafter, mutual notification was required of future treaties or contracts of the
same nature within sixty days after their conclusion.[96] The
Chinese government agreed to do the same.[97] It should be
noted that the powers concerned were not limited to the nine
signatories but also included the adherents to this Resolution
or Agreement.[98]

3. Indecision on the Revocation of Japan's Twenty-one Demands

The Twenty-one Demands made by Japan in 1915 were condemned not only by the Chinese people but also by enlightened Japanese statesmen and intellectuals. [99] It should be recalled that the powers at the Paris Peace Conference turned a deaf ear to China's appeal for their abrogation. The Chinese delegation submitted the case once more to the Washington Conference on December 15, 1921. During the debate at the Committee on Pacific and Far Eastern Questions, Baron Shidehara of Japan declared, at its thirtieth meeting on February 2, 1922, that China's attempted revocation of her treaty commitments in this regard would establish "an exceedingly dangerous precedent" in international relations.[100] In his reply on the following day, Chung-hui Wang of the Chinese delegation stated:

"A still more dangerous precedent will be established with consequences upon the stability of international relations which cannot be estimated, if, without rebuke or protest from other Powers, one nation can obtain from a friendly, but in a military sense, weaker neighbor, and under circumstances such as attended the negotiation and signing of the treaties of 1915, valuable concessions which were not in satisfaction of pending controversies and for which no quid pro quo was offered." [101]

Japan's Twenty-one Demands were undoubtedly in conflict with the letter and spirit of the Open Door Policy and the Covenant of the League of Nations,[102] as well as the principles observed by the Washington Conference. In order to pacify public opinion, the Japanese delegation was ostensibly prepared to consider certain concessions, which were made known on February 2, 1922: first, no future negotiations on Group V of the Twenty-one Demands would be required; second, certain railway loans and loans secured by taxes in South Manchuria and Inner Mongolia would be open to international financing; third, Japan would not insist on supplying all kinds of advisers in South Manchuria; and fourth, all questions relating to Shantung had been settled to the satisfaction of both countries. [103] In reality, there was nothing new in the Japanese offer.

On the subject of the Twenty-one Demands, Western
powers merely exchanged views, but did not recommend any
measures to alter their status. The United States merely
reiterated the doctrine of equality for nationals of all countries and the principles of the newly concluded Nine-Power
Treaty.[104] Consequently, the Conference adopted no resolution
on the subject, but only recorded in the minutes the statements made by various delegates at its sixth plenary session.
Thus China had to reserve the right to seek a satisfactory
solution of this whole question at a future date,[105] which did
occur two decades later. When Japan surrendered in September 1945, all unequal treaties previously concluded between
the two countries were terminated.

VII. EVALUATION OF THE WASHINGTON CONFERENCE
AND ITS AFTERMATH

1. Appraisal of the Conference's Resolutions
relating to China

At Washington, the United States and Great Britain went
a long way in supporting China's cause within the limits of
their own national interests. It was the first time since the
1840's that Western powers had simultaneously realized the
importance of reconciliation with China, largely because of
the rise of Chinese nationalism as manifested in the mass
movement and party policies, as well as the potential danger
of Japan's exclusive influence in the Far East. On many occasions, Western and Chinese diplomats joined hands vis-à-
vis the position of the Japanese delegation. Although moderation was not the virtue of Japanese military leaders, the
statesmen then in power at Tokyo held a comparatively liberal
and conciliatory policy toward international affairs. Otherwise, the limitation of naval armament and settlement of the
Shantung question might not have been possible. It must be
admitted that Japan did make some concessions in both cases.

Turning to specific questions relating to China, the powers
showed restrained sympathy toward her domestic difficulties
and national aspirations. However vague its stipulations might

be, the Nine-Power Treaty went much further than any previous agreement or declaration in respecting China's political independence and territorial integrity. As to its lack of provisions to sanction violators, this Treaty was not essentially different from many other international conventions. An international treaty helps the political force maintain order, but cannot be solely relied upon to eliminate breaches of order completely. The effectiveness of sanctions depends mainly on the determination of the signatories. Moreover, the termination of the Anglo-Japanese alliance consequent to the conclusion of the Four-Power Treaty weakened the position of China's adversary in the Far East, even though this action took place much too late to block the expansion of Japan.

In addition to the restoration of former German rights in Shantung, what China actually gained from the Washington Conference was the periodic revision of the customs tariff and promises from Great Britain and France to return Weihaiwei and Kuangcho-wan. Measures were also adopted to fulfill, step by step, China's demands for relinquishment of extraterritoriality, withdrawal of foreign armed forces, and elimination of foreign postal agencies and wireless stations. There is no doubt that the powers concerned were not prepared to relinquish all these rights immediately. On the other hand, China's domestic situation at the time by no means helped the settlement of these issues. The impotence of the Peking government, intermittent civil strife, and increasing dissatisfaction of the Chinese people with the warlord domination of the North failed to strengthen the position of Chinese diplomats abroad. Internal dissension even threatened the work of the Chinese delegation at Washington. [106] Disunity in the country and lack of substantial progress in administrative and judicial fields had, more or less, dissipated the powers' sympathy for and confidence in the Chinese government.

In spite of the precarious situation in China, the powers agreed, in the Nine-Power Treaty, "to provide the fullest and most unembarrassed opportunity to China to develop and maintain for herself an effective and stable Government" and "to refrain from taking advantage of the present conditions in order to seek special rights and privileges...." [107] One of the most disappointing features of the Washington

Conference was its attitude toward treaty commitments of and with respect to China. What the powers decided upon was the registration and publicity but not reconsideration of the existing commitments. Worst of all was that the Conference discussed but did not decide on China's request for the cancellation of the Twenty-one Demands. Lack of support from the Western powers in this regard had in effect strengthened Japan's position in Manchuria. Less than a decade after the Conference, this Chinese territory was invaded by Japan in defiance of the Nine-Power Treaty, the League Covenant, and the Kellogg-Briand Pact. [108]

In conclusion, Western powers adopted a conciliatory policy toward China at the Washington Conference. The concessions they made were, however, insufficient to satisfy the Chinese people. In any event, their goodwill came too late to change the course of events in China. The Soviet Union had already begun a war of propaganda to court Chinese friendship by issuing the Karakhan Declaration on July 25, 1919; [109] the Chinese Communist Party had already been formed on July 1, 1921, [110] and Sun Yat-sen had become disillusioned with Western powers after the Paris Peace Conference and prepared to cooperate with the Soviet Union. [111] In other words, China was on the eve of another revolution, resorting to drastic policies toward foreign powers. [112]

2. Unfavorable Outcome of the Tariff Conference and the Extraterritorial Commission

The Washington Conference decided to hold a special conference for the discussion of Chinese customs tariff and set up a special commission on extraterritoriality to investigate legal and judicial systems in China. In accordance with the Treaty relating to the Revision of the Chinese Tariff of February 6, 1922, a Special Tariff Conference was to be convened within three months after its coming into force. [113] When the ratifications of all its signatories were deposited with the Government of the United States on August 5, 1925, the Chinese government extended invitations to the powers concerned to attend the Special Tariff Conference in Peking on October 26, 1925. [114] The Conference was held in time to consider China's request for tarrif autonomy effective January 1, 1929, and the interim arrangements. On her part,

China promised to abolish likin simultaneously with the enforcement of the Chinese National Tariff Law.[115]

For several months, proposals and counter-proposals were
presented to the subcommittee meetings. It was finally
agreed, on November 13, 1925, to recommend the conclusion
of a treaty, in which the powers concerned were to recognize
China's right to remove all treaty restrictions on tariff and
to enforce the Chinese National Tariff Law upon the abolition
of likin on January 1, 1929. For the interim period, a surtax was to be imposed on all dutiable goods under seven classes. According to the schedule submitted by American, British,
and Japanese delegates as an amendment to the original
Chinese proposal,[116] the new tariff rates after the charge of
the surtax were to range from 7-1/2% to 27-1/2%.[117]

Unfortunately, because of a change of government, most of
the Chinese delegates left Peking in April 1926, and the
Conference could no longer conduct formal discussions.[118] It
was adjourned on July 3 of that year, but the delegates of the
foreign powers "expressed a unanimous desire to proceed
with the work of the Conference at the earliest possible moment when the delegates of the Chinese Government are in a
position to resume discussion with the foreign delegates of
the problems before the Conference."[119] Although the Conference was never resumed, the efforts of the subcommittee
were not entirely in vain. The informal recognition of China's
right of tariff autonomy by the powers concerned and the discussion of surtax rates served as a basis for the conclusion
of the Sino-American Treaty on July 25, 1928.[120]

In pursuance of the Resolution adopted by the Washington
Conference on December 10, 1921, regarding extraterritoriality in China, the proposed commission should have met in
Peking within three months after the adjournment of the Conference. For various reasons, however, it was not convened
until January 12, 1926.[121] Composed of one member each
from the nine signatories of the Resolution and also Denmark,
Peru, Spain, and Sweden, the Commission made practical
investigations and held twenty-one sessions. Its report, in
four parts, was completed on September 16, 1926. The first
three dealt with the practice of extraterritoriality, the existing judicial and prison systems, as well as the administration
of justice in China; the findings were generally unfavorable

to immediate relinquishment of extraterritoriality under the prevailing conditions in China.[122]

The fourth part of the report contained lengthy recommendations for the improvement of China's legal, judicial, and prison systems; codification and enforcement of civil, criminal, and commerical codes; extension of modern courts, prisons, and detention-houses; and protection of judicial independence from any civil or military interference. According to the report, relinquishment of extraterritoriality in China had to be gradual. During the transitional period, the powers concerned were urged to take the following steps: application of Chinese laws and regulations, wherever appropriate, in their extraterritorial courts; reform of mixed cases and mixed courts; prevention of illegal protection of Chinese nationals, as well as to business and shipping interests; periodic registration of their nationals; improvement of judicial assistance; and requirement of their nationals to pay legitimate taxes imposed by the competent authorities of the Chinese government.[123] In making the recommendations, the Commission stated in the report:

"The commissioners are of the opinion that, when these recommendations shall have been reasonably complied with, the several powers would be warranted in relinquishing their respective rights of extraterritoriality.

"It is understood that, upon the relinquishment of extraterritoriality, the nationals of the powers concerned will enjoy freedom of residence and trade and civil rights in all parts of China in accordance with the general practice in intercourse among the nations and upon a fair and equitable basis."[124]

When the Commission conducted investigations and prepared the report, China was in the midst of civil strife. Warlords occupying different regions of China frequently disregarded human rights and judicial independence. It would be unfair to blame the foreign powers alone for the delay in relinquishing extraterritoriality. On the other hand, the Chinese people were by no means satisfied with the slow process of its abolition in accordance with the Commission's recommendations.

At that time, the Nationalist Party in Canton was resolved to unify the country by destroying the warlords in the North and to terminate the extraterritorial system by speedy improvement of all prerequisite conditions. It may be recalled that, less than one month after the completion of the Commission's report, the revolutionary forces occupied Wuhan. With the establishment of the National Government in Nanking on April 19, 1927, a new move to conduct negotiations for the abolition of unequal treaties, including extraterritoriality, soon followed. [125]

NOTES TO CHAPTER 7

1. For the correspondence between Secretary of State Charles Evans Hugues and American envoys for initiating the Conference, see U. S. For. Rel., 1921, I, pp. 18-21, 27. For Japanese reaction to the American sponsorship of the Conference, see ibid., pp. 52-53.

2. A brief description of the negotiations for the limitation of naval armament, including the 5:5:3 ratio of capital ships for the United States, Great Britain, and Japan respectively, can be found in M. J. Pusey, Charles Evans Hughes (New York, 1951, 2 vols.), II, pp. 479-481; H. O. Yardley, The American Black Chamber (Indianapolis, 1931), Ch. 16.

3. The United States raised strong objections to Japan's long occupation of Eastern Siberia. Eventually Japanese troops evacuated Siberia in 1922 and northern Sakhalin in 1925. See M. H. Pusey, op. cit., II, p. 542.

4. For American attitude toward Japan's mandate of former German islands in the Pacific, see U. S. For. Rel., Paris Peace Conference, II, pp. 512-515. See also R. L. Buell, The Washington Conference (New York, 1922), pp. 52-53.

5. The Chinese government appointed four delegates: Sao-ke Alfred Sze, V. K. Wellington Koo, Chung-hui Wang, and Chao-chu Wu. Sze headed the delegation. An important member of the revolutionary government in Canton, Wu was selected by the Peking government to demonstrate national unity, but he did not come to Washington.

6. For the text of the ten points, see Conference on the Limitation of Armament, Washington, November 12, 1921 to February 6, 1922 (Washington: Government Printing Office, 1922; hereafter cited as Washington Conference, 1921-22), pp. 866-868; Senate Doc., 67th Cong., 2nd Sess., 1921-22, Vol. 10, pp. 443-445.

7. Besides Hughes and Root, there were two other American delegates: Henry Cabot Lodge and Oscar Underwood.

8. See ibid., pp. 450-451.

9. Washington Conference, 1921-22, p. 900.

10. See W. W. Williughby, China at the Conference: A Report (Baltimore, 1922), pp. 43, 197.

11. The signatories were Belgium, France, Great Britain, Italy, Japan, the Netherlands, Portugal, the United States, and China. For the text of the Treaty, see League of Nations, Treaty Series, No. 982 (1925), Vol. 38, P. 278; U. S. Treaty Series, No. 723; British Treaty Series, No. 42 (1925); Carnegie, Treaties, pp. 89-93.

12. In accordance with the resolution adopted by the Conference on February 4, 1922, a Board of Reference was to be established to deal with any questions in connection with Arts. III and V of the Nine-Power Treaty of February 6, 1922. For the text of the resolution, see Senate Doc No. 124, 67th Cong., 2nd Sess., p. 37; Carnegie, Treaties, p. 80.

13. For details of spheres of influence in China, see supra, pp. 49-50.

14. For the text of the Four-Power Treaty or Treaty relating to Insular Possessions and Insular Dominions in the Pacific Ocean, with Declaration, see Senate Doc. 124, 67th Cong., 2nd Sess., 1921-1922, p. 23; U. S. For. Rel., 1922, I, pp. 33-37; Carnegie, Treaties, pp. 58-61.

15. See U. S. For. Rel., 1922, I, p. 335.

16. In October 1920, the British government appointed an ad hoc committee to study the problem. In January 1921, the committee unanimously recommended that the alliance be terminated and substituted by a tripartite entente of Great Britain, Japan, and the United States. See Rohan Butler and J. P. T. Bury (eds.), Documents on British Foreign Policy 1919-1939 (London, 1966), First Series, Vol. 14, pp. 467-470.

17. Art. I of the Treaty of December 13, 1921. See also the Supplementary Treaty of February 6, 1922 (Senate Doc. No. 124, 67th Cong., 2nd Sess., p. 26).

18. In his address to the Congress on March 8, 1922, President Harding stated that "the so-called Lansing-Ishii agreement has no binding effect whatever, either with respect to the past or to the future, which is in any sense inconsistent with the principles and policies declared in the nine-power treaty." U. S. For. Rel., 1922, II, p. 593. See also the Memorandum sent by the Japanese Embassy to the State Department on December 27, 1922 (ibid., II, pp. 597-598). For the original agreement of 1917, see supra, p. 51. The text of Exchange of Notes cancelling the Agreement can be found in U. S. Treaty series, No. 667; Carnegie, Treaties, p. 130.

19. For the Paris Peace Conference and the Shantung question, see supra, pp. 160-163.

20. In accepting the American invitation to the Conference on July 26, 1921, Japan emphasized that questions "as are of sole concern to certain particular Powers or such matters that may be regarded accomplished facts should be scrupulously avoided." See U. S. For. Rel., 1921, I, p. 45. In his interview with Secretary of State Hughes on July 21, 1921, Baron Shidehara, Japanese Ambassador to the United States, requested the American government to persuade China to conduct bilateral negotiations with Japan for the settlement of the Shantung question. See ibid., I, pp. 613-615.

21. Ibid., 1922, I, p. 935.

22. See the Chinese Delegation to the Washington Conference, Conversations between the Chinese and the Japanese Representatives in regard to the Shantung Question (Washington, 1923), pp. 3-4. Among the observers were John V. A. MacMurray and Miles W. Lampson, who later became American and British Ministers to China respectively.

23. Japan proposed a long-term loan from Japanese financiers, who would recommend a chief engineer, a traffic manager, and a chief accountant, all of Japanese nationality, for the duration of the loan. On the other hand, China offered payment by Chinese government treasury notes and the appointment of a Japanese chief engineer. See U. S. For. Rel., 1922, I, pp. 682, 686, 940-943, 945, 961-963; the Japanese Delegation to the Washington Conference, Conversations between the Chinese and Japanese Representatives in regard to the Shantung Question: Minutes of the Proceedings (Washington, 1923), pp. 12, 151, 153-154, 160, 175, 199. For details of the negotiations, see Wunsz King, China at the Washington Conference 1921-1922 (New York, 1963), pp. 6-25.

24. For its text, see British and Foreign State Papers, Vol. 116, p. 676; Carnegie, Treaties, pp. 80-88.

25. See also the Sino-Japanese Agreement between Delegates of the Japanese and Chinese Governments for the Withdrawal of the Japanese Troops Along the Line of the Shantung Railway, March 28, 1922. British and Foreign State Papers, Vol. 116, p. 686; Carnegie, Treaties, pp. 100-101.

26. For the text of the Agreement Governing Details of Arrangements for the Settlement of Outstanding Questions in Connection with Shantung, with Annex and Exchange of Memoranda,

December 1, 1922, see League of Nations, Treaty Series, No. 559 (1924), Vol. 22, p. 257; British and Foreign State Papers, Vol. 120, p. 115; Carnegie, Treaties, pp. 114-126.

27. For the text of the Agreement on Detailed Arrangements for the Settlement of Outstanding Questions relative to Tsingtao-Tsinanfu Railway, see League of Nations, Treaty Series, No. 560 (1924), Vol. 22, p. 315; British and Foreign State Papers, Vol. 120, p. 134; Carnegie, Treaties, pp. 127-129. More information about the Shantung question at the Washington Conference can be found in Willoughby, I, Ch. X.

28. For the lease of Weihaiwei, see supra, p. 48. For the text of the Exchange of Notes between the Heads of the British and Chinese Delegations regarding the Retrocession of Weihaiwei on February 3/5, 1922, see British Parliamentary Papers, Misc., No. 1 (1922), Cmd. 1627, p. 86; British and Foreign State Papers, Vol. 116, p. 435; Carnegie, Treaties, pp. 76-78. For further information, see infra, p. 320. In a note from the Colonial Office to the Foreign Office on September 15, 1921, Winston Churchill expressed hostility to the surrender of British leased territories in China, but Balfour explained to Lloyd George that the announcement of restituting Weihaiwei at the Washington Conference "would have most striking effect and make the greatest appeal to general public." See Rohan Butler and J. P. T. Bury, Documents on British Foreign Policy 1919-1939, First Series, Vol. 14, pp. 501-502, 627-628.

29. See supra, pp. 110-111.

30. See Senate Doc., 67th Cong., 2nd Sess., 1921-1922, Vol. 10, pp. 469-471. For V. K. Wellington Koo's six proposals brought before the Sub-Committee on Chinese Revenue on November 29, 1921, see Conference on the Limitation of Armament: Subcommittees, Washington, November 12, 1921-1922 (Washington, 1922; hereafter cited as Washington Conference, Subcommittees), p. 546.

31. For the text, see League of Nations, Treaty Series, No. 981 (1926), Vol. 38, p. 268; U. S. Treaty Series, No. 724; British Treaty Series, 1925, No. 43; Carnegie, Treaties, pp. 93-97.

32. Arts. I, IV of the Treaty. See also supra, p. 111.

33. See Arts. II, VII. For the inland taxation of linkin, see supra, p. 111. The treaties in question were: Art. VIII of the Sino-British Treaty of September 5, 1902 (Chinese Customs, Treaties, I, pp. 543-568; Hertslet, Treaties, I, pp. 171-188; MacMurray, Treaties, I, pp. 342-355; also supra, p. 111.); Arts.

IV, V of the Sino-American Treaty of October 8, 1903 (Chinese Customs, Treaties, I, pp. 745-763; Hertslet, Treaties, I, pp. 566-578; MacMurray, Treaties, I, pp. 423-450); Art. I of the Sino-Japanese Supplementary Treaty of October 8, 1903 (Chinese Customs, Treaties, II, pp. 617-636; Hertslet, Treaties, I, pp. 383-391; MacMurray, Treaties, I, pp. 411-412).

34. See Arts. II, III. For the Special Conference, see infra, pp. 203-204.

35. See Arts. V, VI.

36. Japan, in particular, objected to a higher rate. See W. W. Willoughby, China at the Conference: A Report, p. 64; Washington Conference, Subcommittees, pp. 560-568.

37. See Senate Doc., 67th Cong., 2nd Sess., 1921-22, Vol. 10, p. 656.

38. For the text of the resolution, see Carnegie, Treaties, p. 73; Senate Doc. No. 124, 67th Cong., 2nd Sess., 1922, p. 42. See also W. W. Willoughby, China at the Conference: A Report, pp. 62, 110.

39. For foreign supervision of China's customs, see supra, pp. 107-109. In an editorial of the London Times of November 26, 1921, it was stated that China's desire to increase the tariff rate would undermine the customs. For the text of the Chinese declaration on February 6, 1922, see British and Foreign State Papers, Vol. 116, p. 596; British Parliamentary Papers, Misc., No. 1 (1922), Cmd. 1627, p. 52; Carnegie, Treaties, p. 89.

40. This Treaty was to come into force on the date of deposit of all ratifications. Due to the Sino-French controversy over the 'Gold Franc', France's ratification was delayed until August 5, 1925. In accordance with Art. I of the Treaty, the revision of customs tariff was to become effective as soon as possible. It was actually completed in 1922.

41. See supra, pp. 112-116.

42. Chinese Customs, Treaties, I, pp. 543-568; Hertslet, Treaties, I, pp. 171-188; MacMurray, Treaties, I, pp. 342-355.

43. Chinese Customs, Treaties, I, pp. 745-763; Hertslet, Treaties, I, pp. 566-578; MacMurray, Treaties, I, pp. 423-450.

44. Chinese Customs, Treaties, II, pp. 617-636; Hertslet, Treaties, I, pp. 383-391; MacMurray, Treaties, I, pp. 411-412.

45. Carnegie, Treaties, p. 57.

46. For the text of the resolution see ibid., pp. 56-58; Senate Doc. No. 124, 67th Cong., 2nd Sess., p. 37.

47. See U. S. For. Rel., 1922, I, pp. 290-291.

48. For the Chinese statement on this subject made at the Committee on Pacific and Far Eastern Questions on November 28, 1921, see Washington Conference, 1921-22, p. 982.

49. For the text, see Senate Doc. No. 124, 67th Cong., 2nd Sess., p. 39; Carnegie, Treaties, pp. 71-72.

50. See U. S. For. Rel., 1922, I, p. 292.

51. For details, see supra, pp. 116-123.

52. See U. S. For. Rel., 1922, I, p. 295; Carnegie, Treaties, p. 74.

53. For the text, see ibid., pp. 73-74; Senate Doc. No. 124, 67th Cong., 2nd Sess., p. 41. On February 4, 1922, the nine powers also adopted a resolution that diplomatic consultation be made to promote better administration of the Chinese Eastern Railway with a view to securing more efficiency of service and protection to the railway and its personnel. See ibid., p. 44.

54. See supra, pp. 88-89.

55. For the practice of appointing a French national to be Co-Director General, see supra, p. 109.

56. For the text of the Resolution, see Carnegie, Treaties, p. 71; Senate Doc. No. 124, 67th Cong., 2nd Sess., p. 39.

57. For the text of the resolution, see ibid., p. 40; Carnegie, Treaties, pp. 69-70.

58. For the text of the Chinese declaration, see ibid., p. 70.

59. For details, see supra, pp. 48-49.

60. See supra, p. 70.

61. For the text of the Declaration, see British Parliamentary Papers, Misc., No. 1 (1922), Cmd. 1627, p. 63; British and Foreign State Papers, Vol. 116, p. 586; Carnegie, Treaties, p. 56; Washington Conference, 1921-22, p. 908.

62. Koo's statement was similar to that contained in 'Questions for Readjustment' submitted to the Paris Peace Conference.

For its text, see ibid., pp. 1060-1062; Senate Doc. 67th Cong., 2nd Sess., 1921-22, Vol. 10, p. 540. See also ibid., p. 552. The subject of foreign concessions and settlements was not brought before the Washington Conference for discussion. For their origin and status, see supra, pp. 70-74.

63. See W. W. Willoughby, China at the Conference: A Report, pp. 181-192; also supra, pp. 190-192.

64. See infra, p. 320.

65. See, for instance, the alleged rights of the American Siems-Carey Company to build a railway in China granted by a certain governor-general of the provinces of Hunan and Hupeh, and of the French government to extend a loan for the construction of a railway and a mining enterprise in Kwangsi, granted by a governor of that province. See Willoughby, I, pp. 3-4.

66. See supra, p. 124.

67. For details, see supra, pp. 154-159.

68. For instance, the Agreement regarding Cooperation of Japanese and Chinese Armies of May 16, 1918 (MacMurray, Treaties, II, pp. 1411-1412); the Supplement to Military Agreement, Explanatory of Certain Important Points, September 6, 1918 (ibid., II, pp. 1413-1414); the Agreement regarding Cooperation of Japanese and Chinese Navies of May 19, 1918 (ibid., II, pp. 1412-1413); the Supplement to the Sino-Japanese Joint Military Defense Pact of February 5, 1919 (ibid., II, p. 1414); the Supplement to the Sino-Japanese Joint Naval Defense Pact of March 1, 1919 (ibid., II, pp. 1414-1415); and the Agreement for Purchase of Arms of July 31, 1918 (ibid., II, pp. 1414-1415). These agreements were later cancelled by the two countries through an Exchange of Notes on January 28, 1921. For the text, see Peking Leader, January 27, 30, 1921; Carnegie, Treaties, pp. 45-47.

69. See Arts. 19(4) and 35 of the Provisional Constitution of the Republic of China, March 11, 1912. In spite of domestic turmoil, this 1912 Constitution had been legally the fundamental law of China from 1912 to 1923. See Willoughby, I, p. 5. The text of the Constitution can be found in William L. Tung, The Political Institutions of Modern China, pp. 322-325. Yüan Shih-k'ai's dissolution of the Parliament on January 10, 1914 and his promulgation of the Constitutional Compact on May 1, 1914 were regarded as unconstitutional and condemned by the Chinese people. Thus President Li Yüan-hung proclaimed, on

June 29, 1917, the formal restoration of the Provisional Constitution of 1912 and the original Parliament. For details of political and constitutional disputes in China during that period, see ibid., Chs. 3-4.

70. Hertslet, Treaties, I, p. 583; MacMurray, Treaties, I, pp. 54-55.

71. Ibid., I, pp. 266-267.

72. Ibid., I, pp. 204-205; Hertslet, Treaties, I, pp. 586-589.

73. Ibid., I, pp. 591-596; MacMurray, Treaties, I, pp. 263-267.

74. Hertslet, Treaties, I, pp. 608-614; MacMurray, Treaties, I, pp. 522-526.

75. Ibid., I, p. 640.

76. Ibid., I, pp. 657-658.

77. Ibid., I, pp. 674-678.

78. Ibid., I, pp. 770-771.

79. Ibid., I, pp. 803-804.

80. Ibid., II, pp. 1327-1328.

81. Ibid., II, pp. 1394-1396.

82. Carnegie, Treaties, pp. 32-36.

83. See supra, pp. 49-50, 51, 124-125.

84. These were the Agreement relating to China and Korea, January 30, 1902 (Hertslet, Treaties, I, pp. 597-598; MacMurray, Treaties, I, pp. 324-325); the Agreement respecting Integrity of China, etc., August 12, 1905 (ibid., I, pp. 516-519); and the Agreement respecting the Integrity of China, the General Peace of Eastern Asia and India, and the Territorial Rights and Special Interests of the Parties in Those Regions, July 13, 1911 (ibid., I, pp. 900-901).

85. According to the list submitted by the Chinese delegation, the dates of their conclusion were: July 30, 1907; July 4, 1910; and July 8, 1912. The texts were not available at the time of the Washington Conference.

86. February 20, 1917; MacMurray, Treaties, II, p. 1169.

87. February 21, 1917; ibid., II, pp. 1167-1168.

88. March 1, 1917; ibid., II, pp. 1168-1169.

89. March 28, 1917; ibid., II, p. 1169.

90. See supra, pp. 160-163.

91. Point 3 of China's proposals (Washington Conference, 1921-22, pp. 866-868).

92. Ibid., p. 4

93. Art. 18 of the League Covenant reads: "Every treaty or international engagement entered into hereafter by any Member of the League shall be forthwith registered with the Secretariat and shall as soon as possible be published by it. No such treaty or international engagement shall be binding until so registered."

94. This Sino-Russian Treaty was supplied to the Committee at its twenty-fifth meeting. The text can also be found in MacMurray, Treaties, I, pp. 81-82.

95. For the text, see Senate Doc. No. 124, 67th Cong., 2nd Sess., p. 43; Carnegie, Treaties, pp. 74-75.

96. In the case of contracts, notification was to be made by the powers concerned after the receipt of information of their conclusion. The contracts to be filed included those involving "any concession, franchise, option or preference with respect to railway construction, mining, forestry, navigation, river conservancy, harbor works, reclamation, electrical communications, or other public works or public services, or for the sale of arms or ammunition," or "a lien upon any of the public revenues or properties of the Chinese Government or of any of its administrative subdivisions." Art. II of the Resolution.

97. Lists of treaties and contracts were supplied by the signatories. Most of these can be found in MacMurray, Treaties; Hertslet, Treaties; W. M. Malloy, Treaties, Conventions, International Acts, Protocols, and Agreements between the United States and Other Powers, 1776-1923 (Washington, 1919-1923, 3 vols.).

98. Invitations to adhere to this Agreement were extended to states which had treaty relations with China, including Bolivia, Brazil, Chile, Denmark, Germany, Norway, Persia, Peru, Spain, Sweden, and Switzerland.

99. For details of these Demands, see supra, pp. 154-159. In his book, Japan and Her Destiny, Mamoru Shigemitsu, Japan's wartime Foreign Minister, frankly pointed out that these Demands constituted "a serious blunder that had an irretrievable effect on Japan's future path." English translation by Oswald White (New York, 1958), p. 39. See also Yamato Ichihashi, The Washington Conference and After (Stanford, 1928), pp. 191, 289. This Japanese author and professor was usually biased against China. To qualify these Demands, however, he used the adjectives 'infamous' and 'notorious'. See Wunsz King, China at the Washington Conference 1921-1922, p. 49.

100. See U. S. For. Rel., 1922, I, p. 357; Senate Doc., 67th Cong., 2nd Sess., 1921-22, Vol. 10, p. 754.

101. Ibid., p. 777. See also U. S. For. Rel., 1922, I, p. 359.

102. Art. 20 of the League Covenant provided:

"1. The Members of the League severally agree that this Covenant is accepted as abrogating all obligations or understandings inter se which are inconsistent with the terms thereof, and solemnly undertake that they will not hereafter enter into any engagements inconsistent with the terms thereof.

"2. In case any Member of the League shall, before a Member of the League, have undertaken any obligations inconsistent with the terms of this Covenant, it shall be the duty of such Member to take immediate steps to procure its release from such obligations."

103. See U. S. For. Rel., 1922, I, p. 358.

104. See W. W. Willoughby, China at the Conference: A Report, pp. 182-183.

105. According to Art. 19 of the League Covenant, "the Assembly may from time to time advise the reconsideration by Members of the League of treaties which have become inapplicable and the consideration of international conditions whose continuance might endanger the peace of the world." On September 11, 1929, China requested the tenth session of the League Assembly to establish a committee to study the means for applying this article. France raised a strong objection to this proposal lest Germany should resort to it for the revision of the Treaty of Versailles. No practical step was taken by the League Assembly to effect the Chinese request. For the Assembly's resolution on September 25, 1929, see League of Nations Doc. A.91.1929.V.

106. See U. S. For. Rel., 1922, I, pp. 275-276; T. L. Yuan, "Huang Fu's Part in the Washington Conference: A Retrospect," Collection of Essays in Memory of the Late Huang Fu (1879-1936), p. 116, as cited in Wunsz King, China at the Washington Conference 1921-1922, p. 16. See also ibid., pp. 34-35.

107. Art. I(2,4) of the Nine-Power Treaty.

108. The Mukden incident occured on September 18, 1931. See infra, pp. 257-259. For the text of the Kellogg-Briand Pact or the General Treaty for the Renunciation of War of 1928, see League of Nations, Treaty Series, Vol. 94 (1929), pp. 56-74. For resort to war under international treaties, see William L. Tung, International Organization under the United Nations System (New York, 1969), pp. 210-212.

109. See infra, pp. 219-220.

110. See infra, pp. 224-225.

111. See infra, pp. 227-229.

112. See infra, pp. 229-230.

113 Art. II of the Treaty.

114. In addition to the nine signatories of the treaty, Denmark, Norway, Spain, and Sweden were also invited to attend the Conference. For China's Note of Invitation of June 24, 1925 and the powers' Reply on September 4, 1925, see Chinese Social and Political Science Review, Vol. 9, No. 4 (October 1925), pp. 842, 845; Carnegie, Treaties, pp. 153-154, 157-160.

115. See U. S. For. Rel., 1925, I, pp. 839-840, 862.

116. The Chinese proposal was that, effective three months after the signing of the tariff treaty, the rates of the surtax would be 5% on ordinary goods, 20% on grade B luxuries, and 30% on grade A luxuries (wine and tobacco).

117. Although the proposed treaty was never concluded, a surtax of 2-1/2% was imposed by Chinese local authorities. In its memorandum to the powers concerned on December 16, 1926, the British government urged the powers to recognize the fait accompli. See Wunsz King, China at the Washington Conference 1921-1922, p. 47; Foreign Policy Association, Information Service, Vol. IV, No. 15 (1928-29), pp. 302-303, 311. For details of the Tariff Conference, see also The China Year Book, 1926-1927, pp. 1106-1146.

118. After the civil war in the winter of 1924, Tuan Ch'i-jui became the Provisional Chief Executive of the Peking government. He was compelled to resign on April 20, 1926, when Chang Tso-lin, the warlord in Manchuria, decided to assume power by himself. See William L. Tung, The Political Institutions of Modern China, pp. 78-82.

119. Joint statement issued by the foreign delegates at the time of the Conference's adjournment. Willoughby, p. 838.

120. For the text, see U. S. Treaty Series, No. 773; Treaties between the Republic of China and Foreign States, 1927-1957 (Taipei: Ministry of Foreign Affairs, 1958; hereafter cited as Chinese Republic, Treaties), pp. 648-649; Carnegie, Treaties, pp. 230-231. See infra, p. 254. Further information on the Tariff Conference can be found in Stanley F. Wright, China's Struggle for Tariff Autonomy (Shanghai, 1938), pp. 461-491.

121. At first, China wanted more time for necessary preparation. Later, the French government used the postponement of the Commission as a weapon to force China to accept French terms for the settlement of the 'Gold Franc' controversy between the two countries. See Willoughby, II, p. 678.

122. In signing this report, Wang Chung-hui, the Chinese delegate, attached a statement to the effect that he was not in agreement with certain portions of its first three parts. See ibid., p. 679.

123. For the text of the recommendations, see American Journal of International Law, 1927, Supplement, pp. 58-66; Carnegie, Treaties, pp. 181-184.

124. Ibid., pp. 181-182.

125. See infra, pp. 255-257.

Chapter 8
VICISSITUDES OF CHINA'S REORIENTED FOREIGN RELATIONS

I. ESTABLISHMENT OF SINO-SOVIET RELATIONS

1. Soviet Declarations of Friendship with China

Contrary to Japanese allegations, Bolshevik propaganda had nothing to do with the May fourth Incident of 1919, which was a spontaneous expression of Chinese patriotism against Japanese imperialism and pro-Japanese officials.[1] While the incident created a movement favorable to the spread of revolutionary ideas, it was not instigated or organized by any political party. There was actually little contact between China and the Soviet Union before the Karakhan Declaration to be analyzed below. Even though letters were exchanged between Sun Yat-sen and George V. Chicherin, Soviet Commissar for Foreign Affairs, in the fall of 1918, their communications merely conveyed mutual greetings and good wishes. At that time, Sun had not yet been able to establish a solid revolutionary base in the Southwest,[2] and the Russian Bolsheviks were still confronted with Allied intervention and civil strife. In concluding his letter, however, Chicherin expressed the hope that efforts would be made to "close the ranks in the great fight for the common interests of the world proletariat." [3]

On July 25, 1919, Leo M. Karakhan, Deputy Commissar for Foreign Affairs, addressed a declaration "to the Chinese people and to the Governments of North and South China."[4] In both tone and content, the Karakhan Declaration clearly manifested the Soviet intention to reverse Czarist policy by taking the following steps: to abrogate the Sino-Russian Treaty of 1896,[5] the Final Protocol of 1901,[6] and all Russo-Japanese agreements concerning China concluded between 1907 and 1916;[7] to return to China everything taken from her by the Czarist government independently or together with Japan and the Allies;[8] to renounce all territorial acquisitions in Manchuria and other areas obtained by the Czarist government;[9] to revert, without compensation, the Chinese Eastern Railway (CER) and the mining, timber, gold, and other concessions seized by the Russians under previous regimes;[10] to disclaim the remaining portion of the Boxer indemnity;[11] and to disclaim the right of extraterritoriality and all special privileges, as well as Russian factories in China.[12] In addition to the principal points stated above, the Soviet government indicated its willingness to establish official relations and discuss other questions with Chinese representatives.

The Karakhan Declaration, issued only one month after the Paris Peace Conference failed to return former German rights in Shantung, demonstrated a vivid contrast between the attitudes of the Soviet Union and other powers toward China. Although the Peking government hesitated to take any action in response to the Soviet offers, Chinese people of various organizations and professions rejoiced at this friendly declaration. Due to the inaction of the Peking government at the time and subsequent consolidation of Bolshevik power, the Soviet government made no immediate efforts to implement its promises. Yet Chinese enthusiasm generated by the Karakhan Declaration remained in the minds of many intellectuals, who had long been disillusioned with the warlord rule in the North and imperialistic policies of Japan and many Western powers.

After the Peking government sent a special delegation to Moscow for preliminary negotiations, the Soviet government issued, on September 27, 1920, another declaration signed by Karakhan, reasserting the proposals contained in the 1919 declaration except for reservations concerning the Chinese Eastern Railway.[13] Following the 1920 declaration, a number of Soviet representatives, including M. I. Yurin, A. K. Paikes, and Adolph A. Joffe went to Peking for exploratory talks. Because the questions of Outer Mongolia and the Chinese Eastern Railway could not be solved in a manner satisfactory to both governments, nothing was resolved until the conclusion of two agreements between Peking and Moscow in 1924.

2. Sino-Soviet Agreements of 1924

Soviet strategy toward China in the 1920's was to support the revolutionary forces in the South and negotiate with the Peking government for the establishment of diplomatic relations. Following his second declaration, Karakhan addressed a note to the Chinese Minister of Foreign Affairs on October 27, 1920, proposing the conclusion of an agreement embodying general principles and a special one regulating the Chinese Eastern Railway. Finally, formal negotiations took place between Karakhan and C. T. Wang of the Peking government. On March 14, 1924, the two plenipotentiaries signed the completed treaty. Unexpectedly, however, Wang's signature was disavowed by his own government largely due to the pressure from France, Japan, and the United States. These powers looked with disfavor on China's unilateral entrance into any agreement with the Soviet government detrimental to their interests. [14]

Appealing to public opinion, Karakhan released the text of the signed treaty. Meanwhile, Michael M. Borodin made an attempt to negotiate locally with Chang Tso-lin, virtual ruler of Manchuria, where the Chinese Eastern Railway was located. Soon afterward, V. K. Wellington Koo, Chinese Foreign Minister, resumed talks with Karakhan. On May 31, 1924, two agreements were concluded, not essentially different from the repudiated treaty.

The Agreement on General Principles for the Settlement of the Questions, with Six Declarations and Exchange of Notes, contained the following provisions for the resumption and regulation of diplomatic relations between the two countries: [15]

(1) annulment of all conventions, treaties, agreements, protocols, contracts, etc. concluded between China and the Czarist government and negotiation for new ones to replace them "on the basis of equality, reciprocity and justice, as well as the spirit of the Declarations of the Soviet Government of the years 1919 and 1920" (Art. III);

(2) Soviet promise to terminate all treaties, agreements, etc. concluded between the Czarist government and any third party or parties which affected the sovereign rights or inter-

ests of China, and mutual guarantee not to conclude any treaties or agreements prejudicial to the sovereign rights or interests of either of them (Art. IV);

(3) Soviet recognition of Outer Mongolia as "an integral part of the Republic of China," respect for "China's sovereignty therein," and withdrawal of Soviet troops then in Outer Mongolia (Art. V);

(4) mutual pledge not to permit any organized activities within their territories or engage in any propaganda against either of the contracting parties (Art. VI);

(5) maintenance of the present boundaries pending redemarcation and regulation of navigation of waterways bordering the contracting parties on the basis of equality and reciprocity (Arts. VII, VIII);

(6) Soviet renunciation of the Russian portion of the Boxer indemnity, extraterritoriality, as well as other special rights and privileges relating to all concessions in China acquired by the Czarist government (Arts. X-XII);

(7) conclusion of a commercial treaty and formulation of a customs tariff on the basis of equality and reciprocity (Art. XIII); and

(8) settlement of the question of the Chinese Eastern Railway in accordance with Article IX of this agreement and a special agreement for that purpose.

The above were the essential points of this general agreement. Detailed arrangements were to be worked out by conferences between the two contracting parties.[16] Whatever the actual development in later years might be, the agreement itself was not only equal in terms but also significant in that it settled three major issues: first, Soviet recognition of China's sovereignty over Outer Mongolia; second, termination of all concessions, special rights and privileges acquired through unequal treaties, including extraterritoriality and tariff restrictions; third, acknowledgment of China's right to the Chinese Eastern Railway. For a nation which suffered unequal treatment from major powers for eight decades, this agreement undoubtedly created great excitement in China.

The Chinese Eastern Railway was constructed and operated in accordance with the Sino-Russian Bank (Russo-China

Bank, later known as Russo-Asiatic Bank) Contract of September 8, 1896.[17] It was ostensibly a jointly-managed commercial enterprise; but, for all practical purposes, Russia exercised control of the line to further her political and economic penetrations into Manchuria. During the Bolshevik Revolution, China notified the Bank concerned to assume provisional control of CER pending the establishment of a new government in Russia recognized by her. An agreement was signed with the Bank on October 2, 1920, as a supplement to the 1896 contract.[18] For the settlement of the status and operation of the railway, the Soviet Union and China concluded, on May 31, 1924, the Agreement for the Provisional Management of the Chinese Eastern Railway, with Declaration,[19] supplementary to the provisions of Article IX of the Sino-Soviet Agreement on General Principles of 1924.

The contracting parties agreed that the Chinese Eastern Railway, as a purely commercial enterprise, was only concerned with matters pertaining to its business operations, and could be redeemed by the Chinese government with Chinese capital under conditions settled at a conference.[20] For the provisional management of the railway, the two governments were to appoint five members each to constitute the board of directors, with one Chinese director as its president and director-general and one Russian director as its vice-president and assistant director-general. There was also to be a board of auditors, composed of two Chinese and three Russian auditors; its chairman was to be elected from among the Chinese auditors. For the general administration of the railway, the board of directors was to appoint one manager (Russian) and two assistant managers (one Russian and one Chinese). Other employees, including the chiefs and assistant chiefs of departments, would be appointed by the board of directors on the principle of equitable representation between nationals of the two contracting parties. The statutes of the railway, approved by the Czarist government on December 4, 1896, were to be revised in accordance with the new provisions of the 1924 agreements.[21] The above detailed description is necessary because of the extreme importance of the Chinese Eastern Railway in international politics.

Although the terms for the settlement of CER had not been faithfully carried out, the signing of the two agreements in 1924 marked a turning point in China's modern relations with foreign powers. The sympathetic attitude of the Soviet Union toward oppressed nations as repeatedly declared at that time also gave impetus to the spread of socialism and the growth of the Communist Party in China. While negotiating for the establishment of diplomatic relations with Peking, the Soviet Union simultaneously dispatched advisers to Canton to help Sun Yat-sen reorganize the Nationalist Party for the intensification of the anti-warlord and anti-imperialist movement.

II. CONVERGENCE OF CHINA'S REVOLUTIONARY FORCES

1. Formation of the Chinese Communist Party

In the search for new ideas and programs for national salvation, Chinese intellectuals were attracted not only by the revolutionary principles of Sun Yat-sen but also by other radical approaches from ultra-nationalism[22] to communism. Led by Ch'en Tu-hsiu and Li Ta-chao, yung liberals began to study Marxism as successfully introduced in Russia. The Karakhan Declaration abolishing all unequal treaties with China greatly inspired Chinese interest in socialist ideas. Then, in May 1920, the Communist International sent Gregori Votinsky to China to organize Marxist societies in Shanghai, Peking, and other places.[23] The most important leaders in charge of various socialist groups at that time were Ch'en Tu-hsiu in Shanghai, Li Ta-chao in Peking, and Mao Tse-tung in Hunan. Chou En-lai and Ch'en Yi led similar activities among the Chinese residing in France.

In pursuance of the policy laid down by its second world congress held in the fall of 1920, the Third International intensified the promotion of communism in China. With the assistance of its representative, G. Maring,[24] the Chinese Socialist Youth Corps later known as the Chinese Communist Youth[25] was soon organized in Shanghai. On July 1, 1921, the Chinese Communist Party was founded in Shanghai. Although the Party's first congress was only attended by twelve delegates representing less than sixty members in the country, [26] it marked a new chapter in the history of China. Ch'en Tu-hsiu, then in Canton, was elected secretary-general of the Party; Mao Tse-tung became secretary of its Hunan branch in October of the same year.27 Stimulated by Communist activities, the awakened workers in China soon formed the All-China Labor Federation, which held its first congress in Canton in May 1922.

The position of the Chinese Communist Party toward foreign powers was elaborately presented in the manifesto of its second congress,28 which was convened in July 1922. After condemning imperialist aggression against China for the past eighty years, the manifesto made the following analysis of the international situation:

"There are two trends in the present-day world politics which run directly counter to each other: (1) the capitalist-imperialist powers of the world which are jointly attempting to subjugate the proletariat and the oppressed peoples throughout the world; (2) the revolutionary movement which aims at the overthrow of international capitalist imperialism, that is, the world revolutionary movement and the oppressed peoples' national revolutionary movement, both led by the Communist International and Soviet Russia — the vanguard of the world proletariat.

"The revolutionary forces of these two movements against capitalist imperialism — the proletarian revolution and the national revolution — become more closely united with each passing day. These united revolutionary forces are bound to throw the decaying corpse of world capitalism into the grave that it has dug for itself. In the past few decades, the forces of the Chinese people that arose to resist imperialist oppression have grown considerably — and will continue to grow in even greater measure. But the anti-imperalist movement of the Chinese people must join forces with the national revolution of all the oppressed peoples of the world and unite with the world proletarian revolutionary movement in order to overthrow quickly the common oppressor — international capitalist

imperialism. This is the only path for the toiling
masses in China to take if they are to liberate
themselves from imperialist oppression." [29]

In conclusion, the manifesto called for the overthrow of
the warlords in order to establish peace in China and the
liquidation of imperialist oppression so as to achieve national
independence. The Communist congress adopted a rather conciliatory policy toward the Nationalist Party. Meanwhile, it
decided to join the Communist International to promote world
revolution. Thus, in 1922, shortly after the adjournment of the
Washington Conference, all signs in China pointed to a relent-
less struggle against domestic warlords and imperialist powers. At its third national congress, held in Canton in June 1923,
the Chinese Communist Party resolved to carry out this mission under the banner of the Chinese Nationalist Party, which
was recognized as the central force of national revolution at
that time.[30]

2.   Adversities of the Nationalist Party, 1912-1923

From 1912 to 1923, the Chinese Nationalist Party had
undergone many changes in the midst of China's political
turmoil. When the Republic was established in 1912, the
revolutionary organization T'ung-meng Hui merged with other
political groups to form the Nationalist Party (Kuomintang),
which controlled a majority of votes in the Parliament. The
party was disbanded by President Yüan Shih-k'ai in November
1913, consequent to the failure of the 'Second Revolution'
raised by its leaders in the Southeast.[31] In order to meet the
changing situation, Sun Yat-sen reorganized it into the Chinese Revolutionary Party (Chung-hua Ko-min Tang) on July
8, 1914.

Sun commanded high respect from his followers, but many
members did not join the new party owing to their objection
to the required oath of personal loyalty. Meanwhile, overseas
branches still used the traditional name to avoid registration
difficulties with local authorities. In consideration of these
factors, Sun decided, on October 10, 1919, to change the party
title to the Chinese Nationalist Party (or the Nationalist Party
of China — Chung-kuo Kuomintang), generally known as the

Nationalist Party or Kuomintang. The renamed party was still under the absolute leadership of Sun, who remained its Director-General (Tsung-li or Leader) for the rest of his life.[32]

The political situation in China during that period was extremely unstable. For a short span of two years and four months after the death of Yüan Shih-k'ai on June 6, 1916, the Presidency of the Peking government changed hands three times. The substitution of a new Parliament and the drafting of a new constitution in Peking were resented by many leaders in the Southwestern provinces, where Sun established his power base and conducted military expeditions against the North in the name of protecting the Provisional Constitution of 1912 and restoring the old Parliament.[33] On August 25, many members of the old Parliament convened an emergency session in Canton, and decided to organize a Military Government. On September 1, Sun was elected Generalissimo of the new regime. Soon after his assumption of the new office, however, several important members of the Military Government secretly negotiated for a compromise with the Peking government. Under the circumstances, Sun submitted his resignation and went to Shanghai.

Realizing the inadequate organization of the Military Government and its lack of leadership after Sun's resignation, the Emergency Session of Parliament decided to launch a formal government in Canton and then elected Sun as its President. Sun took over his new office on May 5, 1921, and concentrated his efforts on the task of the northern expedition. Then, on June 16, 1922, his subordinate, Ch'en Ch'iung-ming, engineered a coup d'etat.[34] Sun was eventually compelled to leave Canton for Shanghai, and did not return until February 11, 1923. By that time, the government in Canton was again reorganized and reverted to the Generalissimo system.[35] What has been said about Sun's political activities reflected the upheaval of China's domestic situation on the eve of his vital decision to ally with the Soviet Union and to admit the Chinese Communists into the Nationalist Party.

In 1919, Sun was still hopeful that the Paris Peace Conference would right the wrongs inflicted on China by foreign powers in the past. He even presented to the Western governments an elaborate plan for the material reconstruction of China, as embodied in his book, The International Development of China, 36 but his hope for their assistance was not fulfilled. Then the failure of the Paris Peace Conference to return the Shantung rights to China, the continuing disturbances in the North and the South, and the inability of the loosely organized Nationalist Party to carry out the revolutionary mission made him fully realize the necessity of a drastic change in his domestic and foreign policies. As previously stated, the success of the Washington Conference in 1921-1922 was insufficient to meet the expectations of the Chinese people and too late to turn the political tide in China. Both the Nationalist and Communist parties were leaning toward the Soviet Union for guidance and cooperation.

3. Nationalist Cooperation with the Soviet Union and the Chinese Communists

It was in December 1922 that Sun Yat-sen and Adolph A. Joffe met together in Shanghai and exchanged views on the world situation and domestic problems of China. On January 26, 1923, they issued a joint manifesto, which reads, in part, as follows:

"Dr. Sun Yat-sen holds that the Communist order or even the Soviet system cannot actually be introduced into China, because there do not exist here the conditions for the successful establishment of either Communism or Sovietism. This view is entirely shared by Mr. Joffe, who is further of the opinion that China's paramount and most pressing problem is to achieve unification and attain full national independence, and regarding this great task he has assured Dr. Sun Yat-sen that China has the warmest sympathy of the Russian people and can count on the support of Russia." 37

The Sun-Joffe manifesto laid down the foundation of Nationalist cooperation with the Soviet Union. In July 1923, Sun dispatched Chiang Kai-shek to Russia for an investigation of Soviet political and military conditions. After receiving first hand information from Chiang on current developments in China, Chicherin wrote to Sun on December 4, emphasizing mass organization and effective propaganda as important means to achieve the revolutionary task.[38] Moscow had earlier sent Michael M. Borodin to Canton as Sun's political adviser to assist in preparing for party reorganization, which was effected at its first national congress in Canton in January 1924.

Several important decisions adopted by the congress occupied an important place in China's recent political history. Among these were the so-called three great policies: (1) cooperation with the Soviet Union, (2) admission of the Chinese Communists to the Nationalist Party, and (3) organization of peasants and workers as the backbone of the mass movement. Sun Yat-sen was anxious to solicit Soviet cooperation in carrying out his revolutionary programs,[39] but had not the slightest idea of introducing Communism in China as explicitly stated in his joint manifesto with Joffe. In order to avoid any possible misunderstanding, he emphatically pointed out: "The Comunists are joining our Party in order to work for the national revolution.... In any case, if the Communists betray the Kuomintang, I will be the first to propose their expulsion."[40] In his policies toward peasants and workers, Sun preferred peaceful cooperation to class struggle.[41] For the training of a revolutionary army, he founded the Whampoa Military Academy in May 1924, with Chiang Kai-shek as its President. Among the Soviet military advisers in Canton was General Galens, known as Marshal Blücher while leading the Soviet Far Eastern Army after the outbreak of the Sino-Japanese War. All these events had a significant bearing on China's foreign relations in later years.

The first national congress of the Nationalist Party issued a manifesto, which laid down, among many other things, the guidelines of China's foreign policies for the observance of the Party and the government. The following were the essential points: (1) abrogation of all unequal treaties; (2) conclusion of new treaties on the basis of absolute equality and mutual respect for sovereign rights; (3) granting of the most-favored-nation treatment to treaty powers which would voluntarily renounce their special rights and privileges; (4) revision of other treaties prejudicial in any way to the interests of China; (5) assignment of the remaining Boxer indemnities for educational purposes; and (6) repayment of legitimate foreign loans, but not those previously contracted by the irresponsible governments in Peking to the detriment of the political interests and public welfare of the Chinese people. [42] This manifesto has been considered an extremely important document in the history of Chinese revolution, because all the points summarized above have served as the bases of China's foreign policies for several decades.

Sun Yat-sen died on March 12, 1925. The abolition of unequal treaties was stressed in his testament. The importance of Sun's will warrants its reproduction in English as follows:

"For forty years I have devoted myself to the cause of National Revolution, the aim of which is to secure for China a position of independence and equality among nations. The accumulated experience of these forty years has fully convinced me that to attain this goal, it is necessary to awaken the mass of our own people and associate ourselves with those peoples of the world who treat us on a footing of equality in the common struggle.

"At present, the work of the Revolution is not yet achieved. Let all my comrades follow my writings, 'The Program of National Reconstruction,' 'The Outline of National Reconstruction,' 'The Three People's Principles,' and 'The Manifesto of the First National Congress of the Party,' and work unceasingly for their ultimate realization. Above all, the convocation of a National People's Convention and the abolition of unequal treaties, which I have recently advocated, should be accomplished within the shortest possible time. This is my last will." [43]

At its second national congress held in Canton, in January 1926, the Nationalist Party formally accepted Sun's will as the fundamental charter of party programs, to be recited at the opening of every public meeting under Nationalist rule. In spite of numerous setbacks, the party's determination to abolish unequal treaties had been carried out. The following chapter will describe, in detail, the slow but steady process and the final achievement of this difficult task.

III. CONFRONTATION BETWEEN NATIONALISM AND IM-
PERIALISM

1. Causes and Consequences of the
May 30th Incident

The decision of the first national congress of the Nationalist Party in 1924 to admit the Chinese Communists formed the so-called first united front of China's revolutionary forces. Notwithstanding internal frictions, the two parties worked hard, jointly and individually, to organize the mass movement. Membership of peasant associations in South China was considerably expanded within a year. Meanwhile, the All-China Labor Federation decided, at its second national congress in Canton, to intensify union activities.[44] As always, students were eager to take part in any patriotic crusade.

The year 1925 was marked with numerous strikes of both political and economic nature. The May 30th incident, in particular, generated nation-wide sentiment against imperialism. It originated at the memorial service of Ku Chunghung at the International Settlement in Shanghai. A laborer at a Japanese textile mill in Yangtzepoo, Shanghai, Ku was killed during the course of a strike at the mill in the middle of the month. Many students and workers attended the service to demonstrate their sympathy to the deceased and their anger at Japanese brutality. The British police first arrested some forty demonstrators, then opened fire on the others who went to the police station demanding their release. The seriousness of the May 30th incident was fully stated in the note sent by the Chinese Ministry of Foreign Affairs to the Diplomatic Body at Peking on June 3. In addition to those arrested, the note pointed out that "four were killed outright, six seriously wounded, of whom two succumbed a little while afterward, and seventeen slightly wounded, three of whom died later."[45] In contrast, the police suffered no casualties. This proved that the demonstrators did not resort to violence and hence the shooting could not be justified.

At the request of the diplomatic representatives in Peking, an international commission of judicial inquiry was set up for the purpose of investigating the incident. It was composed of E. Finley Johnson (American), K. Suga (Japanese), and H.G. Gollan (British). Since American authorities were not involved in the incident, Judge Johnson's report was noteworthy for its objectivity. He first traced the long-standing causes of Chinese dissatisfaction with the International Settlement in Shanghai. These included: (1) extraterritoriality and the status of the Mixed Court; (2) no representation in the municipal council and hence loss of sovereign right over that part of Chinese territory; and (3) extension of roads beyond the bounds of the International Settlement.

Among the immediate and proximate causes were the failure to prosecute the Japanese responsible for the killing of the Chinese laborer and to release the students arrested by the police. Then lack of appropriate compensation to the wounded and to the familes of the dead and the resort to still more shooting further infuriated the Chinese. Above all, Judge Johnson pointed out "the failures on the part of the foreigners in China to realize that the Chinese people have made greater advancement during the past ten years in civics, in the fundamental principles of government and in the better understanding of individual rights under the law, than they have made in any one hundred years during their entire history." [46]

Because there was no settlement of the May 30th incident through diplomatic channels, strikes and boycotts extended to other parts of the country. Another serious incident took place on June 23 of the same year in the British and French concessions in Canton, locally known as Shameen. When a procession of Chinese demonstrators passed Shakee Street, British and French authorities ordered the police to open fire. Consequently, according to an estimate of the Chinese local government, over one hundred were killed and wounded. The British consul-general claimed, however, that the attack came from the Chinese side first. Failure to reach a settlement resulted in an intensified strike against Hongkong and a boycott of British goods. Although the Chinese party and government leaders made known their indignation at British brutality and stubbornness both prior to and after the June 23rd incident,[47] the demonstration and subsequent strike were spontaneous expressions of Chinese patriotism against imperialist oppression.

2. Conciliatory Policies of the
United States and Great Britain

After consolidating its power in Kwangtung province, the Nationalist Party formally established a National Government in Canton on July 1, 1925. As Commander-in-Chief of the National Revolutionary Forces, Chiang Kai-shek directed military campaigns against the warlords. Beginning in May 1926, the Northern Expedition became so successful that, within a few months, Central and Southeast China fell under Nationalist control and the National Government moved from Canton to Wuhan. Both the United States and Great Britain realized the irresistible trend of the nationalistic awakening of China. On January 27, 1927, the Department of State declared that the American government was ready "to continue the negotiations on the entire subject of the tariff and extraterritoriality." The statement also reminded the Chinese people that the United States "holds no concessions in China and has never manifested any imperialistic attitude toward that country." [48]

On the same day, the British government addressed proposals for treaty modification to the Chinese authorities at Peking and Wuhan. To Great Britain, a realistic approach in response to Chinese nationalism was more urgent than to the United States. The strike against Hongkong was over, but anti-British emotions had not yet dissipated. During the course of the Northern Expedition, British concessions in Hankow and Kiukiang were taken over by the Chinese authorities. In the proposals, the British government expressed its willingness to modify extraterritorial rights and the administration of British concessions and settlements in China. In his communication to Foreign Minister Chen Yu-jen of the Nationalist government in Wuhan, British representative O'Malley stressed that immediate steps would be taken to effect the proposals if the Nationalist government could reach a satisfactory settlement of the controversy over British concessions in Hankow and Kiukiang and give assurances not to alter the status of other concessions and settlements except by negotiations. [49]

Concerned with the possible repetition of the seizure of Hankow and Kiukiang concessions in Shanghai, the British government dispatched troops to China to safeguard the International Settlement. In its letter to the Secretary-General of the League of Nations on February 8, 1927,[50] the British government complained about anti-British agitation in China and expressed its readiness to welcome the good offices of the League in settling outstanding questions with the Chinese authorities. Fortunately, Shanghai fell to the Nationalists in March without any armed conflict between Chinese and British troops. There were two important factors contributing to the peaceful situation. First, the Nationalists were then more restrained and preferred negotiations to confrontation with foreign powers. At that time, the relationship between Chiang Kai-shek and the Communists was worsening. Second, British statesmen were earnestly searching for a fair and conciliatory policy based on the new situation in China. Agreements between the two countries had already been reached for the rendition of the British concessions in Hankow (February 19) [51] and Kiukiang (February 20/March 2).[52] The Chinese government issued regulations governing the administration of these places to the satisfaction of all parties concerned.[53]

3. The Nanking Incident and Its Settlement

An unfortunate incident took place in Nanking on March 24, 1927, when Nationalist troops defeated the Northern army and entered the city. As a consequence of armed distrubances caused by undisciplined soldiers, rebels, or agents provocateurs, foreign lives and property suffered injuries and damages and several consulates were intruded into. American and British warships stationed in the Yangtze River bombarded the city, resulting in a loss of Chinese lives and property. The United States, Great Britain, Japan, France, and Italy simultaneously protested to the Chinese authorities and demanded punishment of those responsible for the disturbances, complete reparations for personal injuries and material damage, as well as an apology in writing with assurances of preventing all forms of violence in the future.[54]

The Nationalist government, in its separate replies, expressed profound regret for the incident. While mainly complying with their demands, it condemned the naval bombardment and reminded the powers that the root of anti-foreign sentiment was the unequal treaties. [55] In his note to American Minister MacMurray on March 30, 1928, for the settlement of the Nanking incident, General Huang Fu, then Foreign Minister of the Nationalist government in Nanking, stated that "although it has been found, after investigation of the incident, that it was entirely instigated by the Communists prior to the establishment of the Nationalist government at Nanking, the Nationalist government nevertheless accepts the responsibility therefor."[56] Notes were also exchanged with other powers concerned to the same effect.[57] Thus the Nanking incident was amicably closed.

4. Japan's Armed Intervention in Tsinan

Japan was the last of the five powers to reach agreement with China on the settlement of the Nanking incident,[58] and the only country which used force to obstruct the unification movement of China. The incident in question occurred in Tsinan on May 3, 1928. After the return of former German rights in Shantung to China, Japan had kept some mining and other interests in that province. When the Chinese revolutionary forces marched northward near Shantung, Japan dispatched a substantial number of troops to Tsinan, ostensibly for the protection of Japanese lives and property. Hostilities began immediately after the Nationalist conquest of Tsinan on May 1. The Chinese forces did everything possible to avoid serious conflict, but the Japanese troops shelled the city and shot to death many disarmed soldiers and civilians on May 3. Even the Chinese Commissioner of Foreign Affairs, Ts'ai Kung-hsi, and his staff stationed in the city were slaughtered. All party and government officials, including Foreign Minister Huang Fu, were compelled to leave the city for safety. [59]

In order to justify the atrocities resulting from her armed intervention, Japan tried to shift the responsibility to the Chinese side. The Japanese commander even insisted on the following demands: (1) apology from the Chinese Commander-in-Chief; (2) punishment of Chinese officers responsible for the incident; and (3) suspension of hostilities, propaganda, and military activities within seven miles of Tsinan and the Shantung (Tsinan-Tsingtao) Railway. Japan's intervention was

evidently intended to hamper the advances of the revolutionary army to Peking. For the purpose of avoiding further
conflict, the Nationalist authorities yielded to the demands
and continued the task of the Northern Expedition.[60] The
Tsinan incident was not settled until the two countries signed
an agreement on May 28, 1929, by which Japan promised to
withdraw her troops from Shantung within two months.[61]

At this juncture, mention should also be made of Japan's
determination to prevent Nationalist forces from entering
Manchuria. On May 18, 1928, China was warned that should
the Nationalist army pursue Chang Tso-lin's into Manchuria,
Japan would disarm the troops of both sides. China's unification was achieved at the end of 1928 by peaceful arrangement
with Chang Hsueh-liang, who succeeded his deceased father
as commander of the Manchurian forces.[62]

5.   Enmity to All, Friendship to None

Domestically unified in 1928, China was diplomatically
isolated under the slogan 'Down with Imperialism'. Agitation
against Great Britain and other Western powers became the
maxim of the Chinese Communists, who exercised great
influence on the foreign policies of the Nationalist government in Wuhan. Although Western powers reacted with moderation to the Nanking incident, China demanded nothing less
than the abolition of all unequal treaties. Because of the
Tsinan incident, animosity between China and Japan deepened.
After the Nationalist purification movement against the Chinese Communists, Sino-Soviet friendship began rapidly deteriorating.

The Nationalist government lost no time in conducting
individual negotiations with the powers concerned to terminate unequal treaties, which will be fully discussed in the following chapter. In the case of the Chinese Eastern Railway,
there developed a direct confrontation between the local administration in Manchuria and the Soviet Union. On the ground
of Soviet dissemination of Communist propagands in violation
of the 1924 agreements, the Chinese authorities raided Soviet
consulates in several cities along the railway. Then China
took control of CER on July 11, 1929. In retaliation, Soviet
troops resorted to military operations against the Manchur-

ian army in the fall of 1929. Although the dispute was eventually settled by the Khabarovsk Protocol of December 22, 1929,[63] the Chinese Eastern Railway crisis caused extreme anxiety to many Western powers at the time.

Since both China and the Soviet Union were signatories to the General Treaty for the Renunciation of War or the Kellogg-Briand Pact of 1928, the United States, Great Britain, France, Italy, and several other nations reminded the disputing parties of their obligation not to resort to war.[64] The Soviet Union refuted the idea that any signatory could assume the role of guardian of the Pact and, in its note to the United States, questioned the American right to render advice and direction in this respect especially since no official relations existed between the two countries.[65] According to Max Beloff, "the whole incident, and the Russian note in particular, served to revive American memories of Russian imperialist aggressiveness."[66] It is important to note that, throughout the crisis, Japan maintained a rather neutral position, even though her interest in Manchuria was in direct conflict with the Soviet Union.

In the 1930's, China stood almost alone in the international community. Perhaps not entirely due to its own fault, the Nationalist government forstered a general mood of distrust in, if not enmity to, most of the major powers, but cultivated close friendship with none of them. It is understandable that, having suffered from decades of the bondage of unequal treaties, the Chinese people could not be expected to change their attitude overnight. In international politics, however, there are no permanent friends or enemies. National security and interest, not emotional or ideological considerations, should be the guiding principle for the formulation of foreign policies. Weakened by years of civil war and bordering on two strong neighbors, China should have at least maintained cordial relations, if not an alliance, with either Japan or the Soviet Union.[67] It was extremely unwise for her to defy both at the same time.

With respect to the Western powers, the United States had been sympathetic to China's nationalistic awakening, but she was geographically too far and politically unprepared to render any effective assistance at the time of emergency during the prewar period. Probably due to circumstances beyond her control, China did not succeed in establishing close ties with other Western powers, individually or collectively. Therefore, when Japan invaded Manchuria in 1931 and North China in the ensuing years, the Nationalist government had to endure the consequences of its isolated position. This intolerable situation was not perceptibly changed until the outbreak of World War II.

NOTES TO CHAPTER 8

1. Based upon his personal observations in nine provinces of China during the period of the May Fourth Movement, John Dewey concluded that "I have yet to find a single trace of direct Russian influence." See his "New Culture in China," Asia (July 1921), p. 584. For details of the May Fourth Movement, see supra, pp. 164-166.

2. For Sun's resignation from the office of the Generalissimo of the Military Government in Canton and his difficulty with the opportunistic militarists in the Southwest, see William L. Tung, The Political Institutions of Modern China, pp. 73-74.

3. In his letter to Sun Yat-sen on August 1, 1918, Chicherin wrote: "Like you, we are encountering incredible difficulties on our path. Surrounded by an iron ring of the bayonets of the imperialist Government, the hirelings of the bourgeoisie, the Czechoslovak hordes, and the Russian bourgeoisie, who desire to restore the monarchy in Russia, we are cut off from our friends, the proletariat of South China." For the text of the letter, see Jane Degras (ed.), Soviet Documents on Foreign Policy (New York, 1951, 3 vols.), I, pp. 92-93.

4. For the text of Karakhan Declaration of 1919, see ibid., I, pp. 158-161.

5. See supra, pp. 49, 75-76, 120.

6. See supra, pp. 53-54.

7. These include the Political Convention of July 30, 1907 (supra, pp. 50, 76, 77); the Convention in regard to Manchuria of July 4, 1910 (supra, p. 77); and the Convention in regard to Cooperation in the Far East of July 3, 1916 (supra, Ch. 4, note 38).

8. According to the Karakhan Declaration, the Soviet Union opened negotiations with the Peking government, for the return of Czarist acquisitions from China and the abrogation of all Czarist treaties detrimental to China; but, because of Allied pressure on Peking not to establish relations with Moscow, the negotiations were suspended in March 1918. See Louis Fischer, The Soviets in World Affairs 1917-1929 (Princeton, 1951, 2 vols.), II, p. 539.

9. The peoples in these areas would have the option of choosing which state they wish to dwell "and what form of government they wish to establish in their own countries." The passage in quotes was later omitted in any Russian text of the Declaration.

10. This item was omitted in any subsequent Russian text of the Declaration, but it appeared originally in the English translation from the French text as published by the Chinese Ministry of Foreign Affairs. The omitted passage reads as follows:

> "The Soviet Government returns to the Chinese people without demanding any kind of compensation, the Chinese Eastern Railway, as well as all the mining concessions, forestry, gold mines, and all the other things which were seized from them by the government of Tsars, that of Kerensky, and the Brigands, Hovat, Semenoff, Koltchak, the Russian Ex-generals."

The China Year Book, 1924-25, p. 869. For the complete text of the Declaration, see ibid., pp. 868-870.

11. The Declaration denounced the use of the Boxer indemnity to defray the expenses of the Czarist legation and consulates in China, and urged the Chinese people to expel the Czarist representatives. On September 23, 1920, the Peking government issued a Presidential mandate to terminate its relations with the Czarist Minister, Prince Koudacheff, and consuls in China. See The China Year Book, 1921-1922, p. 626.

12. In giving up the right of extraterritoriality, the Declaration emphasized that "not one Russian official, priest, or missionary shall be able to interfere in Chinese affairs."

13. For the English text, see ibid., 1924-1925, pp. 870-872; Allen S. Whiting, Soviet Policies in China, 1917-1924 (New York, 1954), Appendix c, pp. 272-275.

14. France protested any alteration of the management of the Chinese Eastern Railway, because the Russo-Asiatic Bank which financed the railway had been put under French protection consequent to the revolutionary turmoil in Russia. Japan claimed an immense investment of supplies in the railway for transporting Japanese troops to Siberia. The United States was concerned with the adverse effect on foreign interests which might result from a Sino-Soviet agreement. See Louis Fischer, op. cit., II, p. 545.

15. For the text, see League of Nations, Treaty Series, No. 955 (1925), Vol. 37, p. 176; Carnegie, Treaties, pp. 133-140. Re-establishment of diplomatic and consular relations were stipulated in Art. I.

16. See Art. II of the agreement.

17. See supra, Ch. 4, note 26; p. 120. For the text of the 1896 contract, see MacMurray, Treaties, I, pp. 74-79.

18. For the text, see Carnegie, Treaties, pp. 29-31.

19. For the text, see ibid., pp. 141-144.

20. See Art. IX (1-7) of the 1924 Agreement on General Principles.

21. See Arts. I-V, IX of the 1924 Agreement for the Provisional Management of the Chinese Eastern Railway. For the text of the 1896 statutes, see MacMurray, Treaties, pp. 84-88.

22. The Chinese Youth Party stood for nationalism and democracy. It was first founded on December 23, 1923, by a group of Chinese students in France. Among its leaders were Tseng Chi and Li Huang. Originally under the name of China Nationalist Youth Corps, the party adopted the present title at its fourth national congress in September 1929. Some traced its origin to 1918, when students in China and Japan organized the Young China Study Association. One of the two minor parties in Taiwan today, the party is anti-Communist and in close cooperation with the Nationalist Party. In the West, it is also known as the Young China Party. See China Handbook (Taipei, Taiwan), 1960-1961, p. 100.

23. Votinsky, also known as Wu T'ing-k'ang, came to China with his wife, a Russian secretary, and a Chinese interpreter, Yang Ming-chai. Yang devoted ten years to work and study in Russia, but was never active in the party organization after his return to China. See Tse-tsung Chow The May Fourth Movement, pp. 243-244, note (j).

24. G. Maring, alias H. J. F. M. Sneevliet, also visited Sun Yat-sen in the Southwest in the winter of 1921. See the Centeral Reform Committee of the Nationalist Party, Selected Works of the Director-General [Chiang Kai-shek] of the Nationalist Party (in Chinese; Taipei, 1952), p. 230.

25. The name was changed in 1925. Chou En-lai and several other Chinese students in France set up a similar organization in Paris in February 1921, four months after the establishment of the Shanghai Corps. See Po-tsan Chien and others, Concise History of China (Peking, 1964), p. 148.

26. The delegates attending the first congress of the Communist Party included Mao-Tse-tung, Tung Pi-wu, and Chang Kuo-t'ao. See Chiao-mu Hu, Thirty Years of the Communist Party of China (Peking, 1959), pp. 7-8.

27. For a brief description of the founding of the Chinese Communist Party, see Benjamin I. Schwartz, Chinese Communism and the Rise of Mao (Cambridge, 1961), pp. 31-36.

28. For the text of the manifesto, see Hua Hu and others (eds.), Source Materials of the History of the Chinese Revolution under China's New Democracy (in Chinese; Shanghai, 1951), pp. 69-84. An abridged text can be found in Conrad Brandt and others (eds.), A Documentary History of Chinese Communism (Cambridge, 1959), pp. 63-65.

29. English translation from Sheng Hu, Imperialism and Chinese Politics, p. 271.

30. For the text of the Manifesto of the Third National Congress of the Chinese Communist Party, see Hua Hu, op. cit., pp. 86-87.

31. See supra, pp. 153-154.

32. For details, see William L. Tung, The Constitutional and Political Systems of Prewar China, pp. 75-78.

33. See Yu-chiung Yang, Legislative History of Modern China (in Chinese; Shanghai, 1936), pp. 260-262.

34. For Sun's own statement about the coup d'etat, see Hsieh-ch'in Lei, Thirty Years of Turmoil in China (in Chinese; Hongkong, 1955), Vol. I, pp. 12-13. The following is an excerpt of his statement:

> "I and my comrades have fought a life and death struggle for the republic for about thirty years, suffering numerous ups and downs; yet never did we experience such a crushing failure. In the past, we frequently encountered setbacks at the hands of our enemies. This time, however, the enemy in the North had already been defeated, but a new enemy arose in the person of Ch'en Ch'iung-ming, who had been under my tutelage for more than ten years. His treachery and cruelty surpass that of any outside enemy. This is not only a misfortune for the Republic, but it indicates the degredation of morality in the country."

See also Sun's Declaration of the Second Constitution-Protecting Movement, The Collected Works of Sun Yat-sen, Vol. IV, under "Political Declaration through the Years," pp. 21-26.

35. See Lu Tsou, The Manuscript of the History of the Nationalist Party of China (in Chinese; Shanghai, 1929), Vol. II, p. 1077, Tuan-sheng Ch'ien and others, History of the Political Insti-

tutions under the Chinese Republic (in Chinese; Shanghai, 1939), Vol. I, p. 166.

36. Its English text was published by Putnam's Sons, New York, in 1922.

37. The China Year Book, 1924, p. 863. This manifesto can also be found in The Collected Manifestoes of the Nationalist Party (in Chinese), published by the Special Committee of the Mass Meeting at Nanking on the Memorial Day of Sun Yat-sen in 1928.

38. In his letter to Sun Yat-sen, Chicherin wrote:

> "We think that the fundamental aim of the Kuomintang Party is to build up a great powerful movement of the Chinese people and that therefore propaganda and organization on the biggest scale are its first necessities. Our example was significant: our military activities were successful because a long series of years had elapsed during which we organized and instructed our followers, building up in this way a great organized party throughout the whole land, a party capable of vanquishing all its adversaries. The whole Chinese nation must see the difference between the Kuomintang, a popular organized mass party, and the military dictators of the various parts of China."

Louis Fischer, The Soviets in World Affairs, Vol. II, p. 635.

39. See Hsieh-ch'in Lei, op. cit., pp. 20-21.

40. Leang-li T'ang, The Inner History of the Chinese Revolution, p. 178. In explaining the reasons for the Communists' decision to join the Nationalist Party, Li Ta-chao, one of the most important Communist leaders, stated:

> "Before joining it, we have made a detailed study both of the theories and of facts. Dr. Sun has given us permission to retain our relationship with the China branch of the Third International. Consequently, our joining this Party and at the same time keeping our membership in the Communist Party is an open and honorable action, not a surreptitious move. On the contrary, since we have joined the Party and so long as we remain its members, we shall carry out its political program and abide by its constitution and by-laws. We shall obey the disciplin-

ary measures or punishment imposed by this Party
in case we fail to do so."

Chiang Chung-cheng [Chiang Kai-shek], Soviet Russia in China,
p. 27.

41. See Sun's Labor Day Speech in 1924 under the title, "The Sufferings of the Chinese Workers from Unequal Treaties," and
also his speech before the Government Institute for the Training
of Workers for the Peasant Movement in Canton, August 23,
1924. Their text can be found in The Collected Works of Sun
Yat-sen (in Chinese; Shanghai: New Cultural Press, 21st ed.,
1929), Vol. III, pp. 189-196, 337-342.

42. For the text of the manifesto, see The Collected Laws of the
Chinese Republic (compiled by the Legislative Yuan of the
National Government, in Chinese; Shanghai, 1934), Vol. I, p. 24.
Its English translation can be found in Min-ch'ien T. Z. Tyau,
Two Years of Nationalist China (Shanghai, 1930), pp. 29-30.

43. The Collected Works of Sun Yat-sen (in Chinese; Shanghai,
Tai-chung Press, 1929), Vol. 4, Appendix, p. 13. Sun is also
revered by the Chinese Communists on the mainland as one of
China's great revolutionary heroes. For details, see William L.
Tung, The Political Institutions of Modern China, p. 106, note
2. The resistance to foreign aggression and abolition of unequal treaties were emphatically stated in Article 4 of 'The
Outline of National Reconstruction', formulated by Sun Yat-sen
on April 12, 1924. This Outline was one of Sun's writings listed in his last will, which was solemnly received by the Nationalist Party at the third plennary session of its Central Committee on May 2, 1925.

44. Its first congress was held in Canton in May 1922. Within a year,
there were more than a hundred strikes in various cities and
industrial areas. A bloody incident occured on February 7, 1923,
when General Wu Pei-fu's soldiers opened fire on railway
workers on strike in Hankow and Changhsintien, protesting
Wu's suppression of their attempt to organize the General
Trade Union of the Peking-Hankow Railway Workers. About
forty of them were killed and many injured. This massacre
reinforced their conviction to resist "armed counter-revolution
by armed revolution." Chiao-mu Hu, op. cit., pp. 10-11.

45. See The China Year Book, 1926-1927, p. 930.

46. Ibid., 1926-1927. p. 948.

47. Although French authorities were also involved in the incident,
Great Britain evidently became the main target. Besides pro-

tests from the Nationalist authorities in Canton, the Chinese Communist Party issued a declaration to the workers on strike in Hongkong and Canton on August 8, 1926. For its text, see Hua Hu and others, op. cit., pp. 141-143. For details of the Great Strike of Hongkong and Canton, see also Harold R. Isaacs, The Tragedy of the Chinese Revolution (Stanford, 1961), pp. 70-72, 106-107.

48. Carnegie, Treaties, pp. 196-197. For the full text of the American statement, see ibid., pp. 193-197; Congressional Record, 69th Cong., 2nd Sess. (February 21, 1927), p. 4387.

49. For the text of the British proposals, see League of Nations, Official Journal, Vol. 8, No. 3 (March 1927), p. 294; Carnegie, Treaties, pp. 197-198.

50. For the text, see League of Nations, Official Journal, Vol. 8, No. 3 (March 1927), p. 292; Carnegie, Treaties, pp. 199-202.

51. For the Agreement with regard to the British Concession at Hankow, see British Parliamentary Papers, China No. 3 (1927), Cmd. 2869, pp. 3-4, 12-14; Chinese Social and Political Science Review, Vol. 11, No. 2 (April 1927), Documents, p. 115; Carnegie, Treaties, pp. 203-205.

52. For the Agreement with regard to the British Concession at Kiukiang, see British Parliamentary Papers, China No. 3 (1927), Cmd. 2869, p. 3; The China Year Book, 1928, p. 739; Carnegie, Treaties, pp. 213-215.

53. For the Regulations of the Municipal Bureau of the Special Administrative District No. 3 of Hankow, February 19, 1927, see British Parliamentary Papers, China No. 3 (1927), Cmd. 2869, p. 4; Chinese Social and Political Science Review, Vol. 11, No. 2 (April 1927), Documents, p. 119; Carnegie, Treaties, pp. 205-213.

54. For the text, see British Parliamentary Papers, China No. 4 (1927), Cmd. 2953, p. 27; The China Year Book, 1928, p. 730; Carnegie, Treaties, p. 216.

55. For the replies by Nationalist Foreign Minister Eugene Chen to the British, American, and Japanese notes on April 14, 1927, see The China Year Book, 1928, pp. 731, 732, 733, respectively.

56. Carnegie, Treaties, p. 224. In a personal letter to General Huang on April 9, 1929, American Minister MacMurray wrote: "I believe that the settlement is one that does honor to both sides; and I realize how much credit for the result is due to your courage in doing what you felt to be right, regardless

of the opposition and criticism which you would encounter in some quarters by doing so.'' Yeh-yün Shen (Mrs. Huang Fu), Recollections of Yeh-yun (in Chinese; Taipei, 1968, 2 vols.), Vol. II, p. 358.

57. For the settlement of the Nanking incident, China exchanged notes with the United States on April 2, 1928 (Carnegie, Treaties, pp. 223-226); with Great Britain on August 9, 1928 (Chinese Social and Political Science Review, Vol. 12, No. 4, October 1928, p. 67); with Italy on September 24/30, 1928 (North China Herald, October 20, 1928, p. 81); with France on October 1/9, 1928 (loc. cit.); and with Japan on May 2, 1929 (Carnegie, Treaties, pp. 278-279).

58. See supra, note 14, for the dates when the Nanking incident was settled with the five powers.

59. For details of the Tsinan incident, see Yeh-yün Shen, op. cit., Vol. II, pp. 367-399; William L. Tung, Imperialism and China, Pt. II, pp. 57-68.

60. See Yeh-yün Shen, op. cit., Vol. II, pp. 385-386; Foreign Policy Association, Information Service, The Rise of Kuomintang (Vol. IV, No. 8), p. 182.

61. For the text of the Agreement in Settlement of the Tsinan Incident of May 3, 1928, see Carnegie, Treaties, pp. 274-275.

62. When Chang Tso-lin retreated from Peking to Manchuria, his train was bombarded. It was an open secret that Japan did not want him in Manchuria. He was seriously injured and died soon afterward. Disregarding Japanese warnings, Chang Hsueh-liang decided to join the Nationalist government for the unification of the country. For details of Japanese interests in Manchuria and its later development, see supra, pp. 75-77. infra, pp. 257-262.

63. This Protocol was preceeded by a provisional agreement, signed at Nikolsk on December 3, 1929. For the text of both documents, see J. W. Wheeler-Bennett and others (eds.), Documents on International Affairs (London: Royal Institute of International Affairs, 1928-1929), pp. 280-284. On October 11, 1930, representatives of China and the Soviet Union conducted negotiations at Moscow for the settlement of CER dispute, in accordance with the 1924 agreements. The conference was, however, postponed indefinitely after the Japanese invasion of Manchuria on September 18, 1931. The status of CER subjected to further changes after Japan's occupation of Manchuria. Disregarding China's protest, the Soviet Union sold the railway to

Japan's puppet state, Manchukuo, through an agreement on March 23, 1935. See The China Year Book, 1935, pp. 138-147.

64. See U. S. For. Rel., 1929, II, pp. 186-435.

65. See J. W. Wheeler-Bennett and others, op. cit., 1929, pp. 274-280.

66. Max Beloff, The Foreign Policy of Soviet Russia 1929-1941 (London, 1947, 2 vols.), Vol. I, p. 75. Soviet subversive activities in China were revealed in documents seized in the 1929 raid of the Soviet consulates. See Chinese Social and Political Science Review, Vol. 13, No. 4 (October 1929), Public Documents Supplement.

67. The Soviet Union broke off relations with the Peking government in April - May 1927, when the Soviet envoy was recalled in protest against the raid upon the Soviet Embassy in Peking by Chang Tso-lin. Sino-Soviet relations were not resumed until December 13, 1932. See The China Year Book, 1933, pp. 656-657.

Chapter 9
CHINA'S DIPLOMACY IN PEACE AND WAR FOR THE ABOLITION OF UNEQUAL TREATIES

I. BILATERAL NEGOTIATIONS PRIOR TO WORLD WAR II

1. China's Treaty Relations with Foreign Powers in 1928

As previously stated,[1] both the Nationalist and Communist parties sought the abolition of unequal treaties. At the time of its inauguration on July 1, 1925, the National Government in Canton reaffirmed its determination to achieve this objective. The year 1928 marked the reunification of China, with Nanking as the capital of the nation. In June of that year, altogether twenty-three countries had entered into treaty relations with China:[2] Austria,[3] Belgium,[4] Bolivia,[5] Brazil, [6] Chile, [7] Denmark,[8] Finland,[9] France, [10] Germany,[11] Great Britain,[12] Italy,[13] Japan,[14] Mexico, [15] the Netherlands, [16] Norway,[17] Persia, [18] Peru,[19] Portugal,[20] the Soviet Union, [21] Spain, [22] Sweden,[23] Switzerland,[24] and the United States. [25] As a consequence of World War I, China had already terminated unequal treaties with Austria, Germany, and Russia, and replaced these with new treaties based on the principles of equality and reciprocity.[26] On the same footing were the treaties China concluded with Bolivia, Chile, Finland, and Persia. Thus there were actually sixteen countries which enjoyed extraterritoriality and other unilateral privileges in China. Table III lists countries having treaty relations with China in 1928. Those entitled to treaty rights of extraterritoriality or restricted tariff rates are duly indicated.

TABLE III
COUNTRIES HAVING TREATY RELATIONS
WITH CHINA IN 1928

Those marked with * and/or § indicate countries entitled to treaty rights of extraterritoriality and/or restricted tariff rates as of June 1928.

Belgium*§	Netherlands*§
Brazil*	Norway*§
Denmark*§	Peru*
France*§	Portugal*§
Great Britain*§	Spain*§
Italy*§	Sweden*§
Japan*§	Switzerland*§
Mexico*	U.S.A.*§

For the abrogation of unequal treaties, the National Government in Nanking intended to negotiate new treaties on the bases of equality and reciprocity. During the transitional period, it promulgated, on July 7, 1928, Provisional Regulations governing Relations with Foreign Countries and Their Nationals. These included: (1) protection of foreign nationals and their property in China according to Chinese law; (2) obligation of foreign nationals residing in China to be amendable to Chinese law and subject to the jurisdiction of Chinese courts; (3) payment of the prevailing customs tariff pending the application of the Chinese national tariff; and (4) compliance of foreign nationals residing in China with Chinese revenue laws, paying all taxes on the same basis as the Chinese.[27] The steps taken by the Chinese government were not unilateral denunciations but bilateral negotiations, which differed from the multilateral approaches undertaken at the Paris Peace Conference of 1919 and the Washington Conference of 1921-1922. Early attempts were made by the Peking government to abrogate several treaties which had been concluded without the approval of the Chinese Parliament. The National Government at Nanking concentrated on negotiating new treaties to replace those due to expire or subject to revision.

2. Treaties not Having the Approval of the Chinese Parliament

On principle, a treaty comes into effect when it is ratified by the appropriate authorities of the signatory states, unless otherwise agreed upon. [28] The signing of a treaty imposes on the contracting parties a moral but not legal obligation to ratify it. Accordingly, the Peking government held that the failure of the Chinese Parliament to approve certain treaties constituted a valid ground for their renunciation. Although negotiations in this regard took place before the Nationalist Party came into power, these efforts served as a useful reference for the adoption of other means by the National Government to implement its objectives, and, therefore, deserve a brief review at this juncture.

The granting of extraterritoriality to Switzerland was based upon the Declaration attached to the Sino-Swiss Treaty of Amity of June 13, 1918. [29] In the process of its formal ratification in October 1921, the Chinese Parliament failed to approve the terms in the attached Declaration. Nonetheless, Switzerland insisted on the validity of this provision. Under the same category were the Sino-Japanese Treaties of May 25, 1915, [30] which failed to gain the approval of the Chinese Parliament. After informing the Japanese government of the situation on March 10, 1923, the Chinese Ministry of Foreign Affairs declared that, with the exception of those items already settled by the two countries or withdrawn by the Japanese government, all the provisions of these treaties have become null and void. The Japanese government ignored the Chinese declaration, and insisted upon its rights under the 1915 treaties. Thus, in both cases, China's arguments were not accepted by the contracting parties.

3. Treaties Due to Expire or Subject to Revision

The test case under this category was the Sino-Belgian Treaty of Commerce of November 2, 1865, [31] which was to expire on November 2, 1926. Six months before the date of its expriation, the Chinese government notified the Belgian government to that effect and requested the conclusion of a new treaty. The Belgian government argued that Article 46 of the Treaty empowered only Belgium to propose its revision. [32]

Since further negotiations did not yield an agreement, the Chinese government declared the Treaty non-operative on November 6, and turned down a Belgian proposal to submit the case to the Permanent Court of International Justice for judicial settlement on the ground that the dispute was essentially political in nature.[33] Upon the request of the Belgian government, however, the Court took jurisdiction of the case and issued a Provisional Order on January 8, 1927. When a new Sino-Belgian Treaty was concluded on November 22, 1928,[34] the Belgian government withdrew the case from the Court.[35] The new treaty was a compromise, under which the Belgian government recognized the Chinese right of tariff autonomy but would not relinquish extraterritoriality until the majority of states enjoying that right should agree to do so.[36]

The Sino-Franco Treaty of Commerce of April 25, 1886,[37] was to expire on August 7, 1926. According to Article 18 of the Treaty, a revision could be made ten years after the date of its conclusion. On March 4, 1926, the Chinese government requested the French government to negotiate for its revision.[38] The two governments began to discuss the matter on January 26, 1927, but did not reach a settlement. In the case of the Sino-Swedish Treaty of July 2, 1908,[39] the Chinese government informed the Swedish government, on November 2, 1928, that, in view of its impending expiration on June 14, 1929, negotiations for a new treaty were in order. In reply to the Chinese proposal on November 15, the Swedish government requested postponement of this consideration.

China's negotiations with Italy, Denmark, and Brazil yielded favorable results. In its note to the Italian government on June 30, 1928, the Chinese government expressed an intention to negotiate for a new treaty to replace the Sino-Italian Treaty of October 26, 1866,[40] which was due to expire. The two countries concluded a Preliminary Treaty of Amity and Commerce on November 27 of the same year,[41] in which the Italian government recognized China's tariff autonomy and promised to relinquish extraterritoriality as soon as other powers participating in the Washington Conference of 1921-1922 would agree to do so.[42] Similar provisions concerning tariff and extraterritoriality were stipulated in the Sino-Danish Preliminary Treaty of Amity and Commerce of December 12, 1928,[43] which was to replace the expiring Sino-

Danish Treaty of July 13, 1863.[44] Since the Sino-Brazilian Treaty of October 3, 1881[45] was to expire on June 3, 1932, the Brazilian government expressed its willingness to negotiate for a new treaty along the lines of the Sino-Italian Treaty of 1928. Due to China's preoccupation with the Japanese invasion, however, this proposed new treaty was not signed until 1943. [46]

In the 1930's, neither Great Britain nor the United States complied with China's requests for treaty revisions. On December 23, 1933, the Chinese government served notice to the British government of the expiration dates of two treaties: (1) October 24, 1930, for the Treaty of Tientsin of June 26, 1858;[47] and (2) July 28, 1933, for the Commercial Treaty of September 5, 1902.[48] Because the Sino-American Treaty of October 8, 1903[49] was due to expire on January 13, 1934, the Chinese government requested the United States government to consider its revision in a note dated December 23, 1933. Both the British and American governments agreed to open negotiations, but their unwillingness to relinquish extraterritoriality in the immediate future postponed any agreement with China.

One unique case was China's treaty relations with Spain. In pursuance of Article 23 of the Sino-Spanish Treaty of October 10, 1864,[50] China notified Spain of her intention to revise it. The Spanish government insisted that the proposed revision should be limited to tariff and commercial matters. Failing to reach an agreement, the Chinese government denounced the treaty on November 11, 1927. A Preliminary Treaty of Amity and Commerce was later concluded between the two countries on December 27, 1928,[51] almost identical to the Sino-Italian Treaty of November 27, 1928, in respect of tariff and extraterritoriality. [52] When civil war broke out in Spain in 1937, Spanish diplomats and consular officials left China. Seizing this opportunity, the Chinese government terminated Spain's right of extraterritoriality as she did in the case of Russia in 1920.

Protracted negotiations between China and Japan for treaty revision proved fruitless. In accordance with Article 26 of the Sino-Japanese Treaty of Commerce of July 21, 1896,[53] a revision could be made every ten years. At China's initiative, the two governments opened discussions on January 21, 1927.

The treaty in question should have expired on April 20, 1927, but was extended pending negotiations. Meanwhile, the Chinese government informed the Japanese government of the approaching expiration of the Sino-Japanese Supplementary Treaty of Commerce of October 8, 1903.[54] Because of the complicated relationships between the two countries, nothing resulted from the bilateral conferences.

Contrary to the attitudes of Japan and several other countries, Mexico was most cooperative with China in their negotiations for the replacement of the Sino-Mexican Treaty of December 14 of 1899,[55] which was due to expire on November 30, 1928. The Mexican government readily agreed to relinquish the right of extraterritoriality by an Exhange of Notes with the Chinese government on November 12, 1929.[56] Mexico was, therefore, the second country after the Soviet Union to renounce this right. The new Treaty of Amity, concluded on August 1, 1944, was entirely based upon the principles of equality and reciprocity.[57]

4. China's Achievement of Tariff Autonomy

After the adjournment of the Tariff Conference held at Peking in 1925-1926,[58] the American government reiterated its readiness to continue negotiations on the subject. This attitude was openly declared by Secretary of State Frank B. Kellogg on January 27, 1927.[59] The United States consequently concluded the first treaty with China restoring the latter's right of tariff autonomy on July 25, 1928, not long after the establishment of the National Government in Nanking.[60] It annulled all previous provisions relating to "rates of duty on imports and exports of merchandise, drawbacks, transit dues and tonnage dues in China," and applied "the principle of complete national tariff autonomy."[61]

In the same year, identical provisions were provided in China's tariff treaties with Norway (November 12),[62] the Netherlands (December 19),[63] and Sweden (December 20).[64] The same was embodied in China's preliminary treaties of amity and commerce of 1928 with Italy (November 27),[65] Denmark (December 12),[66] Portugal (December 19),[67] and Spain (December 27).[68] In the same year, China concluded tariff treaties with Great Britain (December 20),[69] and

France (December 22),[70] both of which attached certain reservations. Beginning with February 1, 1929, the Chinese National Tariff should have become operative,[71] but was left in abeyance until the tariff treaty with Japan went into effect on May 16, 1930.[72] Among the twelve countries entitled to the treaty right of restrictive tariff rates, the United States led and Japan concluded the list of new agreements with China for the restoration of her tariff autonomy as shown in Table IV.[73]

TABLE IV
FOREIGN POWERS WHICH CONCLUDED TREATIES
RELATING TO TARIFF AUTONOMY WITH
CHINA AND THEIR DATES OF SIGNATURE

(Listed according to dates of signature.)

Name of Country	Date of Signature
U.S.A.	7/25/1928
Norway	11/12/1928
Belgium	11/22/1928
Italy	11/27/1928
Denmark	12/12/1928
Netherlands	12/19/1928
Portugal	12/19/1928
Great Britain	12/20/1928
Sweden	12/20/1928
France	12/22/1928
Spain	12/27/1928
Japan	5/6/1930

5. Further Negotiations for Relinquishing
Extraterritoriality

Originally there were nineteen countries which enjoyed the right of extraterritoriality in China, namely, Austria-Hungary, Belgium, Brazil, Denmark, France, Germany, Great Britain, Italy, Japan, Mexico, the Netherlands, Norway, Peru, Portugal, Russia, Spain, Sweden, Switzerland, and the

United States.[74] Austria-Hungary and Germany lost this right as a consequence of World War I, and the Soviet Union voluntarily relinquished it after the Bolshevik Revolution in Russia. Thus, by 1928, sixteen countries still retained this much hated privilege in China. Consequent to the conclusion of treaties of amity and commerce in November and December of 1928, Belgium, Denmark, Italy, Portugal, and Spain agreed to its termination when other participating states of the Washington Conference of 1921-1922 or the majority of states enjoying extraterritoriality should give consent to the same.[75] Meanwhile, negotiations for a similar treaty with Japan were in progress.[76] There remained, therefore, ten more nations to be dealt with by the Chinese government.

On April 27, 1927, the Chinese government addressed identical notes to Great Britain, the United States, France, the Netherlands, Norway, and Brazil, expressing China's earnest desire to abolish extraterritoriality and "assume jurisdiction over all nationals within her domain."[77] It was hoped that once the consent of the six powers with comparatively greater interests in China could be obtained, the other four countries — Mexico, Peru, Sweden, and Switzerland — would follow suit.[78] Again, the attitudes of Great Britain, France, and the United States would be pivotal to the success or failure of negotiations. In their replies, these major powers stated that the existing conditions in China did not warrant the surrender of their nationals to the jurisdiction of Chinese courts, because the recommendations adopted by the Commission on Extraterritoriality had not been fully carried out. On the other hand, they had no objection to China's desire to choose January 1, 1930, as the starting point for the abolition of extraterritoriality.[79]

On December 28, 1928, the Chinese government issued a mandate, proclaiming that, beginning with January 1, 1930, "all foreign nationals in the territory of China who are now enjoying extraterritorial privileges shall abide by the laws, ordinances, and regulations duly promulgated by the Central and Local Governments of China."[80] In his statement two days later, Foreign Minister C. T. Wang implied that the actual application of the mandate would be effected by individual negotiations. The French government was adamantly opposed to the Chinese action and insisted that any revision of treaty rights had to be based upon mutual consent.[81] Consequently, Sino-French discussions yielded no progress.

Great Britain and the United States indicated their willingness to relinquish extraterritoriality through a gradual process to be applied first to civil cases and minor police offenses. They also attached conditions for a transitional period, including the engagement of foreign legal advisers, establishment of special chambers in Chinese courts, and temporary exclusion of Shanghai and other reserved areas. As a result of exchanges of proposals and counter-proposals, Great Britain and the United States made concessions to meet Chinese viewpoints.[82] Brazil, Norway, and the Netherlands also expressed their willingness to comply with Chinese wishes through exchanges of notes.[83] When agreements on the subject were almost in sight, Japan invaded Manchuria on September 18, 1931. Consequently, negotiations were temporarily suspended for the duration of China's national emergency.[84] It turned out that, among the sixteen countries, Mexico was the only one which actually agreed to relinquish extraterritoriality in China prior to World War II.[85]

Although treaty powers were not yet prepared to relinquish extraterritoriality in the immediate future, they did make one minor concession to China by accepting her proposal of reorganizing the Provisional Court at Shanghai on February 17, 1930. Subsequent to the rendition of the Mixed Court to the Kiangsu Provincial Government,[86] a Provisional Court was established for a period of three years. After the reorganization, a District Court for the Special Area in Shanghai and the Second Branch of the Kiangsu Provincial Court were created. Both courts were to apply Chinese laws and regulations, substantive and procedural. This new feature marked the beginning of the complete elimination of foreign interference with China's judicial system.[87]

II. SINO-JAPANESE HOSTILITIES (1931-1937)

1. Japan's Invasion of Manchuria

Ever since the termination of the Russo-Japanese War and the conclusion of the Sino-Japanese Convention and its Supple-

mentary Agreement on December 22, 1905,[88] Japan's influence in Manchuria had been rapidly increasing.[89] Group II of
the Twenty-one Demands fully revealed Japan's political and
economic designs in Manchuria, with territorial acquisition as
her ultimate objective.[90] When the Nationalist forces marched
to North China in 1928, the Japanese government even warned
that, should they pursue Chang Tso-lin's troops into Manchuria, both armies would be disarmed.[91] After Chang was
killed as a result of a Japanese plot on his way from Peking
to Mukden on June 4, 1928,[92] Japan exerted strong pressures
on Chang Hsueh-liang, known as the Young Marshal, who
succeeded his father as the virtual leader of Manchuria.
By persuasion and threats, Japanese officers tried to prevent
Manchuria from joining the National Government in Nanking
and to obtain for Japan the right to construct five more railways in Manchuria by local agreements.[93] Much to Japan's
indignation, Chang finally decided to take orders from Nanking
and surrender none of China's territorial sovereignty.

Japan's aggressive designs in China were intensified, when
General Giichi Tanaka, leader of the Seiyuka Party, became
Prime Minister in 1927. When the Minseito Party came to
power in 1929, the Japanese government adopted a conciliatory policy toward China. Foreign Minister Kijuro Shidehara
intended to settle various Sino-Japanese issues through negotiations. Because of the dual system of government, however, the army and navy were not entirely under the control
of the prime minister.[94] Frustrated by the changing situation
in Manchuria favorable to China's unification and disappointed
with the moderate policy of the civilian government in Tokyo,
the Japanese Kwantung Army stationed in Manchuria contemplated drastic action to turn the tide of events. China suffered the largest scale of civil war in 1930 and the most disas-
trous flood along the rich area of the Yangtze Valley in 1931.
Recognizing China's adversity as Japan's opportunity, the
belligerent officers decided to occupy Manchuria by military
means. In order to create a pretense, they carefully planned
an explosion on a railroad junction of the South Manchuria
Railway near Mukden on September 18, 1931. Japanese forces
immediately attacked Chinese barracks, and occupied first
Mukden and then other parts of Manchuria.[95]

Military operations of the Kwantung Army were originally
undertaken without orders from Tokyo; in the beginning, the

Japanese government tried to restrict troop movements to defensive purposes only. To avoid provocation, the Chinese forces received instructions not to resist. There was, therefore, no question of self-defense to justify Japan's action. Because of its inability to control the army and the Western powers' preoccupation with their own domestic affairs, the Japanese government later acquiesced in the fait accompli, and concentrated on consolidating its position in Manchuria and vindicating its action internationally. At that time, the United States had not yet recovered from the depression, and Great Britain was confronted with a currency problem leading to the abandonment of the gold standard. It was most unlikely that there would be any Anglo-American joint front against Japan. The Soviet Union was then not strong enough to defy Japan; nor could she solicit support from France or other powers to intervene in Japan's territorial conquest as Czarist Russia did in 1895. Pressed by the belligerent attitude of her army officers, Japan continued to carry out its expanionist policy, regardless of world public opinion. In the past, Japan had limited her action in China to the conclusion and execution of unequal treaties; but, after September 18, 1931, she resorted to direct invasion, in violation of the League Covenant, the Nine-Power Treaty, and the Kellogg-Briand Pact.

2. China's Appeal to the League of Nations

Both China and Japan were original members of the League of Nations,[96] and should have been bound by the provisions of the Covenant in the settlement of their disputes. [97] The Mukden incident came to the attention of the League Council on the day after it occurred. On September 21, Saoke Alfred Sze, the Chinese delegate,[98] requested the Council, under Article 11 of the Covenant, [99] to take whatever action necessary to restore peace in Manchuria, and indicated China's willingness to abide by League decisions. At its meeting on September 28, he proposed an investigation of the situation by a neutral commission with a view to effecting the early withdrawl of Japanese troops from Manchuria.[100] A resolution to appoint a Commission of five members was adopted by the Council meeting of December 10, "to study on the spot and to report to the Council on any circumstances which, affecting international relations, threatens to disturb peace between China and Japan, or the good understanding between them, upon which peace depends.''[101]

As formally constituted in the middle of January 1932, the Commission of Enquiry was headed by Lord Lytton (British), with Count Aldrovandi (Italian), General Henri Claudel (French), Major-General Frank R. McCoy (American), and Dr. Heinrich Schnee (German) as members.[102] China and Japan designated V. K. Wellington Koo and Isaburo Yoshida, respectively, as assessors. Not a member of the League of Nations but having a traditional interest in the Far East, the United States attached special importance to the crisis and agreed to participate in the Commission. At this juncture, mention should also be made of the famous Stimson doctrine of non-recognition of any situation created by forcible means. On January 7, 1932, Secretary of State Henry L. Stimson addressed to the Chinese and Japanese envoys at Washington identical notes, in which he pointed out the following:

"The American Government deems it to be its duty to notify both the Government of the Chinese Republic and the Imperial Japanese Government that it cannot admit the legality of any situation de facto nor does it intend to recognize any treaty or agreement entered into between these governments, or agents thereof, which may impair the treaty rights of the United States or its citizens in China, including those which relate to the sovereignty, the independence, or the territorial and administrative integrity of the Republic of China, or to the international policy relative to China, commonly known as the open door policy; and that it does not intend to recognize any situation, treaty, or agreement which may be brought about by means contrary to the convenants and obligations of the Pact of Paris of August 27, 1928, to which treaty both China and Japan as well as the United States are parties." [103]

Disregarding American policy and League resolutions, Japan created the puppet state 'Manchukuo' on February 18, 1932. With respect to non-recognition of 'Manchukuo', the Stimson doctrine was incorporated in the Assembly resolution of March 11, 1932,[104] and the Assembly report of February 24, 1933.[105] In this connection, an explanation should be made about the functions of the League Council and Assembly. According to the Covenant, both organs could deal with any matter within the competence of the League or affecting the peace of the world.[106] As a permanent member of the Council, Japan could exercise more influence on that body dominated by great powers, which generally laid stress on international reality rather than law and justice. In addition to Article 11, China then invoked Articles 10 and 15 of the Covenant, [107] and requested the transfer of the Sino-Japanese controversy to the Assembly. On March 3, 1932, a special session of the Assembly was convened to deal with the situation under Article 15.[108] It was also the Assembly which later considered the Lytton Report.

The Commission of Enquiry went to the Far East at the end of February 1932, and conducted a thorough investigation on the spot. Released on October 1,[109] the Report recommended ten principles as general bases for the final settlement of the dispute between the two countries.[110] In the main, the Report upheld China's territorial sovereignty in Manchuria, where the special interests of Japan would be recognized. It also proposed the promotion of Sino-Japanese relations and international cooperation in conformity with existing multilateral treaties.

The Report was later transmitted to the Assembly by the Council. On December 9, the Chinese delegate, Tai-chi Quo, stated that, on the bases of previous resolutions and in conformity with pertinent provisions of international treaties, China was ready to accept the recommendations, together with the resolution of March 11th, as the basis for practical negotiations. The Assembly adopted a resolution on the same date to set up a Special Committee of Nineteen to search for conciliatory measures for the settlement of the dispute. Because of Japan's insistence on recognizing 'Manchukuo' as an accomplished fact, no solution could be found. After the failure of its attempts at conciliation,[111] the Assembly adopted, on February 24, 1933, a draft report prepared by the Special Committee with suggestions based on the Lytton Report. [112] China voted for its adoption, but Japan notified the League of her intention to withdraw from this international organization on March 27, 1933. Since Japan's withdrawal would not take effect until two years later in accordance with the provisions of the Covenant, her obligations under the Covenant and resolutions of the League remained legally binding even though they went practically unfulfilled.[113]

3. Extension of Conflicts to Shanghai and North China

Before the arrival of the Lytton Commission in China, Japan waged the first battle of Shanghai on January 28, 1932. Because of the clash of a group of Japanese and an anti-Japanese mob at Chapei, a Chinese section of Greater Shanghai, the Japanese consul-general delivered an ultimatum to the mayor, demanding full satisfaction of all conditions, including the immediate disbanding of all anti-Japanese organizations. The terms were accepted, but the Japanese navy chose to use force anyway.[114] During the debate at the League Council, the Chinese delegate, W. W. Yen, bluntly pointed out that "Japan does not want to see China united and strong," as evidenced by her intrigues in recent decades. [115] The Chinese army offered stout resistance in Shanghai. The Lytton Commission observed that "the Shanghai affair undoubtedly exercised considerable influence on the situation in Manchuria," as "everywhere opinion hardened, and the spirit of resistance increased." [116] In pursuance of the resolution adopted by a special session of the Assembly convened in March, the British, French, and Italian diplomatic representatives in China helped the disputing parties conclude an armistice agreement on May 5, for the cessation of hostilities in Shanghai.[117]

Following the battle of Shanghai, Japan carried out more military ventures in North China. In 1933, the Japanese army conquered Jehol, and penetrated into Hopei. Subsequent to intensive fighting along the Great Wall, a truce agreement was signed at Tangku, by representatives of Chinese and Japanese commanders, on May 31, 1933,[118] and a demilitarized zone was set up in Hopei. After a one-year breathing spell, a new threat of Japanese aggression in North China compelled the Chinese government to sign the Ho-Umezu Agreement on July 6, 1935, which set the stage for the evacuation from Hopei province of all branches of the Nationalist Party and Chinese forces under the direct control of the Central Government.

On November 25, Japan created a semi-independent regime in Eastern Hopei. Meanwhile, an attempt was made to foment autonomous movements in Hopei, Shantung, Shansi, Chahar, and Suiyuan. Because of the firm but tactful attitude of the Chinese leaders and the British and American concern with new Japanese intrigues, this five-province autonomy did not materialize. Tokyo decided to be temporarily contented with the establishment of the Hopei-Chahar Council.[119] Nevertheless, the feeling prevailed that the Chinese people must be prepared to fight against the invader in order to save themselves.

4. Student Demonstrations in December 1935

Witnessing the unfolding of tragic events in a country under the oppression of domestic warlords and foreign imperialists, Chinese students had long been leaders of all patriotic movements as demonstrated by the May Fourth and the May Thirtieth incidents.[120] To carry out their longstanding struggle, students in Peking again endured sacrifices on March 18, 1926.[121] During the Northern Expedition from 1926 to 1928, they acted either independently or jointly with organized peasants and workers to help the revolutionary forces unify the country. Many of them were, however, disillusioned with the break-up of the first united front between the Nationalists and Communists. The Tsinan incident revived their anti-imperialist spirit,[122] which was further hardened by the Manchurian crisis.[123] Students from all over the country went to Nanking, petitioning the government to fight against the aggressor; colleges and universities in Peking and Shanghai became strongholds of this patriotic movement. There was a brief period of inactivity between 1932 and 1935, but the deteriorating situation in North China demanded their vehement action again.

When Japan pressured the provincial authorities in North China to set up an autonomous regime, students in Peking were deeply concerned with the possibility of the creation of another 'Manchukuo'. Having revived their student union in November 1935, they decided to march to the headquarters of General Ho Yin-ch'in on December 9. As Chiang Kai-shek's trusted lieutenant, Ho had just arrived in Peking to consult with local

leaders on how to save the situation. The main objective of
the students was to oppose Japan's device of setting up autonomous regimes to further encroach upon Chinese territory, [124]
because they suspected that the impending establishment of
the Hopei-Chahar Political Council, headed by General Sung
Che-yüan, might be a preliminary step in detaching the Northern provinces from the control of the Central Government.
Led by Yenching and Tsinghua universities, approximately
one thousand students representing fifteen institutions were
involved in the December 9th demonstration. Non-partisan and
genuinely patriotic, they marched in an orderly procession.
General Sung's soldiers and local police met them with force,
even though they did not resort to violence. This unfortunate
incident on December 9 resulted in many casualties and arrests. [125]

Indignant at police brutality, students immediately started
to prepare a large-scale demonstration, which took place on
December 16, with about eight thousand participants from over
forty institutions. Some Nationalist and Communist members
and sympathizers were also involved. Sung's troops dealt with
them severely. It was reported that three hundred and seventy
students received different degrees of injury and thirty-three
were arrested or missing. The Hopei-Chahar Political Council still emerged on December 18, two days later than originally planned. Japan put strong pressure on local authorities
to cope with student activities. The demonstration in Peking
was eventually halted,[126] but the national salvation movement
quickly spread throughout the country.

5. The Sian Incident and the
Nationalist-Communist Reconciliation

While the Nationalist-Communist reconciliation was
prompted by the Sian incident, the rising nationalism and
patriotism in China, constantly spurred by the student movement, actually contributed to the formation of a united front
of all anti-Japanese forces. [127] When student delegates from
various cities assembled in Nanking in November 1935,
Chiang Kai-shek assured them that the government would
never conclude secret agreements with Japan in detriment
to China's national sovereignty even if armed resistance were

necessary. The National Salvation Association was soon organized by the leftists in Shanghai. Many students went to work in the Northwest, where Chang Hsueh-liang's troops were confronted with the Communists'. Sian, China's Capital for many dynasties, became the center of political activities in that region.

The so-called Sian incident occurred on December 12, 1936, when Chiang Kai-shek was forcibly detained by Chang Hsueh-liang and Yang Hu-cheng. The latter was then in charge of the security of Shensi province. Personal relationships between the two generals and Chiang had been deteriorating for some time. Chang's soldiers came from Manchuria and longed to return to their home land instead of fighting the Communists, who seized every opportunity to agitate their defection from Nanking. Chang and Yang claimed that the coup de'etat was aimed at persuading Chiang to divert the anti-Communist campaign to a war of resistance against Japan.

The turn of events in China did not suit Soviet policy at the time. To avoid a two-front war against both Germany and Japan, then already bound together by an Anti-Comintern Pact of November 25, 1936, Stalin hoped that Japan would be deeply involved in a prolonged conflict with a united China. The Chinese Communist Party had not yet recovered from heavy losses suffered prior to and during the Long March from Kiangsi to Yenan.[128] Nobody realized the Communist weaknesses better than Mao Tse-tung, who would have everything to gain by a truce with the Nationalists. Because only Chiang could lead the country in resisting Japan at the time, both Moscow and Yenan considered it opportune to reconcile with Chiang in the face of an imminent struggle against their common enemy.[129]

Unable to get support from the Communists and other military leaders and threatened by an impending attack from the government forces, the rebels finally repented and released Chiang on December 26, with the understanding that Chiang was to take necessary steps to stop the civil strife and prepare for an eventual war against Japan.[130] Although the Sian incident was ill-conceived, subsequent developments prepared the way for Chiang to consolidate the country at a time of national emergency. As a prelude to full-scale war between

China and Japan, this event has often been considered a turning point in the modern history of the Far East.

III. DIPLOMATIC ACCOMPLISHMENTS AND FRUSTRATIONS DURING THE SINO-JAPANESE WAR (1937-1945)

1. International Reaction to Japan's Undeclared War

Having failed to control North China by local intrigues and concerned with the Nationalist-Communist reconciliation after the Sian incident, Japanese militarists were determined to crush China by force before she had time to consolidate her defensive power. It is never difficult for an aggressor to find a convenient excuse for any offensive action. On the night of July 7, 1937, Japanese troops demanded entrace into Wanping to search for a missing soldier. This Chinese district was located at the southern end of Loukou-ch'iao (Marco Polo Bridge) along the Peiping-Tientsin Railway, where the stationing of foreign troops was permitted by the Final Protocol of 1901.[131] When the Chinese commander refused the demand, Japanese troops opened fire and started an eight-year war with China. Whatever pretense Japan might concoct for propaganda purposes, the fighting was conducted on Chinese territory, a large part of which subsequently fell into the invader's grip.

As the signatories of the Nine-Power Treaty of February 6, 1922, agreed "to respect the sovereignty, the independence, and the territorial and administrative integrity of China," [132] Japan's resort to war violated not only the Kellogg-Briand Pact and the League Covenant but also the Nine-Power Treaty.[133] On July 16, 1937, China dispatched circular notes to the signatory powers of the Treaty other than Japan, and also to Germany and the Soviet Union, pointing out Japan's violation of the three international instruments and expressing her own readiness to settle the dispute by pacific means. [134] Evidently the Chinese government expected the calling of a Nine-Power Conference to discuss the matter. Secretary of State Cordell Hull stated, on the same day, that the United

States would respond to cooperative efforts by peaceful methods to solve the international controversy.

On November 3, the Nine-Power Conference was held at Brussels. Nineteen nations having interests in the Far East took part in the Conference. Japan and Germany declined to attend. The Conference did not resolve the differences, but, on November 15, issued a declaration, which reaffirmed the principles of the Nine-Power Treaty of respecting China's sovereignty and territorial integrity. By that time, any means short of force could not possibly stop Japan's aggression, but the signatory powers were then not ready to impose effective sanctions against her. After adopting a vague report on November 24, the Conference decided to adjourn temporarily but was never reconvened.[135]

The call of the Brussels Conference was endorsed by the League of Nations, to which China appealed again on September 12, 1937. The Chinese government invoked Articles 10, 11, and 17 of the Covenant. Due to Japan's act of aggression against China's "territorial integrity and existing political independence" within the meaning of Article 10, the Chinese government requested the Secretary-General of the League of Nations to summon a meeting of its Council. Article 16 dealt with economic and military sanctions against a member,[136] while Article 17 applied the same to a non-member.[137] Japan was then no longer a member of the League, which was thus called upon to invite her to assume obligations as an ad hoc member under Article 17. Rejecting the invitation of the League, the Japanese government intensified its land and air warfare in China.[138]

At that time, the prestige of the League was at a low ebb. Germany had withdrawn from it, and occupied the Rhineland in violation of the Treaty of Versailles. Italy had defied the League resolutions and economic sanctions to conquer Ethiopia. What the eighteenth Assembly of the League did was to adopt two reports on October 6, 1937, condemning Japan's aggression in violation of her obligation under the Nine-Power Treaty and the Kellogg-Briand Pact, and recommending moral and material aid to China.[139]

The Sino-Japanese controversy was brought up again by the Chinese delegate, V. K. Wellington Koo, on September 16, 1938, when the nineteenth Assembly was in session. As expected,

Japan declined the Council's invitation to participate in the League's discussion of the subject.[140] Accordingly, sanctions as provided in Article 16 should have applied to Japan, because of the latter's refusal "to accept the obligations of Membership in the League for the purposes of such dispute" and "resort to war against a Member of the League."[141] Finally, on September 30, the Council adopted a draft report by its President. In equivocal terms, the report deemed it appropriate to apply individual sanctions even though coordinated action had not yet been assured.[142]

It is needless to say that, with the increasing tension in Europe, no coordinated sanctions were ever enforced against Japan. The impotence of the League in solving the Sino-Japanese dispute was really not the fault of the organization, but was due to the lack of determined efforts of its constituent members. In particular, Great Britain and France purposely refrained from imposing sanctions against the strongest power in the Far East, while European security was being threatened by the militant policies of Germany and Italy.

2. China's Relationships with Wartime Allies

Throughout the Sino-Japanese hostilities, the United States was most sympathetic to China. President Roosevelt's 'quarantine' speech at Chicago on October 5, 1937, was clearly aimed at Japan,[143] but American public opinion was not ready to 'quarantine' the political epidemic in the Far East. Both the United States and Great Britain had, however, extended economic assistance to China. After the fall of Canton in October 1938, overland routes became the only supply lines, largely through the roads connecting Burma and the Soviet Union, as well as the railway from Yunnan to Indochina. Due to Japan's strong pressures, France stopped the arms traffic through the railway, and then the Burma Road was closed in 1940.

During the early stage of the war, China did receive substantial aid from the Soviet Union. It should be recalled that the formation of the second united front between the Nationalists and the Communists opened the way for Sino-Soviet reconciliation, and the two countries signed a Non-Aggression

Pact on August 21, 1937.[144] The supply from the northern route did not last long, however, because the Soviet Union was later preoccupied with the war on the Western front. After Pearl Harbor, China became a full-fledged ally of the Western powers, but 'Europe first' strategy had delayed a major offensive in Asia.

When Chiang Kai-shek conferred with President Roosevelt and Prime Minister Churchill at Cairo in November 22-26, 1943, China was promised that a large-scale amphibious campaign, designated Operation ANAKIM, would be launched to relieve her from the Japanese onslaught. This plan was however, abandoned after the Teheran Conference, because OPERATION OVERLAND required all landing craft for the cross-channel invasion.[145] Lack of immediate Allied support notwithstanding, China did obtain a firm commitment from the American and British leaders with respect to restoring Chinese territories forcibly taken by Japan since 1895. In the Cairo Declaration of December 1, 1943, Roosevelt, Churchill, and Chiang, speaking on behalf of their respective governments, proclaimed:

> "It is their purpose that Japan shall be stripped of all the islands in the Pacific which she has seized or occupied since the beginning of the first World War in 1914, and that all the territories Japan has stolen from the Chinese, such as Manchuria, Formosa, and the Pescadores, shall be restored to the Republic of China. Japan will also be expelled from all other territories which she has taken by violence and greed. The aforesaid three great powers, mindful of the enslavement of the people of Korea, are determined that in due course Korea shall become free and independent." [146]

The Declaration further stated that "with these objects in view the Three Allies, in harmony with those of the United Nations at war with Japan, will continue to persevere in the serious and prolonged operations necessary to procure the unconditional surrender of Japan."[147] The terms of the Cairo Declaration were reaffirmed in the Postdam Proclamation Defining Terms for Japanese Surrender of July 26, 1945. [148] After Japan surrendered in September 1945, the Allied powers did carry out all the conditions prescribed in the Declaration, including the restoration of Chinese territories and the independence of Korea. For all practical purposes, all unequal treaties previously imposed on China by Japan were terminated by the war.[149]

In contrast to the spirit of the Cairo Declaration, the Yalta Agreement on the Far East inflicted a most serious blow on China. Roosevelt and Churchill met Stalin at Yalta from February 4 to 11, 1945. They discussed four principal subjects: (1) establishment of the United Nations, (2) the problem of Germany, (3) Eastern Europe, and (4) Soviet entrance into the war against Japan. With the exception of the Kurile Islands, the southern part of Sakhalin and the islands adjacent to it, the Agreement regarding Japan was entirely concerned with China,[150] but no invitation was extended to Chiang Kai-shek to participate in the deliberations. The terms pertaining to China are summarized as follows: (1) preservation of the status quo in Outer Mongolia (the Soviet sponsored regime of the Mongolian People's Republic); (2) internationalization of the commercial port of Daiern with safeguard of Soviet preeminent interests, and restoration of the former Russian base of Port Arthur to the Soviet Union; and (3) establishment of a joint Soviet-Chinese company to operate the Chinese Eastern Railway and the Southern Manchurian Railway.[151]

In order to understand the effects of the Yalta Agreement on China, a brief review of the historical development of the above-mentioned places and railways is necessary. Outer Mongolia was an integral part of China as explicitly recognized in the Sino-Soviet Agreement of 1924.[152] Russia obtained the lease of Dairen and Port Arthur from China in 1898 for twenty-five years, and then transferred it to Japan after the Russo-Japanese War without consulting China.[153] The Chinese Eastern Railway was arbitrarily sold by the Soviet Union to the Japanese sponsored puppet state of 'Manchukuo' under China's protest.[154] The Japanese South Manchurian Railway [155] together with the Chinese Eastern Railway and the two ports should have been rightfully restored to China after the defeat of Japan.

Disregarding China's rights, the Yalta Agreement consented to all Soviet demands. The three leaders realized, however, that "the agreement concerning Outer Mongolia and the Ports and railroads referred to above will require concurrence of Generalissimo Chiang Kai-shek.'' The President of the United States was entrusted to ''take measures in order to obtain this concurrence on advice from Marshal Stalin.'' Furthermore, ''the Heads of the three Great Powers have agreed that these claims of the Soviet Union shall be unquestionably fulfilled after Japan   has been defeated.''[156] It appeared as if China were an enemy rather than an ally, and would be treated like a vanquished state after the war.

The conclusion and enforcement of an agreement vitally affecting China's territorial integrity and national sovereignty without her prior knowledge and consent was allegedly to shorten the war with Japan and thereby to save many American lives.[157] This act of sacrificing justice for expediency in violation of the Nine-Power Treaty proved unnecessary, since the United States government had already possessed reliable information of the imminent collapse of Japan. [158] In conclusion, the commitments made by the United States and Great Britain with the Soviet Union at the expense of China were morally wrong, politically unwise, and legally intolerable. The Chinese felt they were once again being mistreated by the Western powers, or to speak precisely in this case, by her wartime allies. At a time when China was determined to terminate all unequal treaties, the major powers foolishly sowed new seeds of discord and distrust, which the postwar world has been reaping since the emergence of Communist power on China's mainland.

3. Termination of Unequal Treaties

Negotiations for relinquishing extraterritoriality were suspended after the Mukden incident. While China was still fighting alone against Japan, the State Department exchanged notes with the Chinese Ministry of Foreign Affairs in May 1941, expressing the American intention to resume discussions on the subject after the restoration of peace. The British government made the same assurance about two months later. After Pearl Harbor, China became one of the major allies. Although the United States and Great Britain could not render effective military assistance to China owing to the pressure of the Western front, they believed it politically expedient to comply with China's long held desire to abolish extraterritoriality. Thus, on October 10, 1942, both countries declared their readiness to open diplomatic consultations for the immediate relinquishment of extraterritoriality.

Once the principles were agreed upon, it did not take long to complete technical procedures. Consequently, on January 11, 1943, China simultaneously concluded, with the United States at Washington[159] and with Great Britain at Chungking,[160] the Treaty for the Relinquishment of Extraterritorial Rights in China and the Regulation of Related Matters. These treaties together with exchanges of notes not only renounced extraterritoriality but also other unilateral rights and privileges previously acquired by unequal treaties.

Led by the United States and Great Britain, other treaty powers soon followed suit: Belgium, Brazil, the Netherlands, Norway, and Sweden concluded new treaties with China on the bases of equality and reciprocity during the war; [161] Denmark, France, Portugal, and Spain did likewise soon afterward. Japan and Italy lost their treaty rights as a consequence of the war. Thus China finally liberated herself from the century old bondage of unequal treaties. The recovery of lost territories and sovereign rights resulting from the abolition of unequal treaties will be discussed in the following chapter.

One of the most tragic events during World War II was the Yalta Agreement on the Far East, which produced damaging effects on postwar China. Compelled by Allied pressures and practical circumstances, the Chinese government grudgingly concluded with the Soviet Union the Treaty of Friendship and Alliance on August 14, 1945.[162] Coming into effect ten days later, the Treaty embodied an Exchange of Notes, Agreement on the Chinese Changchun Railway, Agreement on the Port of Dairen with Protocol, Agreement on Port Arthur with Annex, and Agreement on Relations between the Soviet Commander-in-Chief and the Chinese Administration Following the Entry of Soviet Forces into the Territory of the Three Eastern Provinces of China in Connection with the Present Joint War Against Japan. Also included were the Minutes of the Meeting between Stalin and T. V. Soong, President of the Chinese Executive Yuan, on July 11, 1945, on the evacuation of Soviet troops from Chinese territory after the capitulation of Japan.[163]

The Sino-Soviet Treaty and related documents merely confirmed what had been decided by Roosevelt and Churchill with Stalin at Yalta. The Chinese Changchun Railway represented a new railway system to be formed by the combination of the main trunk lines of the Chinese Eastern Railway and the South Manchurian Railway leading from Manchouli to Pogranichnaya and from Harbin to Dairen and Port Arthur. [164] Like the former Chinese Eastern Railway, this new railway system, ostensibly under Sino-Soviet joint operation, was actually under the control of Soviet officials.[165] The agreement on this railway system was to remain in force for thirty years, after which its ownership would revert to China. The same period was applied to the Soviet use of Dairen and Port Arthur. China had to recognize the independence of Outer Mongolia within her existing frontiers after a plebiscite.[166] In compariosn, the Soviet Union under Stalin exacted from China the same territorial and political rights as Czarist Russia did, including those transferred to Japan after the Russo-Japanese War. In the case of Outer Mongolia, Moscow went further in detaching it from China not only in fact but also in treaty form.[167] What a contrast of policies the Soviet Union displayed in shifting from the Karakhan Declaration and the 1924 Agreement to the demands made by Stalin at Yalta! [168]

China fought Japan for eight years, while the Soviet Union entered into the war only on the verge of Japan's collapse. Under what rules of international law could Moscow claim rights over Dairen, Port Arthur, and the Manchurian railways, which should have legitimately been reverted to China? In this regard, the Allied commitments at Yalta were much more unjust than the transfer of the Shantung rights to Japan by the Paris Peace Conference.[169] What China obtained from the Soviet Union was the vague promise of non-interference in internal affairs, including the prevailing situation in Sinkiang, as well as extending moral and material support to the National Government.[170] Later events revealed that Moscow did not abide by these commitments. In every respect, this Sino-Soviet Treaty of 1945 was a new unequal treaty, the title of friendship and alliance notwithstanding.

The refusal of the Peking government to sign the Treaty of Versailles was eventually vindicated at the Washington Conference of 1921-1922.[171] The National Government should never have signed that Treaty in 1945. Commentators on Far Eastern affairs considered China's lack of resistance to Allied pressure a diplomatic blunder of the first magnitude. Although the Allied leaders committed themselves to secure the concurrence of the Chinese government for the execution of the Yalta Agreement, what compulsory measures could they apply to force China's acceptance without violating the letter and spirit of the newly signed United Nations Charter? [172] Allied submission to Soviet demands was probably motivated by an earnest desire for postwar peace in the Far East by limiting, under the terms of a treaty, exactly how far Moscow could go. But could the Soviet Union venture to encroach upon China's territorial integrity and national soverignty by force if the Allied powers were determined to maintain justice, law, and order?

Subsequent developments in China proved that appeasement did not stop Moscow from assisting the Chinese Communists in coming to power. On the other hand, the Soviet Union would never have exacted such harsh terms from China if the latter were united and strong. In retrospect, China's troubles were largely due to her own weaknesses. It was on February 25, 1953, long after the Chinese Communists took over the Mainland, that the National Government in Taiwan declared null and void the Sino-Soviet Treaty of 1945, because the Soviet Union failed to carry out its terms.[173] Although the actual restoration of Dairen, Port Arthur, and the railway rights in Manchuria took place only after painful negotiations between Peking and Moscow,[174] China had technically put an end to the humiliating era of unequal treaties and resumed the status of a major power in international affairs.[175] The world is now facing a temporarily disunited but potentially strong nation, whose long-suffered wounds from imperialism have not yet healed and whose unwavering aspirations for terra irredenta remain to be fulfilled.

NOTES TO CHAPTER 9

1. See supra, pp. 224-228.

2. The date of the first treaty concluded by each of the twenty-three countries with China and its sources are cited in the footnotes. Unless a second treaty is listed or otherwise indicated, the right of extraterritoriality was granted to that country by the first treaty.

3. Treaty of Peking, September 2, 1869 (Chinese Customs, Treaties, II, pp. 457-476, 495-504; Hertslet, Treaties, I, pp. 215-222).

4. Imperial Rescript of July 25, 1845, Granting Trade Privileges under Provisions of Existing Treaties (Chinese Customs, Treaties, II, p. 3; Hertslet, Treaties, I, p. 223); extraterritoriality granted by the Treaty of Peking of November 2, 1865 (Chinese Customs, Treaties, II, pp. 4-22; Hertslet, Treaties, I, pp. 223-234).

5. Treaty of Friendship of December 3, 1919 (Carnegie, Treaties, pp. 22-23; G. Fr. de Martens, Nouveau recueil général de traités, 3rd series (Lepzig, 1927), Vol. 16, p. 643) − without extraterritoriality.

6. Treaty of Tientsin of October 3, 1881 (Chinese Customs, Treaties, II, pp. 813-823; Hertslet, Treaties, I, pp. 234-240).

7. Treaty of Amity of February 18, 1915 (MacMurray, Treaties, II, pp. 1190-1191) − without extraterritoriality.

8. Treaty of Tientsin of July 13, 1863 (Chinese Customs, Treaties, II, pp. 313-330; Hertslet, Treaties, I, pp. 249-258).

9. Treaty of Amity of October 29, 1926 (Carnegie Treaties, pp. 185-186) − without extraterritoriality.

10. Treaty of Whampoa of October 24, 1844 (Chinese Customs, Treaties, I, pp. 771-790; Hertslet, Treaties, I, pp. 258-269).

11. Treaty of Tientsin of September 2, 1861 (Chinese Customs, Treaties, II, pp. 115-138; Hertslet, Treaties, I, pp. 331-342).

12. Treaty of Nanking of August 29, 1842 (ibid., I, pp. 7-12; Chinese Customs, Treaties, I, pp. 351-356); Extraterritoriality explicitly provided in the General Regulations under Which the British Trade Is to be Conducted at the Five Ports of Canton

Amoy, Foochow, Ningpo, and Shanghai, July 22, 1843 (ibid., I, pp. 383-389).

13. Treaty of Peking of October 26, 1866 (ibid., II, pp. 403-420; Hertslet, Treaties, I, pp. 354-361).

14. Treaty of Tientsin of September 13, 1871 (Chinese Customs, Treaties, II, pp. 507-514, 572-575, 642-648); extraterritoriality more fully provided in the Treaty of Commerce and Navigation of July 21, 1896 (ibid., II, pp. 604-614, 720-731; Hertslet, Treaties, I, pp. 373-382; MacMurray, Treaties, I, pp. 68-74.

15. Treaty of Washington of December 14, 1899 (ibid., I, pp. 214-220; Chinese Customs, Treaties, II, pp. 833-843; Hertslet, Treaties, I, pp. 399-407).

16. Treaty of Tientsin of October 6, 1863 (ibid., I, pp. 407-415; Chinese Customs, Treaties, II, pp. 399-351).

17. Treaty of Commerce of March 20, 1847 (ibid., II, pp. 45-71; Hertslet, Treaties, I, pp. 527-540).

18. Treaty of Friendship of June 1, 1920 (League of Nations, Treaty Series, No. 240 (1922), Vol. 9, p. 19; Carnegie, Treaties, pp. 26-27) − without extraterritoriality.

19. Treaty of Tientsin of June 26, 1874 (Chinese Customs, Treaties, II, pp. 798-807; Hertslet, Treaties, I, pp. 415-420).

20. Treaty of Tientsin of August 13, 1862 (ibid., I, p. 422; Chinese Customs, Treaties, II, pp. 251-272); not ratified at the time, but later revived by the Treaty of Peking of December 1, 1887 (ibid., II, pp. 272-294; Hertslet, Treaties, I, pp. 423-433). This latter treaty was preceded by the Protocol of Lisbon of March 26, 1887, governing relations with Macao (ibid., I, pp. 422-423; Chinese Customs, Treaties, II, p. 273).

21. Agreement of General Principles for the Settlement of the Questions, May 31, 1924 (Carnegie, Treaties, pp. 133-140; League of Nations, Treaty Series, No. 955 (1925), Vol. 37, p. 176), by which the Soviet Union renounced the right of extraterritoriality in China. The first treaty between China and Russia was the Treaty of Nerchinsk of August 27, 1689 (Chinese Customs, Treaties, I, pp. 3-13; Hertslet, Treaties, I, pp. 437-439), but extraterritoriality was not granted to Russia till the Treaty of Tientsin of June 13, 1858 (ibid., I, pp. 455-461; Chinese Customs, Treaties, I, pp. 85-100).

22. Treaty of Tientsin of October 10, 1864 (ibid., II, pp. 359-377; Hertslet, Treaties, I, pp. 512-522).

23. Treaty of Commerce of March 20, 1847 (ibid., I, pp. 527-540; Chinese Customs, Treaties, II, pp. 45-71).

24. Treaty of Amity of June 13, 1918 (MacMurray, Treaties, II, pp. 1429-1430).

25. Treaty of Wanghia of July 3, 1844 (Chinese Customs, Treaties, I, pp. 677-690).

26. See the Sino-German Declaration, Agreement, and Exchange of Notes concerning the Reestablishment of Freindly and Commercial Relations, May 20, 1921 (Carnegie, Treaties, pp. 47-53; League of Nations, Treaty Series, No. 261 (1922), Vol. 9, pp. 283, 285-289); the Sino-Soviet Agreement on General Principles for the Settlement of Questions, May 31, 1924 (cited in supra, note 21); and the Sino-Austrian Treaty of Commerce of October 19, 1925 (Carnegie, Treaties, pp. 165-169; League of Nations, Treaty Series, No. 1301 (1926), Vol. 55, p. 19).

27. See Min-ch'ien T. Z. Tyau, Two Years of Nationalist China, p. 101. See also U. S. For. Rel., 1928, II, pp. 416-417.

28. A comprehensive discussion on this subject can be found in José S. Camara, The Ratification of International Treaties (Toronto, 1949); Francis O. Wilcox, The Ratification of International Conventions (London, 1935). For a brief discussion of the conclusion and ratification of treaties, see William L. Tung, International Law in an Organizing World, pp. 332-337.

29. For its text, see supra, note 24.

30. See supra, pp. 154-157.

31. For the text of the Sino-Belgian Treaty of 1865, see Chinese Customs, Treaties, II, pp. 4-22; Hertslet, Treaties, I, pp. 223-234.

32. Art. 46 of the Sino-Belgian Treaty was identical to Art. 27 of the Sino-British Treaty of June 26, 1858, and corresponding articles of other treaties. The article reads:

> "It is agreed that either of the High Contracting Parties to this Treaty may demand a further revision of the Tariff, and of the Commercial Articles of this Treaty, at the end of ten years; but if no demand be made on either side within six months after the end

of the first ten years, then the tariff shall remain
in force for ten years more, reckoned from the end
of the preceding ten years; and so it shall be, at the
end of each successive ten years."

33. In reply to the Belgian proposal of November 10, 1926, the
Chinese government stated the following in its Note to the
Belgian Minister at Peking on November 16, 1926:

"As regards the proposal of the Belgian Government to bring the question of the interpretation of
Article 46 of the Treaty of 1865 before the Permanent Court of International Justice, the Chinese
Government, mindful of their obligations under Article 36 of the Statute of the said Court, would be
prepared to discuss the possibility of invoking jointly
with the Belgian Government the services of this
highest international tribunal, if the Belgian Government had indicated a willingness to seek a solution
on the broad basis of the universally recognized principle of equality in international intercourse and that
of ex aequo et bono. For the point at issue between
the two Governments is not the technical interpretation of Article 46 of the Treaty of 1865, an article
which is a striking symbol of the inequalities in the
entire instrument. This technical point had more than
once been waived by the Belgian Government when it
agreed to put an end to the Treaty of 1865 and conclude
a new one to take its place. The real question at bot-
tom is that of the application of the principle of
equality of treatment in the relations between China
and Belgium. It is political in character and no nation
can consent to the basic principle of equality between
States being made the subject of a judicial inquiry.
A submission of the question of interpretation of
Article 46 of the Treaty of 1865 to the aforesaid
Court would serve merely to stress Belgium's desire
to maintain in her favor the regime of inequality in
China, and would in no way remove the obstacle
which had stood in the way of the successful completion of the recent negotiations."

34. For the text, see Chinese Republic, Treaties, pp. 19-23;
League of Nations, Treaty Series, Vol. 87 (1929), pp. 287-295.

35. For the judgment of the Permanent Court of International
Justice, see Publications of the Permanent Court of International
Justice, Series A, No. 8, Denunciation of the Treaty of November
2nd, 1865, between China and Belgium; A.D. MacNair and H.

Lauterpacht, Annual Digest of Public International Law Cases, 1927-1928, Case Nos. 350, 351.

36. See Art. 1 and Annex I respectively.

37. For the text, see Chinese Customs, Treaties, I, pp. 913-924; Hertslet, Treaties, I, pp. 301-311.

38. In the same Note, the Chinese government expressed its intention to revise the Sino-Franco Convention Complementary to the Additional Commercial Convention of 1887. That Convention was concluded on June 20, 1895. For its text, see Chinese Customs, Treaties, I, pp. 937-941; Hertslet, Treaties, I, pp. 323-327.

39. For the text, see Chinese Customs, Treaties, II, pp. 97-112; MacMurray, Treaties, I, pp. 740-747.

40. For the text, see Chinese Customs, Treaties, II, pp. 403-420; Hertslet, Treaties, I, pp. 354-361.

41. For the text, see Carnegie, Treaties, pp. 243-246; Chinese Republic, Treaties, pp. 213-217.

42. See Art. I of the Treaty and the attached Exchange of Notes.

43. See, respectively, Art. I and Annex I of the Treaty, which can be found in Carnegie, Treaties, pp. 246-249; Chinese Republic, Treaties, pp. 77-81.

44. The Chinese government informed the Danish government of its impending expiration on June 30, 1928. For the text of the 1863 Treaty, see Chinese Customs, Treaties, II, pp. 313-330; Hertslet, Treaties, I, pp. 249-258.

45. In accordance with the terms of that treaty, a revision could be made after ten years. For its text, see Chinese Customs, Treaties, II, pp. 813-823; Hertslet, Treaties, I, pp. 234-240.

46. See the Sino-Brazilian Treaty of Amity, August 20, 1943 (Chinese Republic, Treaties, pp. 41-42).

47. For the text, see Chinese Customs, Treaties, I, pp. 404-421; Hertslet, Treaties, I, pp. 18-35.

48. For the text, see Chinese Customs, Treaties, I, pp. 543-568; Hertslet, Treaties, I, pp. 171-188; MacMurray, Treaties, I, pp. 342-355.

49. For the text, see Chinese Customs, Treaties, I, pp. 745-763; Hertslet, Treaties, I, pp. 566-578; MacMurray, Treaties, I, pp. 423-450.

50. For the text, see Chinese Customs, Treaties, II, pp. 359-377; Hertslet, Treaties, I, pp. 512-522.

51. For the text, see Carnegie, Treaties, pp. 270-273; Chinese Republic, Treaties, pp. 426-431.

52. See Art. I and Annex I of the Sino-Spanish Treaty of December 27, 1928.

53. For the text, see Chinese Customs, Treaties, II, pp. 604-614, 720-731; Hertslet, Treaties, I, pp. 373-382; MacMurray, Treaties, I, pp. 68-74.

54. For the text, see Chinese Customs, Treaties, II, pp. 617-636; Hertslet, Treaties, I, pp. 383-391; MacMurray, Treaties, I, pp. 411-422.

55. For the text, see Chinese Customs, Treaties, II, pp. 833-843; Hertslet, Treaties, I, pp. 399-407; MacMurray, Treaties, I, pp. 214-220.

56. For the text, see Chinese Republic, Treaties, pp. 311-313.

57. See ibid., pp. 313-316. Art. VI(1) of the Treaty reads:

    "The nationals of each of the High Contracting Parties, as well as their property, in the territory of the other, shall be subject to the laws and regulations of the latter and to the jurisdiction of its courts."

58. See supra, pp. 203-204.

59. See Congressional Record, 69th Cong., 2nd Sess. (February 21, 1927), p. 4387. See also supra, p. 233.

60. For the text of the Sino-American Treaty regulating Tariff Relations of July 25, 1928, see Carnegie, Treaties, pp. 230-231; Chinese Republic, Treaties, pp. 648-649.

61. Art. I of the Treaty.

62. For the text, see Carnegie, Treaties, pp. 237-238; Chinese Republic, Treaties, pp. 355-356.

63. For the text, see Carnegie, Treaties, pp. 249-250; Chinese Republic, Treaties, pp. 319-322.

64. For the text, see Carnegie, Treaties, pp. 263-265; Chinese Republic, Treaties, pp. 442-444.

65. See supra, p. 279, note 41.

66. See supra, p. 279, note 43.

67. For the text, see Carnegie, Treaties, pp. 252-256; Chinese Republic, Treaties, pp. 405-411.

68. See supra, p. 280, note 51.

69. For the text, see Carnegie, Treaties, pp. 257-263; Chinese Republic, Treaties, pp. 527-535. In the Exchange of Notes between Chinese Foreign Minister C. T. Wang and the British Minister to Nanking Miles W. Lampson on December 20, 1928, it was agreed that "the ad valorem rates of duty or the specific rates based thereon in the National Customs Tariff to be adopted by the National Government are the same as the rates which were discussed and provisionally agreed upon at the Tariff Conference of 1926 and that these are the maximum rates to be levied on British goods; furthermore, that these will remain the maximum rates on such goods for a period of at least one year from the date of enforcement of the tariff; and that two months notice will be given of the coming into force of the said tariff." In the same Notes, the Chinese government expressed its intention to take necessary steps "to abolish likin, native customs dues, coast-trade duties, and all other taxes on imported goods whether levied in transit or on arrival at destination." See Annex III of the Treaty.

70. For the text, see Carnegie, Treaties, pp. 265-270; Chinese Republic, Treaties, pp. 107-113. In signing the Treaty, the French government attached a few conditions: minimum tariff on certain merchandise exported to France; abolition of likin; provision for the service of certain loans; and maintenance of present rates of reduction on tariff duties of merchandise imported to and exported from Indochina pending the conclusion of a new convention to replace the Sino-Franco conventions of April 25, 1886 (Chinese Customs, Treaties, I, pp. 913-924; Hertslet, Treaties, I, pp. 301-311), of June 26, 1887 (Chinese Customs, Treaties, I, pp. 933-936; Hertslet, Treaties, I, pp. 311-314), and of June 20, 1895 (Chinese Customs, Treaties, I, pp. 937-941; Hertslet, Treaties, I, pp. 323-327; MacMurray, Treaties, I, pp. 28-30).

71. Promulgated on December 7, 1928, the new tariff rates ranged from 7-1/2% to 27-1/2%, corresponding to the rates of interim surtax proposed at the Tariff Conference of 1925-1926. See supra, p. 204. Covering 718 items, the new tariff schedule charged an excise of 32-1/2% on cigars and cigarettes, and contained a free list for such items as books and periodicals.

72. The Treaty was signed on May 6, 1930. For the text, see Chinese Republic, Treaties, pp. 233-243. Japan also attached conditions to the tariff treaty, including the maintenance of the tariff rates on merchandise listed in Pts. I and II of the annexed schedule for a period from one year to three years, and a speedy consolidation of unsecured and inadequately secured obligations of China due to Japanese creditors. See Annexes I, IV of the Treaty.

73. In the Sino-German Treaty of Friendship and Commerce, August 17, 1928 (Carnegie, Treaties, pp. 232-233; Chinese Republic, Treaties, pp. 194-195), Art. I specified China's right of tariff autonomy. Although Germany no longer had any unequal treaty with China, the reason for this provision was that imports from Germany were previously permitted to pay the prevailing rates of customs duties pending the operation of the Chinese National Tariff. It should be recalled that, since the conclusion of the Agreement for the Reestablishment of Friendship and Commercial Relations on May 20, 1921 (Carnegie, Treaties, pp. 47-53), Sino-German relationships had been on a footing of equality and reciprocity.

74. See supra, p. 112.

75. Belgium alone agreed to relinquish extraterritoriality when the majority of states enjoying that right so decided.

76. See Min-ch'ien T.Z. Tyau, Two Years of Nationalist China, p. 107.

77. U. S. For. Rel., 1929, II, p. 561.

78. Sweden and Switzerland had no major interests in China. Peru had no nationals in China at the time. See Wesley R. Fishel, The End of Extraterritoriality in China (Los Angeles, 1952), p. 148. Mexico voluntarily relinquished the right of extraterritoriality by an Exchange of Notes on November 12, 1929. See supra, p. 280, note 56.

79. See The China Year Book, 1931, pp. 486-487; U. S. For. Rel., 1929, II, pp. 665-667.

80. The China Year book, 1931, p. 487.

81. See U. S. For. Rel., 1930, II, p. 356.

82. For details, see U. S. For. Rel., 1929, II, pp. 665-667; 1930, II, pp. 471-480, 485-489, 497; 1931, III, pp. 726-730, 789, 813-827; Wesley R. Fishel, op. cit., pp. 147, 172-183; Tsien, pp. 154-157.

83. For the text of exchanges of notes between China with the Netherlands and Norway on April 25, 1931, see Yin-ching Chen (ed.), Treaties and Agreements between the Republic of China and Other Powers, 1929-1954 (Washington, D. C., 1957; hereafter cited as Chen, Treaties), pp. 72-75, 76, respectively. Brazil was willing to conclude a treaty with China similar to the Sino-Italian Treaty of 1928. See supra, p. 253.

84. The Chinese government originally declared its intention to enforce regulations concerning the exercise of Chinese jurisdiction over foreigners in China as of January 1, 1932. Because of the Mukden Incident, this contemplated action had to be postponed.

85. See supra, p. 280, note 56.

86. For details, see supra, p. 114.

87. The reorganization of the Provisional Court was achieved through negotiations with the same six powers concerned with the abolition of extraterritoriality. Arrangemements for the establishment of Chinese courts at the International Settlement and the French Concession in Shanghai were agreed upon on February 17 and July 28, 1931, respectively. The duration of the agreements was three years, but could be extended. For details, see Tsien, pp. 117-120; Chen, Treaties, pp. 29-35; Chinese Republic, Treaties, pp. 135-142.

88. On the same date, the two countries also signed secret protocols granting Japan the right of railway construction and mining interests in Manchuria. For the text of the Convention and its Supplementary Agreement, see Chinese Customs, Treaties, I, pp. 636-641, 734-735; Hertslet, Treaties, I, pp. 391-396; MacMurray, Treaties, I, pp. 549-553. For a summary of the Protocols, see ibid., I, pp. 554-555.

89. For details, see supra, pp. 76-77.

90. See supra, pp. 156-157.

91. See supra, p. 236.

92. Both Chinese and Japanese sources are now available, describing the details of the plot. For a summary, see Chin-tun Liang, Historical Description of the September 18th Incident (in Chinese; Hongkong, 1964), pp. 211-220. This work also appears in English in an abridged form, under the title, The Sinister Face of the Mukden Incident (New York, 1969). See pp. 10-44, in particular.

93. The five railways in question were: (1) Tunhwa to Tuman, (2) Changchun to Talai, (3) Kirin to Wuchang, (4) Yenki to Hailin, and (5) Taonan to Solun. Negotiations for the construction of these railways began with Chang Tso-lin, but were not completed by the time of his death.

94. For details of the development in Manchuria, see A. J. Toynbee, Survey of International Affairs, 1932, pp. 432-470.

95. According to the Report of the League of Nations Commission of Enquiry, under the Chairmanship of Lord Lytton (hereafter cited as Lytton Report), "an action undoubtedly occurred on or near the railroad between 10 and 10:30 P.M. on September 18th, but the damage, if any, to the railroad did not in fact prevent the punctual arrival of the South-bound train from Changchun, and was not in itself sufficient to justify military action." Lytton Report, p. 71. For the railroad explosion and Japan's responsibility for the Mukden Incident, see Chin-tun Liang, op. cit., pp. 15-24.

96. China refused to sign the Treaty of Versailles on account of the unfair settlement of the Shantung Question; but, as a signatory to the Peace Treaty of St. Germain with Austria on September 10, 1919, she became an original member of the League of Nations.

97. See, in particular, Arts. 11-15 of the League Covenant.

98. Sze was then Chinese Minister to Great Britain. China was newly elected as a non-permanent member of the League Council, of which Japan had been a permanent member until her withdrawal from the League in March 1933.

99. Art. 11 of the League Covenant reads:

"1. Any war or threat of war, whether immediately affecting any of the Members of the League or not, is hereby declared a matter of concern to the whole League, and the League shall take any action that may be deemed wise and effectual to safeguard the peace of nations. In case any such emergency should arise, the Secretary-General shall, on the request of any Member of the League, forthwith summon a meeting of the Council.

"2. It is also declared to be the friendly right of each Member of the League to bring to the attention of the Assembly or of the Council any circumstance whatever affecting international relations which threatens to disturb international peace or the good understanding between nations upon which peace depends."

100. See League of Nations, Official Journal, Vol. 12 (1931), Pt. II, p. 2291.

101. Ibid., Vol. 12 (1931), Pt. II, p. 2374.

102. The Commission members were recommended by the respective governments and appointed by the League Council. Walker D. Hines was first proposed as the American member, but he declined to serve.

103. Department of State, Peace and War: United States Foreign Policy 1931-1941 (Washington, 1943), Doc. 793-94/3437A, pp. 159-160. The text of Stimson's statement can also be found in League of Nations, Official Journal, Special Supplement, No. 101, p. 155. This doctrine was reasserted in his open letter to Senator William E. Borah, Chairman of the Foreign Relations Committee, on February 23,1932. Secretary Stimson had earlier hoped that Japanese statesmen would exert efforts to find a peaceful solution of the controversy. See his Far Eastern Crisis (New York, 1936), pp. 42-44.

104. China repeatedly denounced acquisition of territory by conquest, and wholeheartedly supported the Assembly resolution of March 11, 1932. The Chinese government reiterrated its position in a statement by Foreign Minister Wen-kan Lo, on August 29, 1932. See League of Nations, Official Journal, Special Supplement, No. 102, p. 39.

105. See infra, p. 287, note 111.

106. For respective functions of the League Assembly and Council, see William L. Tung, International Organization under the United Nations System, pp. 22-23.

107. Art. 10 of the League Covenant reads:

"The Members of the League undertake to respect and preserve as against external aggression the ter-

ritorial integrity and existing political independence
of all Members of the League. In case of any such
aggression or in case of any threat or danger of such
aggression, the Council shall advise upon the means
by which this obligation shall be fulfilled."

Art. 15 provided for detailed procedures for the Council and
the Assembly in the pacific settlement of international disputes. Paragraph 10 of Art. 15 stipulates the following:

"In any case referred to the Assembly, all the provisions of this Article and Article 12 relating to the
action and powers of the Council shall apply to the
action and powers of the Assembly, provided that a
report made by the Assembly, if concurred in by the
Representatives of those Members of the League
represented on the Council and of a majority of the
other Members of the League, exclusive in each
case of the Representatives of the parties to the dispute, shall have the same force as a report by the
Council concurred in by all the members thereof
other than the Representatives of one or more of the
parties to the dispute."

108. At that time, Japan's invasion of China went beyond Manchuria.
      On January 28, 1932, the Japanese navy began military oper-
      ations in Shanghai, to be described in the section below.

109. The Report was completed and signed by the members of the
      Commission on September 4, 1932. To counter the Commis-
      sion's efforts, the Japanese government concluded a treaty
      of alliance with the puppet state 'Manchukuo' on September
      15, before the official release of the Report. The Chinese
      government afforded the Commission all facilities to obtain
      necessary information with the hope that it would function on
      the bases of equity and existing treaty provisions. See Memor-
      anda presented to the Lytton Commission by V. K. Wellington
      Koo, Assessor (New York, 1932, 3 vols.), Vol. 1, pp. 66-67.

110. The ten principles were as follows: (1) compatibility with the
      interests of both China and Japan, (2) consideration for the
      interests of U.S.S.R., (3) conformity with existing multilateral
      treaties, (4) recognition of Japan's interests in Manchuria,
      (5) establishment of new treaty relations between China and
      Japan, (6) effective provision for the settlement of future
      disputes, (7) Manchurian autonomy, (8) maintenance of internal
      order and security against aggression, (9) encouragement of an
      economic rapprochement between China and Japan, and (10) in-
      ternational cooperation in Chinese reconstruction. The princi-

ple of Manchurian autonomy meant that the government of Manchuria should be modified in such a way as to secure, consistently with the sovereignty and administrative integrity of China, a large measure of autonomy designed to meet special conditions of the area. For the full text of the Report, see League Doc. C.663.M.320.1932.VII.

111. The President of the League Assembly reviewed the failure of conciliation at its sixteenth plenary meeting on February 21, 1933, in the following words:

> "Such, then, is the situation with which the League of Nations is faced today. Since September 21st, 1931, first the Council and then the Assembly have endeavoured to settle the dispute in agreement with the parties, in accordance with the articles of the Covenant in virtue of which the matter was referred to them. For exactly seventeen months the efforts at conciliation have been pursued. At the outset of the dispute, the Council received an assurance that the withdrawal of the Japanese troops into the zone of the South Manchurian Railway, which had already been begun, would be pursued as rapidly as possible in proportion as the safety of the lives and property of Japanese nationals was effectively assured, and that Japan hoped to carry out this intention in full as speedily as possible.

> "Today, the Three Eastern Provinces are occupied; Japanese troops have crossed the Great Wall and attacked Shanhaikwan; it is announced that operations are being prepared for the occupation of the province of Jehol.

> "The procedure of conciliation is, of course, not yet closed. It cannot be formally closed until the adoption by the Assembly of the report provided for in Article 15, paragraph 4, of the Covenant. I hesitate, however, to make a new appeal with a view to conciliation, for it would be necessary not only that fresh proposals which the Assembly could accept should be made to it, but also that it should receive an assurance that the existing situation would not be aggravated and that no fresh military operations would be undertaken."

League of Nations, Official Journal, Special Supplement, No. 112, p. 13.

112. The report was prepared in pursuance of Art. 15(4) of the Covenant. For its text, see League Doc. A.(Extr).22.1933.VII.

113. According to Art. 1(3), "Any Member of the League may, after two years' notice of its intention so to do, withdraw from the League, provided that all its international obligations and all its obligations under this Covenant shall have been fulfilled at the time of its withdrawal." In his statement of March 28, 1932, V. K. Wellington Koo presented the view of the Chinese government as follows:

"As applied to Japan's announced withdrawal, it means that all the resolutions adopted by the Council and the Assembly of the League of Nations even since the League was seized of the Sino-Japanese dispute are still binding on her and that equally binding on her will be all decisions or resolutions which may be adopted by the League in this matter at any time before her secession may be regarded as a fact in law. It also means that Japan is not entitled to the right to withdraw from the League unless and until she has carried out not only all the resolutions and decisions of the League of Nations in respect to the present dispute and the other obligations under the Covenant but also all obligations under those international agreements, the provisions of which have also been proclaimed by the League as guiding principles for the settlement of the dispute. In short, if Japan claims the right to withdraw from the League, it is her duty to implement all the provisions of the Paris Pact and the Nine Power Treaty as well as those of the Covenant within the two years after she notified her withdrawal to the League of Nations. If she fails to do so, she remains a member of the League and will be as much subjected to its authority as every other Member State. The just and equitable settlement of the Sino-Japanese question by the League is, therefore, in no way prejudiced by the step which the Japanese Government has taken."

Quoted from Wunsz King, China and the League of Nations: The Sino-Japanese Controversy (New York, 1965), pp. 60-61.

114. See ibid., pp. 30-33.

115. See League of Nations, Official Journal, March 1932, Pt. I, p. 366.

116. Lytton Report, pp. 86-87.

117. For the text of the Agreement, see Chinese Republic, Treaties, pp. 243-246; Chen, Treaties, pp. 84-88.

118. For the text, see Chinese Republic, Treaties, p. 247; Chen, Treaties, pp. 95-96. The Agreement was signed by Lieutenant-General Hsiung Pin, Chief of Staff to the Peiping Branch Military Council, under authorization from General Ho Ying-chin, Chairman of that Council, and Major-General Nej-i Okamura on behalf of General Muto, Commander-in-Chief of the Japanese Kwantung Army. For details, see Chien-min Wang, "General Hsiung Pin and the Tangku Truce Agreement," Biographical Literature (in Chinese), Vol. 12, No. 6 (June 1968), pp. 6-9.

119. Established on December 18, 1935, the Council was not completely independent of the Central Government, and was quite different from Japan's original design of setting up an autonomous regime of the five provinces in North China. See U. S. For. Rel., 1935, III, pp. 342, 351, 390, 404, 420, 423-424, 426, 434, 448, 464, 468, 480. The attitude of Chinese leaders in Nanking toward Japan's new threat of aggression could be characterized by the following well-known slogan: "Not to forsake peace until peace is proved unattainable; not to talk lightly about sacrifice unless there is no alternative." For a more detailed account of the Japanese-directed autonomous movement in North China, see Chin-tun Liang, "The Autonomous Movement in North China," Biographical Literature (in Chinese), Vol. 12, No. 5 (May 1968), pp. 22-31; No. 6 (June 1968), pp. 10-22.

120. See supra, pp. 164-166, 231-232.

121. This was generally known as the March 18th Massacre, when the troops of Tuan Ch'i-jui, Provisional Chief Executive of the Peking government, opened fire on the students who conducted orderly demonstrations against his pro-Japanese policy. For a summary of the Chinese student movement up to 1926, see John Israel, Student Nationalism in China (Stanford, 1966), pp. 1-6.

122. See supra, pp. 235-236.

123. See supra, pp. 257-259.

124. In their petition to the government, the students listed six demands: (1) opposition to the so-called autonomous movement, (2) open conduct of Sino-Japanese relations, (3) prohibition of arbitrary arrests, (4) safeguard of territorial sovereignty, (5) cessation of civil strife, and (6) freedom of speech, press, and assembly. The leaflets were directed against Japanese aggression, with no evidence of anti-government literature. Similar observations were reported in T.

290 CHINA AND THE FOREIGN POWERS

A. Bisson's Japan in China (New York, 1938), and John
Israel's work just cited. See also Hao-jan Chu, "The De-
cember 9th Movement," The China Quarterly, No. 30 (April-
June 1967), pp. 173-174; Jessie G. Lutz, "December 9, 1935:
Student Nationalism and the Chinese Christian Colleges,"
The Journal of Asian Studies, Vol. 26, No. 4 (August 1967),
pp. 627-648.

125. For details, see John Israel, op. cit., pp. 111-123. Several
works in English have since been written on the subject,
such as Hubert Freyn, Prelude to War: The Chinese Students
Rebellion of 1935-1936 (Shanghai, 1939); Helen F. Snow (Nym
Wales), Notes on the Chinese Student Movement (Madison,
Conn., 1959). Estimates of the number of students involved
in the December 9th demonstration vary from eight hundred
to two thousand.

126. For the December 16th incident and its aftermath, see Chin-
tun Liang, "The Autonomous Movement in North China,"
Biographical Literature (in Chinese), Vol. 12, No. 6 (June
1968), pp. 17-21; John Israel, op. cot., pp. 125-156.

127. See Edgar Snow, Journey to the Beginning (New York, 1958),
pp. 142-143, 146.

128. See Mao Tse-tung: Selected Works (New York, 1954-1962, 5
vols.), Vol. 1, p. 193; William L. Tung, The Political Institutions of Modern China, p. 162.

129. H.H. K'ung, then Acting President of the Executive Yuan of
the National Government, analyzed fully the positions of
Stalin and Mao in his "A Memoir of the Sian Incident," in
The Collection of Speeches of H.H. K'ung (New York, 1960,
2 vols., in Chinese), Vol. II, pp. 657-704.

130. According to Mao Tse-tung, Chiang accepted the following
terms prior to his release from Sian: (1) to reorganize the
Kuomintang and the National Government by expelling the pro-
Japanese clique and admitting the anti-Japanese elements;
(2) to release the patriotic leaders in Shanghai and all other
political prisoners and to guarantee the freedom and rights
of the people; (3) to end the policy of 'annihilating the Communists' and to enter into an alliance with the Red Army to
resist Japan; (4) to convoke a national salvation conference of
all parties, all groups, all circles, and all armies to decide
on the line for fighting Japan and saving the nation from
extinction; (5) to establish relations of cooperation with
countries sympathetic to China's resistance to Japan; and
(6) to adopt other specific ways and means for national

salvation. See Mao Tse-tung: Selected Works, Vol I, p. 255.

On the othe hand, Chiang flatly denied that he had ever entered into any agreement with Chang and Yang or with the Communists. In all probability, they discussed verbally how to consolidate the nation for an eventual war with their common enemy. Thus Chiang declared, at the time of his departure from Sian, that all promises would be kept and actions resolutely taken. For further details, see Chiang Kai-shek and Madame Mei-ling (Sung) Chiang, Sian: A Coup D'etat, which is also available in English under the title, General Chiang Kai-shek; the Account of the Fortnight in Sian When the Fate of China Hung in the Balance (Garden City, N.Y., 1937). Further information on the Sian incident and the united front can be found in Lyman P. van Slyke, Enemies and Friends: The United Front in Chinese Communist History (Stanford, 1967), Chs. 4-8; James M. Bertram, Crisis in China: The Story of the Sian Mutiny (London, 1937).

131. See supra, pp. 53-54, 84.

132. Art. I (1) of the Treaty. For the text, see Carnegie, Treaties, pp. 89-93; British Treaty Series, No. 42 (1925); U. S. Treaty Series, No. 723; League Of Nations, Treaty Series, No. 982 (1925).

133. Japan never declared war throughout the Sino-Japanese hostilities; China did so on December 9, 1941. According to the Hague Convention on Opening Hostilities of 1907, the contracting parties were required not to commence hostilities "without previous and explicit warning, in the form either of a reasoned declaration of war or of an ultimatum with conditional declaration of war." Several states, especially Japan, have not always followed the Hague stipulations. In the present case, Japan tried to avoid the legal implications of violating treaty obligations. Nonetheless, an armed conflict of considerable extent and prolonged period should be considered a war in a material sense, with or without a declaration and equally accountable in case of violation of international conventions or other commitments.

134. For details of the Nine-Power Treaty of 1922, see supra, pp. 187-189.

135. Completely disappointed with the result of the Conference, Arnold Toynbee was very critical of the attitudes of its participating powers as frankly expressed in the following remarks: "The spectacle of international anarchy moved them not to try to put an end to it but simply to try to keep out of it;

and in their eager anxiety to make sure of avoiding a hero's death they took flight from Brussels in November 1937 as ignominiously as Joseph Sedley had fled from the same city in June 1815 at the intimidating sound of the guns at Waterloo." Survey of International Affairs, 1937, pp. 52-53. For details, see Tsien Tai, China and the Nine Power Conference at Brussels in 1937 (New York, 1964), pp. 1-20.

136. Art. 16 of the League Covenant reads:

"1. Should any Member of the League resort to war in disregard of its covenants under Articles 12, 13 or 15, it shall ipso facto be deemed to have committed an act of war against all other Members of the League, which hereby undertake immediately to subject it to the severance of all trade or financial relations, the prohibition of all intercourse between their nationals and the nationals of the covenant-breaking State, and the prevention of all financial, commercial or personal intercourse between the nationals of the covenant-breaking State and the nationals of any other State, whether a Member of the League or not.

"2. It shall be the duty of the Council in such case to recommend to the several Governments concerned what effective military, naval or air force the Members of the League shall severally contribute to the armed forces to be used to protect the covenants of the League.

"3. The members of the League agree, further, that they will mutually support one another in the financial and economic measures which are taken under this Article, in order to minimize the loss and inconvenience resulting from the above measures, and that they will mutually support one another in resisting any special measures aimed at one of their number by the covenant-breaking State, and that they will take the necessary steps to afford passage through their territory to the forces of any of the Members of the League which are cooperating to protect the covenants of the League.

"4. Any Member of the League which has violated any covenant of the League may be declared to be no longer a Member of the League by a vote of the Council concurred in by the Representatives of all the other Members of the League represented thereon."

137. According to Art. 17(1), "in the event of a dispute between a Member of the League and a State which is not a member of the League, or between States not members of the League, the State or States not members of the League shall be invited to accept the obligations of membership in the League for the purposes of such dispute, upon such conditions as the Council

may deem just.'' Should the non-member accept such invitation, the same Article stipulated that "the provisions of Articles 12 to 16 inclusive shall be applied with such modifications as may be deemed necessary by the Council.''

138. In accordance with Art. 17(3), "if a State so invited shall refuse to accept the obligations of membership in the League for the purposes of such dispute, and shall resort to war against a Member of the League, the provisions of Article 16 shall be applicable as against the State taking such action.'' While China relied on the League to settle the dispute through pacific means, Japan replied with a gigantic scale of military operations. Japanese aircraft bombarded not only open towns and civilians but also British and American gunboats in the Yangtze River. In August 1937, the British Ambassador to China, Sir Huge Knatchbull-Hugesson, was injured on his way from Nanking to Shanghai, while his car flying the union jack was machine-gunned by the Japanese air force.

139. For details, see Wunsz King, China and the League of Nations, pp. 85-86.

140. For details, see League of Nations, Monthly Summary, September 1938, p. 216.

141. See supra, note 138, for Art. 17(3) of the League Covenant.

142. The important points of the report were contained in the following passage:
"In view of Japan's refusal of the invitation extended to her, the provisions of Article 16 were, under Article 17, Paragraph 3, applicable in present conditions, and the Members of the League were entitled to act as before on the basis of that finding, and also to adopt individually the measures provided for in Article 16. As regards coordinated action in carrying out such measures, it was evident from the experience of the past that all elements of cooperation which were necessary were not yet assured.''

League of Nations, Monthly Summary, September 1938, p. 217.

143. In his Chicago speech, President Franklin D. Roosevelt commented on the spread of the epidemic of world lawlessness in the following manner: ''When an epidemic of physical disease starts to spread, the community approves and joins in a quarantine of the patients in order to protect the health of the community against the spread of the disease.... There must be positive measures to preserve peace.'' Department of State, Peace and War: United States Foreign Policy, 1931-1941, Doc. 93, pp. 383-387. For a critical examination of the

United States policy toward the Far East from Japan's occupation of Manchuria and Jehol to her full-scale war with China, consult Dorothy Borg, The United States and the Far Eastern Crisis of 1933-1938 (Cambridge, 1964).

144. For the text, see Chen, Treaties, pp. 113-114; Chinese Republic, Treaties, pp. 486-487. A Sino-Soviet Commercial Treaty was signed on June 16, 1939 (ibid., pp. 488-499).

145. See Julius W. Pratt, A History of United States Foreign Policy, p. 684. For a detailed description of Allied military plans against Japan, see Chin-tun Liang, The Cairo Conference and China (in Chinese; Hongkong, 1962), pp. 52-59, 65-115.

146. Chen, Treaties, P. 174. For the full text of the Cairo Declaration, see ibid., pp. 173-174; Department of State Bulletin, Vol. 9 (December 4, 1943), p. 393.

147. Chen, Treaties, p. 174.

148. No. 8 of the Postdam Proclamation reads: "The terms of the Cairo Declaration shall be carried out and Japanese sovereignty shall be limited to the islands of Honshu, Hokkaido, Kyushu, Shikoku and such minor islands as we determine." For the full text of the Proclamation, see ibid., pp. 216-217.

149. For further clarification of effect of war on treaties, see William L. Tung, International Law in an Organizing World, p. 432.

150. For the text of the Yalta Agreements, see Chen, Treaties, pp. 194-195.

151. See Arts. 1-3 of the Yalta Agreement regarding Japan.

152. See Art. V of the Sino-Soviet Treaty on General Principles for the Settlement of Questions between the Countries Concerned, May 31, 1924 (supra, p. 240. note 15). For Russia's designs in Outer Mongolia, see supra, pp. 81-83.

153. For details, see supra, pp. 48-49.

154. See supra, p. 246, note 63. For the construction and subsequent development of the Chinese Eastern Railway, see supra, pp. 116, 120, 220-223.

155. See supra, pp. 121-122.

156. Quotes from the Yalta Agreement (Chen, Treaties, p. 195). The United States government authorized Ambassador Hurley to

inform Chiang Kai-shek of the Yalta Agreement on June 15, 1945.

157. Prime Minister Churchill deemed that the Yalta Agreement regarding Japan was primarily an American affair, and signed it against the advice of Foreign Secretary Anthony Eden. See Winston S. Churchill, Triumph and Tragedy (Boston, 1953), p. 390. For further comments on Soviet designs in China and the Yalta Agreement, see Dean Acheson, Present at the Creation: My Years in the State Department (New York, 1969), p. 202; John Leighton Stuart, Fifty Years in China (New York, 1954), pp. 177, 179, 180, 272, 313.

158. Prior to the Yalta Agreement, intelligence reports from the United States Army, Navy, and Air Force reached the same conclusion. See Julius W. Pratt, op. cit., p. 690; Herbert Feis, The China Tangle: The American Effort in China from Pearl Harbor to the Marshall Mission (Princeton, 1953), p. 236.

159. For the text of the Sino-American Treaty and Exchanges of Notes, which came into effect on May 20, 1943, see Chinese Republic, Treaties, pp. 659-669; Chen, Treaties, pp. 149-159.

160. For the text of the Sino-British Treaty and the Exchanges of Notes, which entered into force on May 20, 1943, see Appendix D; Chen, Treaties, pp. 140-148; Chinese Republic, Treaties, pp. 589-599.

161. The Sino-British Treaty of January 11, 1943, also applied to Canada, which, however, chose to conclude a separate treaty to the same effect with China on April 14, 1944. For its text, see ibid., pp. 50-56; Chen, Treaties, pp. 179-183.

162. For the text of the Treaty and related documents, see ibid., pp. 218-234; Chinese Republic, Treaties, pp. 505-523.

163. At their fifth meeting, Stalin repeatedly assured Soong that the evacuation would be completed within three months. See ibid., p. 523; Chen, Treaties, p. 233.

164. For details of the railway systems in Manchuria, see supra, pp. 116-120, 121-123, 156-157.

165. See Chinese Republic, Treaties, pp. 512-515; Chen, Treaties, pp. 223-226. For a comparison of the administration of the Chungchun Railway with that of the Chinese Eastern Railway under the 1896 Statutes and the 1924 Sino-Soviet Agreement, see supra, pp. 120, 222-223.

166. The question of Outer Mongolia was provided for in the Exchange of Notes between the Chinese Foreign Minister Wang Shih-chieh and the Soviet Foreign Minister V. Molotov, on the same date as the Treaty. On October 20, 1945, a plebiscite was held in Outer Mongolia under the supervision of the Soviets. Under the circumstances, almost all the Mongolians voted for independence as expected. China had no alternative but to extend formal recognition of the existing situation in January of the following year.

167. Cf. supra, pp. 81-83.   Under Art. V of the Sino-Soviet Treaty of 1924, the Soviet Union "recognizes that Outer Mongolia is an integral part of the Republic of China and respects China's sovereignty therein."

168. Cf. supra, pp. 219-222.

169. For details, see supra, pp. 160-163.

170. See Art. 5 of the 1945 Treaty and Arts. 2-3 of the Exchange of Notes, in which the Soviet Union agreed to recognize only the National Government as the Central Government of China.

171. See supra, pp. 162-163, 190-192.

172. The Charter was adopted on June 26, 1945, by the United Nations Conference on International Organization at San Francisco, of which the United States, Great Britain, the Soviet Union, and China were the sponsoring states. For the obligations of member states, see, in particular, Art. 2(4) of the Charter.

173. For a statement of this date by the Chinese Foreign Minister to that effect, see Chen, Treaties, pp. 233-234; Chinese Republic, Treaties, pp. 523-524.

174. See infra, pp. 320-321.

175. For China's past predominance on the Asiatic mainland, see supra, pp. 1-2.

Chapter 10
CHINA IN TRANSITION AFTER EMANCIPATION FROM UNEQUAL TREATIES

I. FOREIGN INVOLVEMENT IN THE MIDST OF NATION-ALIST-COMMUNIST CONFLICTS

1. American Mediation and Economic Aid
Prior to the Nationalist Debacle

After eight years of war against Japan, China eventually won the victory with her Allies and emerged as one of the major powers. Domestically, however, the nation was deeply immersed in an unprecedented civil strife, which indirectly involved both the United States and the Soviet Union. Actually, wartime relationships between the Nationalists and Communists proved at best an uneasy truce.

The United States made an attempt to serve good offices with a view to improving the situation. Accompanied by American Ambassador Patrick J. Hurley,[1] Mao Tse-tung flew from Yenan to Chungking, China's wartime capital, on August 28, 1945. He discussed with Chiang Kai-shek several vital issues, including the nationaliziation of armed forces, democratization of political institutions, and participation of Communist forces in accepting the surrender of Japanese troops in China. Although the views of both parties were frankly exchanged and clarified, their conversations did not lead to substantial agreement for harmonious cooperation.[2] Barely one month after the Japanese surrender, the so-called second united front completely broke down and armed conflicts intensified.

Extremely concerned with the worsening situation, President Harry S. Truman dispatched General George C. Marshall as his special envoy to China for the purpose of persuading

297

"the Chinese Government to call a national conference of representatives of the major political elements to bring about the unification of China.'[3] In his statement on United States policy toward China on December 15, 1945, President Truman emphasized that "a strong, united and democratic China is of the utmost importance to the success of this United Nations organization and for world peace." It was his firm belief that "a China disorganized and divided either by foreign aggression, such as that undertaken by the Japanese, or by violent internal strife, is an undermining influence to world stability and peace, now and in the future.'[4]

Thus the Marshall Mission had two major objectives: first, to achieve a unified and integrated China by recognizing the National Government as the only legal government of China, in accordance with the Cairo Declaration and the Potsdam Proclamation; and, second, to attain peace and democracy by broadening the bases of the National Government so as to include Communists and other political elements in the country and to integrate existing autonomous forces into the Chinese National Army.[5] Before the end of the year and prior to the arrival of General Marshall, Communist troops penetrated deep into Manchuria and North China. In view of American-Soviet potential rivalry in the Far East and Moscow's great influence on the Chinese Communist Party at that time, Chiang Kai-shek had serious doubts as to whether "Moscow would agree to let the United States succeed in its mediation efforts" between the Nationalists and the Communists.[6] Marshall's efforts to render good offices and mediation were then accepted by leaders of both parties, even though no final agreement on the restoration of peace and unity could be reached.

Failing to accomplish the objectives of his mission, General Marshall left China for Washington in January 1947,[7] to become Secretary of State. On January 7, General Marshall issued a statement, blaming both parties for their overwhelming suspicion of each other: on the Nationalists, "the leaders of Government are strongly opposed to a communistic form of government;" on the Communists, they insisted that "they are Marxists and intend to work toward establishing a communistic form of government in China."[8] Nonetheless, he launched a great hope in the adoption by the National Assembly, on December 25, 1946, of a new democratic constitution, "which to all major respects is in accordance with the principles laid down by all-party Political Consultative Conference of last January." In his opinion, "it is unfortunate that the Communists did not see fit to participate in the Assembly since the Constitution that has been adopted seems to include every major point that they wanted."[9]

American aid to China after V-J Day was fairly substantial. In 1946, the United States signed agreements with China to forward lend-lease supplies[10] and to sell military and civilian war surplus property at a nominal price.[11] The new Sino-American Treaty of Friendship, Commerce and Navigation of November 4, 1946 provided a model of equal and reciprocal relationships between China and foreign powers. [12] This Treaty was followed by the signing of the Agreement concerning the United States Relief Assistance to the Chinese People of October 27, 1947.[13] Although the failure of Marshall's mission had adversely affected the American attitude toward the National Government, Congress eventually enacted the China Aid Act which became law on April 3, 1948.[14] Consequently, the Economic Aid Agreement was concluded between the two countries on July 3 of the same year.[15] Other agreements to effect educational exchange[16] and the establishment of the Joint Commission on Rural Reconstruction[17] were signed in 1947 and 1948 respectively.

The unique feature of American economic and technical aid to China was that the United States did not actually expect anything in return. Certain quarters of the Chinese government complained of its insufficiency comparable to the magnitude of China's problems and also the lack of substantial military aid to suppress the Communist rebellion. [18] In all fairness, however, the postwar treaty relationship between China and the United States is not only technically equal but also materially beneficial to the recipient country. To a nation at the mercy of unequal treaties for a century, American economic assistance demonstrated a sharp contrast with the unilateral exactions by imperialist powers in the past. It was true that, in rendering assistance to the National Government, the United States did not intend to go so far as to be directly or actively involved in the Chinese civil war. [19] The causes for the subsequent fall of the mainland to the Chinese Communists were many, and the major responsibility should not be shifted to the prevailing policy of the American government.[20]

2. Comparison of Communist and Nationalist Foreign Policies

Dissensions between the Chinese Communists and Nationalists are largely in political ideologies and domestic programs rather than in fundamental foreign policies. No matter which party is in power, national interests generally govern China's relations with foreign countries. Anti-imperialism was elaborately pronounced in the manifesto of the Communist Party's second national congress in 1922.[21] Ever since its formation in 1920, the Party had relied on Moscow for guidance and assistance until its open split with the Soviet leadership. [22]

When the Chinese Soviet Republic was created at Juichin, Kiangsi province, basic principles of foreign relations were stipulated in its constitution of November 7, 1931.[23] This first fundamental law of the Chinese Communist regime avowed to abolish all political and economic privileges previously obtained by imperialist powers through unequal treaties and to confiscate or nationalize all foreign enterprises with the exception of those permitted by Chinese laws.[24] It offered asylum to foreign revolutionaries and equal rights to all alien toilers residing in China.[25] Finally, as provided in this constitution, "the Soviet regime of China declares its readiness to form a united revolutionary front with the world proletariat and all oppressed nations, and proclaims the Soviet Union, the land of proletarian dictatorship, to be its loyal ally." [26]

Either outlawed by, or in opposition to, the government, the Chinese Communist Party was not in the position to carry out its foreign policies until it came to power by the end of 1949. Of course, its close relationship with Moscow had long been maintained. On the eve of its victory on the mainland, it convened the Chinese People's Political Consultative Conference (CPPCC) in Peking on September 21-30, 1949, represented by delegates from all friendly political parties, groups, and organizations.[27] As the constituent body of the People's Republic for the creation of the Central People's Government, CPPCC adopted the Common Program as the fundamental law of the land prior to the enactment of a constitution in 1954.[28]

This Common Program declared China's opposition to imperialist aggression; cooperation with all peace-loving countries, especially with the Soviet Union;[29] "protection of the independence, freedom, integrity of territory and sovereignty of the country";[30] and maintenance of friendly and commercial relations with foreign governments on the bases of equality and mutual benefit and respect.[31] While safeguarding the right of law-abiding aliens in China[32] and granting asylum to foreign political refugees,[33] the Common Program stressed the utmost importance "to protect the proper rights and interests of Chinese residing abroad."[34] With respect to treaties previously concluded between China and foreign powers, it decided to "recognize, abrogate, revise, or re-negotiate them according to their respective contents."[35]

For the implementation of a constitutional government on a wider base but Communist oriented, Peking convoked the First National People's Congress on September 15-28, 1954. Of the total number of 1,226 deputies, all were selected from different localities except 150 from national minorities, 60 from the armed forces, and 30 from the Chinese overseas.[36] As the supreme organ of state authority and the highest legislative body of the People's Republic, the Congress adopted the Constitution of the People's Republic of China to replace the Common Program as the fundamental law of the land.[37] Mainly dealing with the organization and functions of the government, the Constitution reasserted its basic policy of maintaining friendly relations with socialist and other peace-loving countries, particularly with the Soviet Union, based on "the principle of equality, mutual benefit and mutual respect for each other's sovereignty and territorial integrity."[38]

Another important document with provisions on Peking's foreign policies prior to the strain in Sino-Soviet relations must be mentioned. It is the Constitution of the Communist Party of China, adopted by its Eighth National Congress on September 26, 1956.[39] This Party Constitution reaffirmed China's solidarity with socialist countries under the leadership of the Soviet Union, and advocated peaceful coexistence among countries with different political systems. It emphatically stated that "the Party must work together with the people of the whole country to bring about the liberation of Taiwan."[40]

The foreign policies embodied in the above-mentioned documents were formulated by the Communist regime from 1931 to 1956, serving as guidelines for its foreign relations with other countries. In comparison with the policies of the Nationalist government, the Communist emphasis on friendship with socialist countries marked, among others, one important difference, which, however, no longer holds true after the Sino-Soviet open split. Political asylum is usually granted by nations in accordance with international law and practice, with or without specific provisions in domestic laws. As to the abolition of unequal treaties, establishment of friendly and commercial relations with other nations on the basis of equality and reciprocity, maintenance of territorial integrity and national sovereignty against imperialist aggression, as well as protection of overseas Chinese and of aliens residing in China, the Communist Party has shared almost similar views as those long advocated by the Nationalist Party. [41]

Although ideology played an important role in Peking's foreign relations in early years, Chinese nationalism still prevailed over international communism whenever there were conflicts between the two. This has been proved by later developments of Peking's relationships with the Soviet Union, Outer Mongolia, and most of the Eastern European states. The new constitution and program of the Chinese Communist Party, adopted at its Ninth National Congress in April 1969, condemned modern revisionism and the reactionaries of all countries. It seems that Peking is now more antagonistic to the Soviet Union than to the United States. [42]

Leased territories, foreign concessions and settlements, and other unilateral rights and privileges in China were terminated after the abolition of unequal treaties. The most crucial issue confronting China today is the recovery of territories previously lost to foreign powers and not yet restored to China. To achieve this objective, the Chinese Communists have been in accord with the established policy of the Nationalists. In enumerating lost territories in his important work,

The Three People's Principles, Sun Yat-sen included those within China's own territorial domain and other areas traditionally under her influence.[43] Decrying the break-up of the Chinese territory by imperialist powers in the past century, Chiang Kai-shek warned that "the people as a whole must regard this as a national humiliation, and not until all lost territories have been recovered can we relax our efforts to wipe out this humiliation and save ourselves from destruction."[44] Mao Tse-tung has adopted the same policy both before and after he came to power. As early as 1936, he told Edgar Snow that "it is the immediate task of China to regain all our lost territories."[45] In his Chinese Revolution and Chinese Communist Party, written in December 1939, Mao listed Chinese territories ceded or leased after the Opium War and condemned imperialist exploitations in China.[46]

Aside from former tributary states and areas under Chinese influence, China's lost territories generally include those ceded to foreign powers, such as Formosa, the Pescadores, Hongkong, Macao, and several areas along the Sino-Russian border now under Soviet control.[47] Chinese students were so taught about the lost territories in history and geography classes long before the establishment of the People's Republic. Notwithstanding divergent opinions on domestic politics among the Communists, the Nationalists, and people of other convictions, there has never been any disagreement among them concerning the importance and necessity of recovering lost territories and abolishing unequal treaties.[48] Although Peking has contested China's seat at the United Nations now held by the Republic of China, leaders of both sides objected to the so-called two-China plan. In other words, Taiwan is a part of China and should not be treated as a separate entity under any circumstances. This reveals another point of Communist-Nationalist accord in the field of foreign policies. [49]

With respect to the delimitation of boundaries, Nationalist China recognized its importance as early as 1929, when the Political Program of the National Government during the Period of Political Tutelage was promulgated. The Program laid down four points: (1) to establish a committee to study boundary treaties, (2) to make boundary maps, (3) to ascertain the breath of the maritime belt and that of the straits, and (4) to delimit the uncertain boundaries.[50] By the Sino-British Exchange of Notes of April 9, 1935,[51] a Yunnan-Burma Commission was established to delimit the boundary between Burma and China's Yunnan province. Because the National Government was then preoccupied with negotiations for the abolition of unequal treaties and later with the war against Japan, this important task of demarcating boundaries with neighboring countries had to be postponed. Among the unsettled boundaries, the National Government specified the following:

> "The southernmost and westernmost boundaries remain to be settled as the Pamirs on the west constitute an undemarcated area among China, the U.S.S.R. and the British Empire, and the sovereignty of the Tuansha Islands (the Coral Islands) on the south are contested among China, the Commonwealth of Philippines and Indo-China. The northern section of the boundary between China and Burma remains to be demarcated." [52]

The boundary treaties concluded between Communist China and several neighboring countries were, in fact, the continuation of the program initiated by the National Government but not yet accomplished. The Sino-Indian boundary disputes and the Sino-Soviet territorial controversies confronting Peking in recent years would probably have occurred no matter which Chinese government were in power, even though the means for settlement might be sought in a less hostile manner. After a comparison of Communist-Nationalist foreign policies, it is safe to conclude that, with the exception of Communist ultimate desire for world revolution, which has been reflected in Peking's conduct of foreign affairs, they are largely similar in many practical aspects, differences in tone and expression notwithstanding. In this connection, it must be emphasized that the present discussion is chiefly limited to fundamental policies, with special reference to the abolition of unequal treaties and the recovery of lost territories and rights. Tactics for the execution of foreign policies are subject to constant changes so as to be adaptable to the international situation in general as well as domestic programs, particularly the political alignment, economic development, and military strength.[53] All these important factors vary at different times, and the consequences of the variations will affect the foreign relations of a nation even under the same government.[54]

3. Soviet Assistance to Communist China
Despite the 1945 Treaty

In domestic and foreign affairs, the Chinese Communists have been known both for their flexibility and for their regidity, depending upon the issues and circumstances. When they engaged in civil war from 1945 to 1949 and domestic reconstruction in the ensuing decade,[55] Mao Tse-tung deemed it expedient to adhere to his declared policy of lean-to-one-side in close cooperation with the Soviet Union. Indeed, the military capabilities of the Chinese Red Army were greatly strengthened due to the Soviet transfer of Japanese arms and equipment captured in Manchuria. After taking control of Northeast and North China, Mao proclaimed the inauguration of the Central People's Government in Peking on October 1, 1949. Only one day later, the Soviet Union formally recognized the new regime, in spite of her Treaty of Friendship and Alliance with the Nationalist Government in 1945.[56] General N. Roshin, former Soviet Ambassador to the Nationalist Government, was appointed first Soviet Ambassador to the newly created People's Republic.

Once Moscow set the example, other Communist countries, such as Albania, Bulgaria, Czechoslovakia, East Germany, North Korea, Outer Mongolia, Poland, and Rumania, followed suit. Their prompt establishment of diplomatic relations with Communist China was in response to Peking's policy of socialist solidarity. In the following year, other nations, including Great Britain, Sweden, Norway, Denmark, Finland, the Netherlands, Switzerland, Afghanistan, Burma, Ceylon, India, Indonesia, and Israel,[57] extended recognition to the new regime. In this respect, Soviet initiative encouraged these states to hasten their decisions and enhanced the international status and prestige of the People's Republic at the time of its inception.

Mao Tse-tung went to Moscow in December 1949. As a result of his extensive discussions with Stalin, the Sino-Soviet Treaty of Friendship, Alliance, and Mutual Assistance was concluded on February 14, 1950,[58] accompanied by a series of subsidiary agreements.[59] Meanwhile, the Soviet Union unilaterally nullified her Treaty of Friendship and Alliance with the Nationalist Government, signed on August 14, 1945. The new Treaty cemented the two Communist giants into a military alliance. They agreed that "in the event of one of the contracting parties being attacked by Japan or any state allied with her and thus being involved in a state of war, the other contracting party shall immediately render military and other assistance by all means at its disposal." [60]

On the date of the conclusion of the new Treaty, Moscow and Peking entered into the Agreement concerning the Chang-chun Railway, Port Arthur, and Dairen,[61] which will be fully discussed later.[62] By another agreement, the Soviet Union simultaneously promised to extend credits to the Chinese People's Republic up to the amount of $300,000,000.[63] In the Exchange of Notes between Foreign Ministers Chou En-lai and Andrei Y. Vyshinsky, on the occasion of the signing the above mentioned Treaty and Agreements, Peking recognized the independence of Outer Mongolia, and Moscow agreed to transfer the Japanese assests in Manchuria acquired by Soviet economic agencies to the Chinese government without compensation. [64]

Sino-Soviet economic and technical cooperation was later expanded into different areas on various subjects: formation of joint stock companies for the operation of civil avaiation and exploitation of petroleum and non-ferrous metal resources in Sinkiang;[65] trade agreements for exchange of goods, material, and equipment; exchange of scientific information; installation of long-distance telephone service; establishment of a common railway passenger and freight system; renovation and construction of 141 projects by 1959; additional loans of $130,000,000;[66] and free navigation of merchant ships in their common waterways.[67] At the end of 1957, Peking recorded Soviet assistance in the construction of 211 major industrial projects in China, providing not only financial aid but also technical experts ranging from 7,000 to 10,000.[68] More Soviet industrial goods, machinery, and equipment were sent to China in 1958, in exchange for Chinese textiles, tungsten, tin, tung oil, soya-beans, and other commodities.[69] In the same year, Moscow agreed to assist Peking in the construction and expansion of 47 industrial enterprises, including "important metallurigical enterprises, giant turbine works, turbo-generator works, precision instruments works, power plants, coal mines, an oil refinery, chemical works, timber works, and a special metal products plant." [70]

On February 7, 1959, Khrushchev and Chou En-lai concluded new agreements in Moscow, raising the number of
industrial projects by another 78, to be completed in the
next eight years. Included in these projects were "metallur-
igical, chemical, coal, petroleum, machine building, electrical machinery, radio, building materials, and other industries
and power stations." [71] According to a trade protocol signed
on February 26, 1959, Sino-Soviet trade volume in 1959 was
expected to reach 7,200 million roubles. [72] In view of the above,
Peking commended Soviet aid to China as "one of the important factors that made rapid progress in our country
possible." [73] Of course, Communist China had also many
complaints in her relations with the Soviet Union, but all
grievances, political or economic, were concealed at the
time. In spite of interparty strains not long after Khrushchev's ascendancy to power, Moscow and Peking maintained
close relations until their open split in 1960. [74]

Because of Moscow's recognition of the People's Republic
in Peking, the National Government, having retreated to
Canton, declared its severance of diplomatic relations with
the Soviet Union on October 3, 1949. The active assistance
by Moscow to Peking was definitely in violation of the 1945
Treaty of Friendship and Alliance, which unequivocally stip-
ulated that Soviet "support and assistance will go exclusively
to the National Government as the Central Government of
China." [75] Thus the National Government of the Republic of
China brought before the United Nations a complaint of Soviet
breach of treaty obligations. At its sixth session in 1950, the
General Assembly discussed the issue and decided that
"U.S.S.R., in its relations with China since the surrender of
Japan, has failed to carry out the Treaty of Friendship and
Alliance between China and the U.S.S.R. of 14 August 1945." [76]
In this resolution, the United Nations delivered an important
verdict against Soviet action in China, but it alone could not
reverse the situation. As stated before, the Soviet Union continued to extend aid to Communist China until their relations
were openly ruptured.

According to President Chiang Kai-shek, Soviet actions in
Manchuria violated the terms of the 1945 Treaty soon after
its conclusion. This might partly explain why he twice turned
down Stalin's invitations in that year to meet in person either
in Moscow or on the Sino-Soviet border. [77] Chinag's flat re-

fusal might have also strengthened Stalin's determination to crush the Nationalists, who had long been leaning to the side of the United States. The rivalry of interests between the Soviet Union and the United States, temporarily laid aside during World War II, came to the surface again in the midst of China's civil strife. Meanwhile, basic contradictions also existed between the two Communist giants. Later events will reveal that the Peking-Moscow friendship lasted only one decade, even though their 1950 Treaty of Alliance remains technically in effect.

II. PEACE TREATIES WITH JAPAN AND ITALY

1. Exclusion of China from Peace Treaty Negotiations

With respect to territorial or other acquisitions in China previously obtained by the Axis Powers, Germany had lost them all as a result of the Treaty of Versailles of 1919,[78] but those amassed by Japan and, to a small extent by Italy, remained to be dealt with after the termination of World War II. Through prolonged negotiations by the Foreign Ministers of Great Britain, France, the United States, and the Soviet Union, a peace treaty with Italy was signed in Paris, on February 10, 1947,[79] under which Italy relinquished all her unilateral rights and privileges in China.[80] In the case of Japan, the United States military occupation necessitated by circumstances postponed the conclusion of a treaty of peace.

It was not until the midst of the Korean War that John Foster Dulles was authorized by President Truman to search for an agreement among the Allied powers on the terms for a peace treaty with Japan. After preparing a draft treaty· acceptable to most of the major powers, the United States extended invitations to fifty-four nations to attend the Peace Conference with Japan at San Francisco, on September 4, 1951. Among the Allied powers at war with Japan, China fought singlehandly for a long period and suffered the heaviest losses. Nevertheless, the rivalry between two governments in Taipei and Peking damaged her international image. On the ground that there was not a single voice speaking for the whole nation, China was excluded from the peace conference. Because Burma, India, and Yugoslavia declined the American invitations, only fifty-two nations, including the United States, attended the San Francisco Conference. After her proposed amendments were rejected, the Soviet Union together with Czechoslovakia and Poland did not sign the Peace Treaty as concluded by representatives of forty-nine nations at San Francisco, on September 8, 1951.[81]

In the Sino-Soviet Treaty of Friendship, Alliance, and Mutual Assistance of February 14, 1950, both Moscow and Peking agreed to conclude a peace treaty with Japan at the earliest moment.[82] As events developed, the Soviet Union refused to sign the San Francisco Treaty in 1951. Under circumstances prevailing at the time, Peking and Tokyo were not in a position to reach any political settlement. On the other hand, the National Government of the Republic of China and the Japanese government mutually agreed to negotiate for a peace treaty, which was finally concluded in Taipei on April 28, 1952.[83] Although Peking and Moscow declared that neither of them would be bound by any treaty to which it was not a party,[84] territorial and other arrangements beneficial to China would be most likely acquiesced in by the Chinese Communists.

2. Retrocession of Territories 'Stolen'[85] by Japan

Territorial readjustments were provided for in the San Francisco Treaty of 1951. Among others, Japan renounced "all right, title and claim to Formosa (Taiwan) and the Pescadores (Penghu),"[86] as well as "the Spratly Islands and the Paracel Islands."[87] This renunciation was reaffirmed in the Sino-Japanese Peace Treaty of 1952.[88] In the San Francisco Treaty, Japan also renounced "all right, title and claim to the Kurile Islands and to that portion of Sakhalin and the islands adjacent to it over which Japan acquired sovereighty as a consequence of the Treaty of Portsmouth of September 5, 1905."[89] These provisions merely formalized the actual state of affairs, as the Chinese and Russian territories ceded to Japan in 1895 and 1905 were respectively restored to the two countries after World War II.

The growing power of the People's Republic on the mainland caused a fear in the West that Formosa and the Pescadores, now under the control of the Republic of China, might be forcibly taken over by the Chinese Communists. It was thereby argued that the renunciation of Japan's claim to these territories would not automatically confer their titles to China. In other words, the future destiny of these islands originally belonging to China remains to be settled. This attempt at distorting the legal and actual situation for the sake of international expediency cannot stand an objective scrutiny of documentary evidence.

Consequent to the Peace Treaty of Shimonoseki of 1895, China was compelled to cede Formosa and the Pescadores to Japan.[90] In the Cairo Declaration of 1943, the "Three Great Allies" agreed that "all the territories Japan has stolen from the Chinese, such as Manchuria, Formosa, and the Pescadores, shall be restored to the Republic of China."[91] The leaders of the Allied Powers reaffirmed, in the Potsdam Proclamation Defining Terms for Japanese Surrender on July 26, 1945, that "the terms of the Cairo Declaration shall be carried out."[92] When the Peace Treaty with Japan was concluded by the forty-nine states at San Francisco in 1951, the Signatories agreed that "Japan will recognize the full force of all treaties now or hereafter concluded by the Allied Powers for terminating the state of war initiated on September 1, 1939, as well as any other arrangements by the Allied Powers for or in connection with the restoration of peace."[93]

The Potsdam Proclamation was undoubtedly the most important document with respect to final arrangements for the restoration of peace in the Far East. In his capacity as the Special Representative of the United States President to negotiate for the Peace Treaty, John Foster Dulles made a statement on the subject at San Francisco, on September 5, 1951.[94] He explained the reasons for the incorporation, in Article 8 of the Peace Treaty with Japan of 1951, of the Potsdam surrender terms, because these "constitute the only definition of peace terms to which, and by which, Japan and the Allied Powers as a whole are bound."[95]

It is granted that China was not a party to the San Francisco Treaty of Peace with Japan, but "by Article 26,[96] China is given the right to a treaty of peace with Japan, on the same terms as the present treaty.''[97] As stated before, the Republic of China did sign a peace treaty with Japan to that effect in 1952.[98] After all, Formosa and the Pescadores were 'stolen' by Japan from China, not from any other country, and, therefore, these islands should be restored to the original owner from whom Japan detached them in 1895. Legally speaking, there is little room for argument to the contrary.[99] Practically, China has retaken possession of these islands since Japan's surrender in 1945,[100] as the Soviet Union recaptured the Kurile Islands and the portion of Sakhalin and other adjacent islands acquired by Japan from Russia in 1905.

Unfortunately, overemphasis of national interests or consideration of international expediency sometimes overshadow the legal position of a problem. To prevent the possibility of using force by Peking to occupy Taiwan after the outbreak of the Korean War, President Truman declared the neutralization of the Formosa Strait on June 27, 1950. Simultaneously, he deemed it fit to state that "the determination of the future status of Formosa must await the restoration of security in the Pacific, a peace settlement with Japan, or consideration by the United Nations."[101] The reason for the unilateral issuance of such a statement by the head of a state signatory to both the Cairo Declaration and the Potsdam Proclamation, in conflict with previous commitments solemnly made by the major Allies during the war, cannot be explained in any way other than the security strategy of the United States in the Far East at the time.

Since the termination of the Korean War and the conclusion of the Treaty of Peace with Japan, neither the United States nor the United Nations has ever raised the question of the status of Taiwan. On December 2, 1954, the United States government signed a treaty with the Republic of China for the mutual defense of Taiwan and the Pescadores.[102] Legally, without the authority of the United Nations or a regional organization, the United States has no obligation under a bilateral treaty to defend a territory if it is not her own or belongs to the other signatory. It is, therefore, clear that the real concern of the United States is not the legal status of Taiwan but the possible occupation of this strategic island by the Communist forces from Peking.[103]

3. Termination of Unilateral Rights and Privileges in China

In the Peace Treaty of February 10, 1947, Italy agreed to renounce her concession at Tientsin and also all rights and privileges in the international settlements at Shanghai and Amoy. [104] With respect to the special rights and privileges accorded to Italy by the Final Protocol of 1901 for the settlement of disturbances arising out of the Boxer Uprising, the Italian government agreed to relinquish all these benefits, including the remaining portion of the indemnity. [105] The Chinese government was entitled to reparations against Italy for damages sustained during World War II, [106] but voluntarily waived this right and limited its claims to losses suffered by Chinese nationals in Italy and the expenses incurred by the Chinese government for the maintenance of Italian nationals in China. [107]

In the Sino-Japanese Treaty of Peace of 1952, it was recognized that "all treaties, conventions and agreements concluded before December 9, 1941, between China and Japan have become null and void as a consequence of the war." [108] This comprehensive provision included the Final Protocol of 1901, treaties incorporating the Twenty-one Demands, and all others by which Japan obtained various concessions, rights, privileges, and benefits. [109] Thus Japan's acquisitions in China through half a century of aggression were wiped out completely.

With respect to reparations, the San Francisco Peace Treaty provided that Japan was to enter into negotiations with Allied Powers which suffered war damages, "with a view to assisting to compensate those countries for the cost of repairing the damage done, by making available the services of the Japanese people in production, salvaging and other work." [110] In view of the duration and extent of Japan's invasion of her vast territory, resulting in heavy loss of lives and immense damage to public and private property, China was entitled to demand the largest share of reparations. In the Protocol annexed to the Sino-Japanese Peace Treaty of 1952, however, the Chinese government voluntarily waived the benefit of the above-mentioned services to be made available by Japan, "as a sign of magnanimity and good will toward the Japanese people." [111] The generosity manifested by China in this peace treaty was quite a contrast to Japan's demands for a large amount of reparations consequent to the first Sino-Japanese War,[112] and for all other harsh terms exacted from China in the following decades.[113]

When the National Government of the Republic of China signed this peace treaty with Japan on April 28, 1952, it had already lost the control of the mainland. In the Sino-Japanese Exchanges of Notes of the same date, the two contracting parties agreed that "the terms of the present Treaty shall, in respect of the Republic of China, be applicable to all the territories which are now, or which may hereafter be, under the control of its Government."[114]

With the existence of two governments in China for the past two decades,[115] it would be most difficult for Japan to lean to one side. Tokyo has to take into serious consideration the prevailing international alignment, particularly the United States policy in the Far East. While maintaining diplomatic relations with the National Government in Taiwan, Japan has been carrying out trade with Communist China through unofficial channels. This attempt on the part of the Japanese government to keep friendship with both Taipei and Peking has been appreciated by neither.

III. CONSOLIDATION OF BORDER REGIONS

1. Necessity of Consolidation

After eight years of war against Japan, China recovered Taiwan and the Pescadores, but lost Outer Mongolia. As previously described, Czarist Russia and the Soviet Union had long-range designs in Outer Mongolia, whose independence was demanded by Stalin at the Yalta Conference and subsequently formalized in the Sino-Soviet Treaty of 1945.[117] In order to safeguard the territorial integrity of other border regions, Peking encouraged large-scale migration of Chinese population from the interior to Sinkiang, Inner Mongolia, Tibet, and adjacent areas, where efforts for further consolidation have been continuously made through effective administration. [118] Chinese migrants, including many trained engineers, managers, doctors, and nurses, serve double purposes in these under-developed areas: to expedite economic development and to assimilate the minorities. [119] Consideration of national security has also prompted China's determination to strengthen her control of the border regions.

2. Sinkiang

Strategically located and rich in mineral resources, Sinkiang had long been coveted by Russia.[120] During the Republican period, the Chinese Central Government was seldom strong enough to exercise direct control of that remote province. Local affairs were practically left in the hands of the provincial governor, whose political life depended much upon his skillful handling of cordial relations with Russia. Once the Czar even made plans to annex the northern half of the region, but the outbreak of World War I prevented the fulfillment of his ambition. [121] Not long after the Bolshevik Revolution, Moscow resumed activities in the area. From the time of Japan's invasion of Manchuria to the replacement of Governor Sheng Shih-ts'ai in 1943, the Soviet Union managed to dominate a large part of the region politically and economically. [122] It was said that Moscow rendered material support to a local revolt in Kuldja in 1944. [123]

Soviet designs in Sinkiang became a deep concern to China. Posing as a trustworthy friend to reciprocate China's consent to the lavish terms stipulated in the 1945 Treaty of Friendship and Alliance, Moscow decided to retreat from Sinkiang for the time being. Thus, in the Exchange of Notes between the Chinese and Soviet Foreign Ministers on August 14, 1945, particular mention was made of recent events in Sinkiang. As an assurance to China, "the Soviet Government confirms that, as stated in Article 5 of the Treaty of Friendship and Alliance it has no intention of interfering in the internal affairs of China." [124] The situation in Sinkiang was temporarily stabilized after its occupation by the Chinese Communist Army in 1949. [125] Although Sino-Soviet joint projects in economic and industrial fields were in operation for a while, China has taken direct control of these enterprises since 1955.[126] To solicit minority support, Peking created the Sinkiang Uighur Autonomous Region in the same year.[127]

It is doubtful whether 'sinification' of the area would be the ultimate aim of the Chinese Communist government, even though dissident elements from minority groups occasionally crossed the border to take refuge in Soviet territory. Peking denounced Moscow's complicity in the Ili incident in 1962, resulting in the exodus of a large number of minority group members to the Soviet Union. [128] In the open letter of the Central Committee of the Communist Party of China (CPC) to the Central Committee of the Communist Party of the Soviet Union (CPSU) on February 29, 1964, Moscow was accused of carrying on subversive activities in Sinkiang by "trying to sow discord among China's nationalities by means of the press and wireless, inciting China's minority nationalities to break away from their motherland, and inveigling and coercing tens of thousands of Chinese citizens into going to the Soviet Union." [129] In spite of Sino-Soviet border incident of June 10, 1969 and other sporadic skirmishes along the border of Sinkiang,[130] it is most unlikely that China would initiate serious hostilities along this strategic region where Chinese nuclear installations are located, unless the Soviet Union is determined to destroy them by waging a preventive war.

3. Manchuria

Manchuria had long been subject to territorial, political, and economic intrusions by Japan and Russia. From the conclusion of the Russo-Japanese War in 1905 to the termination of World War II, Japan dominated this region for forty years. As a consequence of the Yalta Agreement and Soviet entrance into the war in the Far East, this eventful area was again at the mercy of Moscow. [131] It was not until the conclusion of the Sino-Soviet Treaty of 1950 and other agreements in the ensuing years that territorial sovereignty of Manchuria had reverted to China.

Railways were always important instruments of international politics in Manchuria. The formation and significance of the Changchun Railway after World War II has already been discussed.[132] The control of this railway by a foreign power, like a dagger in one's heart, could not be long tolerated by Peking. In accordance with an agreement of February 14, 1950, the Soviet Union promised to transfer to China without compensation all rights under the joint administration and all the property of the Changchun Railway, upon the conclusion of a peace treaty with Japan but not later than the end of 1952. [133] The transfer was effected on the date as scheduled.[134] On that account, Mao Tse-tung cabled Stalin to express Chinese gratification for the transfer.[135]

With the evacuation of the Soviet garrison from Port Arthur in 1955 and the transfer of the administration of Dairen, as well as the reversion of joint-stock companies to Chinese control, Moscow took a long stride in retreating from Manchuria.[136] This strategic area is, however, not entirely free from external threat as evidenced by the recurrence of border clashes, which will be discussed later. [137]

4. Tibet

The status of Tibet as an integral part of China and British intrusions on that territory have been described before. [138] Due to the preoccupation of the Chinese central government with civil and foreign wars from 1912 to 1949, Tibet, like several provinces in the interior, was almost left alone in the administration of local affairs. Lapse of central control over a part of China's territory does not, however, waive her right to exercise legal authority in that region.

After the Chinese Communists came into power on the mainland, the Central People's Government advised Lhasa to send local representatives to Peking for consultation on administrative and security matters. Suspecting foreign implications in the prolonged delay of their journey, Peking dispatched army units to Tibet in October 1950, and took effective control of the area.[139] The Tibetan representatives finally reached Peking and signed an agreement on May 23, 1951.[140] Under the terms of the Agreement, the people in Tibet are to enjoy the right of regional autonomy under the Central People's Government, which has the authority to handle external affairs respecting the area of Tibet.[141] The local government was replaced by the Preparatory Committee for the Tibetan Autonomous Region, appointed by the State Council of the Central People's Government at Peking.142

It has been argued that the use of force by Peking to incorporate Tibet as one of China's autonomous regions constituted a violation of international law. The question of international law would indeed arise if the Chinese control of Tibet invoked one of the following: (1) conquest of an independent state, (2) annexation of a territory of another state, (3) intrusion on the interests of a third party, or (4) threat to or breach of international peace.

First, in the records of recent history, Tibet was not an independent state. Nor has the international community recognized it as such.

Second, modern suzerainty generally applies to a political entity which is internally autonomous but externally under the control of the suzerain state. Whatever distinctions between sovereignty and suzerainty the British and Russian governments might wish to make in their treaties concerning China's relationship with Tibet, none of them has denied China's authority over Tibet. As stated before, Tibet never belonged to any state other than China. When the Chinese Empire was on the verge of dismemberment during the latter part of the nineteenth century, Great Britain had political and economic designs in Tibet. By defining Chinese-Tibetan relationship under the term 'suzerainty', the British government expected to exercise more freedom of action in this long coveted area. To the Chinese government and people, however, Tibet has always been considered an integral part of China and is so defined in various constitutional documents.

Thirdly, India, as successor to British interests in Tibet, was probably the only third state directly concerned with Peking's move in that region. In its Note to the Central People's Government on October 21, 1950, the Indian government only expressed its anxiety that Peking's military operations might adversely affect the problem of the Communist representation at the United Nations.143 In reply, Peking reaffirmed the status of Tibet as an inalienable part of Chinese territory and rejected any interference in China's domestic affairs by foreign powers. To the Chinese Communists, the problem of Tibet had noting to do with the problem of Chinese representation at the United Nations. [144]

On November 24, 1950, the Tibetan question was brought before the General Committee of the General Assembly, but consideration was indefinitely deferred by a British proposal, which was supported by Indian and other delegates. In addition to the need for further clarification, views were also expressed that the issue was essentially of domestic nature. [145]

As a result of extensive discussions between Indian and Chinese representatives in Peking, from December 31, 1953 to April 29, 1954, the two countries agreed on principles governing their relations in general and with Tibet in particular. [146] On the closing day of their negotiations, they signed the Agreement on Trade and Intercourse between the Tibet Region of China and India, which came into effect on June 3, 1954. [147] According to this Agreement, India was to withdraw garrisons originally stationed at Yatung and Gyantse for the protection of Indian trade with Lhasa and to transfer to China all postal, telegram and telephone installations and equipment owned or operated by the Indian government in Tibet. All these concessions in Tibet had previously been acquired by Great Britain and were passed on to India. [148] In return, China was to permit the establishment of Indian trade agencies in Yatung, Gyantse, and Gartok, and to grant other facilities, including commercial and pilgrim traffic between India and Tibet. [149] Thus any problem consequent to China's action in Tibet affecting the interests of a third party was amicably settled. [150]

Fourthly, clarification must be made as to whether China's action in Tibet constituted a threat to or breach of international peace. To determine the existence of such a situation, the United Nations and particularly the Security Council should be the proper authority in accordance with the Charter. [151] On March 19, 1959, there was an insurrection in Lhasa, but it was soon suppressed by the Chinese garrison. [152] The Dalai Lama fled to India at the end of March to seek political asylum, which was promptly granted by the Indian government. On October 20 of the same year, the Tibetan question was brought before the Fourteenth Session of the General Assembly. While several delegates condemned the Chinese activities in Tibet as an infringement on human rights, the resolution adopted on October 21 did not imply that Tibet was not a part of Chinese territory. [153]

Another resolution adopted by the General Assembly on December 20, 1961, was chiefly concerned with the human rights of the Tibetan people[154] At its Nineteenth Session, several delegates requested the General Assembly to consider the question of Tibet,[155] which was, however, postponed for discussion until the next session. The constitutional relationship of Tibet as an integral part of China was not at issue. The resolution adopted on December 18, 1965,[156] merely appealed to states to use their best endeavors to achieve the respect for human rights and fundamental freedom in Tibet."[157] In other words, the United Nations organs had neither challenged China's territorial title over Tibet nor condemned Peking's military operations in Tibet as a threat to or a breach of international peace.

From the analysis of all relevant points, it can be seen that Peking's undertaking in Tibet was essentially a matter within the domestic jurisdiction of a state. It was deplorable that internal dissensions could not always be solved through peaceful means, and human rights and fundamental freedoms were not fully respected in the Tibetan situation. [158] Nonetheless, the use of force to settle domestic disputes was not uncommon in other countries, including those which condemned the Chinese Communists in the present case. In view of imperialist encroachments on China's border regions in the past and particularly the circumstances leading to the detachment of Outer Mongolia, any central government in control of China would understandably use any means at its disposal to maintain her territorial integrity, Tibet being no exception. The exercise of constitutional rights without the violation of international law cannot be questioned by other states.

IV. RECOVERY OF TERRITORIAL AND SOVEREIGN RIGHTS

1. Restitution of Ceded and Leased Territories

Among the ceded territories, only Formosa (Taiwan) and the Pescadores (Penghu) were restored to China in 1945. [159]

Others included Macao under Portugal, and Hongkong and a portion of Kowloon under Great Britain. This ceded portion of Kowloon was effected by the Sino-British Convention of Peking, October 24, 1860,[160] subsequent to the Anglo-Franco Second Expedition against China,[161] while the leased territory of Kowloon was granted for a period of ninety-nine years in accordance with the Sino-British Convention for the Extension of Hongkong, June 9, 1898.[162]

Japan and Great Britain obtained the above-mentioned ceded territories through war, but Macao's formal transfer to Portugal in 1887 was due to a diplomatic blunder on the part of China.[163] Through diplomatic pressures and threats of use of force, Czarist Russia compelled Imperial China to redemarcate boundaries between the two countries and thereby acquired immense areas of Chinese territory. This historical injustice has seriously strained present Sino-Soviet relations, and will be fully discussed below.[164]

In their struggle for concessions and spheres of influence since 1898, foreign powers had forced China to lease several strategic areas for twenty-five to ninety-nine years.[165] The transfer of the leased territory of Kiaochow from Germany to Japan and its subsequent restitution to China by the Sino-Japanese Agreement of December 1, 1922, have already been described.[166] At the Washington Conference of 1921-1922, Great Britain expressed her readiness to retrocede Wihaiwei to China, but no agreement was reached until 1930.[167] With respect to the lease of the Kowloon extension, Arthur J. Balfour, speaking on behalf of the British delegation, declined to waive it in consideration of the security of Hongkong.[168] Thus Kowloon remained under the control of Great Britain. On the same occasion, M. Viviani of France declared that the French government would return the leased territory of Kuangchou-wan to China if other powers holding leaseholds in China should promise to do the same.[169] The rendition of Kuangchou-wan did not take place until the conclusion of the Sino-Franco Convention of August 18, 1945.[170]

Dairen and Port Arthur were first leased to Russia in 1898 for twenty-five years, and then were transferred by Russia to Japan in 1905. As a result of the Yalta Agreement and the Sino-Soviet Treaty of August 14, 1945, the Soviet Union regained control of these two important ports.[171]

After the Chinese Communist Party came to power on the mainland, Mao Tse-tung went to see Stalin in Moscow. Consequent to their extensive consultations, the Treaty of Friendship, Alliance, and Mutual Assistance was concluded on February 14, 1950.[172] While abrogating the 1945 Treaty signed by the Nationalist government, this new Treaty did not immediately terminate Soviet rights in Manchuria. They agreed, however, that Soviet troops garrisoned at Port Arthur, which was then under Sino-Soviet joint operation, would be withdrawn upon the conclusion of a peace treaty with Japan but not later than 1952.[173] Although the question of Dairen would be examined after the conclusion of such a peace treaty, the administration of this important port was turned over to China under the terms of the 1950 Treaty.[174]

Subsequent to the signing of the San Francisco Peace Treaty with Japan on September 4, 1951,[175] Peking and Moscow decided to postpone the withdrawal of the Soviet garrison from Port Arthur until their conclusion of peace treaties with Japan.[176] It was soon realized, however, that prospects for signing such peace treaties between the two Communist powers and Japan were not in sight. Hence, on October 12, 1954, a joint declaration was issued in Peking to effect the evacuation of Soviet troops from Port Arthur before May 31, 1955. All installations in that area were also to be transferred to the People's Republic at that time.[177] Negotiations for the return of leased territories in China were thus completed except for Kowloon under Great Britain.

2. Restoration of Sovereign Rights

While an area assigned for foreign residence in the name of a concession or a settlement remained legally a part of Chinese territory, it, nevertheless, gradually fell under foreign control and became a virtual imperium in imperio in China.[178] The continuing existence of foreign concessions and settlements was long regarded by the Chinese as a symbol of national humiliation.[179] The forcible seizure of several foreign concessions by the revolutionary mass during the course of the Northern Expedition was mentioned before.[180] The National Government considered their formal rendition extremely important for the readjustment of China's relations with foreign powers.

When the anti-imperialist movement ran high in the early years of the Nationalist rule, Great Britain accepted what would be the inevitable and decided to relinquish her concessions in the following cities: Hankow and Kiukiang in 1927,[181] Chinkiang in 1929,[182] and Amoy in 1930.[183] Belgium returned her concession in Tientsin in 1929.[184] Others were restored to China during and after World War II: British concessions in Tientsin and Canton in 1943,[185] French concessions in Shanghai, Tientsin, Hankow, and Canton in 1946,[186] and Italian concession in Tientsin in 1941.[187] Japan held the largest numbers of concessions, which were all abolished as a result of war with China and the subsequent peace treaties.[188] The return of the international settlements in Shanghai and Amoy was effected by the Sino-American and Sino-British treaties of 1943 and other treaties between China and the powers concerned.[189] Thus this century-old institution, abnormal in international relations and irritating to Chinese sentiment, was completely abolished.[190]

The dates of the rendition of the above-mentioned concessions and settlements, including those reverted to China before, are shown in Table V.

After the United States and Great Britain took the lead to relinquish extraterritoriality,[191] all other rights and privileges unilaterally acquired by foreign powers in China were abolished either simultaneously or soon afterward. These included treaty ports, stationing of foreign warships, coastal trade and inland navigation, as well as foreign pilotage. As a consequence of the abrogation of the Final Protocol of 1901, concluded between China and the foreign powers for the settlement of the Boxer disturbances, the Legation Quarter at Peking and the right to station armed forces along the communication lines from Peking to the sea were terminated. The remaining portions of the Boxer indemnities were either cancelled or assigned for educational or other constructive purposes.[192] Great Britain and France also abandoned their treaty rights to recommend their own nationals to the respective posts of Inspector-General of the Chinese Maritime Customs and Co-Director General of the Chinese Postal Administration.[193] Table VI shows the dates of the termination of extraterritoriality and other unilateral rights and privileges enjoyed by the treaty powers in China.

TABLE V
DATES OF RENDITION OF FOREIGN CONCESSIONS
AND SETTLEMENTS IN CHINA

Countries	Location	Dates of Rendition
Austria	Tientsin	8/14/1917*
Belgium	Tientsin	1/15/1931
France	Canton, Hankow, Shanghai, Tientsin	6/8/1946
Germany	Hankow, Tientsin	8/14/1917*
Great Britain	Hankow	2/19/1927
	Kiukiang	2/27/1927
	Chinkiang	11/15/1929
	Amoy	9/17/1930
	Canton, Tientsin	5/20/1943
Italy	Tientsin	12/9/1941*
Japan	Amoy, Canton, Hangchow, Soochow, Tientsin, etc.	12/9/1941*
Russia	Hankow, Harbin, Tientsin	9/23/1920
International Settlements:	Amoy, Shanghai	5/20/1943

NOTE: (1) When the rendition was effected by a treaty, the date of the treaty's ratification, not that of its signature, is indicated; (2) those marked with asterisks represent the dates when China declared war against the countries concerned; (3) Russian concessions were terminated by the Presidential mandate of the Chinese government of September 23, 1920; (4) the formal termination of foreign rights over the international settlements in Shanghai and Amoy was effected by the treaties enumerated in supra, note 189; and (5) Chinese ports or cities where foreign concessions or settlements were situated are indicated under the column 'Location'.

With the abolition of all unequal treaties, the most lamentable century in Chinese history stained by unprecedented humiliations had, therefore, come to an end. As to what role China will play after her emancipation from the imperialist yoke, it depends upon both domestic and international developments, particularly her relations with other major powers.

TABLE VI
DATES OF THE TERMINATION OF EXTRATERRITORIALITY
AND OTHER RIGHTS AND PRIVILEGES ENJOYED
BY FOREIGN POWERS IN CHINA

Numerical symbols under the column of unilateral rights and privileges represent the following: (1) extraterritoriality, (2) treaty ports, (3) stationing of foreign warships, (4) coastal trade and inland navigation, (5) foreign pilotage, and (6) the Final Protocol of 1901.

Countries	Unilateral Rights and Privileges	Dates of Termination
Belgium	(1), (2), (4), (6)	11/20/1943
Brazil	(1)	8/1/1943
Denmark	(1), (2), (4), (5)	5/20/1946
France	(1), (2), (3), (4), (5), (6)	2/28/1946
Great Britain	(1), (2), (3), (4), (5), (6)	1/11/1943
Mexico	(1)	10/31/1929
Netherlands	(1), (2), (3), (4), (5), (6)	5/29/1945
Norway	(1), (2), (3), (4), (5)	11/10/1943
Portugal	(1), (2), (4), (5)	4/1/1947
Sweden	(1), (2), (3), (4), (5)	4/5/1945
Switzerland	(1)	3/13/1946
U.S.A.	(1), (2), (3), (4), (5), (6)	1/11/1943

NOTE: Unilateral rights and privileges formerly enjoyed by Austria, Germany, Italy, and Japan were terminated by China as a consequence of the two world wars. Those enjoyed by Czarist Russia were renounced by the Soviet Union and formally terminated by the Sino-Soviet Treaty of March 31, 1924. Spain's unilateral rights and privileges were virtually abolished by China during the Spanish Civil War.

NOTES TO CHAPTER 10

1. General Hurley was appointed the President's Personal Representative to China on August 18, 1944. He later became American Ambassador to China, succeeding Clarence E. Gauss, and served in that capacity from November 30, 1944 to November 27, 1945. It was through him that the United States government formally informed Chiang of the Yalta Agreement.

2. At the time of his departure from Chungking to Yenan, Mao issued a statement emphasizing peaceful cooperation:

   "China today has only one road before her, It is peace. Peace is everything. All other considerations are mistaken.

   "In working together, Koumintang, the Chinese Communist Party and other parties and factions need not fear difficulties, as these can all be overcome in conditions of peace, democracy, solidarity and unity under President Chinang's leadership, and upon the implementation of the Three People's Principles."

   Hsinhua [New China] News Agency, October 9, 1945.

   The minutes of the Chiang-Mao meetings were released on October 10. For a summary, see Chiang Chung-cheng, Soviet Russia in China, pp. 137-138. In the ensuing months, mutual distrust made it difficult to implement their agreed points.

3. President Truman's Letter to General Marshall, December 5, 1945, listed as Annex 61 in United States Relations with China, with Special Reference to the Period 1944-1949, issued by the Department of State in August 1949 (Publication 3573, Far Eastern Series 30). Due to the limited number of copies printed by the Government Printing Office, Washington, D.C., this official publication soon became unavailable to the public. The Stanford University Press reprinted it in 1967, with the Original Letter of Transmittal to President Truman from Secretary of State Dean Acheson and also an introduction by Lyman P. van Slyke, under the title The China White Paper, August 1949 (in 2 vols., hereafter cited as The China White Paper). The Stanford edition is identical to the original official publication except for the unnumbered pages ending with the introduction.

4. The China White Paper, Annex 62.

5. For the enforecement of the cease-fire between the Nationalist and Communist troops and the formation of a coalition govern-

ment, "General Marshall put an embargo on the shipment of combat-type military equipment from the United States to China, an action which remained in effect from August, 1946, to May, 1947." Franz H. Michael and George E. Taylor, The Far East in the Modern World (New York, 1964), p. 757.

6. See Chiang Chung-cheng, Soviet Russia in China, pp. 155-156.

7. Earlier, upon recommendation of General Marshall, President Truman appointed J. Leighton Stuart United States Ambassador to China in January 1946, to assist the task of mediation. Stuart remained in that position until the withdrawal of the American Embassy from Nanking subsequent to the establishment of the Communist government in Peking. For further information on the Marshall Mission, see Dean Acheson, Present at the Creation: My Years in the State Department, pp. 139-148, 202-211; John Leighton Stuart, Fifty Years in China, pp. 168-179.

8. For the text of Marshall's statement, see Department of State Bulletin, January 19, 1947, pp. 83-85.

9. All quotes are from General Marshall's statement of January 7, 1947, which can also be found in The China White Paper, Annex 113. In his Letter of Transmittal to President Truman on July 30, 1949, Secretary of State Dean Acheson shared the views of General Marshall concerning the reasons for the failure of his mission:

> "Increasingly he [Marshall] became convinced, however, that twenty years of intermittent civil war between the two factions, during which the leading figures had remained the same, had created such deep personal bitterness and such irreconcilable differences that no agreement was possible. The suspicions and the lack of confidence were beyond remedy. He became convinced that both parties were merely sparring for time, jockeying for military position and catering temporarily to what they believed to be American desires. General Marshall concluded that there was no hope of accomplishing the objectives of his mission." Ibid., I, p. xii.

10. The Sino-American Agreement on the Disposition of Lend-Lease Supplies in Inventory or Procurement in the United States, June 14, 1946, which was followed by another Agreement under Section 3(c) of the Lend-Lease Act, signed on June 28 of the same year. For their text, see Chinese Republic, Treaties, pp. 676-683; Chen, Treaties, pp. 281-288.

11. For the text of the Sino-American Agreement for the Sale of Certain Surplus War Property, August 30, 1946, see ibid., pp. 288-293; Chinese Republic, Treaties, pp. 683-688. According to Secretary of State Dean Acheson, the total procurement cost of over one billion dollars was realized to the United States at 232 million dollars. See The China White Paper, I, p. xv. The Chinese government later found out that a part of the surplus property was not usable.

12. For the text of the Treaty, see Chinese Republic, Treaties, pp. 688-718; Chen, Treaties, pp. 295-323.

13. For the text, see ibid., pp. 365-372; Chinese Republic, Treaties, pp. 738-747.

14. Notes were exchanged regarding the China Aid Act of 1948 between the American Secretary of State and the Chinese Ambassador to Washington on April 30, 1948. See ibid., pp. 401-404; Chinese Republic, Treaties, pp. 753-756.

15. For the text of the Agreement, see ibid., pp. 757-766; Chen, Treaties, pp. 408-418. See also the Economic Cooperation Administration, Economic Aid to China (Washington, D.C., 1949).

16. This was the Agreement for the use of funds made available in accordance with Article 6.b(1) of the Sino-American Surplus War Property Sales Agreement of August 30, 1946. For its text, see Chen, Treaties, pp. 372-377; Chinese Republic, Treaties, pp. 747-753.

17. See the Sino-American Agreement Providing for the Establishment of Joint Commission on Rural Reconstruction in China, August 5, 1948 (ibid., pp. 775-783; Chen, Treaties, pp. 420-423).

18. In his Letter of Transmittal, Secretary of State Dean Acheson stated that "since V-J Day, the United States Government has authorized aid to Nationalist China in the form of grants and credits totaling approximately 2 billion dollars." The China White Paper, I, p. xv.

19. See ibid., p. xvi.

20. Divergent views on the subject can be found from, among others, Anthony Kubek, How the Far East Was Lost: American Policy and the Creation of Communist China, 1941-1949 (Chicago, 1963); Tang Tsou, America's Failure in China 1941-50 (Chicago, 1963), particularly, Pt. III on the limits of a policy of limited as-

sistance. For a brief review of the factors contributing to the Nationalist defeat, see William L. Tung, The Political Institutions of Modern China, pp. 216-218. A general survey of United States policy and the Nationalist collapse can be found in John King Fairbank, The United States and China (Cambridge, 1958), pp. 262-277; Robert C. North, Moscow and the Chinese Communists (Stanford, 1953), Ch. 13. For a critical review of United States financial assistance to China during the war period, reference may be made to Arthur N. Young, China and the Helping Hand, 1937-1945 (Cambridge, 1964). On February 15, 1970, the Senate Internal Security Subcommittee released a two-volume collection of hitherto secret documents, titled 'The Amerasia Case: A Clue to the Catastrophe of China'. Included in the collection is an introduction written by Anthony Kubek. Considering that these documents reveal many principal reasons relevant to the rise of Communism in China, particularly the anti-Nationalist policy of several Far Eastern experts in the United States Department of State, Paul K. T. Sih, Director of the Center of Asian Studies of St. John's University, New York, agreed with Kubek's analysis that American policy toward China was subverted during World War II. According to Sih, this report in many respects "is a documentary refutation of the White Paper on China." Hsu-pai Tseng, one of the foremost political analysts in Taiwan, also supported Kubek's view. For details, see The New York Times, February 15, 1970; The China Tribune, February 20, 1970. Some critical but fair comments on The China White Paper can be found in John Leighton Stuart, op. cit., pp. 261-270.

21. See supra, pp. 225-226.

22. For the assistance rendered by the Communist International to the Chinese Communist Party in its formative period, see supra, p. 224.

23. For its text, see Conrad Brandt and others (eds.), A Documentary History of Chinese Communism, pp. 220-224.

24. See Art. 8.

25. See Arts. 15, 16.

26. Art. 17.

27. For details, see William L. Tung, The Political Institutions of Modern China, pp. 259-269. The Organic Law of the Chinese People's Political Consultative Conference of September 29, 1949 can be found in Albert P. Blaustein (ed.), Fundamental Legal Documents of Communist China (South Hackensack, N.J., 1962), pp. 96-103.

28. The Common Program was adopted by the First Plenary Session of CPPCC on September 29, 1949. For its text, see ibid., pp. 34-53.

29. See Arts. 11, 54.

30. Art. 54.

31. Arts. 56, 57.

32. For the text of the Regulations governing the control of the entry, exit, transit, residence, and travel of foreign nationals in Communist China, adopted on March 13, 1964, see American Consulate-General in Hongkong, Survey of China Mainland Press (hereafter cited as Survey of China Mainland Press), No. 3208 (April 29, 1964), pp. 1-3.

33. See Arts. 59, 60.

34. Art. 58.

35. Art. 55.

36. For the organization and functions of the National People's Congress, see William L. Tung, The Political Institutions of Modern China, pp. 287-291.

37. Adopted at the first session of National People's Congress on September 20, 1954, the Constitution (with Liu Shao-chi's Report on the Drafting) was published in English by Foreign Languages Press, Peking, in 1954.

38. Preamble of the 1954 Constitution.

39. The English text of the Constitution of the Chinese Communist Party can be found in Albert P. Blaustein, op. cit., pp. 55-103.

40. 'General Program' of the 1956 Party Constitution.

41. See Shih-chieh Wang and Ching-yu Hu (eds.), China's Abolition of Unequal Treaties (in Chinese; Taipei, 1967), pp. 117-144; Tsu-hou Yeh, The Abolition of Unequal Treaties (in Chinese; Taipei, 1967), pp. 66-76. For a general discussion of China's foreign policy, reference may be made to Werner Levi, Modern China's Foreign Policy (Minneapolis, 1953), which also covers the first few years of Communist China. In analyzing the aims of Chinese foreign policy, Charles P. Fitzgerald observed that "the Chinese view of the world has not fundamentally changed: it has been adjusted to take account of the modern

world, but only so far as to permit China to occupy, still, the central place in the picture." Fitzgerald, The Chinese View of Their Place in the World, p. 71.

42. See The New York Times, April 2, 28, May 5, 1969. For the text of the draft constitution of the Chinese Communist Party, which was eventually adopted at its Ninth National Congress, see ibid., January 8, 1969. See also infra, pp. 348-357.

43. See Sun Yat-sen, San Min Chu I (English translation from the tenth edition of the Chinese text by Frank W. Price, published by the Commercial Press, Shanghai, 1927), pp. 33-35.

44. Chiang Kai-shek, China's Destiny (English edition published by Roy Publishers, New York, 1947), p. 34.

45. Edgar Snow, Red Star over China (New York: Random House, 1938 ed.), p. 88.

46. See Selected Works of Mao Tse-tung (Peking: Foreign Languages Press, 1961-1965, 4 vols.), II, p. 311.

47. See infra, pp. 352-355.

48. For further information, see E. H. Rawlings, "The Background to China's Foreign Policy," Asian Review, Vol. 59, No. 219 (July 1963), pp. 189-193.

49. For details, see infra, pp. 408-409.

50. For the text of the Program, see The Collected Laws of the Chinese Republic (Shanghai, 1936, 11 vols.), Vol. 1, pp. 10-14.

51. For the text, see League of Nations, Treaty Series, Vol. 163 (1935), pp. 178-183; The China Year Book, 1935, pp. 148-149.

52. China Handbook, 1937-1945 (New York, 1947, compiled by the Chinese Ministry of Information), p. 1.

53. A special survey of Chinese military affairs can be found in The China Quarterly, No. 18 (April-June 1964), pp. 3-173.

54. Further reference on the strategy and tactics of Communist China's conduct of foreign relations can be found in H. Arthur Steiner, The International Position of Communist China: Political and Ideological Doctrines of Foreign Policy (New York, 1958); Peter S. H. Tang, Communist China Today (Washington, D. C., 1961), I, pp. 485-681; DeVerre E. Pentony (ed.), China, the Emerging Red Giant: Communist Foreign Policies

(San Francisco, 1962); Alice Langley Hsieh, Communist China's Strategy in the Nuclear Era (Englewood Cliffs, N.J., 1962); Franklin W. Houn, "The Principles and Operational Code of Communist China's International Conduct," The Journal of Asian Studies, Vol. 27, No. 1 (November 1967), pp. 21-40; Tang Tsou and Morton Halperin, "Mao Tse-tung's Revolutionary Strategy and Peking's International Behavior," American Political Science Review, Vol. 59, No. 1 (March 1965), pp. 80-99; Thomas W. Robinson, "Peking's Revolutionary Strategy in the Developing World: The Failures of Success," The Annals of the American Academy of Political and Social Science Vol. 386 (November 1969), pp. 64-77. See also John K. Fairbank, "China's Foreign Policy in Historical Perspective," Foreign Affairs, Vol. 47, No. 3 (April 1969), pp. 449-463; A. M. Halpern, "China in the Postwar World," The China Quarterly, No. 21 (January-March 1965), pp. 20-45; Michael B. Yahuda, "Chinese Foreign Policy After 1963: The Maoist Phases," ibid., No. 36 (October-December 1968), pp. 93-113; Robert C. North, The Foreign Relations of China (Belmont, Calif., 1969), pp. 72-146. See also American Consulate-General in Hongkong, Current Background, No. 882 (June 16, 1969), for Communist China's foreign policy and posture in 1968.

55. For a survey of the relationship between the Chinese Communists and the Soviet Union during an earlier period, see Charles B. McLane, Soviet Policy and the Chinese Communists, 1931-1946 (New York, 1958).

56. In the Exchange of Notes of August 14, 1945, which constituted a part of the Treaty, V. Molotov stated that "the Soviet Government agrees to render China moral support and assist her with military supplies and other material resources, it being understood that this support and assistance will go exclusively to the National Government as the Central Government of China." Chinese Republic, Treaties, p. 508; Chen, Treaties, pp. 221-222.

57. Israel's recognition of Communist China has never been reciprocated. North Vietnam established diplomatic relations with Peking on January 18, 1950, while other socialist countries did before the end of 1949. Actually, the international status of North Vietnam was not officially established until the conclusion of the armistice agreements in Geneva, on July 20, 1954. See also infra, pp. 394-395.

58. For the text, see Diplomatic Archives of the Chinese People's Republic (edited by the World Cultural Institute, in Chinese; published by the New China Book Co., Peking, since 1957; hereafter cited as CPR, Diplomatic Archives), Vol. 1, pp. 75-77.

59. The English text of the Treaty and Agreements of February 14, 1950 can be found in O. B. van der Sprenkel (ed.), New China: Three Views (New York, 1951), pp. 227-235.

60. Art. 1 of the Treaty of 1950.

61. For the text of the Agreement, see CPR, Diplomatic Archives, Vol. 1, pp. 77-79.

62. See infra, pp. 316, 320-321.

63. At an interest of one percent per annum, the total amount was to be paid out over five annual installments and to be refunded in ten annual installments beginning with December 31, 1954. For the text of the Agreement, see CPR, Diplomatic Archives, Vol. 1, pp. 79-80.

64. See ibid., Vol. 1, p. 75. The dismantling of industrial equipment in Manchuria and its removal to the Soviet Union created devastating effects on the rehabilitation of the region. See Chiang Chung-cheng, Soviet Russia in China, pp. 168-171. Further reference can be made to Edwin W. Pauley, Report on Japanese Assests in Manchuria to the President of the United States, July 1946 (Washington, D.C., 1946).

65. According to the 1950 agreement, the duration of the Sino-Soviet joint stock companies was thirty years. After a short period of experiment, however, friction resulted. By mutual consent, these companies were dissolved in 1954. See the joint communique issued by Mao Tse-tung and Khrushchev on October 12, 1954 (CPR, Diplomatic Archives, Vol. 3, pp. 174-175).

66. See ibid., Vol. 3, p. 175.

67. The Sino-Soviet agreement on this subject was signed in Moscow, on December 21, 1957. The waterways affected were Heilungkiang (Amur), Sungari, Ussuri, Argun, Cherny Irtysk, Ili, and Sungacha rivers, and Lake Khanka. This agreement was designed to facilitate transport "by the cheapest and shortest routes between Harbin and Kiamnsze in northeast China and Khabarovsk and Komsomolsk-on-Amur in the Soviet Far East, between China's Sinkiang Uighur Autonomous Region and Soviet Kazakhastan." Peking Review, No. 3 (March 18, 1958). p. 20. The text of the agreement can also be found in The Collection of Treaties of the Chinese People's Republic (edited by the Ministry of Foreign Affairs, in Chinese; published by the Institute of Legal Publications, and, from volume 11, by the World Cultural Institute; hereafter cited as CPR, Treaties), Vol. 6, pp. 278-282. For an earlier agreement concerning the

navigation on the Amur, Ussuri, and other waterways, signed at Harbin, on January 2, 1951, see ibid., Vol. 1, pp. 9-34.

68. See Peking Review, No. 9 (April 29, 1958), p. 20. According to Li Hsien-nien's report, 'Final Accounts for 1956 and the 1957 state budget,' submitted to the fourth session of the First People's National Congress on June 29, 1957, Peking's indebtedness to Moscow reached US $2.4 billion. For Li's report, see the dispatch from Hsinhua News Agency, Peking, June 29, 1957. It was estimated that the amount due to unbalaneced trade and loans was comparatively small and that military supplies probably amounted to $2 billion, largely used for China's intervention in the Korean War.

69. See Peking Review, No. 9 (April 29, 1958), p. 20.

70. Ibid., No. 37 (November 11, 1958), p. 21.

71. Ibid., No. 7 (February 17, 1959), p. 12.

72. See ibid., No. 9 (March 3, 1959), p. 20.

73. Renmin Ribao (Jen-min Jih-pao or People's Daily), February 14, 1959. For further details of the Sino-Soviet relations before the split, see Szu-k'ai Chin, Communist China's Relations with the Soviet Union, 1949-1957 (Hongkong, 1961); Vidya Prakash Dutt, China and the World (New York, 1966), pp. 58-78.

74. See infra, pp. 348-352.

75. Exchange of Notes (No. 1) between the Soviet Commissar for Foreign Affairs V. Molotov and the Chinese Foreign Minister Wang Shih-chieh, August 14, 1945, which constituted a part of the Sino-Soviet Treaty of 1945. For the text, see Chinese Republic, Treaties, pp. 508-510; Chen, Treaties, pp. 220-221.

76. GA res. 505(VI). See Official Records of the General Assembly, 6th Session, 1st Committee, 502nd and 503rd meetings.

77. See Chiang Chung-cheng, Soviet Russia in China, pp. 146-148.

78. See supra, pp. 160-163.

79. On the same day, peace treaties were concluded with Bulgaria, Finland, Hungary, and Rumania, as a result of extensive consultations by the Council of Foreign Ministers, who met intermittently in London, Moscow, Paris, and New York, from September 1945 to December 1946. For details of the nego-

tiations and the text of these peace treaties, see A. C. Leiss and Raymond Dennett (eds.), European Peace Treaties after World War II, supplementary to Documents on American Foreign Relations (Boston, 1954), VIII, IX.

80. For details, see Arts. 24-26, 79 of the Peace Treaty with Italy, which can also be found in the United Nations, Treaty Series, Vols. 49, 50 (1950), No. 747.

81. For the text of the Peace Treaty with Japan of 1951, see United Nations, Treaty Series, Vol. 136 (1852), No. 1934; Documents on American Foreign Relations, XIII, pp. 458-479.

82. See Art. 2 of the Treaty (CPR, Diplomatic Archives, Vol. 1, pp. 75-77).

83. The Treaty came into force on August 5, 1952. For the text of the Treaty, Protocol, and the Exchange of Notes, See Chinese Republic, Treaties, pp. 248-257; Chen, Treaties, pp. 454-460.

84. See the Sino-Soviet Exchange of Notes of September 15, 1952 (CPR, Diplomatic Archives, Vol. 2, pp. 89-91).

85. This was the wording used in the Cairo Declaration of 1943.

86. Art. 2(b) of the San Francisco Treaty of 1951.

87. Art. 2(f) of the San Francisco Treaty of 1951.

88. Art. 2 of the Sino-Japanese Peace Treaty of 1952.

89. Art. 2(c) of the San Francisco Treaty of 1951.

90. See supra, p. 45.

91. Paragraph 2 of the Cairo Declaration of 1943.

92. See supra, p. 269.

93. Art. 8 of the San Francisco Treaty of 1951.

94. Department of State, American Foreign Policy, 1950-1955: Basic Documents (Washington, D.C., 1957, 2 vols.), I, pp. 448 462.

95. Ibid., p. 453.

96. Art. 26 of the San Francisco Peace Treaty with Japan reads, in part, as follows:

"Japan will be prepared to conclude with any State which signed or adhered to the United Nations Declaration of January 1, 1942, and which is at war with Japan, or with any State which previously formed a part of the territory of a State named in Article 23, which is not a signatory of the present Treaty, a bilateral Treaty of Peace on the same or substantially the same terms as are provided for in the present Treaty, but this obligation on the part of Japan will expire three years after the first coming into force of the present Treaty."

97. Dulles' statement of September 5, 1951 (supra, note 94).

98. See Art. 2 in particular.

99. Among many books on Formosa, reference may be made to the following for divergent views: Joseph P. Ballantine, Formosa: A Problem for United States Foreign Policy (Washington, D.C., 1952); Fred W. Riggs, Formosa under Chinese Nationalist Rule (New York, 1952); W. G. Goddard, Formosa: A Study in Chinese History (East Lansing, 1966); Important Documents concerning the Question of Taiwan (Peking, 1955); Frank P. Morello, The International Legal Status of Formosa (The Hague, 1966); and Lung-chu Chen and Harold D. Lasswell, Formosa, China, and the United Nations (New York, 1967). Further information on the subject can also be found in many valuable articles.

100. In accordance with MacArthur's General Order No.1, Japan surrendered Formosa and the Pescadores to Generalissimo Chiang Kai-shek. The National Government of the Republic of China has since incorporated these islands as an integral part of Chinese territory under the administration of a provincial government.

101. Department of State Bulletin, Vol. XIII, p. 5.

102. See infra, pp. 346-347.

103. For details, see infra, pp. 345-346.

104. See Arts. 25, 26 of the Peace Treaty with Italy, 1947.

105. See Art. 24 of the Peace Treaty with Italy, 1947.

106. See ibid., Art. 79.

107. See the Sino-Italian Exchange of Notes for the Settlement of the Claims for Damages Arising out of the War, July 30, 1947 (Chinese Republic, Treaties, pp. 218-219). The disposal of Italian official assets and property of Italian nationals in China was settled by an Exchange of Notes of the same date (ibid., pp. 220-222). On April 22, 1949, Italy and China signed the Treaty of Amity for the regulation of normal relationships. For the text, see ibid., pp. 222-232; Chen, Treaties, pp. 427-430.

108. Art. IV.

109. See Art. V of the Sino-Japanese Peace Treaty of 1952; Art. 10. of the San Francisco Peace Treaty of 1951.

110. Ibid., Art. 14(a,1). The reason for paying reparations in this manner was in consideration of Japan's limited resources and other obligations.

111. Art. 1(b) of the Protocol (Chinese Republic, Treaties, pp. 251-253; Chen, Treaties, pp. 456-458).

112. See supra, pp. 45-46.

113. See supra, pp. 154-159, in particular.

114. Chinese Republic, Treaties, p. 254; Chen, Treaties, p. 458. In the Minutes, the Chinese and Japanese plenipotentiaries agreed that "the property, rights or interests in Japan of the collaborationist regimes created in China, as a result of the so-called 'Mukden incident' of September 18, 1931, such as 'Manchukuo' and the 'Wang Ching Wei regime', shall be transferred to China upon agreement between the two Parties in accordance with the relevant provisions of the present Treaty and of the San Francisco Treaty." Ibid., p. 460; Chinese Republic, Treaties, p. 257.

115. In his statement made at San Francisco, on September 5, 1951, John Foster Dulles explained the dilemma of the Allied Powers in concluding the peace treaty with Japan without the participation of China: "They could defer any peace with Japan until they could agree that there was in China a government possessed of both legitimacy and authority. It would, however, be wrong, cruel, and stupid to penalize Japan because there is civil war in China and international disagreement regarding China." Department of State, American Foreign Policy, 1950-1955: Basic Documents, Vol. 1, p. 460.

116. For Peking's relationship with Japan, see infra, pp. 397-399.

117. See supra, pp. 81-83, 270-271, 272.

118. See Henry G. Schwarz, "Chinese Migration to Northwest China and Inner Mongolia, 1949-1959," The China Quarterly, No. 16 (October-December 1953), pp. 62-74; Chiao Yu, "About the Problems of Resettlement and Reclamation," Kuang-ming Daily (in Chinese), January 15, 1957. The resettlement of the Chinese in border regions involved many complicated problems. See, for instance, Survey of China Mainland Press, No. 4216 (July 12, 1968), pp. 3-4; No. 4328 (December 3, 1968), pp. 18-19.

119. The national minorities constitute only a small part of Chinese population. According to the census taken in June 1953, their main centers of habitation were as follows: Chuang, 6,600,000 (Kwangsi province); Uighur, 3,700,000 (Sinkiang Uighur Autonomous Region); Hui, 3,600,000 (Kansu and Chinghai provinces); Yi, 3,300,000 (Liangshan Mountains on Szechwan-Yunnan borders); Tibetan, 2,800,000 (Tibet and Chamdo Area and Chinghai province); Miao, 2,500,000 (Kweichow and western Hunan provinces and other regions in central, south and southwest China); Mongolian, 1,500,000 (Inner Mongolian Autonomous Region, Kansu and Chinghai provinces, and Sinkiang Uighur Autonomous Region); Puyi, 1,250,000 (southwestern part of Kweichow province); and Korean, 1,100,000 (Yenpien Korean Autonomous Chou in Kirin province). In comparison with the total number of Hans, approximately 550,000,000 in 1953, the national minorities altogether occupied about 6% of the total population. See Handbook on People's China (Peking, 1957), pp. 14-15. There are still other minorities with smaller populations: T'ung, 600,000 (Southeastern Kweichow and northern part of Kwangsi); Yao, 600,000 (Kwangsi, northern Kwangtung, and southern Hunan); and T'ai, 500,000 (border regions of Yunnan). See People's China, June 1, 1954. Different sources indicate slight variations of the above figures.

120. See supra, pp. 80-81.

121. See Louis Fischer, The Soviets in World Affairs, Vol. 2, p. 534.

122. See W. A. Douglas Jackson, Russo-Chinese Border-Lands (Princeton, 1962), pp. 50-55; Allen S. Whiting and Shêng Shih-ts'ai, Sinkiang: Pawn or Pivot? (East Lanshing, 1958).

123. See Geoffrey Wheeler, "Sinkiang and the Soviet Union," The China Quarterly, No. 16 (October-December 1963), p. 58. The rebels created the so-called 'East Turkish Republic,' but it was short-lived.

124. Item 3 of the Exchange of Notes (I). For the text, see Chinese Republic Treaties, pp. 508-510; Chen, Treaties, pp. 220-221.

125. For further information, see O.S. Fedyshun,"Soviet Retreat in Sinkiang? Sino-Soviet Rivalry and Cooperation, 1950-1955," American Slavic and East European Review, Vol. 16 (April 1957), pp. 127-145.

126. See supra, note 65.

127. For a survey of the progress made in Sinkiang, see American Consulate-General in Hongkong, Current Background (hereafter cited as Current Background), No. 775 (October 29, 1965), special issue on the "Tenth Anniversary of Founding of Sinkiang Uighur Autonomous Region."

128. See The Origin and Development of the Differences between the Leadership of the CPSU and Ourselves (Peking, 1963), p. 47.

129. Seven Letters Exchanged between the Central Committees of the Communist Party of China and the Communist Party of the Soviet Union (Peking, 1964), pp. 22-23. Further condemnation of Soviet subversive activities was made at the Third People's Congress of the Sinkiang Autonomous Region in April 1964. See dispatch from Hsinhua News Agency, Peking, April 28, 1964. Soviet subversion in Sinkiang was also reported at the tenth anniversary of the founding of the Ili Kazakh Autonomous Chou (District). See Peking Review, No. 37 (September 11, 1964), pp. 5, 26.

130. The border incident on June 10, 1969 involved several Chinese herders, one of whom was killed by Soviet fire. Tension was created when both sides concentrated troops on the border. The Chinese Ministry of Foreign Affairs strongly protested against the Soviet action. See Hsinhua News Agency dispatch and The New York Times, June 11, 1969. For the skirmishes on August 13, see ibid., August 14, 1969.

131. For various phases of international politics in Manchuria, see supra, pp. 75-77, 156-157, 236-237, 257-259, 270-271, 272-274.

132. See supra, p. 270.

133. Art. 1 of the Sino-Soviet Agreement concerning the Changchun Railway, Dairen, and Port Arthur, February 14, 1950 (CPR, Diplomatic Archives, Vol.1, pp. 77-79). According to the communiqué issued on September 15, 1952, a joint Sino-Soviet

Commission was to be established in charge of necessary preparations for the transfer. See ibid., Vol. 2, p. 89.

134. For the text of the Protocol to effect the transfer of the Changchun Railway, signed at Harbin, on December 31, 1952, see ibid., Vol. 2, p. 117.

135. For the text, see ibid., Vol. 2, pp. 117-118.

136. See supra, note 65; infra, pp. 320-321.

137. For details, see infra, pp. 352-353.

138. See supra, pp. 77-80. For further information, see Tieh-Tseng Li, Tibet Today and Yesterday (New York, 1960), pp. 33-198.

139. Peking often defended its action in Tibet on the ground of the necessity to liberate the serfs and to enforce reforms in the monasteries. In her When Serfs Stood Up in Tibet (Peking, 1960), Anna Louise Strong attempted to substantiate these arguments. See, particularly, Chs. VIII-XIII.

140. For the text of the Agreement for the Peaceful Liberation of Tibet, see Concerning the Question of Tibet (Peking, 1959), pp. 14-16; D. Foliot (ed.), Documents on International Affairs, 1951 (Oxford, 1954), p. 577. Containing seventeen articles, this constitutional document was signed with the approval of the Dalai Lama and his advisers.

141. See Arts. 3, 14, of the Agreement.

142. For the founding of the Tibet Autonomous Region together with its first session of the First Congress and the final session of its Preparatory Committee, see, respectively, Current Background, No. 771 (September 27, 1965); Survey of China Mainland Press, No. 3531 (September 3, 1965), p. 1.

143. For its text, see CPR, Diplomatic Archives, Vol. 1, p. 166.

144. See the Note of the Central People's Government in Reply to the Indian Government, October 30, 1950 (ibid., Vol. 1, pp. 164-165). In the same Note, Peking implied that the delay of the journey of the Tibetan representatives to Peking was caused by foreign conspiracy.

145. See UN Docs. A/1534, A/1549, A/1565, A/1658.

146. See the Communiqué on Sino-Indian Relations, released at Peking, on September 29, 1954 (CPR, Diplomatic Archives, Vol. 3, pp. 10-11).

147. For the text of the Agreement, see ibid., Vol. 3, pp. 12-14;. The Indian White Paper, 1954-1959, pp. 98-101.

148. See supra, pp. 77-80.

149. For details, see the Sino-Indian Agreement and the Exchange of Notes of April 29, 1954 (CPR, Diplomatic Archives, Vol. 3, pp. 15-19).

150. See Tieh-tseng Li, op. cit., p. 210. Tsepon W.D. Shakabpa, a Tibetan native and high officer, considered that, in signing the 1954 Agreement with Peking, India deprived herself of the 1904 and 1914 treaty rights. See his Tibet: A Political History (New Haven, 1967), p. 309. Shakabpa's interpretation of Tibetan history showed a contrast in many respects from Tieh-tseng Li's work, which was first published by Columbia University Press, New York, in 1956, under the title, The Historical Status of Tibet. In July 1958, Prime Minister Nehru's scheduled visit to Lhasa was cancelled upon Chinese request. See George N. Patterson, Peking Versus Delhi (New York, 1963), pp. 159-160. See also Girilal Jain, Panchsheela and After: A Reappraisal of Sino-Indian Relations in the Context of the Tibetan Insurrection (London, 1960).

151. See Art. 39 of the United Nations Charter.

152. According to a dispatch from Hsinhua News Agency, March 28, 1959, the rebellion in Lhasa was crushed in just over two days.

153. GA res. 1353 (XIV). India was among the twenty-six Member states which abstained from voting.

154. GA res. 1723(XVI). India and twenty-eight other Members abstained from voting.

155. The request was made by a letter of October 30, 1964, from El Salvador, Nicaragua, and the Philippines. See UN Doc. A/5765.

156. GA res. 2079(XX). It was adopted by a vote of 43-26, with 22 abstentions. The Soviet Union and other Communist countries voted against it. The Republic of China, India, and the United States were among those in favor of its adoption.

157. The resolution as finally adopted was an amendment to the original 7-power draft resolution (UN Doc. A/L.473).

158. As to whether the international covenants on human rights or the Genocide Convention could be applied to the Tibetan case, see Alfred Rubin, "The Position of Tibet in International Law," The China Quarterly, No. 35 (July-September 1968), pp. 147-151. Rubin's legal appraoch to the subject is most thorough and objective. For divergent views, see also International Commission of Jurists, The Question of Tibet and the Rule of Law (Geneva, 1959); George Ginsburgs and Michael Mathos, Communist China and Tibet (The Hague, 1964); H. E. Richardson, A Short History of Tibet (New York, 1962), pp. 183-223.

159. See supra, pp. 309-311.

160. Art. 6 of the Sino-British Convention of 1860 provided that China ceded to England "that portion of township of Kowloon in the province of Kwangtung, "which had been previously leased in perpetuity to the latter. For the text of the Convention, see Chinese Customs, Treaties, I, pp. 430-434; Hertslet, Treaties, I, pp. 45-53.

161. For details, see supra, pp. 25-27.

162. For the text, see Chinese Customs, Treaties, I, pp. 539-540; Hertslet, Treaties, I, pp.120-122; MacMurray, Treaties, I, pp. 130-131.

163. The transfer was effected by the Sino-Portuguese Treaty of Peking, December 1, 1887 (Chinese Customs, Treaties, II, pp. 274-294; Hertslet, Treaties, I, pp. 423-433). Further details can be found in Morse, II, pp. 386-388.

164. See infra, pp. 353-357.

165. See supra, pp. 48-49.

166. See supra, pp. 160-163, 190-192.

167. The restitution was effected by the Sino-British Convention for the Rendition of Weihaiwei and Agreement regarding Certain Facilities for the British Navy after Rendition, April 18, 1930. Ratifications were exchanged on October 1, 1930. For the text, see Chinese Republic, Treaties, pp.544-553; Chen, Treaties, pp. 36-43. See also supra, pp. 48, 192.

168. See W. W. Willoughby, China at the Conference: A Report, p. 187.

169. See ibid., pp. 183-184.

170. For the lease of Kuangchou-wan, see supra, p. 48. The text of the Sino-Franco Convention for the Rendition of the Leased Territory of Kuangchou-wan, August 18, 1945, see Chinese Republic, Treaties, pp. 142-145; Chen, Treaties, pp. 235-237.

171. For details, see supra, pp. 48, 49, 50, 156, 270-271, 273.

172. For the text, see CPR, Diplomatic Archives, Vol. 1, pp. 75-77.

173. Art. 2 of the 1950 Treaty, which also provided that the installations in Port Arthur were to be transferred to China on the condition that the expenses incurred by the Soviet Union for their restoration and maintenance since 1945 would be compensated.

174. Art. 3 of the 1950 Treaty. Under the same article, it was agreed that all property temporarily administered or leased by the Soviet agencies was to be taken over by China.

175. For details, see supra, pp. 308-309.

176. See the Sino-Soviet Exchange of Notes of September 15, 1952 (CPR, Diplomatic Archives, Vol. 2, p. 90). It should be noted that, on April 29, 1952, Japan signed the Treaty of Peace with the National Government of the Republic of China. See supra, p. 309. Peking was not expected to be bound by it.

177. For the text of the Joint Communiqué, see CPR, Diplomatic Archives, Vol. 3 p. 179.

178. See supra, pp. 70-74.

179. Due to arrogance or stupidity, foreign municipal administrators in Shanghai once posted in public parks the sign, "Dogs and Chinese not allowed." Even though such abusive regulations were later abolished, the feelings of the local residents had already been hurt. See Paul K. T. Sih, Decision for China: Communism or Christianity (Chicago, 1959), pp. 44, 226; Tse-tsung Chow, The May Fourth Movement, p. 202; Wolfgang Franke, China and the West, p. 125.

180. See supra, p. 233.

181. See supra, p. 234.

182. See the Sino-British Exchange of Notes concerning the Rendition of the British Concession at Chinkiang, October 31,

1929, which came into effect on November 15, 1929 (Chinese Republic, Treaties, pp. 536-540; Chen, Treaties, pp. 18-20).

183. See the Sino-British Exchange of Notes concerning the Rendition of the British Concession at Amoy, which entered into force on September 17, 1930, the same date of signature (ibid., pp. 63-65; Chinese Republic, Treaties, pp. 553-556).

184. See the Sino-Belgian Agreement for the Rendition of the Belgian Concession at Tientsin, August 31, 1929, which did not come into effect until January 15, 1931 (ibid., pp. 23-31; Chen, Treaties, pp. 1-6).

185. See Art. 4(3) of the Sino-British Treaty of January 11, 1943, which came into effect on May 20, 1943 (ibid., pp. 140-148; Chinese Republic, Treaties, pp. 589-603).

186. See Art. 4(3) of the Sino-Franco Treaty of February 28, 1946, which entered into force on June 8, 1946 (ibid., pp. 152-160; Chen, Treaties, pp. 259-265).

187. The Italian concession was actually abolished on December 9, 1941, when China declared war against Italy. The relinquishment was formalized by Art. 25 of the Peace Treaty with Italy, February 10, 1947. See supra, pp. 308, 312.

188. See supra, p. 312.

189. See Art. 3 of the Sino-American Treaty of January 11, 1943, which came into effect on May 20, 1943 (Chinese Republic, Treaties, pp. 659-669; Chen, Treaties, pp. 149-155); Art. 4 of the Sino-British Treaty of January 11, 1943, which came into effect on May 20, 1943 (Chinese Republic, Treaties, pp. 589-603; Chen, Treaties, pp. 140-148); Art. 3 of the Sino-Belgian Treaty of October 20, 1943 (ibid., pp. 160-165; Chinese Republic, Treaties, pp. 33-40); No. 1(6) of the Annex to the Sino-Norwegian Treaty of November 10, 1943 (ibid., pp. 356-364; Chen, Treaties, pp. 167-173); Item 1 of the Sino-Swedish Exchange of Notes, attached to the Treaty of April 5, 1945 (ibid., pp. 196-202; Chinese Republic, Treaties, pp. 448-458); Art. 4 of the Sino-Netherlands Treaty of May 29, 1945 (ibid., pp. 332-341; Chen, Treaties, pp. 203-209); Art. 4 of the Sino-Franco Treaty of February 28, 1946 (Chinese Republic, Treaties, pp. 152-160; Chen Treaties, pp. 259-265); Art. 2 of the Sino-Danish Treaty of May 20, 1946 (ibid., pp. 274-281; Chinese Republic, Treaties, pp. 83-92); Art. 26 of the Peace Treaty with Italy of February 10, 1947 (United Nations, Treaty Series, Vols. 49, 50 (1950), No. 747); and Item 2 of the Sino-Portuguese Exchange of Notes of April 1,

1947 (Chinese Republic, Treaties, pp. 412-415; Chen, Treaties, pp. 338-340).

190. For the list of foreign concessions and settlements, see supra, pp. 71-73, Table I. Different from regular concessions and settlements, the foreign estate at Kuling was administered by the Kuling Estate Council. As a result of an agreement between the Chinese government and the Council, the control of the estate was reverted to China on January 1, 1936. See The China Year Book, 1936, pp. 180-181.

191. See supra, p. 272. For details, see Art. 1 of the Sino-American Treaty of January 11, 1943, and Paragraph 7 of its Exchange of Notes; Art. 2 of the Sino-British Treaty of January 11, 1943, and its Annex 1 (6); Arts. 1, 12 of the Sino-Belgian Treaty of October 20, 1943; Art. 2 and Annex 1 (4,6) of the Sino-Norwegian Treaty of November 10, 1943; Art. 1 of the Sino-Swedish Treaty of April 5, 1945, and Item 7 of its Exchange of Notes; Art. 2 of the Sino-Netherlands Treaty of May 29, 1945, and its Exchange of Notes, I (3); Arts. 2, 9(2,6) of the Sino-Franco Treaty of February 28, 1946; Arts. 1, 2, 12 of the Sino-Danish Treaty of May 20, 1946; the Sino-Swiss Exchange of Notes of March 13, 1946 (Chinese Republic, Treaties, pp. 459-463; Chen, Treaties, pp. 270-272); Nos. 1, 3 of the Sino-Portuguese Exchange of Notes of April 1, 1947. Brazil and Spain also relinquished their extraterritorial rights in China and concluded treaties of amity with China, respectively, on August 20, 1943 (Chinese Republic, Treaties, pp. 41-42; Chen, Treaties, pp. 158-159), and February 29, 1953 (ibid., pp. 469-472; Chinese Republic, Treaties, pp. 431-434). See also supra, p. 253. There was no indication that a similar treaty was concluded with Peru, which had no nationals in China. Peru's enjoyment of unilateral rights and privileges in China was originally based on the most-favored-nation clause. After the relinquishment of these unilateral rights and privileges by all other countries, there should be no question of the application for that clause. For Canada's conclusion of a separate treaty with China for the abolition of extraterritoriality, see supra, Ch. 9, note 161.

192. Treaties pertinent to this matter can be found in supra, notes 190, 191. For further information on the disposal of the Boxer indemnities, see Tsien, pp. 163-168. For the origin of the unilateral rights and privileges under discussion, see supra, pp. 53-54, 69-75, 83-89, 107-116, 125-127.

193. See, respectively, Annex (1,e) to the Sino-British Treaty of 1943; Art. IX(5) of the Sino-Franco Treaty of 1946.

Chapter 11
CRUCIAL PROBLEMS OF CHINA AS A MAJOR POWER

I. CONTROVERSIES OVER AMERICAN COMMITMENTS TO
   TAIWAN

1. Neutralization of the Formosa Strait

After the Nationalist evacuation from the mainland to Taiwan, the American government adopted a wait-and-see policy for a while. This did not imply, however, that Washington would stand still, "should the Communist regime lend itself to the aims of Soviet Russian imperialism and attempt to engage in aggression against China's neighbors." In that event, according to Secretary of State Dean Acheson, the United States and "other members of the United Nations would be confronted by a situation violative of the principles of the United Nations Charter and threatening international peace and security."[1] When North Korean forces invaded South Korea on June 25, 1950, President Truman took immediate action to neutralize the Formosa Strait. He made it clear, on June 27, that "the occupation of Formosa by Communist forces would be a direct threat to the security of the Pacific area and to the United States forces performing their lawful and necessary functions in that area." Therefore, he declared: "Accordingly I have ordered the Seventh Fleet to prevent any attack on Formosa. As corollary of this action I am calling upon the Chinese Government on Formosa to cease all air and sea operations against the mainland. The Seventh Fleet will see that this is done."[2]

The American act might be construed as a meausre of anticipatory self-defense,3 but it was, in effect, a sheer intervention in China's civil war. Strictly speaking, this unilateral declaration was not in conformity with the principle of

345

neutrality under traditional rules of international law, because at that time the Chinese Communists had not yet entered the Korean War. This legal position was, however, changed when Peking took an active part in the war and was condemned by the General Assembly on February 1, 1951, for its commission of an act of aggression.[4] The Chinese volunteers actually fought the forces not only of the United States but also of the United Nations. The hostilities did not come to an end until the conclusion of an armistice agreement on July 27, 1953.[5]

2. The Mutual Defense Treaty of 1954

To safeguard the defense of Taiwan, the United States made available to the National Government military materials and personnel in early 1951.[6] As the Republic of China was not included in any regional organization or arrangements, such as the Southeast Asia Treaty Organization or the United States bilateral security pacts with Australia, New Zealand, Japan, the Philippines, and South Korea, the National Government approached Washington in December 1953, proposing a security treaty. Consequently, the Sino-American Mutual Defense Treaty was concluded on December 2, 1954, and came into effect on March 3, 1955.[7]

The two governments agreed to undertake the mutual defense of Taiwan and the Pescadores and the island territories in the Western Pacific under United States jurisdiction, and "such other territories as may be determined by mutual agreement."[8] It appears that the inclusion of the 'offshore islands' along the China coast would be subject to the consent of both parties. Each signatory would act to meet an armed attack directed against the territories of the other in accordance with its constitutional processes.[9] Under this Treaty, the United States was given the right to dispose such land, air, and sea forces in and about Taiwan and the Pescadores necessary for their defense.[10] By an Exchange of Notes of December 10, 1954, the two governments further agreed that "such use of force will be a matter of joint agreement, subject to action of an emergency character which is clearly an exercise of the inherent right of self-defense."[11]

In his statement before the Senate Foreign Relations Committee on February 7, 1955, Secretary of State John

Foster Dulles went further to clarify the scope of mutual defense with the explanation that "offensive military operations by either party from the territories held by the Republic of China would be undertaken only as a matter of joint agreement."[12] Thus the Republic of China was bound by the Treaty not to take any offensive action against the mainland without the consent of the United States.[13] On the other hand, Peking accused the United States of militarily occupying Taiwan and the Pescadores to prevent their fall to the Communists.

Due to the growing tension in the Formosa Strait, Congress adopted a joint resolution in January 1955,[14] authorizing the President to employ American armed forces to defend Taiwan and the Pescadores. The Congressional resolution served as a restraining influence on Communist China. In June 1956, Chou En-lai even indicated Peking's willingness to improve relations with the United States,[15] but failed to obtain a favorable response from Washington. In the opinion of a noted Indian expert on Chinese affairs, Dulles' inflexibility might have "killed a chance, if there was any accommodation between the U.S. and Communist China."[16]

3. Continued Antagonism in Spite of Warsaw Talks

Following the Chinese Communist intervention in the Korean War and the General Assembly's recommendation to impose arms embargo on strategic shipments to Communist China and North Korea, the United States has vigorously enforced it to cover arms, ammunition, implements of war, atomic energy materials, petroleum, transportation materials of strategic value, and items useful in the production of the above.[17] Meanwhile, the United States began talks with Peking through their diplomatic representatives in Geneva in 1955, and in Warsaw since 1958. Up to January 1968, there were already 134 such irregularly scheduled meetings. Nevertheless, the United States continued to withold recognition of the People's Republic[18] and object to Peking's representation in the United Nations.[19] It is unique in diplomatic history for ambassadors of two governments to conduct authorized discussions on matters of mutual concern over one hundred times, while neither intends to recognize the other. After a two-year suspension, the 135th meeting was held on January 20, 1970; and the 136th meeting, one month later. Each of these sessions lasted one hour and was officially described as a 'useful' exchange of views on 'a number of matters of mutual interest'   and under 'businesslike' atmosphere. [20]

There are formidable obstacles to the establishment of normal relationships between Washington and Peking. These include the problem of recognition, the defense of Taiwan and the Pescadores,[21] the Vietnam War, as well as the seat at the United Nations. Under the prevailing circumstances, no common basis can be found for practical negotiations unless either or both sides should change their antagonistic policies.[22] The United States relaxed restrictions on traveling to Communist China and on imports by tourists of goods produced there, effective July 23, 1969. A further step for partial lifting of an embargo, imposed during the Korean War in December 1950, was taken by the American government on December 19, 1969, by allowing unlimited imports not only for private use, but also for art collectors, scholars, museums, and even zoological gardens. Effective December 22, 1969, this new decision would also permit subsidiaries and affiliates of United States corporations to sell non-strategic goods to China and buy Chinese products for resale on foreign markets.[23] In the opinion of neutral observers, however, these conciliatory moves are still not sufficiently important to improve the relationships between the two countries.

II. PEKING-MOSCOW STRAINS AND CONFLICTS

1. Differences in Ideological Approaches and State Relations

Khrushchev's condemnation of Stalin at the twentieth congress of the Soviet Communist Party in February 1956 marked the beginning of Sino-Soviet controversies over both ideological approaches and practical policies,[24] which came into the open at the General Council of the World Federation of Trade Unions, held in Peking, in June 1960. [25] In the opinion of the Chinese leaders, Stalin made more contributions than mistakes to the world movement of Communist revolution, and Khrushchev's denunciation of his former superior defamed the entire socialist system.[26]

At the same Soviet congress, Khrushchev put forth the thesis of 'peaceful transition', which, in effect, meant orderly competition between the socialist and capitalist countries instead of establishing proletarian dictatorship by drastic revolution. This Soviet approach was condemned by Peking as a revision of Marxist-Leninist teachings,[27] because it implied a compromise with the bourgeois influence internally and capitalist imperialism externally.[28] The well known declaration adopted at the 1957 Congress of world Communist parties in Moscow, in which Mao Tse-tung personally participated, accepted both the policy of peaceful transition and the strategy of non-peaceful revolution, depending upon individual cases and circumstances. This self-contradictory compromise did not, however, assure harmony within the Communist bloc in actual practice.

According to Khrushchev, it would be expedient to build up Communist influence wherever and whenever possible, but to avoid direct military confrontation with the United States. His disposal of the Cuban missile crisis in 1962 was based on this attitude.[29] The summit meeting between Khrushchev and President Eisenhower in September 1959 and the cultivation of the so-called 'Camp David' spirit displeased Mao Tse-tung to no small degree.[30] There was a marked difference between the Soviet and the Chinese stages of development: the former is comparatively highly advanced, while the latter is still struggling for growth. Moscow did not support Peking's policy of liberating Taiwan by forcible means.[31] Under the prevailing circumstances, Mao deemed it erroneous and selfish to forsake proletarian revolution. It was only for the temporary interest of the Soviet Union that unilateral attempts were made to improve her relations with the United States, without thorough consultation with and the prior consent of the Chinese and other fraternal parties. Peking labeled the Soviet act as promoting sectarianism and splittism in the international Communist movement.

A personality clash also had something to do with the Moscow-Peking rivalry. After the death of Stalin, Mao considered himself the foremost leader in the international Communist movement with respect to seniority and prestige rather than Khrushchev, for whom Mao's respect was very limited.[32] Then the U-2 incident occurred on May 1, 1960, just prior to a scheduled summit conference at Paris; it revealed lack of serious efforts on the part of the United States to relax tensions with the Soviet Union, and made Khrushchev's position very awkward and almost untenable. [33]

Within the socialist orbit, the upheaval in Eastern Europe in 1956, especially the Hungarian revolution, inflicted considerable damage on Moscow's position of leadership in the Socialist world. [34] The ideological split between Peking and Moscow was further deepened by the Soviet attempt to cultivate friendship with Tito, an intolerable revisionist according to the Chinese point of view,[35] and by subsequent condemnation of Albania,[36] Peking's closest ally. At the Rumanian Communist Party Congress, held in Bucharest in June 1960, Khrushchev severely criticized the dogmatic policies of Communist China.[37] When Moscow convened the conference of eighty-one Communist parties in November 1960, efforts were made to reach an ideological reconciliation with Peking by issuing a statement, in which the principle of equality and independence of all Communist parties was recognized. The 1957 declaration and the 1960 statement were, however, never strictly observed,[38] and many practical issues increased the tension between the two Communist giants in the following years.[39]

Relationships between Peking and Khrushchev's successors have not improved. To Mao Tse-tung, the new Soviet leadership under Brezhnev-Kosygin has followed the same policy, characterized as Khrushchevism without Khrushchev.[40] Moscow made repeated attempts to convene a world conference of Communist parties to condemn the Chinese Communist Party. After protracted negotiations, the Soviet leaders managed to hold such a conference on June 5, 1969, attended by representatives of seventy-five of the world's Communist parties.[41] In spite of critical remarks made by Soviet and East European leaders against the Chinese Communist Party, the document, as finally approved on June 17, vaguely emphasized the importance of the unity of the international Communist movement, without a word condemning China as Moscow might have hoped.[42] Nonetheless, Peking accused Moscow of holding such a conference "directed frantically against China and Albania."[43]

In the international field, there has been sharp competition between Peking and Moscow in the developing countries of Asia and Africa, as fully evidenced in the preparations for and discussions at the Afro-Asian conferences.[44] When intermittent skirmishes along the Sino-Indian border took place in 1959 but had not yet developed into a serious conflict, the Soviet Union sided with India,[45] a democratic and neutralist country ideologically oriented toward the West. Peking could not forgive the Soviet betrayal of friendship in time of need.

The Chinese leadership believed that the Soviet-American cooperation in concluding a treaty for the partial halting of nuclear tests represented a joint plot to prevent China from developing her own nuclear power.[46] A monopoly of nuclear weapons by a few nations did not appeal to Peking as a guarantee of international peace. While objecting to a partial ban of nuclear tests, Peking advocated total prohibition and destruction of all nuclear weapons,[47] and called for a summit conference of world leaders to conclude an agreement for that purpose.[48] According to Mao Tse-tung, the overthrow of capitalist imperialism should precede disarmament, and the Soviet talks with Western powers on the reduction and control of armaments at Geneva and the United Nations are a revisionist approach to world problems.[49]

Turning to China's domestic policies, Moscow was critical of Peking's commune system and the 'Great Leap Forward' project. To the Chinese leaders, Soviet loans and conditions for trade were far from desirable.[50] Even during the Korean War, Chinese volunteers sacrificed thousands of casulties to fight a war of proxy for the Soviet Union, yet Peking had to repay the short-term loans for the prosecution of the war.[51] Soviet aid to China was rendered largely in the form of trade and was repaid in "goods, gold or convertible foreign exchange for all Soviet-supplied complete sets of equipment and other goods, including those made available on credit plus interest." In this connection, Peking also complained that "the prices of many of the goods we imported from the Soviet Union were much higher than those on the world market."[52]

In October 1957, the Soviet Union promised to assist China in the development of nuclear technology for national defense.

When restionships worsened, Moscow changed its mind in June 1959, and declined to provide a sample of or manufacturing data for an atomic bomb. Then, in July 1960, Moscow renounced all economic and technical agreements and contracts, and recalled all Soviet experts in connection with various projects, thus crippling China's economy and causing agricultural setbacks.[53] Nevertheless, the Chinese leadership refused to bow to Soviet pressures and continued to hold a hard line policy internally and externally.

2. Territorial and Boundary Disputes

Perhaps the most serious obstacle to the resumption of cordial relations between Communist China and the Soviet Union is their long-standing disputes over territorial and boundary questions. Dorment during the period of close cooperation, this issue has always been in the minds of the Chinese people. It should be recalled that immense areas of Chinese territory were lost to Czarist Russia during the latter part of the Ch'ing dynasty. The cessions were effected by several unequal treaties, concluded under diplomatic pressures and threats of force at a time when China's national power and prestige were at a low ebb.

The territorial question was brought to the attention of the Soviet Union in 1954, when Khrushchev and Bulganin visited Peking. According to Mao Tse-tung, they declined to discuss it.[54] In January 1957, Chou En-lai found another opportunity to talk with Khrushchev on the subject, but the result was equally inconclusive.[55] The dispute came into the open after Peking's accusation of Soviet 'adventurism' and 'capitulationism' in the settlement of the Cuban missile crisis in late October 1962. In its editorial of March 8, 1963, commenting on a statement made by the Communist party of the United States, Peking's official newspaper, Renmin Ribao, singled out several unequal treaties formerly imposed on China by foreign powers, including those by Russia.[56] These were the Sino-Russian Treaty of Aigun of 1858,[57] the Sino-Russian Treaty of Peking of 1860,[58] and the Sino-Russian Treaty of Ili of 1881.[59] Also listed was the Treaty of Tientsin of 1858, which was separately concluded by China with Russia, the United States, England, and France.[60] The one signed with Russia dealt mostly with other questions; on territorial matters, the contracting parties agreed to redemaracate undefined frontiers. [61]

It was not until February 25, 1964, that delegations of the two governments discussed boundary questions in Peking. Failing to reach an agreement, the CPC wrote a letter to CPSU on February 29, 1964,[62] presenting, among other things, the following complaint:

"With the stepping up of anti-Chinese activities by the leaders of the CPSU in recent years, the Soviet side has made frequent breaches of the status quo on the border, occupied Chinese territory and provoked border incidents. Still more serious, the Soviet side has flagrantly carried out large-scale subversive activities in Chinese frontier areas...." [63]

Intermittent border skirmishes have been reported along the Sino-Soviet frontiers in recent years. The widely publicized clashes, which occurred in March 1969, were due to a dispute over the territorial sovereignty of an island in the Ussuri River on the northern frontier of Manchuria.[64] The island was called Chenpao in Chinese and Damansky in Russian. According to a Chinese statement, the 1964 Sino-Soviet discussions on border problems in Peking agreed on China's jurisdiction over the island,[65] but Moscow disputed Peking's claim. Hostile actions also took place along the border of Sinkiang on June 11 and August 13, 1969,[66] and again on the Manchurian frontier on July 8, 1969.[67]

Following the March clashes, the Chinese and Soviet governments issued statements on their territorial disputes. In its statement of March 10,[68] Peking specified two unequal treaties, under which China lost immense areas of territory along the Manchurian border to Russia: the Treaty of Aigun of 1858 and the Treaty of Peking of 1860. Centering on the territorial problem along the Northeast frontier where the disputed island is located, this statement did not even mention the Russian acquisition of Chinese territory along the Northwest frontier.

Taking advantage of the Anglo-Franco joint expedition against China in 1858, Russia pressed the Manchu Court to conclude the Treaty of Aigun in that year. By this Treaty, according to the Chinese statement of March 10, 1969, Russia "annexed more than 600,000 square kilometers of Chinese territory north of the Heilunkiang River and placed some 400,000 square kilometers of Chinese territory east of the Ussuri River under the joint possession of China and Russia." [69] The second Anglo-Franco expedition and the resultant occupation of the Chinese Capital gave Russia another opportunity. By forcing the Manchu government to sign the Treaty of Peking,[70] the statement went on to point out that Russia "incorporated all the Chinese territory east of the Ussuri River into Russia."[71] Quoting comments on Czarist encroachments by Marx, Engels, and Lenin, Peking took satisfaction in that all of them "fully exposed the aggressive and unequal nature of the 'Sino-Russian Treaty of Aigun' and the 'Sino-Russian Treaty of Peking' Czarist Russian imperialism had imposed on China." [72]

The Soviet government refuted the Chinese stand on unequal treaties. In its note to Peking on March 29, 1969, it declared that "the Soviet-Chinese border in the Far East, as it exists now, took shape many generations ago and passes along natural boundaries dividing the territories of the Soviet Union and China." In conclusion, it stated that "this border was given legal status by the Aigun (1858), Tientsin (1858), and Peking (1860) treaties." [73] While denouncing the inclusion of vast areas of the Soviet Union in Chinese maps as Chinese territory, the same note urged Peking "to take without delay practical steps to normalize the situation of the Soviet-Chinese frontier." [74]

The above discussion centered on the Northeast frontier. [75] Documents recently published by both sides do not reveal the extent of Chinese territories along the Northwest frontier lost to Czarist Russia. According to the estimate of a neutral authority on the subject,[76] the Treaty of Peking of 1860 also adversely affected the area of Sinkiang. As a result of the redemarcation of the frontier from Shaban-Dabeg to Kokland, "China surrendered her claim to nearly 350,000 square miles."[77] Following the Treaty of Tarbagatai of 1864[78] and subsequent delimitation of boundaries, the Tien-shan region south of Lake Issyk-kul was given to Russia. While the Treaty of St. Petersburg of 1881 only ceded a small area west of the Holkuts River to Russia,[79] China lost more than 15,000 square miles of territory consequent to several boundary agreements in the ensuing years.[80] With respect to the Mongolian territory, Tannu-Tuva, it was annexed by the Soviet Union while Outer Mongolia was still a part of China.[81]

During the boundary talks in Peking in February 1964, China characterized "the 'Chinese Russian Treaty of Aigun', the 'Sino-Russian Treaty of Peking' and other treaties relating to the present Chinese Soviet boundary were all unequal treaties Czarist Russian imperialism imposed on China when power was not in the hands of the peoples of China and Russia."[82] The Soviet delegation refused to discuss "the historically established state frontier that was sealed by the treaties."[83] After reaching an impasse, the two governments agreed to continue their consultations in Moscow, on October 15, 1964. Before this scheduled meeting, Khrushchev deemed it necessary to request the General Assembly of the United Nations on September 1, 1964, to include in the agenda of its nineteenth session an item entitled "Renunciation by States of the use of force for the settlement of territorial disputes and questions concerning frontiers."[84] This proposal was not discussed at that session.[85]

There was no indication from the Chinese Communist government, either in words or in deeds, that it intended to use force to regain all the territories lost to Russia through unequal treaties. Nor did it prepare to do so in the case of Hongkong and Macao. As a matter of fact, the Central Committee of the Chinese Communist Party informed its Soviet counterpart on February 29, 1964, that, pending a general settlement, "the status quo on the border should be maintained."[86]

In the following months, however, both sides accused each other of border violations.[87] Intermittent clashes along the Sino-Soviet frontier did not halt until Premier Aleksei N. Kosigin paid a surprise visit to Peking on September 11, 1969, on his way home from Ho Chi-minh's funeral in Hanoi. As a consequence of their meeting, the two governments commenced deputy-minister level talks (First Deputy Foreign Minister Vasily V. Kuznetsov for the Soviet Union and Deputy Foreign Minister Chiao Kuan-hua for Communist China) in Peking on October 20. Before the arrival of the Soviet delegation, China made her position clear in a formal statement of October 8, which included five important points:

(1) to reaffirm that the present Sino-Soviet boundary was based upon unequal treaties imposed on China by Czarist Russia; (2) to conduct peaceful negotiations on the basis of the existing treaties and prevailing conditions; (3) to return unconditionally territories occupied by either side in violation of existing treaties and make necessary adjustments hereafter through mutual understanding and accommodation; (4) to conclude equal treaties to replace the unequal ones and carry out surveys for boundary demarcation; and (5) to maintain the status quo of the present border and prevent armed conflicts pending an over-all settlement. [88] In his speech of October 27, Lenoid I. Brzehnev stated that the Soviet Union was "in favor of a solution of the frontier between the U.S.S.R. and the Chinese People's Republic on a lasting and just basis in a spirit of equality, mutual respect and consideration of the interests of both countries."[89] In spite of these conciliatory statements, however, the result of the Sino-Soviet negotiations remains to be seen.

It would be most incomprehensible for the two Communist giants with 4,500 miles of common frontier to forsake their socialist fraternity and resort to force in order to settle their territorial and boundary disputes at the risk of sacrificing millions of lives. Since both governments have been reluctant to rely on arbitration or judicaial means to settle international disputes, the only possible and most realistic channel is still through direct negotiations.

Although Moscow claimed that the treaties under discussion have become historical facts, these were, after all, not reciprocal in nature, unequal in substance, and concluded under unusual environment. Because of the vital change of circumstances in both China and Russia and of international practices in general, these treaties should be reviewed and revised with a view to improving future stability of the region and friendly rleations between the two nations. History proves that the theory of pacta sunt servanda without due consideration of the principle of rebus sic stantibus would constitute a formidable obstacle to peaceful readjustment of international situations.

In actual practice of the international community, states bound by unjust commitments cannot be expected to respect the sanctity of these treaties forever, unless the contracting parties are willing to reconsider such provisions "which have become inapplicabe" and such "international conditions whose continuance might endanger the peace of the world."[90] Strict maintenance of the status quo by one contracting party, while strongly and justifiably objected to by the other, will not serve the best interests of the beneficiary in the long run. Of course, revision of the aforesaid Sino-Soviet treaties should be based upon mutual concessions, which require the wisdom and courage of statesmen on both sides of the frontier.

III. DEMARCATION OF NATIONAL BOUNDARIES

As a corollary to her consolidation of border regions, Communist China made serious efforts to negotiate boundary questions with neighboring states. With the exception of the Soviet Union in the north and India in the southwest, Peking succeeded in concluding boundary treaties with the following states: Afghanistan, Burma, Nepal, Outer Mongolia, and Pakistan. Other countries on the border of China, such as North Vietnam and North Korea, have no boundary disputes with Peking.[91] Although Communist China failed in her boundary negotiations with India, the crucial issues and possibilities for future settlement will be discussed.

1. Burma

As a consequence of the Sino-British Convention of July 24, 1886,[92] China was forced to give up all claims over Burma, even though the latter was still allowed to send a tributary mission to Peking every ten years.[93] Frontier areas between China and Burma were later delimited by the Sino-British Conventions of 1894 and 1897,[94] but the boundary between Yunnan province of China and Wa State of Burma remained to be demarcated. Due to her rejection of the Simla Convention of 1914,[95] China never recognized the McMahon Line along the Burma sector. Nor had Peking accepted the Iselin Line,[96] which was accepted by the National Government of the Republic of China in 1941 when the nation was preoccupied with the war of resistance against Japan. Peking-Rangoon relations were further complicated by the presence on Burmese territory of a few thousand Nationalist soldiers, who retreated from the Chinese mainland after the Communist victory. [97]

In spite of these differences, the two governments followed the principle of coexistence and concluded the Treaty of Friendship and Mutual Non-aggression and also the Boundary Agreement in Peking in 1960.[98] The redemarcated boundary was favorable to Burma, possibly due to China's intention to pacify her small neighbors after encountering difficulties with India.[99] In accordance with the Treaty of Friendship and Mutual Non-aggression, either one of the two contracting parties agreed not to take part in any military alliance directed against the other. Thus Burma was committed not to join the Southeast Asia Treaty Organization or ally with India against Communist China.

2. Nepal

Nepal's relations with China have been cordial, and no difficulty was encountered in demarcating the boundaries between the two countries. On March 21, 1960, two agreements were signed in Peking: one on boundary and another on economic aid.[100] These two were soon followed by the conclusion of the Treaty of Peace and Freindship in the same year. [101] Their unsettled claims over the summit of Mt. Everest were solved by the Boundary Treaty of October 5, 1961,[102] which used the vague expression of 'passing through' instead of naming a specific location. Ten days later, the two governments signed an agreement for the construction of a highway in Nepal.[103] The highway was to be built from Katmandu, the Nepalese capital, to the Tiebtan border, linking another road running to Lhasa.[104] The process of demarcating the Sino-Nepalese boundary was completed and formalized in the Boundary Protocol of January 20, 1963. [105]

By cultivating friendly relations with this mountain state, China reasserted her influence across the Himalayas. Recent reports indicated that Nepal terminated her military assistance agreement of 1965 with India and demanded the withdrawal of Indian army personnel from her territory.[106] This event further demonstrated Nepal's inclination to maintain a policy of nonalignment.[107]

3. Afghanistan

The boundary between Afghanistan and China extends for about twenty miles along the Wakhan Corridor. After the first Sino-Indian border clashes in 1959, the two countries concluded the Treaty of Friendship and Mutual Non-aggression at Kabul, on August 26, 1960. [108] In addition to provisions on pacific settlement of disputes and mutual respect for national sovereignty and territorial integrity, they agreed not " to take part in any military alliance directed against the other contracting party." [109] This stipulation was a precautionary measure on the part of Peking to prevent Afghanistan's possible joining the Central Treaty Organization against China. On November 22, 1963, the two governments signed a boundary treaty in Peking, on the basis of mutual understanding and concessions. [110] The conclusion of this treaty might also be designed to isolate India internationally, because it took place not long after the second Sino-Indian border clashes in 1962. [111]

4. Pakistan

The only common frontier between China and Pakistan is that part of Kashmir claimed by the latter but disputed by India. On May 3, 1962, the two governments announced their readiness to discuss boundary questions. [112] Negotiations began on October 12, when Prime Minister Nehru declared his decision to take the offensive against the Chinese frontier guards in control of the Sino-Indian disputed areas. Having agreed on principle before the end of the year, [113] it did not take long for the two governments to sign an agreement in Peking, on March 2, 1963, concerning the boundary between Sinkiang of China and the contiguous areas under actual control and defense of Pakistan. [114]

It was understood that the boundary between the two countries under the aforesaid agreement would be subject to the maintenance of the existing status of Kashmir in its future settlement. While Pakistan was well satisfied with the agreement, India vigorously denounced it. [115] Of course, the conclusion of this boundary agreement further widened the rift between India and Pakistan. [116] The construction of a highway was being planned from Western Sinkiang to the Pakistan-controlled section of Kashmir; its rapid progress caused deep concern to India, which sent protests to both Pakistan and Communist China in June 1969.[117]   In recent years, Peking has also extended generous assistance to Pakistan in economic and technical fields. [118]

5. Outer Mongolia

Russian designs in Outer Mongolia under both Czarist and Soviet regimes and the circumstances surrounding its independence from China have been previously described. [119] When the Chinese People's Republic was established in Peking in October 1949, notes were exchanged between the prime ministers of the two countries for the immediate establishment of diplomatic relations.[120]   In addition to periodical trade agreements, they signed the Agreement on Economic and Cultural Cooperation on October 4, 1952, [121] the Treaty of Friendship and Mutual Assistance on May 31, 1960,[122] and the Treaty of Commerce on April 26, 1961. [123] Serious efforts were exerted by Peking to strengthen Sino-Mongolian relations by extending economic and technical aid, including the assistance of a few thousand Chinese workers for construction projects.

Formerly a part of Chinese territory, Outer Mongolia has a common frontier with China of over 2,500 miles, several sections of which were not delimited. After the Sino-Indian border clashes in 1962, Peking took the initiative in negotiating with Outer Mongolia for a boundary treaty, which was concluded in Peking, on December 26, 1962, and ratified on March 25, 1963.[124]   After the completion of the demarcating process, a boundary protocol was signed in Ulan Bator, on June 30, 1964.[125]   Sandwiched between two Communist giants, Outer Mongolia was put in a difficult position, when Sino-Soviet relations were worsening. [126]   Ulan Bator decided to side with Moscow; Peking retaliated by stopping, for a time, all transit trade across China to Mongolia. [127] Chinese workers were then ordered out of the country by Ulan Bator. [128]   On the basis of the Soviet-Mongolian Mutual Assistance Pact of 1966, Moscow dispatched troops to Outer Mongolia at the Chinese frontier; border tensions have since been growing. [129]   It is evident that Ulan Bator's attitude twoard Peking is largely determined by the changing status of Moscow-Peking relations.

Both Moscow and Ulan Bator are deeply suspicious of Peking's intention to reassert China's sovereignty over Outer Mongolia. In an interview with a group of Japanese socialists in Peking, on July 10, 1964, Mao Tse-tung was quoted as saying that "in accordance with the Yalta Agreement, the Soviet Union, under the pretext of assuring the independence of Mongolia, actually placed the country under its domination." [130] On September 9, the Mongolian News Agency was authorized to issue a statement, accusing China of cherishing the hope of "turning the MPR into a subordinate outlying district of China." As evidence, the statement quoted the following remarks made by Mao to Edgar Snow in 1936: "With the victory of the people's revolution in China, the MPR 'will automatically become' a part of China." [131]

A statement made in 1936 when Mao was engaged in a desperate struggle against the Nationalists would not necessarily represent the official view of the Chinese People's Republic a few decades later. According to a Soviet source, however, Mao did bring up the status of Outer Mongolia with Khrushchev in Peking in 1954, but the latter declined to discuss it. [132] At the world congress of seventy-five Communist and workers' parties in Moscow in June 1969, Premier Yumzhagiin Tsedenbal of Outer Mongolia responded to the Soviet condemnation of Peking on June 13, and renouncing Mao's intention of annexing his country by force. [133]

The question has been raised as to how long Peking will tolerate a hostile state on China's border closely aligned with Moscow. When China was compelled by circumstances to accept the secession of Outer Mongolia from her territorial domain, it was hoped that the latter would become a free and independent nation, acting as a buffer state between the two major powers. The present situation is beyond the original expectation of China and detrimental to her national interests. The National Government in Taiwan has already taken the position that, in view of the changing situation, Outer Mongolia should be deemed a part of Chinese territory. [134] There is no doubt that self-determination should remain the basic principle to guide the future of Outer Mongolia, but the acutal application of this principle will depend upon whether the Mongolians can really exercise free will in the conduct of domestic and foreign policies.

6. India

The boundary disputes between India and Communist China, which first flared up in 1959, reached serious dimensions in late October 1962. [135] The areas under contention comprise three sectors: western, middle, and eastern. As summarized by the Indian side, [136] the western sector is the boundary between Jammu and Kashmir of India and Sinkiang and the Tibet region of China; the middle sector divides the states of Punjab, Himachal Pradesh and Uttar Pradesh of India and the Ari district of the Tibet region of China; and the eastern sector separates the North East Frontier Agency of India and the Tibet region of China. India has also been concerned with the northern boundaries of Bhutan and Sikkim along the Tibet region of China. [137]

According to India's official estimate, "the boundary between India and China extends over 2,200 miles." With respect to the northern side, "the boundary of Sikkim with the Tibet region of China extends over 140 miles while that of Bhutan extends over 300 miles." [138] In the opinion of the Indian government, "the entire length of this border has been either defined by treaty or recognized by custom or by both," and "the McMahon Line (so called after McMahon, the British representative at the Simla Conference) merely confirmed the natural, traditional, ethnic and administrative boundary in the area." [139]

On the other hand, Communist China declared that her territorial claims were based upon "the traditional customary boundary," which "was not only respected by both China and India over a long period of time, but also reflected in early official British maps." This position was persistently held by China and reaffirmed in Premier Chou En-Lai's letter to the leaders of Asian and African countries on November 15, 1962, [140] in which Chou further explained Peking's position on the scope of areas belonging to China in accordance with the traditional customary boundary and also on the legal status of the McMahon Line: the western sector consists mainly of

Aksai Chin in China's Sinkiang and a part of the Ari district of Tibet, covering a total area of 33,000 square kilometers;[141] the middle sector in dispute is located east of the traditional customary line, covering an area of 2,000 square kilometers; the eastern sector involves the controversial McMahon Line, which has never been recognized by China.

The chief reason for Peking's strong objection to the McMahon Line, as explained by Premier Chou, is due to the fact that it was drawn up by the British plenipotentiary Henry McMahon at the Simla Conference in 1914, "behind the back of the representative of the Chinese Central Government" and "through a secret exchange of letters with the representative of the Tibet local authorities, attempting thereby to annex 90,000 square kilometers of Chinese territory to British India." In view of this historical background, Chou cautioned that "the Sino-Indian boundary dispute is a legacy of British imperialist aggression," hence "China and India ought to have cast away the entire legacy of imperialism and established and developed their relations of mutual friendship on a completely new basis." [142]

After the clashes between Indian and Chinese patrol parties in October 1959, Premier Chou wrote to Prime Minister Jawaharla Nehru on November 7, proposing that "the armed forces of China and India each withdraw 20 kilometers at once from the so-called McMahon Line in the east, and from the line up to which each side exercises actual control in the west."[143] In the same letter, he suggested that they should meet together to resolve their differences in the immediate future. Chou went to New Delhi in April 1960, with the hope of negotiating a settlement with Prime Minister Nehru. As a result of a series of meetings on April 19-25, the two leaders agreed to appoint officials of their respective governments to examine and study all historical documents, records, accounts, maps, and other materials relevant to the boundary question.

The officials appointed for that purpose promptly undertook the task. They met in Peking, New Delhi, and Rangoon, but failed to agree on the basic issues. The Chinese officials declined to discuss the border question involving that part of Kashmir under the control of Pakistan and the boundaries of Tibet with Sikkim and Bhutan. Under the circumstances, they

decided to write a separate report by each side, to be submitted jointly to the two governments before the end of the
year. [144]

Unsuccessful in the diplomatic field, Prime Minister Nehru
was concerned with the possibility of a prolonged war with
Communist China. [145] With the advance of Indian reinforcements and the establishment of more outposts, Prime Minister Nehru requested the Parliament to give him a free hand
in dealing with the situation on August 14, 1962. [146] Hostilities resumed on September 8; Indian troops received orders,
on October 12, to drive the Chinese forces out of the disputed
areas. [147] Then the Cinese countered with a major offensive
on October 20, [148] and advnaced much deeper into the disputed regions by the middle of November. One Western
expert on Asian affairs characterized the Indian defeat as a
"Himalayan miscalculation," because "India precipitated war
with a stronger enemy." [149] Of course, the Indian government
accused Communist China of the act of aggression. [150] In all
fairness, both sides should be responsible for the development of the unfortunate events. The use of force to settle
a boundary dispute by two governments whose leaders advocated the plausible principles of peaceful coexistence was
most regretable. Probably neither side really wanted to wage
a bloody war, [151] but national dignity, prestige, and strategic
considerations made it difficult for the disputing parties to
accept a compromise.

In his letter to Prime Minister Nehru on October 24,
1962, Premier Chou submitted three proposals as a concession on the part of China: (1) to reaffirm the principle of
peaceful settlement of the Sino-Indian boundary question
through negotiations; (2) to withdraw the Chinese "frontier
guards in the Eastern sector of the border to the north of the
line of actual control, and, on the part of India, to refrain
from crossing "the line of actual control, i.e., the traditional
customary line, in the middle and western sectors of the
border"; and (3) to seek a friendly solution of the boundary
question by further consultations between the Prime Ministers
of the two governments in Peking or New Delhi. [152] To clarify
the expression, "the line of control", Chou meant the one of
1959 and not that of 1962. By doing so, "the Chinese forces
will have to withdraw much more than 20 kilometers from
their present position in the Eastern sector." [153] Meanwhile,

Chou wrote to the leaders of Asian and African countries to request their good offices and mediation for a peaceful settlement of the dispute. [154]

To seek a conciliatory settlement through bilateral negotiations or a third-party mediation, Peking ordered a unilateral cease-fire and withdrew its forces 20 kilometers behind the "line of control" as previously proposed. Prime Minister Nehru had, however, serious doubts about China's intentions. In his letter to Premier Chou on December 1, he pointed out that "the three-point proposals of October 24, 1962 and the statement on cease-fire and withdrawals of 21st November, 1962, clearly aim at securing physical control of areas which were never under Chinese administrative control either on 7th November, 1959 or at any time prior to 8th September, 1962." In his opinion, these proposals "are a definite attempt to prejudice India's position in maintaining its stand as regards the boundary." [155]

In order to reconcile the views of the two governments, Chou then suggested that officials of both sides "meet in January 1963 either in Peking, or in Delhi, or in the capital of a friendly Asian or African country" for the purpose of discussing "such matters as withdrawal arrangements for the disengagement of the armed forces of the two sides, establishment of checkpoints and return of captured personnel." [156] Prime Minister Nehru turned down all the Chinese proposals, and considered submitting the Sino-Indian boundary question to the International Court of Justice for adjudication if necessary. [157]

When bilateral negotiations reached a deadlock, the so-called Colombo proposals were presented to both governments for their consideration. These proposals were produced by a conference held at Colombo, on December 10, represented by Ceylon, Burma, Cambodia, Ghana, Indonesia, and the United Arab Republic. The essential points were as follows: (1) western sector – to carry out China's proposal of 20 kilometers withdrawal of their military posts and to establish a demilitarized zone administered by civilian posts of both sides; (2) eastern sector – to consider the line of actual control in the areas recognized by both governments as a cease-fire line to their respective positions, and to settle the remaining areas for future discussion; and middle sector – to solve their differences by peaceful means without resorting to force. The above proposals, submitted to the two governments on December 15, were purported to "pave the way for discussions between representatives of both parties." [158]

Mme. Sirimavo Bandaranaike, Prime Minister of Ceylon, went to New Delhi and Peking with a delegation of the Afro-Asian group to consult with Indian and Chinese leaders. India accepted the proposals after their further clarification.[159] According to Peking's interpretation, however, the clarifications made by the delegates were not completely in conformity with the original proposals adopted by the Colombo conference. Nevertheless, China still "gave positive response" to the proposals with reservations on such points as the establishment of civilian posts in the demilitarized zone by both sides and lack of provision for Indian withdrawal. In spite of these reservations, Peking indicated its willingness to open direct talks with India to resolve their differences.[160] It is unfortunate that, in the ensuing years, there have been neither direct negotiations between the disputing governments nor follow-up mediation by third parties which might lead to a peaceful settlement of the Sino-Indian boundary dispute.[161] Strained relations between the two countries would affect not only peace and stability in Asia but also their own interests in the international community.[162]

Having examined the historical background of the Sino-Indian boundary question together with the arguments put forth by both sides, with no attempt at passing on their respective merits, the present analysis cannot but conclude that the traditional customary lines dividing the Sino-Indian border are disputable in all three sectors. The McMahon Line drawn up in 1914 is legally not binding upon China, because she was not a party to the Simla Convention as previously explained;[163] on this question, the position of the Chinese Nationalists is identical with that of the Communists.[164] This does not, however, preclude the possibility that certain parts of the McMahon Line may coincide with the traditional customary lines, which remain to be agreed upon by both governments. Thus the crucial issue of the Sino-Indian boundary question is to ascertain first what are the traditional customary lines. After a long cooling-off period of more than six years, this problem may be solved by reopening direct negotiations.

If bilateral talks should prove unsuccessful, it might be advisable to settle the dispute by arbitration. The arbitration tribunal could be composed of five distinguished jurists or statesmen, who are nationals of third states. India and China would, for example, name two persons each, and the fifth one as chairman of the tribunal would be selected by unanimous vote of the four.[165] Prior to arbitration proceedings, the two governments should conclude a special compromis, concerning the substance of the dispute, scope of jurisdiction, guiding principles, and rules of procedure to be followed by the tribunal. The arbiters would examine all the historical evidences with due consideration of the areas under actual occupation and control before and after 1959. The two governments should also agree beforehand that the arbiters may decide the boundary question ex aequo et bono and that the award shall be unconditionally binding upon them.

It is hoped that statesmen of both India and China will take as their primary concern the long-range friendship between the two countries and mutual benefit of their peoples, instead of fighting for certain lines along territories hitherto not under effective occupation, uninhabited or sparsely populated.[166] Any concession made by either government might be unpopular in its country for a time, but temporary popularity of an official act does not necessarily work for the permanent interests of the country.[167]

NOTES TO CHAPTER 11

1. Letter of Transmittal to President Truman from Secretary of State Dean Acheson, The White Paper, p. xvii.

2. Department of State Bulletin, Vol. XIII, p. 5

3. Cf. Art. 51 of the United Nations Charter on individual or collective self-defense against armed attack or aggression. In The Caroline case in 1837, Secretary of State Daniel Webster defined the conditions for a state to exercise the right of self-defense as "instant, overwhelming, and leaving no choice of means, and no moment for deliberation. See J. B. Moore, A Digest of International Law (Washington, D.C., 1906, 8 vols.), II, p. 412. For further details on the right of self-defense and its restrictions, see William L. Tung, International Law in an Organizing World, pp. 416-418.

4. GA res. 498(V).

5. The text can be found in Department of State, Military Armistice in Korea and Temporary Supplementary Agreement (Washington, D.C., 1957).

6. See Sino-American Exchanges of Notes for Military Assistance, January 30/February 9, 1951, and also Décember 29, 1951/ January 2, 1952 (Chinese Republic, Treaties, pp. 794-798, 798-802; Chen Treaties, pp. 439-441, 443-445).

7. For the text, see ibid., pp. 487-489; Chinese Republic, Treaties, pp. 824-827.

8. Art. VI of the Treaty. It should be mentioned that Nationalist forces evacuated Tachens, a comparatively vulnerable island, in February 1955.

9. See Art. V of the Treaty.

10. See Art. VII of the Treaty.

11. The Notes were exchanged between Secretary of State John Foster Dulles and the Chinese Foreign Minister George K.C. Yeh on behalf of their respective governments. For the text, see Chen, Treaties, pp. 489-490. It was not included in the Chinese Republic, Treaties, an official publication of the Chinese government. The text of both the Treaty and Exchange of Notes can be found in Documents on American Foreign Relations, 1954, pp. 360-362, 363-364, respectively. Since Peking

linked the offshore islands to the defense of Formosa, President Eisenhower informed Congress that the Communist position "compels us to take into account closely related localities." Department of State Bulletin, Vol. 32 (February 28, 1955), pp. 329-330.

12. For the text of Dulles' statement, see ibid., February 21, 1955, pp. 287-290.

13. For comments on debarring the Republic of China from invading the mainland, see The New York Times, December 2, 3, 1954.

14. Adopted by the House of Representatives on January 25, by a vote of 409-3, and by the Senate on January 28, by a vote of 64-6. Public Law 4, 84th Cong., 1st Sess. (January 29, 1955).

15. See Chou's address before the Second National Committee of the Chinese Political Consultative Conference on June 28, 1956. People's China, Supplement, No. 14 (July 16, 1956), pp. 3-14.

16. Vidya Prakash Dutt, China and the World (New York, 1966), p. 23. During the Quemoy-Matsu crisis in 1958, the United States would have defended these offshore islands if the Communist attacks were directed at threatening the security of Taiwan. See The New York Times, September 5, 1958. On June 27, 1962, President Kennedy reiterated the American policy set forth by President Eisenhower in 1958 that the United States "would not remain inactive in the face of any aggressive action against the offshore islands which might threaten Formosa." Department of State, Foreign Policy Briefs, Vol. XI, No. 26, July 9, 1962.

17. See World Wide Enforcement of Strategic Trade Controls, the Third Report to Congress, September 27, 1953, of the Administrator of the Mutual Defense Control Act of 1951 (Washington, D.C., 1953), p. 33.

18. In his address before the China Institute of America in New York City on May 18, 1951, Dean Rusk, then Assistant Secretary of State for Far Eastern Affairs, stated that "we recognize the National Government of the Republic of China, even though the territory under its control is severely restricted." The text of the address is available in pamphlet form, reprinted by the Committee of One Million against the Admission of Communist China to the United Nations.

19. The reasons for United States objection were fully explained in the address by Ambassador James J. Wadsworth, Ameri-

can representative to the United Nations, before the General Assembly on October 1, 1960. The address was published as a a pamphlet by the American-Asian Educational Exchange, Inc., N.Y. See also infra, pp. 406-408.

20. See The New York Times, January 21, February 21, 1970. President Nixon's Report to Congress on February 18, 1970, respecting American policy toward China, merely reaffirmed the United States position declared in previous statements. The 135th meeting was a result of informal conversations between American Ambassador Walter J. Stoessel and Chinese Chargé d'Affaires Lei Yang at the Chinese Embassy in Warsaw. See ibid., December 13, 1969. A meeting was originally scheduled for February 20, 1969. It was, however, cancelled by Peking on February 18, ostensibly on the ground that the United States granted political asylum to Liao Ho-shu, who defected to the West from his diplomatic post at The Hague. See ibid., February 19, 1969. In early meetings, the United States representative usually raised three demands: (1) the renunciation of the use of force in the settlement of the Taiwan problem, (2) an accounting of the missing Korean war prisoners, and (3) the release of the Americans held in China. This information was revealed by Secretary Dulles in reply to questions by House Democratic leader John McCormack. See Long Island Press, December 6, 1957. According to Secretary of State William P. Rogers, Ambassador Walter J. Stoessel was instructed to discuss with his Chinese counterpart in Warsaw at the meeting of February 20, 1969, the following questions: (1) an agreement setting forth principles of peaceful coexistence, (2) exchange of newsmen, and (3) a settlement of pending postal and telecommunications problems. See The New York Times, February 19, 1969. After the scheduled meeting was cancelled, Peking resumed attacks on the United States policy toward Taiwan in its official paper, Renmin Ribao. See The New York Times, May 20, 1969.

21. For Peking's attitude toward American defense of Taiwan, see the following official publications by the Foreign Languages Press, Peking, including speeches, editorials, and other documents: Important Documents concerning the Question of Taiwan (1955); Oppose U.S. Military Provocations in the Taiwan Straits Area: A Selection of Important Documents (1958); Oppose U.S. Occupation of Taiwan and "Two Chinas" Plot: A Selection of Important Documents (1958); Oppose the New U.S. Plots to Create "Two Chinas" (1962); and Two Tactics, One Aim: An Exposure of the Peace Tricks of U.S. Imperialism (1960). At the nineteenth anniversary of the founding of the People's Republic of China on October 1, 1968, Marshal Lin Piao reiterated Peking's determination to take possession of Taiwan.

NOTES TO CHAPTER 11

For the English text of his speech, see Current Background, No. 865 (October 18, 1968), pp. 11-12.

22. Further information on American policy toward Communist China can be found in U.S. Policy with Respect to Mainland China, Hearings before the Committee on Foreign Relations, U.S. Senate, 89th Cong., 2nd Sess. (Washington, D.C., 1966); William W. Lockwood (ed.), The United States and Communist China (Princeton, 1965). In these two volumes, several scholars, including Hans Morgenthau and George F. Kennan, advocated the change of the present American policy. Some background information on United States relations with China can be found in John King Fairbank, The United States and China (Cambridge, 1958), pp. 246-277, 307-320; Harold M. Vinacke, United States Policy toward China (Cincinnati, 1961); Meribeth E. Cameron, Thomas H. D. Mahoney, and George E. McReynolds, China, Japan and the Powers (New York, 1960), pp. 462-497. For a review of the events, personalities, and issues affecting American involvement in China, see China and U.S. Far East Policy, 1945-1967 (a publication of Congressional Quarterly, Washington, D.C. 1967), pp. 1-219; Roger Hilsman, To Move a Nation: The Politics of Foreign Policy in the Administration of John F. Kennedy (Garden City, N.Y., 1967). In an airport statement upon his arrival in Taipei, Secretary of State William P. Rogers reaffirmed that "we will continue to meet our treaty obligations to our allies including, of course, our ally of long-standing, the Republic of China." The New York Times, August 2, 1969.

23. There are two essential points in the new regulations announced by the Department of State on July 23, 1969: (1) American citizens traveling abroad are allowed to bring home goods produced in Communist China valued up to $100; and (2) American scholars, students, scientists, doctors, and newsmen are permitted to travel to the Chinese mainland, subject to approval by Peking in each case. See The New York Times, July 22, 1969. For the State Department announcement of December 19, 1969, see ibid., December 20, 1969.

24. As First Secretary of the Soviet Communist Party, Nikita Khrushchev delivered a secret speech on February 25, 1956, condemning Stalin's conduct of state affairs and cult of personality. Its text was made available by the United States Department of State.

25. For details, see Peking Review, No. 24 (June 14, 1960), pp. 13-22; The Origin and Development of the Differences between the Leadership of the CPSU and Ourselves (Peking, 1963), p. 25.

26. See "On the Historical Experience of the Dictatorship of the Proletariat," Renmin Ribao, April 5, 1956.

27. Peking continued its attacks on Soviet 'revisionism' and also on the theory of 'limited sovereignty' advocated by Moscow after Soviet intervention in Czechoslovakia in 1968. See, for instance, a series of articles in Current Background, No. 850 (April 3, 1968); dispatches from Hsinhua News Agency, Peking, March 21, 25, 1969.

28. See "Leninism and Modern Revisionism," an editorial from Hongqui (Hung-ch'i or Red Flag), No. 1, 1963. This editorial was also published in a pamphlet by the Foreign Languages Press, Peking, 1963. See also Robert C. North, Moscow and Chinese Communists (Stanford, 1963), pp. 285-291. Peking's views on revisionism were fully explained in "The Differences between Comrade Togliatti and Us," Renmin Ribao, December 31, 1962. Further discussion on the subject can be found in More on the Differences between Comrade Togaliatti and Us (Peking, 1963).

29. Soviet missiles and bombers were withdrawn from Cuba in late October 1962. For a legal analysis of the crisis, see William L. Tung, International Law in an Organizing World, pp. 388-390. For a further description of the severe strain between Peking and Moscow as a consequence of this Soviet retreat, see Vidya Prakash Dutt, op. cit., pp. 134-146.

30. Upon his arrival in Peking from the United States, Khrushchev spoke at the airport, emphasizing that "everything must be done in order to really clear the atmosphere and create conditions for friendship among nations." See Peking Review, No. 40 (October 6, 1959), pp. 10-11. Peking simply ignored his remarks and did not even give a speech of welcome. For further information on Sino-Soviet disputes, see Donald S. Zagoria, "Strains in the Sino-Soviet Alliance," Problems of Communism, Vol. 9, No. 3 (May-June 1960), pp. 1-11; Zbigniew Brzezinski, "Pattern and Limits of the Sino-Soviet Dispute," ibid., Vol. 9, No. 5 (September-October 1960), pp. 1-7.

31. Art. I of the Sino-Soviet Treaty of 1950 provided that Soviet obligation to render military and other assistance to Communist China would arise only when the latter were attacked by Japan or any state allied with Japan. However, the Soviet Union supported Peking during the Quemoy-Matsu crisis in 1958, even though Moscow did not approve of the use of force to solve the problem. On September 7, Khrushchev wrote to President Eisenhower, warning that "an attack on the People's Republic of China" would be deemed as "an attack on the Soviet Union." The New York Times, September 9, 1958.

32. See Hongqi, 1964, Nos. 2-3, pp. 6-32; No. 6, pp. 2-39; No. 9, pp. 2-33; No. 13, pp. 1-33; No. 14, pp. 1-17; No. 16, pp. 1-6; Nos. 21-22, pp. 1-8. See also Franz Michael, "Khrushchev's Disloyal Opposition; Structural Change and Power Struggle in the Communist Bloc," Orbis, Vol. 7, No. 1 (Spring 1963), pp. 49-76.

33. Khrushchev subsequently broke up the Paris summit conference, which was to be held on May 16, 1960. The Soviet Union brought a complaint of the U-2 flight before the Security Council, which discussed the question on May 23, 1960. See the Repertoire of the Practice of the Security Council, Supplement, 1959-1963, pp. 281-282. The drafting resolution accusing the United States of aggression was rejected at its meeting on May 26, 1960. See ibid., pp. 157-158. For Peking's attitude toward the U-2 incident, see Hongqi, No. 11 (June 1, 1960), pp. 1-3.

34. In January 1957, Chou En-lai went to Moscow and then to Hungary, Poland, and Czechoslovakia to help consolidate the socialist front with due recognition of national autonomy. See Donald S. Zagoria, The Sino-Soviet Conflict, 1956-1961 (Princeton, 1962), pp. 61-62. For Peking's criticism on 'big-nation chauvinism', see Renmin Ribao, December 29, 1956. After Chou's return from Eastern Europe to Moscow, a Sino-Soviet joint communiqué was issued, emphasizing both bloc interest and national equality. See The New York Times, January 19, 1957.

35. Titoism has been repeatedly condemned by the Chinese leadership. In Peking's view, the Khrushchev-Tito declaration of June 20, 1956, was partly responsible for the crisis in Hungary and Poland in 1956. See Renmin Ribao, December 29, 1956. See also Is Yugoslavia a Socialist Country? (Peking, 1963).

36. Khrushchev denounced the Albanian leadership at the twenty-second congress of the Soviet Communist Party, which was held in October 1961. In effect, he called for the overthrow of Enver Hoxha and Mehmet Shehu, to whom the Chinese gave solid support.

37. In reply, the Chinese delegation issued a statement on June 26, 1960. For the text, see The Origin and Development of the Differences between the Leadership of the CPSU and Ourselves, Appendix II.

38. See "Let Us Unite on the Bais of the Moscow Declaration and the Moscow Statement," Renmin Ribao, January 27, 1963.

39. At the twenty-second congress of the Soviet Communist Party in 1961, Chou En-lai continued to criticize Moscow's errors. In

reply, Khrushchev told Chou, in effect, that the support of the Chinese Communist Party was no longer needed and that the Soviet leaders would go their own way. Open letters have since been exchanged by the two fraternal parties, criticizing each other's mistakes. See The Origin and Development of the Differences between the Leadership of the CPSU and Ourselves, pp. 46, 49, 50.

40. For a comprehensive analysis of Sino-Soviet relations both before and after Khrushchev's fall, see Edgar Snow, The Other Side of the River: Red China Today (New York, 1961), pp. 646-672; John Gittings (ed.), Survey of the Sino-Soviet Dispute; a Commentary and Extracts from the Recent Polemics, 1963-1967 (London & New York, 1968); William E. Griffith, "Sino-Soviet Relations, 1964-65," The China Quarterly, No. 25 (January-March 1966), pp. 3-143. See also "Revisionist New Tsars in Moscow Are Chief Anti-Soviet Criminals," Renmin Ribao, March 25, 1969. This article was written by two personnel of the Chinese Liberation Army; its English translation appeared in Survey of China Mainland Press, No. 4387 (April 1, 1969), pp. 23-24.

41. The Chinese and most Asian Communist parties were absent. For details, see The New York Times, June 6-8, 1969.

42. For excerpts from the document, see ibid., June 19, 1969.

43. See the critical comments made by Marshal Lin Piao, China's Defense Minister, in his message of greetings to Beqir Balluku, the Albanian Defense Minister, on the occasion of the twenty-sixth anniversary of the founding of the Albanian Army. Ibid., July 10, 1969.

44. See infra, Ch. 12, note 96. For Moscow's challenge to Peking's activities in developing countries, see Donald S. Zagoria, "Sino-Soviet Friction in Under-developed Areas," Problems of Communism Vol. 10, No. 2 (March-April 1961), pp. 1-13; Robert A. Scalapino, "Sino-Soviet Competition in Africa," Foreign Affairs, Vol. 42 (July 1964), pp. 640-654.

45. See "The Truth About How the Leaders of the CPSU Have Allied Themselves with India against China," Renmin Ribao, November 2, 1963. For details of the Sino-Indian border conflict in 1962, see infra, pp. 362-367.

46. For the Treaty Banning Nuclear Weapon Tests in the Atmosphere, in Outer Space and Under Water, concluded in Moscow, on August 5, 1963, see Disarmament Commission, Official Records (Supplement for January to December 1963, UN Doc. DC/207-208), pp. 53-55.

47. For official statements, editorials, and other documents on the subject, see People of the World, Unite, for the Complete, Thorough, Total and Resolute Prohibition and Destruction of Nuclear Weapons (Peking, 1963). See also Hungdah Chiu, "Communist China's Attitude Towards Nuclear Tests," The China Quarterly, No. 21 (January-March 1965), pp. 96-107.

48. See Peking Review, No. 42 (October 16, 1964), pp. ii-iv. Communist China also denounced the Nonproliferation Treaty, signed in Moscow, London, and Washington, on July 1, 1968. In Peking's view, it was again a Soviet-American attempt at persuading non-nuclear powers to enter into an act of self-abnegation not to develop or acquire nuclear weapons, while the nuclear powers could maintain their advantageous position for all practical purposes. The draft resolution recommending the treaty was adopted by the General Assembly of the United Nations on January 12, 1968. See GA res. 2373(XXII); UN Doc. A/7016/Add.1.

49. For Soviet participation in disarmament talks with the United States and other powers, see William L. Tung, International Organization under the United Nations System, Ch. 8. On July 14, 1963, the Central Committee of CPSU published an open letter to its party members and Communist parties throughout the world, putting the blame on Peking for Sino-Soviet disputes. In reply, the editorial departments of Renmin Ribao and Hongqi published, on September 6, 1963, The Origin and Develâ€‘opemnt of the Differences between the Leadership of the CPSU and Ourselves. The differences included the problem of disarmament. Communist China's objection to disarmament talks at the present time is largely due to her sense of insecurity. So long as the nation is under the threat of the two superpowers, it is not the time to talk about disarmament.

50. See Harold C. Hinton, Communist China in World Politics (Boston, 1966), p. 159.

51. In his "My Ideological Review," Lung YÃ¼n, a member of the Standing Committee of the National People's Congress, wrote:

> "It was unreasonable for China to bear all the expenses of the Korean War.... The Soviet loan ... is repayable in full in ten years. The time is too short and moreover interest has to be paid.... When the Soviet Union liberated our Northeast, it dismantled some machinery equipment in our factories. Was there compensation for it? Will there be repayment?"

Renmin Ribao, July 14, 1957; English translation from Current Background, No. 470 (July 26, 1957). Here the word 'Northeast' meant Manchuria, which is located in the northeastern part of China.

Complaint on the same subject was embodied in the Letter of the Central Committee of the Chinese Communist Party to its Soviet counterpart on February 29, 1964. See Seven Letters Exchanged between the Central Committees of the Communist Party of China and the Communist Party of the Soviet Union (Peking, 1964), pp. 25-26.

52. Ibid., p. 24.

53. The Soviet Union "unscrupulously withdrew the 1,390 Soviet experts working in China, tore up 343 contracts and supplementary contracts concerning experts, and scrapped 257 projects of scientific and technical cooperation, all within the short span of a month." Ibid., p. 26. On the other hand, the Soviet Union blamed the Chinese for the termination of economic cooperation, reduction of trade, as well as suspension of scientific, technical, and cultural exchange. In his address to the Supreme Soviet on July 10, 1969. Foreign Minister Andrei A. Gromyko reported that trade between the two countries 'dropped from about 2,000 million rubles in 1959 to 86 million rubles in 1968." The New York Times, July 11, 1969.

54. This was revealed through an interview between Chairman Mao Tse-tung and the Delegation of the Japanese Socialist Party. See Sekai Shuho (Tokyo), August 11, 1964.

55. See Asahi Shimbun (Tokyo), August 1, 1964, for an interview between Chou and Okada, a Socialist member of the Japanese Diet.

56. See "A Comment on the Statement of the Communist Party of the U.S.A.," Renmin Ribao editorial, March 8, 1963 (published as a pamphlet by Foreign Languages Press, Peking, 1963, p. 12). The statement, issued by CPUSA on January 9, 1963, criticized the attitude of the Chinese Communist Party. For its text, see The Worker (New York), January 13, 1963.

57. For the text, see Chinese Customs, Treaties, I, pp. 81-84; Hertslet, Treaties, I, pp. 454-455; Mayers, Treaties, p. 100. See also supra, p. 27.

58. For the text, see Hertslet, Treaties, I, pp. 461-472; Chinese Customs, Treaties, I, pp. 101-120; Mayers, Treaties, pp. 105-112. See also supra, p. 27.

59. This treaty was signed at St. Petersburg, concerning the territorial dispute over the Ili Valley. See supra, p. 80. For the text, see Chinese Customs, Treaties, I, pp. 168-187; Hertslet, Treaties, I, pp. 483-499.

60. For details of the treaties of Tientsin, see supra, p. 25.

61. For the text, see Chinese Customs, Treaties, I, pp. 85-100; Hertslet, Treaties, I, pp. 455-461.

62. For the text, see Peking Review, No. 19 (May 8, 1964), pp. 7-27; Seven Letters Exchanged between the Central Committees of the Communist Party of China and the Communist Party of the Soviet Union, pp. 21-41.

63. Ibid., pp. 22-23.

64. The border incident occurred first on March 2, followed by other clashes at later dates. For details, see The New York Times, March 3, 12, 14, 16, 31, for the development of the situation and statements by both governments.

65. See ibid., March 12, 1969.

66. See ibid., June 12, August 14, 1969.

67. Skirmishes took place on Pacha Island, called Goldinsky Island by the Russians, in the Amur River. Each side accused the other of malicious provocations. See ibid., July 9, 1969. In 1951, a Sino-Soviet joint commission was formed to regulate shipping on the border rivers of the Amur River basin. The two sides conducted meetings intermittently at the Soviet city of Khabarvsk (Poli), where the commission is located. After the March clashes, they met again on June 18. As a result of a number of sessions, the two sides reached an agreement, on August 8, on certain specific issues relating to navigation on their boundary rivers. See ibid., July 14, August 9, 12, 1969.

68. See ibid., March 12, 1969.

69. The statement issued by the Chinese Ministry of Foreign Affairs in Peking, March 10, 1969 (The New York Times, March 12, 1969). See also Art. I of the Treaty of Aigun of 1858; supra, note 57.

70. See supra, pp. 25-27; also supra, note 58.

71. The Chinese statement of March 10, 1969 (The New York Times, March 12, 1969). See also Art. I of the Treaty of Peking of 1960. Art. II dealt with the delimitation of the northwestern frontier.

72. The Peking statement of March 10, 1969, laid great emphasis on the following remarks made by the highest authorities of socialism:

"As Marx pointed out in 1857 and 1858, the Opium War of 1840 was followed by 'the successful encroachment of Russia from the north on China, and Russia took possession of the banks of the River Amur, the native country of the present ruling race [the Manchus] in China.'

"Furthermore, after the signing of the 'Chinese-Russian Treaty of Aigun,' Engels penetratingly pointed out: 'When at last England resolved to carry the war to Peking, and when France joined her in the hope of picking up something to her advantage,' Russia despoiled 'China of a country as large as France and Germany put together, and of a river as large as the Danube.'

"Lenin also pointed out that the task of the Russian imperialist policy in Asia was 'to seize the whole of Persia, complete the partition of China.'"

The New York Times, March 12, 1969.

73. For the text, see ibid., March 31, 1969. See also supra, notes 57-59.

74. Soviet Note of March 30, 1969 (ibid., March 31, 1969).

75. According to an independent source, more Chinese land along the Northeast frontier was lost to Russia. By the Treaty of Nerchinsk of 1689, "China ceded about 93,000 square miles to the Russians." W. A. Douglas Jackson, Russo-Chinese Border-Lands (Princeton, 1962), pp. 31-32, 111-112. See, however, supra, p. 5. As a result of the Treaty of Kiakhta of 1727, "the Chinese lost nearly 40,000 square miles, between the upper Irtysh and the Sayan Mountains, as well as south and southwest of Lake Baikal." The Supplementary Treaty of Kiakhta of 1768 only made minor changes in the vicinity of boundary posts. See ibid., pp. 33, 112-113. See also supra, p. 5. For the text of these early Sino-Russian treaties, see Chinese Customs, Treaties, I, pp. 3-66; Hertslet, Treaties, I, pp. 437-449.

76. W. J. Douglas Jackson, Professor of Geography at the University of Washington, author of Russo-Chinese Border-Lands, just cited.

77. Ibid., p. 116.

78. See ibid., pp. 38, 116. For the text of the Treaty, see Chinese Customs, Treaties, I, pp. 144-151; Hertslet, Treaties, I, pp. 472-478.

79. See Jackson, op. cit., pp. 39, 116-117. See also Art. 7 of the Treaty of St. Petersburg; supra, note 59.

80. For details, see Jackson, op. cit., p. 117. There are many discrepancies over Sino-Soviet frontier areas between the Chinese and Soviet maps. For a map of the territories in dispute between Communist China and the Soviet Union, see The New York Times, March 12, 1969.

81. Tannu Tuva was detached from Outer Mongolia in 1926, and was secretly incorporated into the Soviet Union in October 1943. See supra, Ch. 2, note 76. It should be noted that Outer Mongolia's formal independence from China did not take place until January 1946.

82. The statement issued by the Chinese government on March 10, 1969 (The New York Times, March 12, 1969).

83. Soviet Note to Peking, dated March 29, 1969. See ibid., March 31, 1969.

84. See UN Docs. A/5751 (Soviet Letter of September 21, 1964), A/5740 (Soviet Letter of October 8, 1964). On December 31, 1963, Khrushchev sent circular notes to various governments on the same subject, the text of which was broadcast by Tass International Service on January 3, 1964. Excerpts from the Note can be found in Dennis J. Doolin, Territorial Claims in the Sino-Soviet Conflict: Documents and Analysis, pp. 33-36.

85. See the Note by the President of the General Assembly on status of agenda of the nineteenth session. UN Doc. A/5884.

86. Seven Letters Exchanged between the Central Committees of the Communist Party of China and the Communist Party of the Soviet Union, p. 22. Although Peking condemned the aforesaid unequal treaties, its position on the Sino-Soviet territorial and boundary disputes as expressed in the official statement of March 10, 1969, was comparatively moderate. See The New York Times, March 12, 1969. For a general survey of the borderlands and the Sino-Soviet relations, see Howard L. Boorman and others (eds.), Moscow-Peking Axis: Strengths and Strains (New York, 1957), pp. 142-197; Francis Watson, The Frontiers of China: A Historical Guide (New York, 1966), pp. 31-53, 169-184; George N. Patterson, The Unquiet Frontier: Border Tensions in the Sino-Soviet Conflict (Hongkong, 1966), which also discusses the historical background of the Sino-Soviet relations with respect to the border disputes.

87. On August 19, Peking accused Moscow of initiating 429 border incidents in June and July 1969; on the other hand, the Soviet

Union charged Communist China, on September 10, with 488 violations of the Sino-Soviet frontier between June and mid-August. See The New York Times, August 20, September 11, 1969. For a chronology of Sino-Soviet border conflicts, see Free China Weekly, November 2, 1969.

88. See The New York Times, October 9, 1969. A day before, Peking reiterated China's intention of peaceful settlement of the Sino-Soviet border dispute and refuted the position of the Soviet government in its statement of June 13. For details, see ibid., October 8, 1969.

89. Ibid., October 28, 1969. See, however, Premier Kosigin's pessimistic report of June 10, 1970 (ibid., June 11, 1970).

90. See Art. 19 of the League Covenant. Treaty revision is also implied in Art. 14 of the Charter of the United Nations. Cf. the views of a Soviet jurist, Fedor Kozhenikov, as embodied in a dispatch from Tass International Service, Moscow, April 8, 1964; originally in Russian, quoted from Dennis J. Doolin, op. cit., pp. 39-40. See also William L. Tung, International Law in an Organizing World, pp. 345-347, 356-359.

91. There was a minor discrepancy between Chinese and North Korean maps concerning the boundary line of the Changpai Peak, but it has never become a dispute. Peking raised no objection to the existing boundaries with North Vietnam and Laos.

92. For the text, see Chinese Customs, Treaties, I, pp. 506-508; Hertslet, Treaties, I, pp. 88-90.

93. See supra, p. 1; Ch. 1, note 1.

94. For the text of the Convention of March 1, 1894 and that of February 4, 1897, see Chinese Customs, Treaties, I, pp. 513-515, 532-538; Hertslet, Treaties, I, pp. 92-94, 113-119. See also supra, p. 47.

95. See supra, pp. 79-80.

96. The Line was named after Colonel Frederic Iselin, a Swiss, who was commissioned to survey the boundary in 1935-1937. See also supra, pp. 303-304.

97. For the complaint by the Burmese government against Nationalist China before the United Nations and subsequent evacuation of approximately seven thousand Nationalist soldiers and their dependents, see William L. Tung, "Have the Permanent Members of the Security Council Fulfilled Their Primary Responsibilities for the Maintenance of International Peace and

Security?" Revue de Droit international de sciences diplomatiques et politiques (Geneva), Vol. 47 (January-March
1969), p. 27.

98. For the text of the Boundary Agreement of January 4, 1960
and its subsequent Exchange of Notes of October 1, 1960,
see CPR, Treaties, Vol. 9, pp. 68-77, 78-79. For the text of
the Treaty of Friendship of January 28, 1960, see ibid.,
pp. 44-45. Its English text can be found in The Collected
Treaties of Amity of the Chinese People's Republic (compiled
by the Ministry of Foreign Affairs, Peking, 1965; hereafter
cited as CPR Collected Treaties), pp. 5-6. As early as June
29, 1954, the Chinese and Burmese Prime Ministers issued a
joint declaration in Rangoon, emphasizing their mutual observance of the five principles of coexistence. See also infra, pp.
389-392.

99. See Alastair Lamb, Asian Frontiers (New York, 1968),
pp. 136-137. Further information can be found in Chinese
People's Institute of Foreign Affairs, A Victory for the Five
Principles of Peaceful Coexistence: Important Documents on
the Settlement of the Sino-Burmese Boundary Questions (Peking, 1960); Maung Maung, "The Burma-China Boundary
Settlement," Asian Survey, Vol. 1, No. 1 (March 1961),
pp. 38-43.

100. For the text of the two agreements, see CPR, Treaties,
Vol. 9, pp. 63-65, 84-86, respectively.

101. The Treaty was signed in Katmandu, on April 28, 1960. Its
English text can be found in CPR. Collected Treaties, pp.
12-13.

102. For the text, see CPR, Diplomatic Archives, Vol. 8, pp.
271-277.

103. For the text, see ibid., Vol. 8, pp. 281-282.

104. See Long Island Press (New York), May 6, 1967; February
21, 1968.

105. For the text, see CPR, Treaties, Vol. 12, pp. 67-120.

106. See The China Tribune (New York, in Chinese), June 27, 1969,
according to an announcement made by Nepalese Premier,
Kirtinidhi Bista, on June 25, 1969. For details, see The
New York Times, June 30, 1969. Insisting that Nepal's action was not due to pressure from Communist China, the
Premier stated that "we are acting on our own initiative in
accordance with a policy of strict nonalignment and peaceful

coexistence." Ibid., July 18, 1969. For Nepal's fear of India, see George N. Patterson, Peking Versus Delhi (New York, 1964), pp. 142-143. Before the end of 1969, India withdrew her military personnel from Nepal. See Long Island Press, December 29, 1969.

107. For further information on Nepal's relations with India and Communist China, see New Development in Friendly Relations between China and Nepal (Peking, 1960); Girilal Jain, India Meets China in Nepal (Bombay, 1959); A. Kashin, "Nepal – Chinese Stepping Stone to India," Institute for the Study of the USSR (Munich), Bulletin, Vol. 12, No. 7 (July 1965), pp. 22-27; M.D. Stevens, "Recent Trends in Sino-Nepalese Relations," Asian Review, Vol. 59 (October 1963), pp. 250-260; Shen-yu Dai, "Peking, Katmandu and New Delhi," The China Quarterly, No. 16 (October -December 1963), pp. 86-98.

108. For the text, see CPR, Collected Treaties, pp. 22-24. In the Exchange of Notes (ibid., pp. 30-32), the contracting parties nullified the Treaty of Friendship of March 2, 1944, signed between Afghanistan and the National Government of the Republic of China (Chen, Treaties, pp. 174-175; Chinese Republic, Treaties, pp. 1-2).

109. See Arts. 1-3.

110. For the text, see CPR, Treaties, Vol. 12, pp. 122-124.

111. In the opinion of Francis Watson, the conclusion of the Sino-Afghan boundary treaty in 1963 might be "closely connected with the encounter with the Soviets on the Sinkiang frontier than with the problem of India." See his The Frontiers of China, pp. 139-140. For further discussion of Sino-Afghan relations, see Shen-yu Dai, "China and Afghanistan," The China Quarterly, No. 25 (January-March 1966), pp. 213-221.

112. See CPR, Diplomatic Archives, Vol. 9, p. 322.

113. For the communiqué on the progress of negotiations issued on December 28, 1962, see CPR, Treaties, Vol. 11, pp. 14-15.

114. For the text, see ibid., Vol. 12, pp. 64-67.

115. See the Indian Notes to Communist China and Pakistan on March 2, 5, 1963, respectively. For the text, see Indian Ministry of External Affairs, Sino-Pakistan "Agreement," March 2, 1963: Some Facts (New Delhi, 1963), pp. 29-31.

116. See W. M. Dobell, "Ramifications of the China-Pakistan Border Politics," Pacific Affairs, Vol. 37, No. 3 (Fall 1964), pp. 283-295; George L. Montagno, "Peaceful Coexistence: Pakistan and Red China," The Western Political Quarterly, Vol. 18, No. 2, Pt. 1 (June 1965), pp. 309-317.

117. In the view of India, this highway had no commercial value and was built solely to facilitate the movement of Chinese troops and military equipment to a threatening position along the cease-fire line in Kashmir. See The New York Times, June 30, 1969.

118. According to Collin McCullough's report from Peking on July 19, 1969, "four years ago, Peking gave an interest-free loan of $60 million repayable in 20 years with a 10-year grace;" and "last year, another economic technical agreement was signed, this time for $40 million, with the same terms." The New York Times, July 20, 1969.

119. See supra, pp. 81-83, 270, 273. For general information on Outer Mongolia after her independence, consult Robert A. Rupen, The Mongolian People's Republic (Stanford, 1966); Owen Lattimore, Normads and Commissars: Mongolia Revisited (New York, 1962); George G. S. Murphy, Soviet Mongolia: A Study of the Oldest Political Satellite (Berkeley, 1966).

120. For the text, see CPR, Diplomatic Archives, Vol. 1, pp. 13-14.

121. For the text, see ibid., Vol. 2, pp. 93-94.

122. For the text, see CPR, Collected Treaties, pp. 14-15.

123. For the text, see CPR, Diplomatic Archives, Vol. 9, pp. 305-308.

124. For the text, see CPR, Treaties, Vol. 11, pp. 19-36.

125. For the text, see ibid., Vol. 13, pp. 78-258.

126. See Robert A. Rupen, "Mongolia in the Sino-Soviet Dispute," The China Quarterly, No. 16 (October-December 1963), pp. 75-85; Michael Dawson Stephens, "A Recent History of Sino-Mongolian Relations," Asian Review, Vol. 1, No. 1 (New Series, April 1964), pp. 45-50.

127. See The New York Times, September 1, 1964.

128. See ibid., August 8, 1965.

129. See ibid., March 16, 1966; January 3, 1967; June 26, 1969. Commercial relations between the two countries have still been maintained. On May 13, 1968, a Sino-Mongolian trade protocol was signed in Peking, See a dispatch from Hsinhua News Agency, Peking, May 13, 1968.

130. Sekai Shūhō (Tokyo), August 11, 1964; quoted from Dennis J. Doolin, op. cit., p. 43.

131. Ibid., p. 62 (based on a broadcast from Montsame International Service, Ulan Bator, in Russian, September 10, 1964).

132. Pravda editorial, September 2, 1964.

133. See The New York Times, June 14, 1969.

134. This attitude was reaffirmed by the National Government's instructions to the Chinese Embassy in Ankara in early July 1969, notifying the Turkish government of the Chinese position. It was rumored that Turkey was contemplating extending recognition to Outer Mongolia. See The Central Daily News (Taipei, in Chinese), July 4, 1969.

135. The dispute had already been known in 1954, but both sides tried to minimize it. See Klaus H. Pringsheim, "China, India, and Their Himalayan Border (1961-1963)," Asian Survey, Vol. 3, No. 10 (October 1963), pp. 474-495. China's territorial claims to the Sino-Indian border regions was stated fully in Premier Chou En-lai's letter to Prime Minister Nehru on September 8, 1959. For its text, see Indian Ministry of External Affairs, White Paper: Notes, Memoranda and Letters Exchanged and Agreements Signed between the Governments of India and China (hereafter cited as Indian White Paper), No. II (September -November 1959), pp. 27-33.

136. See "Statements Leading to the Adoption of the Agenda as Summarized by the Indian Side," in Indian Ministry of External Affairs, Report of the Officials of the Governments of India and the People's Republic of China on the Boundary Question (1961), pp. 4-8.

137. See ibid., p. 4.

138. Indian Ministry of External Affairs, India-China Border Problem (n.d.), p. 1.

139. Ibid., pp. 1-2.

140. For the text, see The Sino-Indian Boundary Question (enlarged ed., Peking, 1962), pp. 9-10. For further information
on the Chinese position, see Documents on the Sino-Indian
Boundary Question (Peking, 1960).

141. The Chinese strategic highway linking western Sinkiang and
western Tibet was built across Aksai Chin in 1956-1957.
It seemed that this highway was only known to India sometime after its completion. See Harold C. Hinton, op. cit.,
p. 285.

142. All quotes from The Sino-Indian Boundary Question, pp. 10,
11, 12. For comments on the Chinese claims, see Alfred P.
Rubin, "The Sino-Indian Border Disputes," The International
and Comparative Law Quarterly, Vol. 9 (January 1960),
p. 125.

143. "Premier Chou En-lai's Letter to Prime Minister Nehru,
November 7, 1959," The Sino-Indian Boundary Question,
p. 49. In the Note sent by the Chinese Ministry of Foreign
Affairs to the Indian Embassy in China on December 26,
1959, Peking enumerated various reasons to justify its claims
in the three sectors of the Sino-Indian border. For the text,
see ibid., pp. 51-92.

144. The reports submitted by the Indian and Chinese officials
were published by the Indian Ministry of External Affairs in
1961, under the title, Report of the Officials of the Governments of India and the People's Republic of China on the
Boundary Question (pp. 1-342 for the Indian part; pp. CR1-
213 for the Chinese part). This Report contains a map of the
Northern Frontier of India and a map of the Southwestern
Frontier of China. Many other maps prepared by both sides
to justify their territorial claims can be found in The Sino-
Indian Boundary Question (enlarged ed., Peking, 1962); and
Indian Ministry of Information and Broadcasting, The Chi-
nese Threat (New Delhi, 1963). For divergent views by dif-
ferent writers on the Sino-Indian boundary dispute, consult
Alastair Lamb, The China-India Border: The Origins of the
Disputed Boundaries (London, 1964), particularly pp. 6-13,
49-54, 75-87; W. F. van Eekelen, Indian Foreign Policy and
the Border Dispute with China (The Hague, 1964); Margaret
W. Fisher and others, Himalayan Battlegound: Sino-Indian
Rivalry in Ladakh (New York, 1963), pp. 81-146; R. A. Hut-
tenback, "A Historical Note on the Sino-Indian Dispute over
the Aksai Chin," The China Quarterly, No. 18 (April-June
1964), pp. 201-207; R. K. Patil, "The India-China Border
Dispute – The Western Sector," Indian Quarterly, Vol. 20,
No. 2 (April-June 1964), pp. 156-179; C. N. Satyapalan,

"The Sino-Indian Border Conflict," Orbis, Vol. 7, No. 2 (Summer 1964), pp. 374-390.

145. See Indian Ministry of External Affairs, Prime Minister on Sino-Indian Relations, Vol. I: In Parliament (New Delhi, n.d.), p. 370.

146. See ibid., Pt. II, pp. 103-121.

147. See The New York Times, October 13, 1962.

148. See Norman D. Palmer, "Trans-Himalayan Confrontation," Orbis, Vol. 6, No. 4 (Winter 1963), pp. 513-527.

149. Harold C. Hinton, op. cit., p. 299.

150. See "Message of October 26/27, 1962, from the Prime Minister of India to Heads of Governments," in Indian Ministry of Information and Broadcasting, Chinese Aggression in War and Peace (New Delhi, 1962), p. 33.

151. In his three lectures at the Delhi China Study Center in June 1965, published under the title, China: Three Facets of a Giant (Bombay, 1966), Henry G. Schwarz gave the impression that military aggression against her southern neighbors was not the policy of Communist China, because her goals could be obtained by other means.

152. See "Letter of October 24, 1962, from Premier Chou En-lai to the Prime Minister of India," in Indian Ministry of Information and Broadcasting, Chinese Aggression in War and Peace, pp. 35-36.

153. "Letter of November 4, 1962, from Premier Chou En-lai to the Prime Minister of India," ibid., p. 38.

154. For Premier Chou's letter of November 15, 1962, see The Sino-Indian Boundary Question, pp. 36-37.

155. Indian White Paper, VIII (October 1962-January 1963), p. 30. Nehru's letter was in reply to Chou's of November 28.

156. "Letter from Premier Chou En-lai to the Prime Minister of India, 30 December 1962," ibid., p. 47. A few months later, China released the Indian prisoners of war.

157. See "Letter from Prime Minister of India to the Prime Minister of China, 1 January 1963," ibid., p. 51.

158. For the text of the Colombo proposals, see "Enclosure to Letter Dated 15 December 1962, from the Prime Minister of

Ceylon,'' ibid., IX (January-July 1963), pp. 184-185; The Sino-Indian Boundary Question, II (Peking, 1965), pp. 41-42.

159. See "Clarifications Given by the Representatives of the Colombo Powers to the Government of India, 13 January 1963,'' Indian White Paper, IX, pp. 185-186; ''Letter from the Prime Minister of India, to the Prime Minister of Ceylon, 26 January 1963,'' ibid., 186-187.

160. See "Letter from Premier Chou En-lai to Prime Minister of India, 3 March 1963,'' ibid., p. 4; joint communiqué of the Ceylonese and Chinese Prime Ministers, Hsinhua News Agency dispatch, January 8, 1963. For further details of the Chinese attitude toward the Colombo proposals and subsequent developments, see Peking Review, No. 5 (February 1, 1963), pp. 10-11; No. 12 (March 22, 1963), pp. 10-14.

161. See "The Indian Government's Refusal of Negotiations under the Smokescreen of 'Acceptance of the Colombo Proposals in Toto','' Renmin Ribao editorial, October 13, 1963.

162. Ever since her open split with the Soviet Union and boundary disputes with India, Communist China has become increasingly isolated in the international community. For Peking's foreign relations immediately after these events, see American Consulate-General, Extracts from China Mainland Publications, Nos. 82 (March 11, 1964), 84 (March 25, 1964), 85 (April 1, 1964), and 90 (May 6, 1964).

163. See supra, pp. 79-80, 363; Alastair Lamb, The McMahon Line: A Study in the Relations between India, China and Tibet, 1904 to 1914 (London, 1966, 2 vols.), II, pp. 505, 530-531. 579-586. In his letter to Prime Minister Nehru on September 8, 1959, Premier Chou reiterated the reasons why China refuted the McMahon Line. See Indian White Paper, II (September-November 1959), p. 29. See, however, L.C. Green, "Legal Aspects of the Sino-Indian Border Dispute,'' The China Quarterly, No. 3 (July-September 1960), pp. 42-58.

164. In a statement of October 29, 1962, issued by the Ministry of Foreign Affairs in Taipei and released in New York by the Permanent Mission of the Republic of China to the United Nations, the National Government condemned the McMahon Line as ''a line unilaterally claimed by the British during their rule over India.''

165. The arbitration tribunal could be composed in any other way upon mutual agreement. Another channel for arbitration is the Permanent Court of Arbitration at The Hague. For the or-

ganization and functions of the Court, see William L. Tung, *International Law in an Organizing World,* pp. 378-379.

166. Sir Edward Grey deemed it absurd to make theoretical claims to territories without extending appropriate administration. See Alastair Lamb, *The McMahon Line,* II, p. 587.

167. In recent years, there were only minor skirmishes along the Sino-Indian border. At a New Year's news conference in 1969, Prime Minister Indira Gandhi indicated that she was ready to open a dialogue with China on the boundary question. It was said, however, that one of India's conditions would be the Chinese withdrawal from the territories occupied in the fall of 1962. See *The New York Times,* January 2, 1969.

Chapter 12

REASSERTION OF CHINA'S POSITION IN ASIA AND BEYOND

I. CONDITIONS FOR PEACEFUL COEXISTENCE

1. Foreign Relations of Communist China in General

Socialist solidarity was originally one of Communist China's fundamental policies, but, in actual practice, Peking soon found out that ideology is not necessarily the determining factor governing international relations. Because of territorial, security, and other vital issues, and due to circumstances not always under its own control, Peking has become increasingly antagonistic not only to the United States but also to the Soviet Union. It has been, however, the intention of the Chinese leaders to maintain friendly relations with those states which are not aligned with the two superpowers. Serious attempts were made to establish close ties with many nations in Asia,[1] Africa,[2] the Middle East,[3] and Latin America.[4] Diplomatic missions were exchanged with a number of European states, including Great Britain and France,[5] but their relationships have been generally limited to trade. With the exception of Albania and Rumania, Eastern European countries have leaned toward Moscow since the Sino-Soviet split. The warm friendship between Peking and Havana did not last long either.

In developing countries of Asia and Africa, Peking exerted maximum efforts within its limited resources to carry out programs of economic and technical aid, even though not all of them were rewarding. Non-Communist governments would naturally abhor any means of propaganda or subversion with the ultimate goal of overthrowing the existing regimes. On several occasions, cordial relations between Peking and some

389

newly established states were suddenly affected by a change of their domestic order or a rapid turn of international events. Peking has also been challenged in Africa and other areas by the National Government of the Republic of China,[6] now in Taiwan but continuously recognized by a majority of nations as the legal government of China.

2. Principles of Peaceful Coexistence

When Chou En-lai raised the banner of peaceful coexistence as the fundamental policy of the Chinese People's Republic in 1954, it attracted world-wide attention. In the Sino-Indian Agreement of April 29, 1954,[7] the two governments agreed on five principles governing their relations: (1) mutual respect for national sovereignty and territorial integrity, (2) non-aggression, (3) non-interference in domestic affairs of other states, (4) equality and reciprocity, and (5) peaceful coexistence.[8] These principles under the general designation of peaceful coexistence were also embodied in the Sino-Burmese joint communiqué of June 29, 1954,[9] the Sino-Soviet declaration of October 11, 1954,[10] and were reaffirmed by the Bandung Conference of Asian-African states in April 1955.[11]

Khrushchev's interpretation of peaceful coexistence as peaceful competition among all the states[12] was, however, refuted by the Chinese Communists, who could not see the possibility of achieving world socialism by means of peaceful competition with capitalist or imperialist countries.[13] The theoreticians in Peking expounded the differences of 'peaceful coexistence between nations' with 'people's revolutions in various countries,'.[14] In their view, peaceful coexistence refers to relations between different nations; revolution means the overthrow of the oppressors as a class by the oppressed people within a country.[15] It seems that Communist China, while stressing continuous revolution against capitalism and colonialsim by oppressed peoples in non-Communist countries, recognizes the inevitability of peaceful coexistence bewteen nations of different political systems.

In any event, coexistence either as a policy or strategy is an international reality with which nations have to reconcile themselves for the time being. The five principles were sponsored by the manifesto of sixty-four Communist and workers' parties in the world in 1957.[16] In slightly different phraseology, a resolution incorporating these principles was adopted by the General Assembly of the United Nations on December 14, 1957.[17]

3. Peaceful Coexistence in Practice

Taking the doctrine at its face value, all five principles are in conformity with the rules of international law and the Charter of the United Nations. The question is how far has Communist China followed this doctrine. Peking's performance in this respect varied according to the attitudes of other parties concerned. In other words, Chinese reactions to international issues generally depended upon the actions of interested powers. The Sino-Indian border conflicts fully demonstrated that peaceful coexistence cannot be achieved without mutual understanding and concessions by both states at dispute.

In his letter to Prime Minister Nehru of India on December 30, 1962, Premier Chou En-lai reiterated China's intention to adhere to the five principles of peaceful coexistence, because "these principles are indeed what the Chinese government has consistently advocated, and for their realization it has made unremitting efforts." Referring to the Sino-Indian controversies over the boundary question, he frankly pointed out that "these differences cannot possibly be resolved if one side attempts to bind the other side with these principles while itself refuses to abide by them."[18] Chou's statement further explained Peking's position that mutual observation of the five principles is the condition for the fulfillment of peaceful coexistence.

Nations hostile to each other may also coexist so long as they maintain a reasonable balance of power, but peaceful relations among states can be realized only by reciprocal efforts toward that common goal. China's success in settling boundary questions with Burma and several other countries can be attributed to the willingness of all parties concerned to seek an amicable solution. After a careful examination of the attitudes of many newly established states in comparison with the practices in the West, an Asian jurist concluded that "the Asian concept of peaceful coexistence is not rigid, less theoretical, unsophisticated, perhaps even naive, but precisely for these reasons its chances of success are greater than the Soviet concept of peaceful coexistence."[19] In the words of a British author, "although it might be said that the Five Principles in themselves did little more than describe a state of international relations normal in time of peace, their formulation was widely interpreted as opening a new phase and marking a new kind of accord."[20]

II. RELATIONS WITH NEIGHBORING STATES

1. Security Zones and Other Areas
Proximate to China

Like many other countries, China deems national security a primary element governing the strategy of foreign relations. For several decades, foreign powers intruded into China's border regions, including Manchuria, Tibet, and Yunnan, from adjacent territories under their control. Although these areas formerly used as imperialist bases for aggression have all become independent, most of them have not yet developed sufficient capabilities for self-preservation in case of major confrontations. Because of their geographical propinquity, historical relationships,[21] and postwar developments, North Korea, North Vietnam, and Laos are considered by Communist China to be within her security zone. Diplomatic or military actions by any unfriendly power in these areas would be vigorously countered by Peking, regardless of cost and consequences. This Chinese attitude can be easily understood by comparing the strong reaction of the United States to the presence of French forces in Mexico in 1862-1867[22] and to the Soviet installation of missiles in Cuba in 1962.[23]

China is also deeply interested in developments in other neighboring states, several of which have concluded treaties with Peking concerning boundary questions, mutual assistance, non-aggression, or economic aid. Peking's relationships with these countries, including Burma, Nepal, Afghanistan, Pakistan, and Outer Mongolia have already been discussed.[24] Sikkim and Bhutan are geographically contiguous to China and traditionally under her influence.[25] Although Great Britain and now India have claimed the right to control the external affairs of the two Himalayan nations, Peking would like to see them become buffers on the Sino-Indian frontier. Not contiguous, but proximate to China, is Japan. As a former victim of Japan's aggression, China would not tolerate the ressurgence of militarism in that country, especially if it is aligned with an unfriendly power.[26] Cambodia's relationship with Communist China is unique in that the former, ostensibly a neutralist country, had nevertheless maintained close ties with Peking.

2. North Korea

The Korean War broke out on June 25, 1950, when North Korean forces crossed the 38th parallel to invade South Korea. Two days later, President Truman ordered the Seventh Fleet to neutralize the Formosan Strait, thus preventing any attempt by Communist China to occupy Taiwan by force.[27] In effect, the United States intervened in the Chinese civil war by her military presence. Following General Douglas McArthur's appointment as Commander of United Nations Forces in Korea and his visit with President Chiang Kai-shek, Peking was keenly concerned with the possibility of using Nationalist troops in Taiwan for concerted operations in Korea. 'Chinese People's Volunteers' secretly crossed the Yalu River into North Korea in the middle of October, but no massive penetration took place until American forces marched near the Manchurian border.

The possible annihilation of the North Korean army and the direct threat to China's heavy industrial center by a hostile power made Peking decide to enter the Korean War by launching a counter-offensive on November 26.[28] Thus, in the words of General McArthur, 'an entirely new war' started and did not end until the signing of an armistice agreement at Panmunjom, on July 27, 1953.[29] Peking and Pyŏngyang have since been bound by a series of commitments, among which is the Treaty of Friendship and Mutual Assistance of July 11, 1961.[30]

3. North Vietnam

North Vietnam is another region vitally important to China's security. Chinese memory is still fresh from the French menace to her Southwestern provinces after the loss of her former dependency Annam.[31] Ever since the Chinese Communist army marched to the Sino-Vietnamese frontier in November 1949, Peking has been extending aid to Ho Chi Minh for his struggle against the French and later the Americans. The termination of hostilities in Korea in 1953 made it possible for China to render large-scale assistance to Hanoi.[32] After the French surrender of Dienbienphu to the Viet Minh troops led by Ho Chi Minh, on May 7, 1954, the French government decided to accept the inevitable and signed armistice agreements with the Communist Vietnam Command on July 20, 1954.[33] Consequently, Laos, Cambodia, and Vietnam achieved their independence, but Vietnam was partitioned along the 17th parallel into two states with the understanding of reunification by 'free elections' scheduled on July 20, 1956. In the Geneva settlement, Communist China played an important role.

In South Vietnam, Ngo Dinh Diem became Chief of State after the deposition of Bao Dai. Due to the extensive activities of the Viet Cong, free elections were not held as originally envisaged at Geneva,[34] and civil strife reached serious proportions.[35] After the Gulf of Tonkin incident in early August 1964, the United States began to conduct direct attacks against the Viet Cong and to bomb North Vietnam on February 7, 1965.[36] Political instability in South Vietnam as evidenced by successive changes of government made it necessary for the United States to reinforce troops.

In spite of their worsening relationships, both Moscow and Peking countered the American action with massive aid to North Vietnam.[37] Communist China repeatedly protested American violations of her air space above land domain and territorial waters, which are twelve miles from the low-water mark of the shore. It seems that all sides concerned have now realized that political aims cannot be achieved solely through force, and are ready to discuss the issues at the conference table. Whatever may be the outcome of peace negotiations between the disputing parties in Paris or elsewhere, any agreement without the tacit or express endorsement of Peking will be only a temporary truce, not a permanent settlement.

4. Laos

Consequent to the Geneva Agreement of 1954, Laos became independent, but domestic dissensions prevailed. The Pathet Lao, supported by Communist China, continuously engaged in a political and military struggle against the rightists. As a compromise, Prince Souvanna Phouma led a neutralist government, which has been under constant pressures from both sides. When a new cabinet was established under Phoui Sananikone in August 1958, Peking denounced it on the grounds of its American support and lack of representation of the Pathet Lao dominated party, Neo Lao Hak Xat.[38] After another coup d'etat in August 1960, Prince Souvanna Phouma resumed the Premiership but encountered periodic setbacks. Peking's chief objective in Laos was to neutralize the country, free of American influence, not only for the consideration of national security but also to safeguard easy access to Thailand.[39]

In order to avert a serious crisis in Laos, a fourteen-nation conference was held in Geneva from May 1961 to July 1962. Foreign Minister Chen Yi of Communist China strongly condemned American and SEATO interference in Laos. The final settlement reached at Geneva met the Communists' terms for the most part, such as the formation of a coalition government and the neutralization of the country.[40] Highways were being built linking China and Laos at Peking's cost for the facilitation of transportation and communications between the two countries.[41] Because of her geographical location and strategic considerations, Peking has considered Laos within the security zone of China.[42]

5. Cambodia

Different from other nations described before, Cambodia has no common frontier with China. Because of the strained relations of his country with Thailand and Vietnam, Prince Norodom Sihanouk solicited Peking for necessary support, including economic and technical aid.[43] Premier Chou En-lai visited Phnom Penh in November 1956, and advised the Chinese residents to observe local laws and regulations. All these preceded the formal establishment of diplomatic relations between the two countries, which took place in July 1958.[44] Their friendship was further strengthened by the conclusion of the Treaty of Friendship and Non-aggression on December 19, 1960, by which each signatory is obliged not "to take part in any military alliance directed against the other Contracting Party."[45]

Cambodia does not belong to SEATO or any other regional arrangement unfriendly to Communist China. On the contrary, Phnom Penh shares with Peking the common sentiment of hostility toward South Vietnam and Thailand. However, after his overthrow by Lt. General Lon Nol on March 18, 1970, Phnom Penh's power alignment has been drastically changed. While the new regime asked military and economic assistance from non-Communist countries, Mao Tse-tung pledged to support the Prince's exiled government formed in Peking, and denounced the United States intervention in Cambodia. Premier Lon Nol tried to avoid any provocation which might worsen his relationships with Communist China, and instructed all public functionaries to protect the Chinese minority in the country.[46] In view of the traditional distrust between the Cambodians and Vietnamese, the continuing occupation of Cambodian territory by South Vietnamese forces has further intensified the already complicated situation in Southeast Asia.

6. Sikkim and Bhutan

At the zenith of her power during the middle of the nineteenth century, Great Britain forced Sikkim and Bhutan to become virtually her protectorates. This legacy was passed to India after the latter's independence. Actually, these two Himalayan states had long been related to Tibet and under the orbit of Chinese influence.[47] Probably on account of this consideration, Communist China declined India's request to discuss boundary questions concerning Sikkim and Bhutan.[48] Peking has, however, no intention to interfere with the affairs of these tiny neighbors, unless they choose to ally themselves with India against China. As buffer states, their destinies depend primarily upon their diplomatic skill in maintaining friendly relationships with both India and China.[49]

China's boundary with Sikkim was delimited by the Sino-British Agreement of March 17, 1890.[50] During the Indian-Pakistani conflict in September 1965, Peking deemed India's military works on the Sino-Sikkim border a threat to China's security and demanded their dismantling to avoid grave consequences.[51] Although there was some small-arms firing on the Sino-Sikkim border at that time,[52] China's action was chiefly designed to support Pakistan.[53]

Since Peking denounced the McMahon Line as illegal, it would not recognize the Sino-Bhutanese border so far as it was based on that line.[54] Notwithstanding the assumptions that Chinese troops had probably crossed the territory claimed by Bhutan during the Sino-Indian border conflicts in 1959 and 1962 and that Bhutan might have concluded a secret boundary agreement with Peking in 1961,[55] no official records are available to verify either. In view of her geographical location with over 200 miles of common frontier with China, Bhutan's national interests will be best served by avoiding antagonism against either Peking or New Delhi.

7. Japan

Sino-Japanese relationships are unique in many respects. For half a century, Japan systematically encroached upon China's territorial and sovereign rights. Chinese casualties and sufferings from the eight years of bloody war are still vivid in people's minds. Thus any step toward the revival of militarism in Japan will be deemed a threat to the security of China.[56] Diplomatically, postwar Japan is an ally of the United States, and continues to recognize the National Government in Taiwan as the legal government of China. From an assumption that a friend of an enemy is an enemy, the official relationship between Peking and Tokyo can be described as cool at best. In the Sino-Soviet Treaty of Friendship, Alliance and Mutual Assistance of February 14, 1950, the two signatories undertook jointly to prevent "the resumption of aggression and violation of peace on the part of Japan or any state that may collaborate with Japan directly or indirectly in acts of aggression."[57] The invocation of this Treaty provision is most unlikely under the prevailing relationship between Peking and Moscow.

Both before and after the San Francisco Conference for the conclusion of the Peace Treaty with Japan of September 8, 1951,[58] Chou En-lai repeatedly declared that the People's Republic of China would not recognize the validity of a treaty without its participation.[59] The Peace Treaty of 1952 between Japan and the Republic of China was also denounced as illegal.[60] Peking has strongly objected to the presence of American troops in Japan after the end of Occupation, on the basis of the United States-Japanese Security Pact of September 8, 1951.[61] Coming into effect on April 28 of the following year, this Pact was renewed on January 19, 1960.[62] Both Peking and Moscow condemned it as a revival of the cold war.[63]

Notwithstanding antagonism to Japan's alliance with the United States, Peking has maintained close contacts with members of the Japanese Socialist Party and Communist Party.[64] The repatriation of approximately 30,000 Japanese left on the Chinese mainland after the war, including technicians and prisoners of war, furthered mutual understanding and communication between the peoples of the two countries.[65] To solicit friendship from the Japanese people, Mao Tse-tung even told the Japanese Socialist delegation on July 10, 1964, that the Kurile Islands "must be returned to Japan."[66]

Economically, an industrially resurgent Japan and Communist China are complementary to each other and will be mutually benefited by the expansion of trade. Japanese businessmen and political leaders have frequently visited Peking, negotiating for trade agreements.[67] The exchange of unofficial representatives and the establishment of liaison offices in Peking and Tokyo for trade purposes were agreed upon in April 1964. During an election campaign in Kyushu on December 13, 1969, Premier Eisaku Sato declared his intention to establish high-level official contacts with Communist China.[68] The National Government of the Republic of China, with which Japan maintains diplomatic relations has abhorred Japanese commercial activities with the mainland. Taking all factors into consideration, Sino-Japanese cooperation in the future will contribute much to the stability and prosperity of East Asia.

III. PROTECTION OF OVERSEAS CHINESE IN SOUTHEAST ASIA

1. Distribution of Overseas Chinese in Different Countries

The reasons for China's special attention to Thailand, Indonesia, Malaysia, Singapore, and several other countries in Southeast Asia are twofold: access to raw materials essential to industrialization and armaments, and protection of over ten million Chinese residents in these areas, [69] which is a rough estimate involving many with complicated status of double nationality. Strict restrictions imposed by local governments on alien ownership of property and business, especially after World War II, forced many overseas Chinese to adopt citizenship of their resident countries, without necessarily giving up their Chinese nationality. [70] Thus official census of local governments is not always reliable in determining the number of Chinese nationals residing therein.

In Southeast Asia, Thailand, Malaya, and Indonesia have the largest number of Chinese nationals, approximately 2.4 million each. Although there are less than a million Chinese in Singapore, they comprise over 75% of its total population. Chinese residents in Vietnam have probably been reduced to 800,000 after the war, mostly concentrated in the South, with only about 50,000 in the North. The distribution of overseas Chinese in Cambodia, the Philippines, British Borneo, and Burma ranges from 230,000 to 320,000. While Laos is strategically important to China, only 10,000 Chinese reside in that country.

Percentage-wise, the relative importance of the Chinese among the total population in Malaya (37.8%) and British Borneo (27%) is only next to Singapore. [71] The destination of Chinese immigrants is not guided by geographical proximity. As a matter of fact, the number of Chinese overseas is comparatively small in areas adjacent to China. Economic opportunities and local environment have been more important factors in choosing their residence outside China.

2. Diplomatic Protection against
Local Discrimination

Through diligence and perseverance, overseas Chinese have successfully established themselves in local communities, especially in retail trade. Most of the areas mentioned above became independent after World War II; with the intense development of nationalism, these countries steadfastly adopted strict measures to uproot Chinese dominance of their economy. Various laws and regulations were enforced by the governments of Thailand,[72] the Philipines, [73] Indonesia,[74] and South Vietnam,[75] to restrict resident aliens in their ownership of property and business activities, as well as the curriculums of schools operated by them. Ostensibly applied to all aliens, these discriminatory acts have been directed against the Chinese. For a time, even Cambodia was inclined to do the same.[76] In Malaysia[77] and Singapore, where people of Chinese descent have an important voice due to their large percentage, the situation is different. The problem there is racial conflict between the Malayans and the Chinese, whose harmonious cooperation may be promoted by developing the common interest of the two races in their newly established countries.

Now the question is how much the Chinese government can do to protect overseas Chinese in Southeast Asia. Diplomatic relations of the aforesaid countries with China come under three categories: Indonesia, Burma, Cambodia, Laos, and North Vietnam extended recognition to the People's Republic in Peking; Thailand, the Philippines, and South Vietnam continue to recognize the Republic of China in Taiwan; Malaysia and Singapore have not established official relations with either. Actually, countries imposing the strictest restrictions over their Chinese residents are Thailand, the Philippines, Indonesia, and South Vietnam under President Ngo Dinh Diem. Like South Korea, South Vietnam has stood with the Republic of China in Taiwan as the staunchest comrades in the anti-Communist front; Siagon has, however, chosen to push unscrupulous measures against the Chinese residents and only modified its position when the local economy was distrupted.

Both the Nationalist and Communist governments have stressed the importance of protecting overseas Chinese,[78] and each of them set up a special commission of cabinet rank to take charge of the matter.[79] In their representative organs, they have apportioned a certain number of seats to overseas Chinese.[80] In practice, there is not much that Taiwan or Peking can do to alter the policies of Thailand, the Philippines, and Indonesia toward Chinese nationals residing in these countries. While Taiwan can only resort to paper protests under the prevailing circumstances, Peking's power is not strong enough to deter their present actions either. Thailand and the Philippines are members of SEATO, and closely aligned with the United States. Because of her insular position, Indonesia is not concerned with China's pressures.[81] Since all these countries have few nationals in China, retaliatory measures of the same kind will produce no effect. The only available means to protect the interests of Chinese abroad is through diplomatic negotiations with the governments concerned, especially at a time when both Nationalist and Communist governments are in keen competition to solicit more friends in the international community.

Without effective diplomatic protection from their home government, overseas Chinese may relieve their own difficulties by adjusting themselves to the native community and seeking redress of any wrongs through local remedies.[82] As to how to solve the problem of double nationality,[83] a bilateral agreement between China and the government concerned may serve the purpose, as the Sino-Indonesian Treaty of April 22, 1955 did to a certain extent.[84] In these countries, however, traditional jealousy of Chinese dominance in their economic life and recent suspicion of Peking's subversion and infiltration are more deep-rooted than the question of double nationality. In truth, overseas Chinese are comparatively conservative, business-minded, but not politically inclined. Certain concerns expressed by foreign governments have proved unfounded.

Nationalism has been flourishing in Southeast Asia in recent decades. Nations, new or old, have gone through a period of revolutionary upheaval, which will mellow before long. Statesmen in these countries will soon realize that equal treatment of nationals and aliens will eventually work for their own benefit. Discriminatory acts will inevitably invoke retaliation, because no government can neglect the responsibility in protecting the interests of their nationals abroad. [85] The number of Chinese nationals residing in countries other than those of Southeast Asia is too small to become an important element in local economy and politics, but still several governments have enforced severe regulations to restrict their immigration, thus inflicting a sense of humiliation on the Chinese both in and outside the government. It must be remembered that international controversies of serious magnitude sometimes develop from the accumulation of such minor frictions, which are, at the least, against international comity and detrimental to mutual understanding.

IV. PARTICIPATION IN WORLD AFFAIRS

1. The Geneva Conferences

The importance of China's role in world politics has been considerably weakened by the rivalry of two governments in the country, each challenging the legitimacy of the other. Peking's first move in the international arena was its armed intervention in the Korean War in November 1950, which was terminated by the Armistice Agreement of July 27, 1953. [86] Since the armistice was only a military act, a conference for the final settlement was held in Geneva from April 26 to June 15, 1954. Two basic differences developed between the Communists on one side and the sixteen nations under the United Nations Command on the other: the authority and competence of the United Nations in Korea and the procedures for a future election for the unification of the country. As a major belligerent at the time of war, Communist China took an active part in the negotiations for peace. Because neither side was willing to accept compromises, the conference adjourned without an agreement.[87] On October 1, 1953, the United States concluded the Mutual Defense Treaty with the Republic of Korea,[88] but a permanent settlement of the Korean problem is as remote as ever.

In Indochina, Peking's material assistance to Ho Chi Minh contributed to his overwhelming victory at Dienbienphu. At the Geneva Conference on Indochina, held from May 8 to July 21, 1954, Communist China strongly backed Cambodia, Laos, and Vietnam in their terms for peace. Other states represented at the Conference were Great Britain, France, the Soviet Union, and the United States. The armistice was actually effected through the conclusion of three separate agreements by the Communist Vietnam Command with (1) the Franco-Vietnamese Command, (2) the Franco-Laotian Command, and (3) the Royal Khmer (Cambodian) Army Command.[89] The United States and Vietnam were not parties to these agreements, signed on July 20, 1954, but Under-Secretary Walter Bedell Smith declared that the American government would refrain from disturbing the agreements.[90]

Peking's voice was heard again at Geneva from May 16, 1961 to July 23, 1962, when fourteen nations met intermittently to seek a solution of the Laosian crisis. On the day of adjournment, the representatives of Great Britain, Communist China, the United States, the Soviet Union, and other participating countries signed the Declaration and Protocol on the Neutrality of Laos.[91] All these conferences at Geneva were convened either for the termination of war or for the avoidance of a crisis. It was only at Bandung in April 1955 that Peking was offered, for the first time, the opportunity to take part in a conference for the promotion of mutual understanding and cooperation.

2. The Afro-Asian Conferences

Sponsored by India, Pakistan, Indonesia, Burma, and Ceylon, an Afro-Asian conference was held at Bandung, Indonesia, on April 18-24, 1955.[92] It was attended by twenty-nine countries from Asia and Africa; an international gathering without the participation of the Western powers was unprecendented. In collaboration with Prime Minister Nehru of India, Premier Chou En-lai became a dominant figure both in and outside the conference. The five principles of peaceful coexistence emboided in the Sino-Indian Agreement of 1954 were reaffirmed. It was also at Bandung that Communist China signed a treaty with Indonesia concerning the problem of dual nationality of Chinese nationals residing in that country.[93] Chou's diplomatic skill almost overwhelmed the leaders of the participating governments, especially in his attempt to impress upon the world Peking's conciliatory attitude toward current problems.[94]

On the same occasion, Chou met Nasser of Egypt and laid the groundwork for the establishment of diplomatic relations between the two countries. The gain of friendship among the Afro-Asian nations at Bandung [95] was later offset by the loss of international sympathy during the period of the Cultural Revolution. The Chinese delegation was received with enthusiasm and respect by members of the First Afro-Asian People's Solidarity Conference in Cairo at the end of 1957. Nonetheless, because of Peking's domestic programs and foreign relations in the ensuing years, the carefully cultivated image of Communist China was adversely affected,[96] her development of nuclear weapons notwithstanding. [97]

The Southeast Asia Treaty Organization is a regional agency, established chiefly for the mutual defense of its member nations against Communist aggression.[98] The Republic of China does not belong to SEATO, but is a member of the Asian and Pacific Council (ASPAC), which is a loosely-knit consultative organ of an anti-Communist nature.[99] At its three-day session at Ito, Japan, in June 1969, however, ASPAC adopted a policy of conciliation rather than confrontation with the Communist countries in Asia. Presiding at the meetings, Kiichi Alchi, Foreign Minister of Japan, even expressed the hope that Communist China, North Korea, and North Vietnam would join the Council.[100] Merely as a diplomatic gesture, his expression probably will not mean much to the three Communist states, whose adherence to ASPAC is most unlikely.

3. The Problem of Recognition

Ever since the establishment of the People's Republic in Peking, on October 1, 1949, the international community has been confronted with the problem of recognition. The existence of a government is independent of recognition, which is granted by states chiefly for mutual convenience. Under normal circumstances, recognition will be extended to a new government when it is in actual control of a defined territory, with the support of the population, and the capability of fulfilling its international obligations. On principle, recognition does not imply approval or disapproval; in practice, however, it has often been resorted to by modern states as an instrument of public policy, involving political and other considerations.[101] Thus the United States withheld recognition of the Soviet Union for almost sixteen years because of her objection to Communist policies and programs.[102] The principles and practices stated above represent the general trend of the international community in dealing with a situation when a new regime has substituted for the old one as the sole government of the country.

In the case of China, the legal government is still properly functioning in Taiwan, even though the territory under its actual control is small in comparison with the mainland. As China remains technically in a state of civil war, the granting of recognition to one government automatically withdraws recognition from the other,[103] because international law precludes the recognition of two governments representing one state at the same time. Thus new nations, which emerged after the establishment of the Chinese People's Republic in October 1949, cannot maintain diplomatic relations with both Peking and Taiwan, but they may choose not to recognize either for the time being. According to the report of the Chinese Foreign Minister to the Legislative Yuan on December 27, 1969, the present status of international alignment of the two governments is as follows:[104]

Recognition extended to:	No. of States	Members of UN
Republic of China in Taiwan	68	64
People's Republic of China in Peking	45	44

Up to the beginning of 1969, twenty-five states remained undecided as to which government in China they would extend recognition. The situation fluctuates every year, because a turn of events sometimes presses a state to change its policy toward China. It is important to note, however, that the determining factor of recognition as practiced by most if not all states is not international morality or friendship but international expediency, which governs the relations among states today.

4. The United Nations Seat and the Two-China Plan

While recognition involves only bilateral relations, the problem of representation as to which government should be seated at the United Nations is a collective decision of the members of the General Assembly. These two different questions are, however, interrelated, because Member states of the United Nations will, in most cases, vote for the government with which they have established diplomatic relations. "Whenever more than one authority claims to be the government entitled to represent a Member state in the United Nations," according to a resolution adopted by the General Assembly on December 14, 1950, "the question should be considered in the light of the purposes and principles of the Charter and the circumstances of each case."[105] Another decision was made by the General Assembly at its sixteenth session that the issue of representation should be classified as an important matter. In other words, any decision on this question requires a two-thirds majority of the General Assembly.[106] Draft resolutions to seat the government of the Chinese People's Republic in place of that of the Republic of China were repeatedly submitted to the United Nations and specialized agencies. The most recent proposal was brought before the twenty-fourth session of the General Assembly, but was defeated again on November 11, 1969. Voting records of the General Assembly on this question from 1950 to 1969 are shown in Table VII.

As a consequence of Peking's armed intervention against the United Nations Forces, the General Assembly adopted a resolution on February 1, 1951, condemning Communist China's act of aggression in Korea.[107] Because of this record

TABLE VII
VOTING RECORDS OF THE GENERAL ASSEMBLY
ON SEATING THE GOVERNMENT OF THE
CHINESE PEOPLE'S REPUBLIC, 1950-1969[108]

Year	For	Against	Abstentions
1950	6	33	10
1951	11	37	4
1952	7	42	11
1953	10	44	10
1954	11	43	11
1955	12	42	6
1956	24	47	8
1957	27	48	6
1958	28	44	9
1959	29	44	9
1960	34	42	22
1961	36	48	20
1962	42	56	12
1963	41	57	12
1964	(no vote as explained in note 108)		
1965	47	47	20
1966	46	57	17
1967	45	58	17
1968	44	58	23
1969	48	56	21

and other factors reflected in Peking's conduct of foreign relations, many delegates deemed that the government of the Chinese People's Republic has not observed the conditions required for members of the United Nations as laid down in the Charter.[109] On the other hand, the Republic of China is a founding member of this Organization and has faithfully fulfilled its obligations. Hence a majority of states has continued to support its seat at the United Nations.[110] Nonetheless, international reality necessitates that the Members of the United Nations reconsider the case every year, especially in view of the impracticability of disarament without the cooperation of Communist China. In order to break the impasse, an increasing number of diplomats and academicians have suggested a two-China plan, which deserves careful examination.

The gist of the two-China plan is to recognize the Communist government in Peking as representing China and to admit Taiwan, where the National Government of the Republic of China is presently located, as a new member of the United Nations.[111] As previously discussed, Taiwan is a part of Chinese territory in both legal and political aspects. [112] Since the present rivalry between Taiwan and Peking resulted from internal dissensions, the future destiny of China, including reunification and other issues, should be appropriately decided by the Chinese themselves. While the two governments differ in almost all respects domestically, they are in accord against the two-China plan.[113] Under such circumstances, it is impossible for the United Nations to adopt this frequently mentioned formula without the consent of the interested parties.

On the assumption that the Taiwanese are not Chinese, a suggestion has been made in some Western circles that Taiwan should belong to the Taiwanese under a new political entity independent from the mainland. The truth of the matter is that the people in Taiwan all came from the mainland at different times. After Taiwan has become one of the Chinese provinces subsequent to Japan's surrender, people from other parts of the country should have had the right to move there both before and after the Communists gained control of the mainland. Like the Constitution of the United States, the fundamental laws of China provide that all Chinese nationals are entitled to freedom of residence and change of residence. To urge the independence of Taiwan under those early migrants corresponds to advocating independence by native-born Americans in Florida and California after the United States acquired these territories. [114]

Twenty years have passed since the multitude of the so-called mainlanders came to Taiwan and their children have been born and raised in Taiwan. While Thomas Liao and several other prominent separatists residing abroad have realized the futility of their independence movement and returned to Taiwan to cooperate with the existing regime, it is surprising that this idea of independence by the Taiwanese still persists in the minds of many Westerners. With regard to a small number of people in Taiwan dissatisfied with the present situation,[115] they may recommend reforms through constitutional process before resorting to drastic action of independence. If every dissatisfaction were allowed to lead to secession, there would be a multiplication of new states, for discontent is prevalent even in the most democratic countries.

Discussion would be incomplete without mentioning a small minority of aborigines, who are indigenous to Taiwan and are now living mostly in mountaneous areas. In view of their background and training, to devise a new state for them would be much more difficult than the formation of an independent state for the American Indians. In conclusion, any discrimination against those Chinese who arrived in Taiwan after World War II is unconstitutional, and any scheme to establish a Taiwanese state independent of China is impracticable. Nor is the argument valid that, because of Peking's growing power and potential threat to the security of the Far East, it is better to make Taiwan independent so as to preclude Communist occupation of this strategic island. Such a proposition is based on international expediency at the expense of China's territorial integrity.

5. Whither China?

After experiencing all the vicissitudes of past decades, the Chinese have become more patient than ever. Right or wrong, they have a deep conviction, on the basis of their long historical records, that China will be reunited. Instead of adopting any hasty formula, which may simply complicate the matter in the future, they choose to await further developments of the situation which would be more favorable to their own destiny, and not merely for the convenience of others.

The existence of two rival governments contesting the legitimacy of representation in the international arena has undoubtedly weakened China's position as a major power. In order to match responsibility with power, all five permanent members of the Security Council were virtually elected as members of the Economic and Social Council. China has, however, lost her seat in that Council in recent elections. Nor has her position as a major power been adequately recognized by other members of United Nations organs and international conferences. Admitting that their internal dissensions have affected the nation's international status, the Chinese cannot refrain from feeling slighted. The often advocated strategy of containment (with or without isolation) has indeed infuriated the Communists; the contemptuous response to the voice of the Chinese delegate at the United Nations on some occasions has equally humiliated the Nationalists.

Because of the tremendous impact of unequal treaties on her national development, China requires a brief period for readjustments; meanwhile, as a resurgent power, she expects to receive due respect and dignity from other members of the international community. Adverse circumstances in the past century have rendered the Chinese people extremely sensitive to any expression of contempt toward them and every move for the containment of their country. For the fulfillment of her national aspirations, all segments of China are prepared to seek international support wherever attainable, but will strongly react to any confrontations if unavoidable. [116]

NOTES TO CHAPTER 12

1. For Communist China's early relations with neighboring states, see S. B. Thomas, Communist China and Her Neighbors (Toronto, 1955). See also Good Neighbors Meet (Peking 1956), which contains a series of speeches made by Soong Ching-ling, Vice-Chairman of the Chinese People's Republic, in India, Burma, and Pakistan in 1955-1956.

2. See the Chinese-African People's Association, The Chinese People Resolutely Support the Just Struggle of the African People (Peking, 1961); W. A. C. Adie, "Chou En-lai on Safari," The China Quarterly, No. 18 (April-June 1964), pp. 174-194. For Peking's efforts to win friends in Africa, see also The New York Times, February 9, 1964; May 10, 1966.

3. For Peking's attitude toward the Arab states, see the Chinese People's Institute of Foreign Affairs, China Supports the Arab People's Struggle for National Independence (Peking, 1958).

4. See Ernst Halperin, "Peking and the Latin American Communists," The China Quarterly, No. 29 (January-March 1967), pp. 111-154; The New York Times, May 25, 1964. For the worsening relationship between Communist China and Cuba, see ibid., February 7, 22, 1966.

5. Great Britain recognized the Chinese People's Republic as early as January 6, 1950. It was not until January 27, 1964 that France decided to establish diplomatic relations with Peking.

6. According to reports from Taiwan, the National Government has undertaken an impressive program of technical aid to the developing countries. From 1959 to 1967, more than 1,000 engineers and technicians were dispatched to Southeast Asia, Africa, the Middle East, and Latin America. It is interesting to note the following information from Taiwan's official sources:

> "In Africa alone, there are 17 Chinese farm demonstration teams with more than 500 men working in Liberia, Libya, the Ivory Coast, Dahomey, Gabon, Rwanda, Senegal, Sierra Leone, Niger, Cameroon, Upper Volta, Chad, Togo, Malawi, Gambia, The Congo (Kinshasa), and the Malagasy Republic. In addition, there are a Chinese veterinarian team in Ethiopia, a fishery team in Cameroon, and a handicraft team in Rwanda. A sugar team helped the Congo to restore a sugar mill in 1962. Libya has the largest number of Chinese technicians. Of the 236 Chinese

technical personnel stationed in the country, there
are 207 nurses, 25 engineers, 3 meteorologists and
a harbor consultant. Other countries receiving tech-
nical assistance include Vietnam, Saudi Arabia, the
Dominican Republic, and Brazil."
Free China Weekly (Taipei), November 19, 1967. See also
Long Island Press, November 26, 1965; The New York Times,
December 25, 1968. For relations between the Republic of
China and many Asian states, see Melvin Gurtov, "Recent
Developments on Formosa," The China Quarterly , No. 31
(July-September 1967), pp. 63-71. A summary of Peking's re-
lations with developing countries can be found in Thomas W.
Robinson, "Peking's Revolutionary Strategy in the Developing
World: The Failures of Success," The Annals of the American
Academy of Political and Social Science, Vol. 386 (November
1969), pp. 64-77.

7. For the text, see CPR, Diplomatic Archives, Vol. 3, pp. 12-14.
    The term 'peaceful coexistence' is known as panch shila in
    Hindi.

8. See the Preamble of the Sino-Indian Agreement of 1954.

9. For the text, see CPR, Diplomatic Archives, Vol. 3, pp.
    115-116.

10. Leaders of other states, such as North Vietnam, Burma,
    Poland, and Yugoslavia also supported these principles in their
    official communiqués. See J. J. G. Syatauw, Some Newly
    Established Asian States and the Development of International
    Law (The Hague, 1961), pp. 206-219.

11. The wording 'live together in peace', incorporated in the
    final communiqué of the Bandung Conference, meant sub-
    stantially the same as 'peaceful coexistence'. For details,
    see China and the Asian-African Conference (Peking, 1955);
    infra, pp. 403-404.

12. See Nikita S. Khrushchev, "On Peaceful Coexistence," Foreign
    Affairs, Vol. 38 (October 1959), pp. 1-18.

13. See The Origin and Development of the Differences between
    the Leadership of the CPSU and Ourselves, pp. 9-10; Tang
    Tsou, "Mao Tse-tung and Peaceful Coexistence," in George
    A. Lanyi and Wilson C. McWilliams (eds.), Crisis and Con-
    tinutiy in World Politics (New York, 1966), pp. 661-672.

14. Marshal Lin Piao advocated that "the socialist countries
    should regard it as their international duty to support the

people's revolutionary struggles in Asia, Africa and Latin America." See his Long Live the Victory of People's War (Peking, 1966), p. 49. For Lin Piao's condemnation of Khrushchev's revisionism, see ibid., p. 61.

15. See Hongqi, No. 8 (April 1960), pp. 1-29. The text also appears in "Peking on Coexistence," Foreign Affairs, Vol. 38 (July 1960), pp. 676-681. See also Tang Tsou, "Mao Tse-tung and Peaceful Coexistence," in Cheorge A. Lanyi and Wilson C. McQilliam (eds.), op. cit., pp. 661-672.

16. See Russel H. Fifield, "The Five Principles of Peaceful Coexistence," American Journal of International Law, Vol. 52 (July 1958), p. 508.

17. UN Doc. A/3802. 'Peaceful and tolerant relations' and 'friendly and cooperative relations' were the expressions embodied in the draft resolution submitted by India, Sweden, and Yugoslavia.

18. Indian White Paper, No. VIII, p. 46.

19. J.J. G. Syatauw, op. cit., p. 219.

20. Francis Watson, The Frontier of China, p. 83.

21. See supra, p. 47.

22. For the United States demand for the withdrawal of French troops from Mexico, see Secretary of State William H. Seward's Note to the Marquis de Montholon. House Ex. Doc. (1261), 39th Cong., 1st Sess., No. 93, pp. 589-598.

23. In retaliation, President Kennedy issued the quarantine proclamation of October 24, 1962, entitled 'Interdiction of the Delivery of Offensive Weapons to Cuba'. For the text, see American Journal of International Law, Vol. 57 (1963), Supp., pp. 512-513.

24. See supra, pp. 357-362.

25. See Alastair Lamb, Asian Frontiers, pp. 138, 142-144.

26. Commenting on President Nixon's Asian trip in late July 1969, Ian Stewart reported that the visit "hardened the Chinese ill-will toward the United States," because "Peking takes the view that Asia is its sphere of influence and that any interference by the United States constitutes a direct challenge to Chinese security." The New York Times, August 2, 1969

27. Department of State Bulletin, Vol. 13, p. 5. See also supra, pp. 345-346.

28. Detailed information on the Chinese volunteers in North Korea can be found in Alexander L. George, The Chinese Communist Army in Action: The Korean War and Its Aftermath (New York, 1967).

29. The Armistice was signed by the Commander-in-Chief of the United Nations Forces on the one hand and the Supreme Commander of the Korean People's Army and the Commander of the Chinese People's Volunteers on the other. Its English, Korean, and Chinese texts can be found in Department of State, Military Armistice in Korea and Temporary Supplementary Agreement (Washington, D.C., 1957), I, pp. 3-127.

30. For the text, see CPR, Diplomatic Archives, Vol. 8, pp. 213-215. Leaders in Peking openly agitated for anti-government movements in South Korea. See their speeches in Support the Just and Patriotic Struggle of the South Korean People (Peking, 1960). For the attitude of North Korea amidst the Peking-Moscow rivalry, see Joseph C. Kun, "North Korea: Between Moscow and Peking," The China Quarterly No. 31 (July-September 1967), pp. 48-58.

31. For details, see supra, p. 47. For the text of the Sino-Franco Convention of Tientsin relating to Annam of May 11, 1884, see Chinese Customs, Treaties, I, pp. 894-896; Hertslet, Treaties, I, pp. 293-294.

32. The spirit of comradeship among the Chinese, Koreans, and Vietnamese Communists was fully expressed in Everlasting Friendship between Korean, Chinese and Vietnamese People: Documents on Goodwill Visits of the Democratic People's Republic of Korea Government Delegation to China and Vietnam (Peking, 1959).

33. For their text, see Background Information relating to Southeast Asia and Vietnam, 89th Cong., 1st Sess. (Washington, D.C., 1965), pp. 28-58.

34. During Ho Chi Minh's visit to Peking in the middle of 1955, he secured a substantial amount of economic aid from Peking. In the joint communiqué of July 7, emphasis was laid on a general election to be held in July 1956. See Hsinghua News Agency dispatch, July 8, 1955. The election has never been held. When Chou En-lai visited Hanoi in November 1956, a joint communiqué was issued by the Chinese and North Vietnamese Prime Ministers, urging the speedy implementation of the

Geneva Agreements. See Vietnam News Agency dispatch, November 22, 1956.

35. For a collection of speeches made by Mao Tse-tung and other Chinese leaders against American support of Saigon, see Statement Opposing Aggression against Southern Viet Nam and Slaughter of Its People by the U.S.-Ngo Dinh Diem Clique (Peking, 1963).

36. Cf. the statement made by Secretary of State John Foster Dulles on May 25, 1954, concerning specific conditions for direct American intervention in Indochina. Dpeartment of State, American Foreign Policy, 1950-1955, II, pp. 2391-2392.

37. In his Long Live the Victory of People's War! (Peking, 1966), Marshal Lin Piao, Vice-Chairman of the Chinese Communist Party and concurrently Minister of Defense, stated: "The determination of the Chinese people to support and aid the Vietnamese people in their struggle against U.S. aggression and for national salvation is unshakable. No Matter what U.S. imperialism may do to expand its war adventure, the Chinese people will do everything in their power to support the Vietnamese people until every single one of the U.S. aggressors is driven out of Vietnam." (p. 66).

38. See Foreign Minister Chen Yi's statement of February 18, 1959, expressing "grave concern over the fact that the United States is openly instigating and supporting the Royal Laotian Government to repudiate the Geneva Agreements, creating tension in Laos and sabotaging the peace in Indochina." Concerning the Situation in Laos (Peking, 1959), p. 3.

39. Peking was much concerned with the possible intervention in Laos by SEATO. For Chen Yi's statement on the subject, see Hsinhua News Agency dispatch, Jakarta, April 4, 1961. For other speeches and documents concerning Laos in 1961, see CPR, Diplomatic Archives, Vol. 8, pp. 12-124; American Consulate-General in Hongkong, "Chronology of Communist Reports on Laos, May 1-July 31, 1961," Current Background, No. 661 (September 13, 1961).

40. For the text of the Declaration and the Protocol of July 23, 1962, see CPR, Diplomatic Archives, Vol. 9, pp. 278-286.

41. For the text of the Agreement of January 13, 1962, see CPR, Treaties, Vol. 11, pp. 132-133. The construction of another motor road was undertaken by Peking in 1961, according to Hsinhui News Agency dispatch, April 25, 1961. An agreement establishing civil air communication between the two coun-

tries was also signed on January 13, 1962. For the text, see CPR, Treaties, Vol. 11, pp. 134-138. According to a report by Charles Mohr to The New York Times on July 11, 1969, the Thais were concerned with a potential Chinese threat because of the highways constructed by the Chinese Communists in Laos. The highways in question are the east-west road across the far northern Laotian province of Phongsaly to connect Yunnan and North Vietnam under the 1962 agreement, and a recent one connecting the southern loop from Southern Yunnan through Muang Sai toward the east-west road. In Mohr's view, "the roads have never played any role in the Laotian civil war." Thus he concluded that "the Chinese can hardly be said to have 'invaded' even Laos, much less posing an invasion threat to Thailand," The New York Times, July 12, 1969. See also ibid., October 16, 29, 1969.

42. For further information, see Brian Crozier, "Peking and the Laotian Crisis: A Further Appraisal," The China Quarterly, No. 11 (July-September 1962), pp. 116-123. With the increasing activities of Pathet Lao guerrillas, its political arm, Neo Lao Hak Xat, recently denounced the Laotian government and the International Control Commission created by the 1962 Geneva Agreement. See The New York Times, July 16, 1969. For military activities of the United States in Laos, see ibid., October 26-28, 1969; February 19, March 6-13, May 19, 1970.

43. As early as June 1956, Peking extended an Ł8 million grant to Cambodia. For the exchange of notes concerning the extension of the economic aid agreement of 1956, see CPR, Treaties, Vol. 7, pp. 90-91.

44. See Hsinhua News Agency dispatch, November 27, 1956; Harold C. Hinton, op. cit., p. 425. The Sino-Cambodian Trade Agreement of 1956 was repeatedly renewed. See CPR, Treaties, Vol. 7, pp. 163-164; Vol. 9, p. 116-117; Vol. 11, pp. 81-82.

45. For the text of the Treaty, see CPR, Collected Treaties, pp. 33-34.

46. For Premier Lon Nol's assurance of protecting the Chinese minority in Cambodia and Mao's statement, see The New York Times, May 20, 21, 1970, respectively. To show Peking's displeasure at the American action, Communist China cancelled the Ambassadorial talks in Warsaw, originally scheduled for May 20, 1970. As Asian Conference on Cambodia was held in Jakarta on May 16-17, 1970, attended by the representatives of twelve nations. Their communiqué emphasized Cambodia's independence and neutrality, and urged the withdrawal of all foreign forces from her territory. See ibid., May 17, 18, 1970.

47. See supra, note 25. For relations of Bhutan and Sikkim with China, Tibet, Great Britain, and later India, see George N. Patterson, Peking Versus Delhi, pp. 200-244. See also Alastair Lamb, The China-India Border: The Origins of the Disputed Boundaries, pp. 29-30.

48. See the "Letter from Prime Minister of China to the Prime Minister of India, 8 September 1959," Indian White Paper, No. II, pp. 29-30.

49. India has extended economic assistance to Sikkim and Bhutan in spite of her own need for large amount of foreign aid. According to recent reports, India granted 56 million rupees (US $7.3 million) to each of the two countries. See The New York Times, November 24, 1968.

50. For the text, see Chinese Customs, Treaties, I, pp. 513-515; Hertslet, Treaties, I, pp. 92-94.

51. See The Christian Science Monitor, September 19, 1965.

52. See The New York Times, September 12-14, 1965.

53. Communist China declared that India's military thrust into West Pakinstan "constituted a grave threat to peace in this part of Asia." Ibid., September 8, 1965. India's later reinforcements stabilized the situation in that region. For details, see ibid., July 4, 1966. See also Klaus H. Pringsheim, "China's Role in the Indo-Pakistani Conflict," The China Quarterly, No. 24 (October-December 1965), pp. 170-175.

54. In the Note of the Chinese Ministry of Foreign Affairs to the Indian Embassy in China on December 26, 1959, Peking stated that there was only a certain discrepancy between the delineations on the Chinese and Bhutanese maps. See The Sino-Indian Boundary Question, p. 88.

55. As India claimed the right to conduct foreign relations for Bhutan, it was rumored that an agreement might be secretly concluded between Communist China and Bhutan without the knowledge of New Delhi to delimit the boundary along Bhutan's northern edge and southern corner. See Harold C. Hinton, Communist China in World Politics, pp. 322-323. See also George N. Patterson, "Recent Chinese Policies in Tibet and Towards the Himalayan Border States," The China Quarterly, No. 12 (October-December 1962), p. 199; Alastair Lamb, Asian Frontiers, pp. 140-141; Francis Watson, op. cit., p. 144.

56. For China's concern over the revival of Japanese militarism, see the following articles: "The Chinese People Firmly Oppose Japanese Latent Imperialism," "A Complete Exposure of the True Face of Japanese Militarism," and "Japanese and U.S. Reactionaries Are Actively Reviving Japanese Militarism," in Renmin Ribao, July 7, 17, 1958; December 7, 1959, respectively. On February 18, 1970, Peking accused Japan of developing rockets to be armed with nuclear warheads. See The New York Times, February 19, 1970.

57. Art. I of the Treaty (CPR, Diplomatic Archives, Vol. 1, pp. 75-77).

58. For details, see supra, pp. 308-309.

59. See the Declarations made by Chou En-lai on December 4, 1950 and August 15, September 26, 1951 (CPR, Diplomatic Archives, Vol. 1, p. 187; Vol. 2, pp. 30-36, 37-40, respectively).

60. For details, see supra, p. 309.

61. For the text, see Department of State, Treaties and Other Acts Series 2491; Documents on American Foreign Relations, 1951, pp. 266-267.

62. For the text of the Pact and related documents, see Documents on American Foreign Relations, 1960, pp. 422-431.

63. The statements made by Mao Tse-tung and other Chinese leaders condemning the Pact were embodied in Support the Just Struggle of the Japanese People against the Japan-U.S. Treaty of Military Alliance (Peking, 1960). For the Soviet attitude, see The New York Times, July 2, 1960.

64. See Sheldon Simon, "Maoism and Inter-party Relations: Peking's Alienation of the Japan Communist Party," The China Quarterly, No. 35 (July-September 1968), pp. 40-57. Further information can be found in Shao-chuan Leng, Japan and Communist China (Kyoto, 1959).

65. See A. Doak Barnett, op. cit., p. 262.

66. Sekai Shūhō (Tokyo), August 11, 1964.

67. For instances of various visits to Peking by Japan's former cabinet ministers and also legislators, see The New York Times, October 8, 1960; August 29, October 5, 1966. Trade agreements have been periodically signed. In 1968, the volume of trade between Communist China and Japan was valued at

$110 million. See Long Island Press, May 22, 1969. In his statement on April 11, 1969, Premier Eisaku Sato defended the trade link. See The New York Times, April 12, 1969.

68. For trade relations and Sato's announcement, see, respectively, Hsinhua News Agency dispatch, April, 1964 and The New York Times, December 14, 1969.

69. For a politically oriented suvey of the Chinese in Malaysia and other parts of Southeast Asia, see C. P. Fitzgerald, The Third China: The Chinese Communities in South-east Asia (Vancouver, 1965). For a general discussion of overseas Chinese in Southeast Asia, see A. Doak Barnett, op. cit., pp. 172-210. Further information on the subject can be found in Victor W. W. S. Purcell, The Chinese in Southeast Asia (London, 1951); Robert S. Elegant, The Dragon's Seed, Peking and the Overseas Chinese (New York, 1959).

70. For modes of losing Chinese nationality and problems of double or multiple nationality, see William L. Tung, China and Some Phases of International Law, pp. 94-100.

71. The figure of Chinese nationals in British Borneo includes those in North Borneo, Sarawak, and Brunei. The number of Chinese people in different parts of Southeast Asia is based on G. William Skinner, "Overseas Chinese in Southeast Asia," The Annals of the American Academy of Political and Social Science, Vol. 321 (January 1959), p. 137. According to the same source, the percentage of Chinese residents to the total population in areas not mentioned in the text is as follows: Thailand (11.3), Cambodia (5.5), South Vietnam (6.2), Laos (0.6), Indonesia (2.7), Burma (1.6), Philippines (1.2), and North Vietnam (0.4). The percentage of Chinese nationals in the Federation of Malaysia, which is composed of Malaya, British North Borneo (Sabah) and Sarawak, to the total population of the Federation may vary slightly from the figure given for Malaya. For a simple map of Southeast Asia indicating the areas where overseas Chinese are concentrated, see The New York Times, November 29, 1959.

72. For Chinese nationals in Thailand, see G. William Skinner, Chinese Society in Thailand: An Analytical History (Ithaca, 1957); David A. Wilson, "China, Thailand and the Spirit of Bandung (Pt. II)," The China Quarterly No. 31 (July-September 1967), pp. 103-107.

73. In his article, "Philippine Communism and the Chinese," ibid., No. 30 (April-June 1967), Justus M. van der Kroef also discussed other problems of the Chinese in the Philippines, particularly in pp. 123-137.

74. A comprehensive discussion of the subject can be found in Donald E. Willmott, The National Status of the Chinese in Indonesia (Ithaca, 1956). See also Robert C. Bone, The Role of the Chinese in Indonesia (Washington, D.C., 1951). The Chinese problem in Indonesia is closely related to the changing relationship between Jakarta and Peking. For the early period, see the American Consulate-General in Hongkong, Sino-Indonesian Relations, covering 1950-1959, 1960-1961. After the failure of an alleged plot of Indonesian Communists to overthrow the military leadership and a subsequent change of government, diplomatic relations between Peking and Jakarta were virtually suspended. See The New York Times, September 15, 26, October 10, 1967. For recent developments, see Justus M. van der Kroef. "The Sino-Indonesian Rupture." The China Quarterly, No. 33 (January-March 1968), pp. 17-46.

75. For Vietnamese restrictions and adverse effects on the country's economy, see Bernald B. Fall, "Viet-Nam's Chinese Problem," Far Eastern Survey, Vol. 27 (May 1958), pp. 65-72.

76. Further information can be found in William E. Willmott, The Chinese in Cambodia (Vancouver, 1967).

77. For conditions required for the Chinese to become citizens of Malaya, according to the 1957 Constitution, see Frank H.K. King, The New Malayan Nation (New York, 1957), pp. 16-17, 36.

78. See supra, p. 302.

79. For Peking's policies, see Sy-sun Lu, Programs of Communist China for Overseas Chinese (Hongkong, 1956). See also the statement made by Ho Hsiang-ning, Chairman of the Commission for Overseas Chinese Affairs, in June 1957. Current Background, No. 467 (July 15, 1957), p. 17.

80. Instances are the National Assembly in Taiwan and the National People's Congress in Peking. In the case of Communist China, overseas representatives were appointed. For details, see ibid., No. 290 (September 5, 1954).

81. After the Indonesian Communist Party's coup of September 30, 1965, Peking was suspected of being behind the plot. Communist China openly condemned the rightist army generals of Indonesia for their bloody purges of Indonesian Communists. See Renmin Riabo, October 20, 1965.

82. In his The Future of the Overseas Chinese in Southeast Asia (New York, 1966), Lea E. Williams suggested political assimi-

lation as a means of self-protection by the overseas Chinese through participation in local government and politics. Actually, this course of action will meet, more often than not, resistance from the Thais, Indonesians, or Philipinos.

83. For the Chinese conception of double or duel nationality, see Survey of China Mainland Press, No. 2438 (February 27, 1961), p. 12.

84. For the text, see CPR, Treaties, Vol. 8, pp. 12-17. After a long delay, the Treaty was ratified by Indonesia and China on January 11 and February 10, 1958, respectively. Due to reluctance on the part of Jakarta, the exchange of ratifications did not take place until January 20, 1960. The essential provision of the Treaty is that a person of both Chinese and Indonesian nationality has to choose either one according to his or her own preference. See Arts. 1, 2. On December 15, 1960, Rules for the application of the Treaty were agreed upon by the two governments. For the text, see ibid., Vol. 8, pp. 58-62. The Treaty might have helped solve the question of double nationality, but not other problems of the Chinese in Indonesia. As early as May 8, 1911, on the occasion of the conclusion of the Consular Convention relative to the Possessions and Colonies of the Netherlands, China and the Netherlands exchanged Notes on the subject, and agreed that the nationality of the Chinese residing in the possessions and colonies of the Netherlands was to be determined by the local legislation in force. For the text of the Convention and Notes, see MacMurray, Treaties, I, pp. 856-860, 861-862, respectively. For later agreement on the nationality of Dutch-born Chinese, see H. F. MacNair, "Chinese Acquisition of Foreign Nationality," Chinese Social and Political Science Review, Vol. 7 (1922), No. 4, pp. 6-7.

85. In his 'Political Report' to the National People's Congress on October 23, 1951, Premier Chou En-lai asserted that the mistreatments of overseas Chinese in several countries "cannot but arouse serious attention and deep concern of the Chinese people." Current Background, No. 134 (November 5, 1951). Although Peking's threatening tone has since been softened, its basic policy remains the same. For a survey of violence and bias against overseas Chinese in Southeast Asia, see The New York Times, April 24, 1966.

86. See supra, p. 393. The test of the Armistice Agreement can also be found in American Foreign Policy, 1950-1955: Basic Documents, pp. 724-750.

87. See the American Assembly, The United States and the Far East (New York, 1956), pp. 87-89.

88. For the text of the Treaty and related documents, see American Foreign Policy, 1950-1955: Basic Documents, pp. 897-912.

89. See supra, p. 394. The text of the agreements can be found in 89th Cong., 1st Sess., Background Information relating to Southeast Asia and Vietnam (Washington, D.C., 1965, pp. 28-58.

90. For Smith's statement, see ibid., p. 61.

91. For the text, see CPR, Diplomatic Archives, Vol. 9, pp. 278-286.

92. Speeches and documents relating to the Conference can be found in China and Asian-African Conference (Peking, 1955).

93. See supra, pp. 389-392, 401.

94. For Chou's speeches, see supra, note 92. For an evaluation of the Bandung Conference, see George McT. Kahin, The Asian-African Conference: Bandung, Indonesia (Ithaca, 1956), pp. 6-7.

95. In his talks with Prince Wan Waithayakon, Foreign Minister of Thailand, Premier Chou gave the assurance that there was no 'Free Thai' movement in Southwest China. They also exchanged views on other subjects in a cordial atmosphere. See David A. Wilson, "China, Thailand and the Spirit of Bandung (Pt. II)," The China Quarterly, No. 31 (July-September 1967), pp. 97-98.

96. The so-called 'Second Bandung Conference' of Afro-Asian nations was to be held in Algeria on November 5, 1965. Largely due to Peking's objection to Soviet participation and its subsequent decision to boycott the parley, the scheduled conference was postponed indefinitely. See The New York Times, October 31, November 2, 1965; Peking Review, No. 44 (October 29, 1965), pp. 5-6. Since 1965, Peking's economic aid to non-aligned nations in Asia and Africa has been considerably reduced. See The New York Times, February 26, 1966. See also Ching-chu Ai, "Some Problems of Economic and Technical Aid to Foreign Countries," Renmin Ribao, May 27, 1964; English translation from Survey of China Mainland Press, No. 3237 (June 12, 1964), pp. 1-8.

97. The first explosion of the Chinese atomic bomb occurred on October 16, 1964. Detailed information on the subject can be found in Morton H. Halperin, China and the Bomb (New York 1965); the same author, "Chinese Nuclear Strategy," The China Quarterly, No. 21 (January-March 1965), pp. 74-86;

William R. Harris, "Chinese Nuclear Doctrine: The Decade Prior to Weapons Development (1945-1955)," ibid., pp. 87-95; Walter C. Clemens, Jr., "China's Nuclear Tests: Trends and Portents," ibid., No. 32 (October-December 1967), pp. 111-131. For further information on recent atomic tests by Communist China and Premier Chou En-lai's declaration of Peking's ultimate aim to seek a nuclear ban, see The New York Times, September 30, October 1, 1969.

98. The signatories of the Southeast Asia Collective Defense Treaty, signed at Manila, on September 8, 1954, are Australia, France, New Zealand, Pakistan, the Philippines, Thailand, the United Kingdom, and the United States. Although Cambodia, Laos, and South Vietnam are not parties to it, they are covered by the collective defense system through a separate Protocol of the same date. For the text of the Treaty and the Protocol, see American Foreign Policy, 1950-1955: Basic Documents, I, pp. 912-916.

99. The members of ASPAC are Australia, New Zealand, Malaysia, Thailand, South Vietnam, the Philippines, the Republic of China, South Korea, and Japan.

100. See The New York Times, June 12, 1969.

101. For further discussion of the subject, consult H. Lauterpacht, Recognition in International Law (Cambridge, England, 1947); T.C. Chen, The International Law of Recognition (New York, 1951). For a brief explanation of various pahses of recognition, see William L. Tung, International Law in an Organizing World, pp. 47-56.

102. The United States did not extend recognition to the Soviet government until 1933. For a short period, the Department of State continued to maintain diplomatic relations with the representative appointed by the Kerensky government. See Salimoff & Co. v Standard Oil Co. of New York, Court of Appeals of New York, 1933. 262 N.Y. 220.

103. Much has been written about the problem of recognition of Communist China. For a comprehensive survey, see Robert P. Newman, Recognition of Communist China? (New York, 1961), pp. 104-288. See also Robert A. Scalapino, "Communist China and Taiwan," from United States Foreign Policy—Asia, submitted to the Senate Foreign Relations Committee by Conlon Associates (Berkeley, University of California, Reprint No. 3, 1960); Yutang Lin and others, "An Analysis of the Conlon Report: Its Fallacies and Contradictions as Viewed by Asians," reprinted from Chinese Culture. Vol. VII, No. 4 (December 1966); Paul

K. T. Sih, Should We Recognize Red China? (a pamphlet distributed by the National Catholic Welfare Conference, Washington, D.C., 1960); Quincy Wright, "Non-recognition of China and International Tensions," Current History (March 1958), pp. 152-157.

104. See The China Tribune, December 29, 1969. For a list of states which have diplomatic relations with Taiwan or Peking, see Department of State, Research Memorandum, REA-23, June 13, 1968.

105. GA res. 396(V). See Repertory of Practice of United Nations Organs (United Nations, 1955, 5 vols., and its Supplements; one additional volume containing table of contents and subject index to Vols. I-V, 1957; Supp. No. 1, 2 vols., 1958; Supp. No. 2, 3 vols., 1963-1964), I, p. 281.

106. See Art. 18(2,3) of the United Nations Charter. For further classification of important matters to be decided by the General Assembly, see William L. Tung, International Organization under the United Nations System, pp. 100-101.

107. GA res. 498 (V).

108. On account of the financial crisis of the United Nations, no vote was taken in the 1964 session of the General Assembly. For details of its 1969 session on the China issue, see The New York Times, November 12, 1969.

109. Conditions required for new membership are: (1) states, (2) peace-loving, (3) acceptance of Charter obligations, (4) capability to undertake these obligations, and (5) willingness to do so. See Art. 4(1) of the United Nations Charter.

110. For divergent views on the representation problem, see Herbert W. Briggs, "Chinese Representation in the United Nations," International Organization, Vol. 5 (1951), pp. 3-31; Benjamin H. Brown and Fred Greene, Chinese Representation: A Case Study in UN Political Affairs (New York, 1955); David Brook, The U.N. and the China Dilemma (New York, 1956); Lincoln P. Bloomfield, "China, the United States, and the United Nations," International Organization, Vol. 20 (1966), pp. 653-676; a Report of a National Policy Panel established by the United Nations Association of the United States of America, "China, the United Nations and United States Policy," ibid., pp. 705-723; Paul K. T. Sih, Red China and the United Nations: The Question of Survival (Washington, D.C., 1961); Myres S. McDougal and Richard M. Goodman, "Chinese Participation in the United Nations," American Journal of

International Law, Vol. 60 (1966), pp. 671-727; The China Institute of International Affairs, China and the United Nations (New York, 1959), Ch. 12; Mostafa Rejai, "Communist China and the United Nations," Orbis, Vol. 10, No. 3 (Fall 1966), pp. 823-838. See also Hungdah Chiu, "Communist China's Attitude toward the United Nations: A Legal Analysis," American Journal of International Law, Vol. 62 (1968), pp. 20-50; Byron S. Weng, "Communist China's Changing Attitudes toward the United Nations," International Organization, Vol. 20 (1966), pp. 677-704.

111. See, for instance, The New York Times, January 20, 1960; July 23, 1962. For arguments against Communist China with respect to problems of recognition and United Nations representation, see Steven C. Y. Pan's editorial in The China Tribune, January 13-16, 1960.

112. See supra, pp. 309-311.

113. It is quite understandable that the National Government of the Republic of China will object to any device for its self-liquidation. For speeches made by the leaders of Communist China and related documents in opposition to the two-China plan, see Ch. 11, note 21.

114. In reviewing W. G. Goddard, Formosa: A Study in Chinese History (East Lansing, 1966), Professor P. T. K. Lin of McGill University pointed out that "a significant part of the Western press alludes to the 'Formosan' as if they were a people with distinct ethnic and cultural indentity and a separate bent, whereas the Chinese refer to the Taiwanese (98 percent of whom are Chinese) in the same sense as Americans refer to Texans." In his view, "the discrepancy might disappear if Americans knew the history of Taiwan as well as they knew that of Texas." The Journal of Asian Studies, Vol. 27, No. 2 (February 1968), p. 394.

115. It is true that there was a riot by the Taiwanese against Governor Ch'en Yi's repressive policy in February 1947, but he was soon removed. For reforms made by the National Government, see Department of State, The Republic of China (Washington, D.C., 1959, Department of State publication 6844), pp. 21-41. For divergent comments on the present situation in Taiwan, see also Mark Mancall (ed.), Formosa Today (New York, 1963), particularly p. 2; Melvin Gurtov, "Recent Developments on Formosa," The China Quarterly, No. 31 (July-September 1967), pp. 59-95. For the escape of a former independence leader, Peng Ming-min, from Taiwan to Sweden, see The New York Times, January 23, February 24, 1970.

116. A. M. Halpern, an American expert on Chinese Communist affairs, commented on Peking's conduct of foreign affairs as generally cautious, but he also pointed out that "when the stakes are high and the threat is imminent, the Chinese are capable of putting everything at risk." See his "China in the Postwar World," The China Quarterly, No. 21 (January-March 1965), p. 45. In pursuance of China's national goals as a great power, one Indian scholar keenly observed that "no sacrifice is too great, no effort too costly to achieve this status." Vidya Prakash Dutt, China and the World, p. 29.

APPENDIX A

The Treaty of Peace, Freidnship, and Commerce between Her Majesty the Queen of Great Britain and Ireland and the Emperor of China, signed at Nanking, August 29, 1842.*

Her Majesty the Queen of the United Kingdom of Great Britain and Ireland, and His Majesty the Emperor of China, being desirous of putting an end to the misunderstandings and consequent hostilities which have arisen between the two Countries, have resolved to conclude a Treaty for that purpose, and therefore named as their Plenipotentiaries, that is to say: —

Her Majesty the Queen of Great Britain and Ireland, Sir Henry Pottinger, Bart., a Major-General in the Service of the East India Company, etc., etc.;

And His Imperial Majesty the Emperor of China, the High Commissioners Keying, a Member of the Imperial House, a Guardian of the Crown Prince and General of the Garrison of Canton; and Elepoo, of the Emperial Kindred, graciously permitted to wear the insignia of the first rank, and the distinction of a Peacock's feather, lately Minister and Governor General, etc., and now Lieutenant-General Commanding at Chapoo:

Who, after having communicated to each other their respective Full Powers and found them to be in good and due form, have agreed upon, and concluded, the following Articles: —

---

*Ratifications exchanged at Hongkong, June 26, 1843; text from Chinese Customs, Treaties, I, pp. 159—164.

427

ARTICLE I.

There shall henceforward be Peace and Friendship between Her Majesty the Queen of the United Kingdom of Great Britain and Ireland, and His Majesty the Emperor of China, and between their respective Subjects, who shall enjoy full security and protection for their persons and property within the Dominions of the other.

ARTICLE II.

His Majesty the Emperor of China agrees, that British Subjects, with their families and establishments, shall be allowed to reside, for the purpose of carrying on their Mercantile pursuits, without molestation or restraint at the Cities and Towns of Canton, Amoy, Foochow-fu, Ningpo, and Shanghai, and Her Majesty the Queen of Great Britain, etc., will appoint Superintendents or Consular Officers, to reside at each of the above-named Cities or Towns, to be the medium of communication between the Chinese Authorities and the said Merchants, and to see that the just Duties and Other Dues of the Chinese Government as hereafter provided for, are duly discharged by Her Britannic Majesty's Subjects.

ARTICLE III.

It being obviously necessary and desirable, that British Subjects should have some Port whereat they may careen and refit their Ships, when required, and keep Stores for that purpose, His Majesty the Emperor of China cedes to Her Majesty the Queen of Great Britain, etc., the Island of Hongkong, to be possessed in perpetuity by Her Britannic Majesty, Her Heirs and Successors, and to be governed by such Laws and Regulations as Her Majesty the Queen of Great Britain, etc., shall see fit to direct.

ARTICLE IV.

The Emperor of China agrees to pay the sum of Six Millions of Dollars as the value of Opium which was delivered up at Canton in the month of March 1839, as a Ransom for the lives of Her Britannic Majesty's Superintendent and Subjects, who had been imprisoned and threatened with death by the Chinese High Officers.

ARTICLE V

The Government of China having compelled the British Merchants trading at Canton to deal exclusively with certain Chinese Merchants called Hong Merchants (or Cohong) who had been licensed by the Chinese Government for that purpose, the Emperor of China agrees to abolish that practice in future at all Ports where British Merchants may reside, and to permit them to carry on their mercantile transactions with whatever persons they please, and His Imperial Majesty further agrees to pay to the British Government the sum of Three Millions of Dollars, on account of Debts due to British Subjects by some of the said Hong Merchants (or Cohong), who have become insolvent, and who owe very large sums of money to Subjects of Her Britannic Majesty.

ARTICLE VI.

The Government of Her Britannic Majesty having been obliged to send out an Expedition to demand and obtain redress for the violent and unjust Proceedings of the Chinese High Authorities towards Her Britannic Majesty's Officer and Subjects, the Emperor of China agrees to pay the sum of Twelve Millions of Dollars on account of the Expenses incurred, and Her Britannic Majesty's Plenipotentiary voluntarily agrees, on behalf of Her Majesty, to deduct from the said amount of Twelve Millions of Dollars, any sums which may have been received by Her Majesty's combined Forces as Ransom for Cities and Towns in China, subsequent to the 1st day of August 1841.

ARTICLE VII.

It is agreed that the Total amount of Twenty-one Millions of Dollars, described in the three preceding Articles, shall be paid as follows: −

Six Millions immediately.

Six millions in 1843. That is: − Three Millions on or before the 30th of the month of June, and Three Millions on or before the 31st of December.

Five Millions in 1844. That is: − Two Millions and a Half on or before the 30th of June, and Two Millions and a Half on or before the 31st of December.

Four Millions in 1845. That is: − Two Millions on or before the 30th of June, and Two Millions on or before the 31st of December; and it is further stipulated, that Interest at the rate of 5 per cent. per annum, shall be paid by the Government of China on any portions of the above sums that are not punctually discharged at the periods fixed.

ARTICLE VIII.

The Emperor of China agrees to release unconditionally all Subjects of Her Britannic Majesty (whether Natives of Europe or India) who may be in confinement at this moment, in any part of the Chinese Empire.

ARTICLE IX.

The Emperor of China agrees to publish and promulgate, under His Imperial Sign Manual and Seal, a full and entire amnesty and act of indemnity, to all Subjects of China on account of their having resided under, or having had dealings and intercourse with, or having entered the Service of Her Britannic Majesty, or of Her Majesty's Officers, and His Imperial Majesty further engages to release all Chinese Subjects who may be at this moment in confinement for similar reasons.

ARTICLE X.

His Majesty the Emperor of China agrees to establish at all the Ports which are by the 2nd Article of this Treaty to be thrown open for the resort of British Merchants, a fair and regular Tariff of Export and Import Customs and other Dues, which Tariff shall be publicly notified and promulgated for general information, and the Emperor further engages, that when British Merchandise shall have once paid at any of the said Ports the regulated Customs and Dues agreeable to the Tariff, to be hereafter fixed, such Merchandise may be conveyed by Chinese Merchants, to any Province or City in the interior of the Empire of China on paying a further amount as Transit Duties which shall not exceed – per cent. on the tariff value of such goods.

ARTICLE XI.

It is agreed that Her Britannic Majesty's Chief High Officer in China shall correspond with the Chinese High Officers, both at the Capital and in the Provinces, under the term "Communication". The Subordinate British Officers and Chinese High Officers in the Provinces under the terms "Statement" on the part of the former, and on the part of the latter "Declaration", and the Subordinates of both Countries on a footing of perfect equality. Merchants and others not holding official situations and, therefore, not included in the above, on both sides, to use the term "Representation" in all Papers addressed to, or intended for the notice of the respective Governments.

ARTICLE XII.

On the assent of the Emperor of China to this Treaty being received and the discharge of the first installment of money, Her Britannic Majesty's Forces will retire from Nanking and the Grand Canal, and will no longer molest or stop the Trade of China. The Military Post at Chinhai will also be withdrawn, but the Islands of Koolangsoo and that of Chusan will continue to be held by Her Majesty's Forces until the money payments, and the arrangements for opening the Ports to British Merchants be completed.

ARTICLE XIII.

The Ratification of this Treaty by Her Majesty the Queen of Great Britain, etc., and His Majesty the Emperor of China shall be exchanged as soon as the great distance which separates England from China will admit; but in the meantime counterpart copies of it, signed and sealed by the Plenipotentiaries on behalf of their respective Sovereigns, shall be mutually delivered, and all its provisions and arrangements shall take effect.

Done at Nanking and Signed and Sealed by the Plenipotentiaries on board Her Britannic Majesty's ship Cornwallis, this twenty-ninth day of August, 1842, corresponding with the Chinese date, twenty-fourth day of the seventh month in the twenty-second Year of Taou Kwang.

[Signatures]

APPENDIX B

The Supplementary Treaty between Her Majesty the Queen of Great Britain and the Emperor of China, signed at Hoomun Chai (The Bogue), October 8, 1843.*

WHEREAS a Treaty of perpetual Peace and Friendship between Her Majesty the Queen of the United Kingdom of Great Britain and Ireland and His Majesty the Emperor of China was concluded at Nanking and signed on board Her said Majesty's ship <u>Cornwallis</u> on the 29th day of August A.D. 1842, corresponding with the Chinese date of the 24th day of the 7th month of the 22nd year of Taou Kwang; of which said Treaty of perpetual Peace and Friendship the Ratifications, under the respective Seals and Signs Manual of the Queen of Great Britain, &c., and the Emperor of China, were duly exchanged at Hongkong on the 26th day of June A.D. 1843 corresponding with the Chinese date, the 29th day of the Fifth month, in the 23rd year of Taou Kwang; And WHEREAS in the said Treaty it was provided (amongst other things), that the five ports of Canton, Fuchow-foo, Amoy, Ningpo and Shanghai should be thrown open for the resort and residence of British Merchants, And that a fair and regular Tariff of Export and Import Duties and other Dues should be established at such Ports; and WHEREAS, various other matters of detail connected with, and bearing relation to, the said Treaty of perpetual Peace and Friendship have been since under the mutual discussion and consideration of the Plenipotentiary and accredited Commissioners of the High Contracting Parties, and the said Tariff and Details having been now finally examined into, adjusted and agreed upon, it has been determined

---

*Published by Proclamation at Hongkong on July 10, 1844; text from Chinese Customs, <u>Treaties</u>, I, pp. 198-207; later amended and incorporated into the Sino-British Treaty of Tientsin, June 26, 1858.

to arrange and record them in the form of a Supplementary Treaty of – Articles, which Articles shall be held to be as binding, and the same efficacy as though they had been inserted in the original Treaty of perpetual Peace and Friendship.

ARTICLE I.

The Tariff of Export and Import Duties which is hereunto attached, – under the Seals and Signatures of the respective Plenipotentiary and Commissioners – shall henceforward be in force at the five Ports of Canton, Fuchowfoo, Amoy, Ningpo. and Shanghai.

ARTICLE II.

The General Regulations of Trade which are hereunto attached, – under the Seals and Signatures of the respective Plenipotentiary and Commissioners, – shall henceforward be in force at the five aforenamed Ports.

ARTICLE III.

All penalties enforced or confiscations made under the III clause of the said General Regulations of Trade shall belong, and be appropriated, to the Public Service of the Government of China.

ARTICLE IV.

After the Five Ports of Canton, Fuchow, Amoy, Ningpo and Shanghai shall be thrown open, English Merchants shall be allowed to trade only at those Five Ports. Neither shall they repair to any other Ports or Places, nor will the Chinese people at any other Ports or Places, be permitted to trade with them. If English Merchant Vessels shall, in contravention of this Agreement, and of a Proclamation to the same purport to be issued by the British Plenipotentiary, repair to any other Ports or Places, the Chinese Government Officers shall be at liberty to seize and confiscate both Vessels and Cargoes, and should Chinese People be discovered clandestinely dealing with English Merchants at any other Ports or Places, they shall be punished by the Chinese Government in such manner as the Law may direct.

ARTICLE V.

The IV clause of the General Regulations of Trade, on the subject of Commercial Dealings and Debts between English and Chinese Merchants is to be clearly understood to be applicable to both Parties.

ARTICLE VI.

It is agreed, that English Merchants and others residing at or resorting to the Five Ports to be opened shall not go into the surrounding Country beyond certain short distances to be named by the local Authorities, in concert with the British Consul, and on no pretence for purposes of traffic. Seamen and persons belonging to the ships shall only be allowed to land under authority and rules which will be fixed by the Consul, in communication with the local officers and should any persons whatever infringe the stipulations of this Article and wander away into the Country, they shall be seized and handed over to the British Consul for suitable punishment.

ARTICLE VII.

The Treaty of perpetual Peace and Friendship provides for British Subjects and their Families residing at the Cities and Towns of Canton, Fuchow, Amoy, Ningpo and Shanghai without molestation or restraint. It is accordingly determined, that ground and houses; the rent or price of which is to be fairly and equitably arranged for, according to the rates pre-

prevailing amongst the people, without exaction on either side; shall be set apart by the local officers, in communication with the Consul, and the number of houses built or rented, will be reported annually to the said local Officers by the Consul for the information of their respective Viceroys and Governors, but the number cannot be limited, seeing that it will be greater or less, according to the resort of Merchants.

ARTICLE VIII.

The Emperor of China having been graciously pleased to grant to all foreign Countries whose Subjects, or Citizens, have hitherto traded at Canton the privilege of resorting for purposes of Trade to the other four Ports of Fuchow, Amoy, Ningpo and Shanghai, on the same terms as the English, it is further agreed, that should the Emperor hereafter, from any cause whatever, be pleased to grant additional privileges or immunities to any of the subjects or Citizens of such Foreign Countries, the same privileges and immunities will be extended to and enjoyed by British Subjects; but it is to be understood that demands or requests are not, on this plea, to be unnecessarily brought forward.

ARTICLE IX.

If lawless Natives of China, having committed crimes or Offences, against their own Government, shall flee to Hongkong or to the English Ships of War or English Merchant Ships for refuge; they shall, if discovered by the English Officers, be handed over at once to the Chinese Officers for trial and punishment; or if, before such discovery be made by the English Officers, it should be ascertained, or suspected, by the Officers of the Government of China whither such criminals and Offenders have fled, a communication shall be made to the proper English Officer, in order that the said criminals and Offenders may be rigidly searched for, seized, and, on proof or admission, of their guilt, delivered up. In like manner, if any Soldier or Sailor or any other person, – whatever his Caste or Country, – who is a Subject of the Crown of England, shall from any cause, or on any pretence, desert, fly, or escape into the Chinese Territory, such Soldier, or Sailor, or other person, shall be apprehended and confined by the Chinese Authorities, and sent to the nearest British Consular, or other Government Officer. In neither case shall concealment or refuge be afforded.

ARTICLE X.

At each of the five Ports to be opened to British Merchants, one English Cruiser will be stationed to enforce good order and discipline amongst the Crews of Merchant Shipping, and to support the necessary authority of the Consul over British Subjects. The Crew of such Ship of War will be carefully restrained by the Officer commanding the Vessel, and they will be subject to all the rules regarding going on shore and straying into the Country, that are already laid down for the Crews of Merchant Vessels. Whenever it may be necessary to relieve such Ships of War by another, intimation of that intention will be communicated by the Consul, or by the British Superintendent of Trade where circumstances will permit, − to the local Chinese Authorities, lest the appearance of an additional Ship should excite misgivings amongst the people; and the Chinese Cruisers are to Offer no hindrance to such relieving Ship, nor is she to be considered liable to any Port Charges or other Rules laid down in the General Regulations of Trade, seeing that British Ships of War never trade in any shape.

ARTICLE XI.

The Posts of Chusan and Koolangsoo will be withdrawn, as provided for in the Treaty of perpetual Peace and Friendship, the moment all the monies stipulated for in that Treaty shall be paid, and the British Plenipotentiary distinctly and voluntarily agrees that all Dwelling Houses, Store Houses, Barracks, and other Buildings that the British Troops or people may have occupied or intermediately built, or repaired, shall be handed over, on the evacuation of the Posts, exactly as they stand, to the Chinese Authorities, so as to prevent any pretence for delay, or the slightest occasion for discussion, or dispute, on those points.

ARTICLE XII.

A fair and regular Tariff of Duties and other dues having now been established,* it is to be hoped, that the system of Smuggling which has heretofore been carried on between English and Chinese Merchants, – in many cases with the open connivance and collusion of the Chinese Custom House Officers, – will entirely cease, and the most peremptory Proclamation to all English Merchants has been already issued on this subject by the British Plenipotentiary, who will also instruct the different Consuls to strictly watch over and carefully scrutinize the conduct of all persons, being British Subjects, trading under his superintendence. In any positive instance of Smuggling transactions coming to the Consul's knowledge he will instantly apprise the Chinese Authorities of the fact, and they will proceed to seize and confiscate all goods, – whatever their value or nature, – that may have been so smuggled, and will also be at liberty, if they see fit, to prohibit the Ship from which the smuggled goods were landed from trading further, and to send her away as soon as her accounts are adjusted and paid. The Chinese Government Officers will, at the same time, adopt whatever measures they may think fit with regard to the Chinese Merchants and Custom House Officers who may be discovered to be concerned in Smuggling.

ARTICLE XIII.

All persons whether Natives of China, or otherwise, who may wish to convey Goods from any one of the five Ports of Canton, Fuchowfoo, Amoy, Ningpo and Shanghai to Hongkong for sale or consumption, shall be at full and perfect liberty to do so on paying the duties on such Goods and obtaining a Pass or Port Clearance from the Chinese Custom House at one of the said Ports. Should Natives of China wish to repair to Hongkong to purchase Goods, they shall have free and full permission to do so, and should they require a Chinese Vessel to carry away their purchases, they must obtain a Pass or

---

*A tariff schedule of 5% ad valorem with certain exceptions was included in the General Regulations, which were attached to this Supplementary Treaty. For the text of these Regulations, see Chinese Customs, Treaties, I, pp. 383–389.

Port Clearance, for her at the Custom House of the Port whence the Vessel may sail for Hongkong. It is further settled, that in all cases these Passes are to be returned to the Officers of the Chinese Government, as soon as the trip for which they may be granted shall be completed.

ARTICLE XIV.

An English Officer will be appointed at Hongkong one part of whose duty will be to examine the registers and Passes of all Chinese Vessels that may repair to that Port to buy or sell Goods, and should such Officer at any time find that any Chinese Merchant Vessel has not a Pass or Register from one of the five Ports, she is to be considered as an unauthorized or smuggling Vessel, and is not to be allowed to trade, whilst a report of the circumstances is to be made to the Chinese Authorities. By this arrangement it is to be hoped, that piracy and illegal traffic will be effectually prevented.

ARTICLE XV.

Should Natives of China who may repair to Hongkong to trade, incur debts there, the recovery of such debts must be arranged for, by the English Courts of Justice on the spot, but if the Chinese Debtor shall abscond and be known to have property real or personal within the Chinese Territory, the rule laid down in the IV Clause of the General Regulations for Trade shall be applied to the case, and it will be the duty of the Chinese Authorities, on application by, and in concert with, the British Consuls, to do their utmost to see justice done between the parties. – On the same principle, should a British Merchant incur debts at any of the five Ports and fly to Hongkong, the British Authorities will, on receiving an application from the Chinese Government Officers accompanied by statements and full proofs of the debts, institute an investigation into the claims, and, when established, oblige the defaulter, or debtor, to settle them to the utmost of his means.

ARTICLE XVI.

It is agreed, that the Custom House Officers at the five Ports shall make a monthly return to Canton of the Passes granted to Vessels proceeding to Hongkong, together with the nature of their Cargoes, and a copy of these Returns will be embodied in one Return and communicated once a month to the proper English Officer at Hongkong. The said English Officer will, on his part, make a similar Return or communication, to the Chinese Authorities at Canton showing the names of Chinese Vessels arrived at Hongkong or departed from that Port, with the nature of their cargoes, and the Canton Authorities will apprise the Custom Houses at the five Ports in order that by these arrangements and precautions all clandestine and illegal trade under the cover of Passes may be averted.

ARTICLE XVII.

Or Additional Article relating to British Small Craft.

Various small Vessels belonging to the English Nation, called Schooners, Cutters, Lorchas, &c. &c., have not hitherto been chargeable with Tonnage Dues. It is now agreed in relation to this class of Vessels which ply between Hongkong and the City, and the City and Macao, that if they only carry passengers letters and baggage, they shall as heretofore pay no tonnage Dues; but if these small craft carry any dutiable articles, no matter how small the quantity may be, they ought, in principle, to pay their full tonnage dues. But this class of small craft are not like the large Ships which are engaged in Foreign Trade; they are constantly coming and going, they make several trips a month, and are not like Foreign Ships which, on entering the Port, cast anchor at Whampoa. If we were to place them on the same footing as the large Foreign Ships the charge would fall unequally, therefore, after this the smallest of these craft shall be rated at 75 Tons, and the largest not to exceed 150 Tons; whenever they enter the Port (or leave the Port with Cargo) they shall pay tonnages dues at the rate of one mace per Ton Register. If not so large as 75 Tons, they shall be considered and charged as of 75 Tons; and if they exceed 150 Tons they shall be considered as large Foreign Ships, and like them, charged tonnage dues at the rate of five mace per Register Ton. Fuchow, and the other Ports having none of this kind of intercourse, and none of this kind of small craft, it would be unnecessary to make any arrangement as regards them.

The following are the Rules by which they are to be regulated.

1st. Every British Schooner, Cutter, Lorcha, &c. shall have a Sailing Letter or Register in Chinese and English, under the Seal and Signature of the Chief Superintendent of Trade, describing her appearance, burthen, &c. &c.

2nd. Every Schooner, Lorcha, and such Vessel, shall report herself, as large Vessels are required to do, at the Bocca Tigris, and when she carries cargo she shall also report herself at Whampoa, and shall, on reaching Canton, deliver up her Sailing Letter or Register, to the British Consul who will obtain permission from the Hoppo for her to discharge her Cargo, which she is not to do without such permission, under the forfeiture of the Penalties laid down in the III Clause of the General Regulations of Trade.

3rd. When the inward cargo is discharged and an outward one (if intended) taken on board, and the duties on both arranged and paid, the Consul will restore the Register or Sailing Letter, and allow the Vessel to depart.

This Supplementary Treaty*; to be attached to the Original Treaty of Peace; consisting of 16 Articles, and one Additional Article, relating to small Vessels, is now written out, forming, with its accompaniments, four pamphlets, and is formally signed and sealed by Their Excellencies the British Plenipotentiary and the Chinese Imperial Commissioner, who, in the first instance, take two copies each and exchange them,

---

*The General Regulations formed part of the Supplementary Treaty. Regulation 13,which provided extraterritorial jurisdiction over disputes between British and Chinese subjects, was amended by Articles XV, XVI, XVII, XXI, XXII, and XXIII of the Sino-British Treaty of Tientsin, June 26, 1858.

that their provisions may be immediately carried into effect. At the same time, each of these High Functionaries having taken his two copies, shall duly memorialise the Sovereign of his Nation; but the two Countries are differently situated as respects distance, so that the Will of the one Sovereign can be known sooner than the Will of the other. It is now therefore agreed that on receiving the Gracious assent of the Emperor in the vermilion pencil, the Imperial Commissioner will deliver the very document containing it, into the hands of His Excellency Hwang, Judge of Canton, who will proceed (to such place as the Plenipotentiary may appoint) and deliver it to the English Plenipotentiary, to have and to hold. Afterwards the Sign Manual of the Sovereign of England having been received at Hongkong, likewise Graciously assenting to and confirming the Treaty, the English Plenipotentiary will despatch a specially appointed Officer to Canton, who will deliver the copy containing the Royal Sign Manual to His Excellency Hwang, who will forward it to the Imperial Commissioner, as a rule and a guide to both Nations for ever, and as a solemn confirmation of our Peace and Friendship.

A most important Supplementary Treaty.

Signed and Sealed at Hoomun Chai on the Eighth day of October 1843, corresponding with the Chinese date of the Fifteenth day of the Eighth moon of the 23rd year of Taou Kwang.

[Signatures]

APPENDIX C

The Treaty of Peace, Amity, and Commerce between the United States of America and the Chinese Empire, signed at Wanghia, July 3, 1844.*

The United States of America and the Ta-Tsing Empire, desiring to establish firm, lasting, and sincere friendship between the two nations, having resolved to fix, in a manner clear and positive, by means of a Treaty or general convention of peace, amity, and commerce, the rules which shall in future be mutually observed in the intercourse of their respective countries; for which most desirable object the President of the United States has conferred full powers on their Commissioner, Caleb Cushing, Envoy Extraordinary and Minister Plenipotentiary of the United States to China, and the August Sovereign of the Ta-Tsing Empire, on his Minister and Commissioner Extraordinary, Kiyeng, of the Imperial House, a Vice-Guardian of the Heir Apparent, Governor-General of the Two Kwangs, and Superintendent-General of the Trade and Foreign Intercourse of the Five Ports:

And the said Commissioners, after having exchanged their said full powers and duly considered the premises, have agreed to the following Articles: —

ARTICLE I.

There shall be a perfect, permanent, and universal peace and a sincere and cordial amity between the United States of America on the one part, and the Ta-Tsing Empire on the other part, and between their people respectively, without exception of persons or places.

---

*Ratifications exchanged at Canton on December 31, 1845; text from Chinese Customs, Treaties, I, pp. 473–486.

ARTICLE II.

Citizens of the United States resorting to China for the purpose of commerce will pay the duties of import and export prescribed by the Tariff which is fixed by and made a part of this Treaty. They shall in no case be subject to other or higher duties than are or shall be required of the people of any other nation whatever. Fees and charges of every sort are wholly abolished; and officers of the revenue who may be guilty of exaction shall be punished according to the laws of China. If the Chinese Government desire to modify in any respect the said Tariff, such modifications shall be made only in consultation with Consuls or other functionaries thereto duly authorized in behalf of the United States, and with consent thereof. And if additional advantages or privileges of whatever description be conceded hereafter by China to any other nation, the United States and the citizens thereof shall be entitled thereupon to a complete, equal, and impartial participation in the same.

ARTICLE III.

The citizens of the United States are permitted to frequent the five ports of Quangchow [Canton], Amoy, Fuchow, Ningpo, and Shanghai, and to reside with their families and trade there, and to proceed at pleasure with their vessels and merchandise to or from any Foreign port and either of the said five ports, and from either of five ports to any other of them; but said vessels shall not unlawfully enter the other ports of China, nor carry on a clandestine and fraudulent trade along the coasts thereof; and any vessel belonging to a citizen of the United States which violates this provision shall, with her cargo, be subject to confiscation to the Chinese Government.

ARTICLE IV.

For the superintendence and regulation of the concerns of citizens of the United States doing business at the said five ports, the Government of the United States may appoint Consuls or other officers at the same, who shall be duly recognized as such by the officers of the Chinese Government, and shall hold official intercourse and correspondence with the latter, either personal or in writing, as occasion may require, on terms of equality and reciprocal respect. If disrespectfully treated or aggrieved in any way by the local authorities, the said officers, on the one hand, shall have the right to make respresentation of the same to the superior officers of the Chinese Government, who will see that full inquiry and strict justice be had in the premises; and on the other hand, the said Consuls will carefully avoid all acts of unnecessary offence to or collision with the officers and people of China.

ARTICLE V.

At each of the said five ports citizens of the United States lawfully engaged in commerce shall be permitted to import from their own or any other ports into China, and sell there, and purchase therein and export to their own or any other ports, all manner of merchandise of which the importation or exportation is not prohibited by this Treaty, paying the duties thereon which are prescribed by the Tariff hereinbefore established, and no other charges whatever.

ARTICLE VI.

Whenever any merchant vessel belonging to the United States shall enter either of the five said ports for trade, her papers shall be lodged with the Consul or person charged with affairs, who will report the same to the Commissioner of Customs, and tonnage duty shall be paid on said vessel at the rate of five mace per ton if she be over one hundred and fifty tons burthen, and one mace per ton if she be of the burthen of one hundred and fifty tons or under, according to the amount of her tonnage as specified in the register; said payment to be in full of the former charges of measurement and other fees, which are wholly abolished. And if any vessel which, having anchored at one of the said ports and there paid tonnage duty, shall have occasion to go to any other of the said ports to complete the disposal of her cargo, the Consul or person charged with affairs will report the same to the

Commissioner of Customs, who on the departure of the said vessel shall note in the port clearance that the tonnage duties have been paid, and report the same to the other Custom Houses; in which case the said vessel on entering another port will only pay duty there on her cargo, but shall not be subject to the payment of tonnage duty a second time.

ARTICLE VII.

No tonnage duty shall be required on boats belonging to the citizens of the United States employed in the conveyance of passengers, baggage, letters, and articles of provision, or others not subject to duty, to or from any of the five ports. All cargo boats, however, conveying merchandise subject to duty shall pay the regular tonnage duty of one mace per ton, provided they belong to citizens of the United States, but not if they are hired by them from subjects of China.

ARTICLE VIII.

Citizens of the United States for their vessels bound in shall be allowed to engage pilots, who will report said vessels at the passes and take them in port; and when the lawful duties have all been paid, they may engage pilots to leave port. It shall also be lawful for them to hire at pleasure servants, compradors, linguists, and writers, and passage or cargo boats, and to employ laborers, seamen, and persons for whatever necessary service, for a reasonable compensation to be agreed on by the parties or settled by application to the Consular officer of their Government, without interference on the part of the local officers of the Chinese Government.

ARTICLE IX.

Whenever merchant vessels belonging to the United States shall have entered port, the Superintendent of Customs will, if he fit, appoint Custom House officers to guard said vessel, who may live on board the ship or their own boats, at their convenience; but provision for the subsistence of said officers shall be made by the Superintendent of Customs, and they shall not be entitled to any allowance from the vessels or owner thereof, and they shall be subject to suitable punishment for any exaction practiced by them in violation of this regulation.

ARTICLE X.

Whenever a merchant vessel belonging to the United States shall cast anchor in either of said ports, the supercargo, master, or consignee will, within forty-eight hours, deposit the ship's papers in the hands of the Consul or person charged with affairs of the United States, who will cause to be communicated to the Superintendent of Customs a true report of the name and tonnage of such vessel, the names of her men, and of the cargo on board, which being done, the Superintendent will give a permit for the discharge of her cargo; and the master, supercargo, or consignee, if he proceed to discharge the cargo without such permit, shall incur a fine of five hundred dollars, and the goods so discharged without a permit shall be subject to forfeiture to the Chinese Government. But if the master of any vessel in port desire to discharge a part only of the cargo, it shall be lawful for him to do so, paying duties on such part only, and to proceed with the remainder to any other ports; or if the master so desire, he may, within forty-eight hours after the arrival of the vessel, but not later, decide to depart without breaking bulk, in which case he will not be subject to pay tonnage or other duties or charges until on his arrival at another port, he shall proceed to discharge cargo, when he will pay the duties on vessel and cargo according to law; and the tonnage duties shall be held due after the expiration of said forty-eight hours.

ARTICLE XI.

The Superintendent of Customs, in order to the collection of the proper duties, will, on application made to him through the

Consul, appoint suitable officers, who shall proceed, in the presence of the captain, supercargo, or Consignee, to make a just and fair examination of all goods in the act of being discharged for importation or laden for exportation on board any merchant vessel of the United States.

And if dispute occur in regard to the value of goods subject to ad valorem duty, or in regard to the amount of tare, and the same cannot be satisfactorily arranged by the parties, the question may, within twenty-four hours, and not afterwards, be referred to the said Consul to adjust with the Superintendent of Customs.

ARTICLE XII.

Sets of standard balances, and also weights and measures, duly prepared, stamped, and sealed according to the standard of the Custom House of Canton, shall be delivered by the Superintendent of Customs to the Consuls of each of the five ports, to secure uniformity and prevent confusion in the measure and weight of merchandise.

ARTICLE XIII.

The tonnage duty on vessels belonging to citizens of the United States shall be paid on their being admitted to entry. Duties of import shall be paid on the discharge of the goods, and duties of export on the lading of the same. When all such duties shall have been paid, and not before, the Superintendent of Customs shall give a port clearance, and the Consul shall return the ship's papers, so that she may depart on her voyage. The duties shall be paid to the shroffs authorized by the Chinese Government to receive the same in its behalf.

Duties payable by merchants of the United States shall be received either in sycee silver or in foreign money, at the rate of exchange as ascertained by the regulations now in force; and imported goods, on their resale or transit in any part of the Empire, shall be subject to the imposition of no other duty than they are accustomed to pay at the date of this Treaty.

ARTICLE XIV.

No goods on board any merchant vessel of the United States in port are to be transhipped to another vessel unless there be particular occasion therefor, in which case the occasion shall be certified by the Consul to the Superintendent of Customs, who may appoint officers to examine into the facts, and permit the transhipment; and if any goods be transhipped without such application, inquiry, and permit, they shall be subject to be forfeited to the Chinese Government.

ARTICLE XV.

The former limitation of the trade of Foreign nations to certain persons appointed at Canton by the Government, and commonly called hong merchants, having been abolished, citizens of the United States engaged in the purchase or sale of goods of import or export are admitted to trade with any and all subjects of China without distinction; they shall not be subject to any new limitations nor impeded in their business by monopolies or other injurious restrictions.

ARTICLE XVI.

The Chinese Government will not hold itself responsible for any debts which may happen to be due from subjects of China to citizens of the United States, or for frauds committed by them, but citizens of the United States may seek redress in law; and on suitable representation being made to the Chinese local authorities through the Consul, they will cause due examination in the premises, and take all proper steps to compel satisfaction. But in case the debtor be dead, or without property, or have absconded, the creditor cannot be indemnified according to the old system of the cohong so called. And if citizens of the United States be indebted to subjects of China, the latter may seek redress in the same way through the Consul, but without any responsibility for the debt on the part of the United States.

ARTICLE XVII.

Citizens of the United States residing or sojourning at any of the ports open to Foreign commerce shall enjoy all proper accommodation in obtaining houses and places of business, or in hiring sites from the inhabitants on which to construct houses and places of business, and also hospitals, churches, and cemeteries. The local authorities of the two Governments shall select in concert the sites for the foregoing objects, having due regard to the feelings of the people in the location thereof; and the parties interested will fix the rent by mutual agreement, the proprietors on the one hand not demanding any exorbitant price, nor the merchants on the other unreasonably insisting on particular spots, but each conducting with justice and moderation; and any desecration of said cemeteries by subjects of China shall be severely punished according to law.

At the places of achorage of the vessels of the United States, the citizens of the United States, merchants, seamen, or others sojourning there may pass and repass in the immediate neighborhood; but they shall not at their pleasure make excursions into the country among the villages at large, nor shall they repair to public marts for the purpose of disposing of goods unlawfully and in fraud of the revenue.

And in order to the preservation of the public peace, the local officers of Government at each of the five ports shall, in concert with the Consuls, define the limits beyond which it shall not be lawful for a citizen of the United States to go.

ARTICLE XVIII.

It shall be lawful for officers or citizens of the United States to employ scholars and people of any part of China, without distinction of persons, to teach any of the languages of the Empire, and to assist in literary labors, and the persons so employed shall not for that cause be subject to any injury on the part either of the Government or of individuals; and it shall in like manner be lawful for citizens of the United States to purchase all manner of books in China.

ARTICLE XIX.

All citizens of the United States in China peaceably attending to their affairs, being placed on a common footing of amity and goodwill with subjects of China, shall receive and enjoy, for themselves and everything appertaining to them, the special protection of the local authorities of Government, who shall defend them from all insult or injury of any sort on the part of the Chinese.

If their dwellings or their property be threatened or attacked by mobs, incendiaries, or other violent or lawless persons, the local officers, on requisition of the Consul, will immediately despatch a military force to disperse the rioters, and will apprehend the guilty individuals and punish them with the utmost rigour of the law.

ARTICLE XX.

Citizens of the United States who may have imported merchandise into any of the free ports of China, and paid the duty thereon, if they desire to re-export the same in part or in whole to any other of the said ports, shall be entitled to make application, through their Consul, to the Superintendent of Customs, who, in order to prevent frauds on the revenue, shall cause examination to be made by suitable officers to see that the duties paid on such goods entered on the Custom House books correspond with the representation made, and that the goods remain with their original marks unchanged and shall then make a memorandum in the port clearance of the goods and the amount of duties paid on the same, and deliver the same to the merchant, and shall also certify the facts to the officers of Custms of the other ports.

All which being done, on the arrival in port of the vessel in which the goods are laden, and everything being found on examination there to correspond, she shall be permitted to break bulk and land the said goods without being subject to the payment of any additional duty thereon.

But if on such examination the Superintendent of Customs shall detect any fraud on the revenue in the case, then the goods shall be subject to forfeiture and confiscation to the Chinese Government.

ARTICLE XXI.

Subjects of China who may be guilty of any criminal act towards citizens of the United States shall be arrested and punished by the Chinese authorities according to the laws of China, and citizens of the United States who may commit any crime in China shall be subject to be tried and punished only by the Consul or other public functionary of the United States thereto authorized according to the laws of the United States; and in order to the prevention of all controversy and disaffection, justice shall be equitably and impartially administered on both sides.

ARTICLE XXII.

Relations of peace and amity between the United States and China being established by this Treaty, and the vessels of the United States being admitted to trade freely to and from the five ports of China open to Foreign commerce, it is further agreed that in case at any time hereafter China should be at war with any Foreign nation whatever, and should for that cause exclude such nation from entering her ports, still the vessels of the United States shall not the less continue to pursue their commerce in freedom and security, and to transport goods to and from the ports of the belligerent parties, full respect being paid to the neutrality of the flag of the United States: Provided that the said flag shall not protect vessels engaged in the importation of officers or soldiers in the enemy's service, nor shall said flag be fraudulently used to enable the enemy's ships with their cargoes to enter the ports of China; but all such vessels so offending shall be subject to forfeiture and confiscation to the Chinese Government.

ARTICLE XXIII.

The Consuls of the United States at each of the five ports open to Foreign trade shall make annually to the respective Governors-General thereof a detailed report of the number of vessels belonging to the United States which have entered and left said ports during the year, and of the amount and value of goods imported or exported in said vessels, for transmission to and inspection of the Board of Revenue.

ARTICLE XXIV.

If citizens of the United States have special occasion to address any communication to the Chinese local officers of Government, they shall submit the same to their Consul or other officer to determine if the language be proper and respectful, and the matter just and right; in which event he shall transmit the same to the appropriate authorities for their consideration and action in the premises. In like manner, if subjects of China have special occasion to address the Consul of the United States, they shall submit the communication to the local authorities of their own Government to determine if the language be respectful and proper, and the matter just and right; in which case the said authorities will transmit the same to the Consul or other functionary for his consideration and action in the premises. And if controversies arise between citizens of the United States and subjects of China which cannot be amicably settled otherwise, the same shall be examined and decided conformably to justice and equity by the public officers of the two nations acting in conjunction.

ARTICLE XXV.

All questions in regards to rights, whether of property or person, arising between citizens of the United States in China shall be subject to the jurisdiction of and regulated by the authorities of their own Government; and all controversies occurring in China between the citizens of the United States and the subjects of any other Government shall be regulated by the Treaties existing between the United States and such Governments respectively, without interference on the part of China.

ARTICLE XXVI.

Merchant vessels of the United States lying in the waters of the five ports of China open to Foreign commerce will be under the jurisdiction of the officers of their own Government, who, with the masters and owners thereof, will manage the same, without control on the part of China. For injuries done to the citizens or the commerce of the United States by any Foreign power, the Chinese Government will not hold itself bound to make reparation.

But if the merchant vessels of the United States, while within the waters over which the Chinese Government exercise jurisdiction, be plundered by robbers or pirates, then the Chinese local authorities, civil and military, on receiving information thereof, will arrest the said robbers or pirates and punish them according to law, and will cause all the property which can be recovered to be placed in the hands of the nearest Consul or other officer of the United States, to be by him restored to the true owner; but if, by reason of the extent of territory and numerous population of China, it should in any case happen that the robbers cannot be apprehended or the property only in part recovered, then the law will take its course in regard to the local authorities, but the Chinese Government will not make indemnity for the goods lost.

ARTICLE XXVII.

If any vessel of the United States shall be wrecked or stranded on the coast of China, and be subjected to plunder or other damage, the proper officers of Government, on receiving information of the fact, will immediately adopt measures for their relief and security, and the persons on board shall receive friendly treatment and be enabled to repair at once to the most convenient of the five ports, and shall enjoy all facilities for obtaining supplies of provisions and water; and if a vessel shall be forced to take refuge in any port other than one of the free ports, then in like manner the persons on board shall receive friendly treatment and the means of safety and security.

ARTICLE XXVIII.

Citizens of the United States, their vessels and property, shall not be subject to any embargo, nor shall they be seized or forcibly detained for any pretence of the public service; but they shall be suffered to prosecute their commerce in quiet, and without molestation or embarrassment.

ARTICLE XXIX.

The local authorities of the Chinese Government will cause to be apprehended all mutineers or deserters from on board the vessels of the United States in China, and will deliver them up to the Consuls or other officers for punishment.

And if criminals, subjects of China, take refuge in the houses or on board the vessels of citizens of the United States, they shall not be harboured or concealed, but shall be delivered up to justice, on due requisition by the Chinese local officers addressed to those of the United States.

The merchants, seamen, and other citizens of the United States shall be under the superintendence of the appropriate officers of their Government.

If individuals of either nation commit acts of violence and disorder, use arms to the injury of others, or create disturbances endangering life, the officers of the two Governments will exert themselves to enforce order and to maintain the public peace by doing impartial justice in the premises.

ARTICLE XXX.

The superior authorities of the United States and of China, in corresponding together, shall do so in terms of equality and in the form of mutual communication (chau-hwui). The Consuls and the local officers, civil and military, in corresponding together shall likewise employ the style and form of mutual communication (chau-hwui). When inferior officers of the Government address superior officers of the other, they shall do so in the style and form of memorial (shin-chin). Private individuals in addressing superior officers shall employ the style of petition (pin-ching). In no case shall any terms or style be suffered which shall be offensive or disrespectful to either party. And it is agreed that no presents under any pretext or form whatever shall ever be demanded of the United States by China or of China by the United States.

ARTICLE XXXI.

Communications from the Government of the United States to the Court of China shall be transmitted through the medium of the Imperial Commissioner charged with the super-intendence of the concerns of Foreign nations with China, or through the Governor-General of the Liang Kwang, that of Min and Chah, or that of Liang Kang.

ARTICLE XXXII.

Whenever ships of war of the United States, in cruising for the protection of the commerce of their country, shall arrive at any of the ports of China, the commanders of said ships and the superior local authorities of Government shall hold intercourse together in terms of equality and courtesy, in token of the friendly relation of their respective nations; and the said ships of war shall enjoy all suitable facilities on the part of the Chinese Government in the purchase of provisions, procuring water, and making repairs, if occasion require.

ARTICLE XXXIII.

Citizens of the United States who shall attempt to trade clandestinely with such of the ports of China as are not open to Foreign commerce, or who shall trade in opium or any other contraband articles of merchandise, shall be subject to be dealt with by the Chinese Government, without being entitled to any countenance or protection from that of the United States; and the United States will take measures to prevent their flag from being abused by the subjects of other nations as a cover for the violation of the laws of the Empire.

ARTICLE XXXIV.

When the present Convention shall have been definitely concluded, it shall be obligatory on both powers, and its provisions shall not be altered without grave cause; but inasmuch as the circumstances of the several ports of China open to Foreign commerce are different, experience may show that inconsiderable modifications are requisite in those parts which relate to commerce and navigation; in which case the two Governments will, at the expiration of twelve years from the date of said Convention, treat amicably concerning the same, by the means of suitable persons appointed to conduct such negotiation.

And when ratified, the Treaty shall be faithfully observed in all its parts by the United States and China, and by every citizen and subject of each; and no individual State of the United States can appoint or send a Minister to China to call in question the provisions of the same.

The present Treaty of peace, amity, and commerce shall be ratified and approved by the President of the United States, by and with the advice and consent of the Senate thereof, and by the August Sovereign of the Ta-Tsing Empire; and the ratifications shall be exchanged within eighteen months from the date of the signature thereof, or sooner if possible.

If faith thereof, we, the respective Plenipotentiaries of the United States of America and the Ta-Tsing Empire as aforesaid, have signed and sealed these presents.

Done at Wanghia, this third day of July in the year of our Lord Jesus Christ one thousand eight hundred and forty-four, and of Taou-Kwang, the twenty-fourth year, fifth month, and eighteenth day.

[Signatures]

APPENDIX D

The Treaty between the Republic of China and the United Kingdom and India for the Relinquishment of Extraterritorial Rights in China and the Regulation of Related Matters, signed at Chungking, January 11, 1943.*

His Excellency the President of the National Government of the Republic of China and His Majesty the King of Great Britain, Ireland and the British Dominions beyond the Seas, Emperor of India:

Being desirous of defining more clearly in a spirit of friendship the general relations between them, and for this purpose to settle certain matters relating to jurisdiction in China;

Have decided to conclude a Treaty for this purpose and to that end have appointed as their Plenipotentiaries:

His Excellency the President of the National Government of the Republic of China:

His Excellency, Doctor Tse Vung Soong, Minister for Foreign Affairs of the Republic of China;

His Majesty the King of Great Britain, Ireland and of the British Dominions beyond the Seas, Emperor of India (hereinafter referred to as His Majesty the King):

For the United Kingdom of Great Britain and Northern Ireland:

His Excellency, Sir Horace James Seymour, K.C.M.G., C.V.O.,

---

*Ratifications exchanged at Chungking, May 20, 1943; text from Chinese Republic, Treaties, pp. 589–603.

His Majesty's Ambassador Extraordinary and Plenipotentiary to the Republic of China;

For India:

Hugh Edward Richardson Esquire, an officer of the Indian Political Service;

Who, having communicated to each other their full powers, found to be in good and due form, have agreed as follows:

ARTICLE I.

(1) The territories of the High Contracting Parties to which the present Treaty applies are, on the part of His Excellency the President of the National Government of the Republic of China, all the territories of the Republic of China; and on the part of His Majesty the King, the United Kingdom of Great Britain and Northern Ireland, India, all colonies, overseas territories, protectorates of His Majesty, all territories under His protection or suzerainty and all mandated territories in respect of which the mandate is exercised by His Government in the United Kingdom. Any reference in subsequent articles of the present Treaty to the territories of one or the other High Contracting Party shall be deemed to relate to those territories of that High Contracting Party to which the present Treaty applies.

(2) In the present Treaty, the term "nationals of the one (or of the other) High Contracting Party" shall in relation to the Republic of China, mean all nationals of the Republic of China; and in relation to His Majesty the King all British subjects and all British protected persons belonging to the territories to which the present Treaty applies.

(3) The expression "companies of the one (or of the other) High Contracting Party" shall for the purpose of the present Treaty be interpreted as meaning limited liability and other companies, partnerships and associations constituted under the law of the territories of that High Contracting Party to which the present Treaty applies.

ARTICLE II.

All those provisions of treaties or agreements in force between His Excellency the President of the National Government of the Republic of China and His Majesty the King which authorise His Majesty or His representatives to exercise jurisdiction over nationals or companies of His Majesty in the territory of the Republic of China are hereby abrogated. The nationals and companies of His Majesty the King shall be subject in the territory of the Republic of China to the jurisdiction of the Government of the Republic of China, in accordance with the principles of international law and practice.

ARTICLE III.

(1) His Majesty the King considers that the Final Protocol concluded at Peking on September 7th, 1901, between the Chinese Governments, including His Majesty's Government in the United Kingdom, should be terminated, and agrees that the rights accorded to His Majesty's Government in the United Kingdom under that Protocol and under the agreements supplementary thereto shall cease.

(2) His Majesty's Government in the United Kingdom will cooperate with the Government of the Republic of China for the reaching of any necessary agreements with the other Governments concerned for the transfer to the Government of the Republic of China of the administration and control of the diplomatic quarter at Peiping, including the official assets and the official obligations of the diplomatic quarter, it being mutually understood that the Government of the Republic of China, in taking over administration and control of the diplomatic quarter, will make provision for the assumption and discharge of the official obligations and liabilities of the diplomatic quarter and for the recognition and protection of all legitimate rights therein.

(3) The Government of the Republic of China shall accord to His Majesty's Government in the United Kingdom a continued right to use for official purposes the land which has been allocated to His Majesty's Government in the United Kingdom in the diplomatic quarter in Peiping, on parts of which are located buildings belonging to His Majesty's Government in the United Kingdom.

ARTICLE IV.

(1) His Majesty the King considers that the International Settlements at Shanghai and Amoy should revert to the admin-

istration and control of the Government of the Republic of China and agrees that the rights accorded to His Majesty in relation to those Settlements shall cease.

(2) His Majesty's Government in the United Kingdom will cooperate with the Government of the Republic of China for the reaching of any necessary agreements with the other Governments concerned for the transfer to the Government of the Republic of China of the administration and control of the International Settlements at Shanghai and Amoy, including the official assets and the official obligations of those Settlements, it being mutually understood that the Government of the Republic of China, in taking over administration and control of those Settlements, will make provision for the assumption and discharge of the official obligations and liabilities of those Settlements and for the recognition and protection of all legitimate rights therein.

(3) His Majesty the King agrees that the British Concession (including the whole British municipal area) at Tientsin and the British Concession at Canton shall revert to the administration and control of the Government of the Republic of China and that the rights accorded to His Majesty in relation to those Concessions shall cease.

(4) The administration and control of the British Concession (including the whole British municipal area) at Tientsin and the British Concession at Canton, including their official assets and official obligations shall be transferred to the Government of the Republic of China, it being mutually understood that the Government of the Republic of China, in taking over administration and control of those Concessions, will make provision for the assumption and discharge of the official obligations and liabilities of those Concessions and for the recognition and protection of all legitimate rights therein.

ARTICLE V.

(1) In order to obviate any questions as to existing rights in respect of or as to existing titles to real property in the territory of the Republic of China possessed by nationals and companies of His Majesty the King, or by His Majesty's Government in the United Kingdom, and in particular questions

which might arise from the abrogation of the provisions of treaties and agreements provided for in Article 2 of the present Treaty, the High Contracting Parties agree that such existing rights or titles shall be indefeasible and shall not be questioned upon any ground except upon proof, established through due process of law, of fraud or of fraudulent or dishonest practices in the acquisition of such rights or titles, it being understood that no right or title shall be rendered invalid by virtue of any subsequent change in the original procedure through which it was acquired. It is also agreed that the exercise of these rights or titles shall be subject to the laws and regulations of the Republic of China concerning taxation, national defense and the right of eminent domain; and that no such rights or titles may be alienated to the government or nationals (including companies) of any third country without the express consent of the Government of the Republic of China.

(2) The High Contracting Parties also agree that if it should be the desire of the Government of the Republic of China to replace by new deeds of ownership existing leases in perpetuity or other documentary evidence relating to real property held by nationals or companies of His Majesty the King or by His Majesty's Government in the United Kingdom, the replacement shall be made by the Chinese authorities without charges of any sort and the new deeds of ownership shall fully protect the holders of such leases or other documentary evidence, and their legal heirs and assigns without diminution of their prior rights and interests, including the right of alienation.

(3) The High Contracting Parties agree further that nationals or companies of His Majesty the King or His Majesty's Government in the United Kingdom shall not be required or asked by the Chinese authorities to make any payments of fees in connection with land transfers for or with relation to any period prior to the effective date of this Treaty.

ARTICLE VI.

His Majesty the King having long accorded rights to nationals of the Republic of China within each of the territories of His Majesty to travel, reside and carry on commerce throughout the whole extent of that territoty, the Government of the Republic of China agrees to accord similar rights to nationals of His Majesty within the territory of the Republic of China. Each High Contracting Party will endeavour to accord in his territories to nationals and companies of the other High Contracting Party in regard to all legal proceedings and in matters relating to the administration of justice and the levying of taxes and requirements in connection therewith treatment not less favorable than that accorded to his own nationals and companies.

ARTICLE VII.

The consular officers of one High Contracting Party, duly provided with exequaturs, shall be permitted to rside in such ports, places and cities of the territories of the other High Contracting Party as may be agreed upon. The consular officers of one High Contracting Party shall have the right within their districts in the territories of the other High Contracting Party to interview, communicate with and to advise the nationals and companies of the former High Contracting Party, and the nationals and companies of one High Contracting Party within the territories of the other High Contracting Party shall have the right at all times to communicate with the consular officers of the former Contracting Party. The consular officers of one High Contracting Party in the territories of the other shall be informed immediately by the appropriate local authorities when any of their nationals are arrested or detained in their consular districts by the local authorities. They shall have the right to visit within the limits of the districts any of their nationals who are under arrest or awaiting trial in prison. Communications from nationals of one High Contracting Party in prison in the territories of the other High Contracting Party addressed to the consular officers of the former High Contracting Party will be forwarded to the appropriate consular officer by the local authorities. Consular officers of one High Contracting Party shall be accorded in the territories of the other High Contracting Party the rights, privileges and immunities enjoyed by consular officers under modern international usage.

ARTICLE VIII.

(1) The High Contracting Parties will enter into negotiations for the conclusion of a comprehensive modern treaty or treaties of friendship, commerce, navigation and consular rights upon the request of either of them or in any case within six months after the cessation of the hostilities in the war against the common enemies in which they are now engaged. The treaty or treaties to be thus negotiated will be based upon the principles of international law and practice as reflected in modern international procedure and in the modern treaties which each of the High Contracting Parties have respectively concluded with other Powers in recent years.

(2) Pending the conclusion of the comprehensive treaty or treaties referred to in the preceding paragraph, if any questions affecting the rights in the territory of the Republic of China of the nationals or companies of His Majesty the King, or of His Majesty's Government in the United Kingdom or of the Government of India, should arise in future and if these questions are not covered by the present Treaty and Exchange of Notes or by the provisions of existing treaties, conventions and agreements between the High Contracting Parties which are not abrogated by or inconsistent with the present Treaty and Exchange of Notes, such questions shall be discussed by representatives of the High Contracting Parties and shall be decided in accordance with the generally accepted principles of international law and with modern international practice.

ARTICLE IX.

The present Treaty shall be ratified and the instruments of ratification shall be exchanged at Chungking as soon as possible. The Treaty shall come into force on the day of the exchange of ratifications.

In witness whereof the above mentioned Plenipotentiaries have signed the present Treaty and affixed thereto their seals.

Done at Chungking this Eleventh day of the First month of the Thirty Second year of the Republic of China corresponding to the Eleventh day of January, 1943, in duplicate in Chinese and English, both texts being equally authentic.

(Signed)   Tse Vung Soong

(Signed)   H. J. Seymour

(Signed)   H. E. Richardson

EXCHANGE OF NOTES

I. Note from Dr. Tse Vung Soong, Chinese Minister for Foreign Affairs, to Sir Horace James Seymour

Chungking, January 11th, 1943

Sir,

During the negotiations for the Treaty signed today between His Excellency the President of the National Government of the Republic of China and His Majesty the King of Great Britain, Ireland and the British Dominions beyond the Seas, Emperor of India, for the United Kingdom of Great Britain and Northern Ireland and India, a number of questions have been discussed upon which agreement has been reached. The understandings reached with regard to these points are recorded in the annex to the present Note, which annex shall be considered as an integral part of the Treaty signed today and shall be considered as effective upon the date of the entrance into force of that Treaty. I shall be glad if Your Excellency would confirm these understandings on behalf of His Majesty's Government in the United Kingdom.

I avail myself of this opportunity to renew to Your Excellency the assurance of my highest consideration.

(Signed)   Tse Vung Soong

His Excellency

Sir Horace James Seymour, K.C.M.G., C.V.O.,

His Majesty's Ambassador,

Chungking.

Annex

1. With reference to Article 2 and Article 82 of the Treaty, it is understood that:

(a) His Majesty the King relinquishes all existing treaty rights relating to the system of Treaty Ports in China. His Excellency the President of the National Government of the Republic of China and His Majesty the King mutually agree that the merchant vessels of the one High Contracting Party shall be permitted freely to come to ports, places and waters in the territories of the other High Contracting Party which are or may be opened to overseas merchant shipping and that the treatment accorded to such vessels in such ports, places and waters shall be no less favorable than that accorded to national vessels and shall be as favorable as that accorded to vessels of any third country. The term "vessels" of a High Contracting Party means all vessels registered under the law of any of the territories of that High Contracting Party to which the Treaty signed this day applies.

(b) His Majesty the King relinquishes all existing treaty rights relating to the special courts in the International Settlements at Shanghai and Amoy.

(c) His Majesty the King relinquishes all existing rights with regard to the employment of foreign pilots in the ports of the territories of the Republic of China.

(d) His Majesty the King relinquishes all existing treaty rights relating to the entry of His naval vessels into the waters of the Republic of China; and the Government of the Republic of China and His Majesty's Government in the United Kingdon shall extend to each other in connection with the visits of the warships of the one High Contracting Party to the ports of the other High Contracting Party mutual courtesy in accordance with ordinary international usage.

(e) His Majesty the King relinquishes any right to claim the appointment of a British subject as Inspector-General of the Chinese Customs.

(f) All the courts of His Majesty the King which have hitherto been sitting in the territories of the Republic of China having been closed down in accordance with Article 2 of the Treaty signed this day, the orders, decrees, judgments and other acts of any of His Majesty's courts in China shall be considered as res judicata and shall when necessary be enforced by the Chinese authorities; further, any cases pending before any of His Majesty's courts in China at the time of the coming into effect of the Treaty shall, if the plaintiff or the petitioner so desires, be remitted to the appropriate courts of the Government of the Republic of China which shall proceed to dispose of them as expeditiously as possible and in so doing shall so far as practicable apply the law which the court of His Majesty would have applied.

(g) His Majesty the King relinquishes the special rights which His vessels have been accorded with regard to coasting trade and inland navigation in the waters of the Republic of China, and the Government of the Republic of China are prepared to take over any properties of His Majesty's nationals or companies which have been used for the purposes of these trades and which the owners may wish to dispose of and pay adequate compensation therefor. The Government of the Republic of China relinquish the special rights which have been accorded to Chinese vessels in respect of naviagation on the river Irrawaddy under Article 12 of the Convention signed in London on March 1st, 1894. Should one High Contracting Party accord in any of his territories the right of coasting trade or inland navigation to the vessels of any third country, such rights would similarly be accorded to the vessels of the other High Contracting Party provided that the latter High Contracting Party permits the vessels of the former High Contracting Party to engage in the coasting trade or inland navigation of his territories. Coasting trade and inland navigation are excepted from the requirement of national treatment and are to be regulated according to the laws of each High Contracting Party in relation thereto. It is agreed, however, that the vessels of either High Contracting Party shall enjoy within the territories of the other High Contracting Party with regard to coasting trade and inland navigation treatment as favorable as that accorded to the vessels of any third country subject to the above mentioned proviso.

2. With reference to the last sentence of Article 5(1) of the Treaty, the Government of the Republic of China declare that the restriction on the right of alienation of existing rights and titles to real property referred to in that Article will be applied by the Chinese authorities in an equitable manner and that, if and when the Chinese Government decline to assent to a proposed transfer, the Chinese Government will, in a spirit of justice and with a view to precluding loss on the part of the nationals or companies of His Majesty

the King whose interests are affected, undertake, if so requested by the national or company of His Majesty to whom
permission to alienate has been refused, to take over the
rights and titles in question and pay adequate compensation
therefor.

3. It is understood that the abolition of the system of the
Treaty Ports will not affect existing property rights and that
the nationals of each High Contracting Party will enjoy the
right to acquire and hold real property throughout the territories of the other High Contracting Party in accordance
with the conditions and requirements prescribed in the laws
and regulations of that High Contracting Party.

4. It is further agreed that questions which may affect
the sovereignty of the Republic of China and which are not
covered by the present Treaty or by the preceeding provisions of the present Note shall be discussed by the Representatives of the Government of the Repbulic of China and
His Majesty's Government in the United Kingdom and decided
in accordance with the generally accepted principles of international law and modern international practice.

II. Note from Sir Horace James Seymour to Dr. Tse Vung
Soong, Chinese Minister for Foreign Affairs

Chungking, January 11th, 1943

Sir,

I have the honour to acknowledge receipt of Your Excellency's Note of today's date reading as follows:

[as in Note I]

I have the honour on behalf of His Majesty's Government
in the United Kingdom to confirm the understandings reached
between us as recorded in the annex to Your Excellency's
Note, which annex shall be considered as an integral part of
the Treaty signed today and shall be considered as effective
upon the date of the entrance into force of that Treaty.

I avail myself of this opportunity to renew to Your Excellency the assurance of my highest consideration.

(Signed)   H.J. Seymour

His Excellency

Dr. Tse Vung Soong,

Minister for Foreign Affairs

of the Republic of China,

Chungking.

III. Note from Dr. Tse Vung Soong, Chinese Minister for Foreign Affairs, to Mr. Hugh Edward Richardson

Chungking, January 11th, 1943

[identical with Note I.]

Hugh Edward Richardson, Esquire,

Indian Agency General,

Chungking.

Annex

[as in Note I]

IV. Note from Hugh Edward Richardson to Dr. Tse Vung Soong, Chinese Minister for Foreign Affairs

Chungking, January 11th, 1943

[identical with Note II]

(Signed)   H. E. Richardson

His   Excellency
> Dr. Tse Vung Soong,
>   Minister for Foreign Affairs
>   of the Republic of China,
>   Chungking.

Agreed Minute

With reference to paragraph 1(a) of the Annex to the Note from the Chinese Minister for Foreign Affairs to His Majesty's Ambassador in connection with the Treaty signed today, it is understood that both High Contracting Parties reserve the right to close any port to all overseas merchant shipping for reasons of national security.

With reference to paragraph 1(g) of the Annex to the Note from the Chinese Minister for Foreign Affairs to His Majesty's Ambassador in connection with the Treaty signed today, His Majesty's Ambassador informed the Chinese Government that trade between India on the one hand and Burma or Ceylon on the other has always been regarded as coasting trade.

(Signed)   Tse Vung Soong

(Signed)   H. J. Seymour

Chungking,

January 11th, 1943.

BIBLIOGRAPHICAL NOTE

This Bibliographical Note does not comprise all the publications cited in the footnotes. For the guidance of general readers, it gives a brief explanation of several important works and some information on other references. As this book is designed chiefly for the Western public, English sources are cited wherever available.

I. TREATIES WITH OR CONCERNING CHINA

Primary sources of this book are drawn from treaties between China and foreign powers and other international agreements concerning China. Vast in number, they are not listed here; instead, a special Index of Treaties is compiled in addition to the Subject Index. This arrangement has the advantage of providing pagination of reference as well as the contracting parties and dates.

II. COLLECTIONS OF TREATIES, DIPLOMATIC CORRESPONDENCE, AND OTHER DOCUMENTS

The following collections are frequently referred to in this book: Treaties and Conventions between China and Foreign States (Shanghai: the Statistical Department of the Inspectorate General of the Chinese Maritime Customs, 2nd ed., 1917, 2 vols., covering the period 1689-1915, with texts in Chinese and other languages; cited as Chinese Customs, Treaties); Treaties, etc., between Great Britain and China; and between China and Foreign Powers; and Orders in Council, Rules, Regulations, Acts of Parliament, Decrees, etc., Affecting British Interests in China (edited by Edward Hertslet, 3rd ed. by Godfrey E. P. Hertslet, covering the period 1689-1907, 2 vols.; London: Harison & Sons, 1908; cited as Hertslet,

Treaties); John V. A. MacMurray, Treaties and Agreements with and concerning China, 1894-1919 (New York: Oxford University Press, 1921, 2 vols.; cited as MacMurray, Treaties).

Two collections of early treaties are occasionally used: William Frederick Mayers, Treaties between the Empire of China and Foreign Powers (London: Trubner & Co., 1877; cited as Mayers, Treaties); William Woodville Rockhill, Treaties and Conventions with or concerning China and Korea, 1894-1904 (Washington, D.C.: Government Printing Office, 1904; an important source of reference before being merged with MacMurray's work; cited as Rockhill, Treaties).

For treaties concluded after the establishment of the Chinese Republic, the following collections are essential: Treaties and Agreements with and concerning China, 1919-1929 (Washington, D.C.: Carnegie Endowment for International Peace, 1929; cited as Carnegie, Treaties); Treaties between the Republic of China and Foreign States, 1927-1957 (Taipei: Chinese Ministry of Foreign Affairs, 1958; two supplementary volumes covering the periods 1958-1961 and 1962-1964, published in 1963 and 1965 respectively; with texts in Chinese and other languages; cited as Chinese Republic, Treaties); Yin-Ching Chen, Treaties and Agreements between the Republic of China and Other Powers, 1929-1954 (Washington, D.C.: Sino-American Publishing Service, 1957; cited as Chen, Treaties); Chung Hua Jen Min Kung Ho Kuo Yu Hao T'iao Yüen Chi or The Collected Treaties of Amity of the Chinese People's Republic (Peking: Ministry of Foreign Affairs, 1965; containing only treaties of amity, with texts in Chinese and other languages; cited as CPR, Collected Treaties); Chung Hua Jen Min Kung Ho Kuo T'iao Yüeh Chi or The Collection of Treaties of the Chinese People's Republic of China (Peking: Institute of Legal Publications; from Volume 11, by World Cultural Institute; up to 1965, 13 vols. published, covering the period 1949-1964; in Chinese only; cited as CPR, Treaties).

other publications of treaties and diplomatic correspondence are also used for supplementary purposes. These include: British Parliamentary Papers (London, 1801-); British and Foreign State Papers (compiled and edited in the Librarian's Department of the Foreign Office, London, 1812-); Papers relating to the Foreign Relations of the United States

(Washington, D.C.: Government Printing Office, 1861-; cited as U. S. For. Rel.); League of Nations Treaty Series; United Nations Treaty Series; British Treaty Series; U.S. Treaty Series.

Reference is also made to numerous government publications on specific issues, for instance, the Indian Ministry of External Affairs, White Paper: Notes, Memoranda and Letters Exchanged and Agreements Signed between the Governments of India and China (New Delhi, 10 vols., covering the period 1959-1964; cited as The Indian White Paper). The Foreign Languages Press in Peking published many booklets and pamphlets on foreign relations in English, such as Seven Letters Exchanged between the Central Committees of the Communist Party of China and the Communist Party of the Soviet Union (1964) and The Sino-Indian Boundary Question (enlarged ed., 1962; one supplementary volume, 1965).

The following Chinese works contain a large number of official documents not available in English: Ch'ou Pan Yi Wu Shih Mo, a collection of official documents relating to China's foreign relations, 1836-1874 (Peking: Palace Museum, 1929-1931, 130 vols.); Ch'ing Chi Wai Chiao Shih Liao, containing diplomatic documents of the last two Reigns of the Ch'ing dynasty, 1875-1911 (compiled by Ne-wei Wang, published by Hsi-yuan Wang in Peking, 1932-1935, 164 vols.). During the Republican period, several collections of Chinese laws and other documents are available, including the edition by the Legislative Yuan of the National Government (Shanghai: Chung Hua Press, 1934, 9 vols., in Chinese) and another edition compiled by P. G. Hsu and P. F. Wu (Shanghai: Commercial Press, 1936, 11 vols., in Chinese). A comprehensive collection of diplomatic documents for the period of the People's Republic of China is Chung Hua Jen Min Kung Ho Kuo Tui Wai Kuan Hsi Wên Chien Chi or Diplomatic Archives of the People's Republic of China (Peking: World Cultural Institute, 10 vols. up to 1965, covering the period 1949-1963; in Chinese; cited as CPR, Diplomatic Archives).

III. OTHER BOOKS, PAMPHLETS, AND PERIODICALS

References other than the above-mentioned collections are numerous. Since their full titles and publishing data are indicated on first appearance in the text, readers are advised to consult specific sources in the footnotes pertinent to various topics. Much space is thus saved by not repeating the listing here. Among many valuable works, the following are particularly useful for general information on China's treaty relations: Hosea Ballou Morse, The International Relations of the Chinese Empire (New York: Longmans, Green & Co., 3 vols.; Vol. I, 1910; Vols. II and III, 1918; cited as Morse); Westel W. Willoughby, Foreign Rights and Interests in China (Baltimore: Johns Hopkins Press, rev. ed., 1927, 2 vols.; cited as Willoughby); Min-ch'ien T. Z. Tyau, The Legal Obligations Arising out of Treaty Relations between China and Other States (Shanghai: Commercial Press, 1917; cited as Tyau); Tai Tsien, Chung Kuo Pou P'ing Têng T'iao Yüen Chi Yüan Ch'i Chi Ch'i Fei Ch'u Chi Ching Kuo or The Origin and Abolition of Unequal Treaties in China (Taipei: Institute for the Study of National Defense, 1961; in Chinese; cited as Tsien).

The yearbooks on China were published under different titles in different places: The China Year Book, published in London, Tientsin, and Shanghai, from 1912 to 1939, edited by H. G. Woodhead; The Chinese Year Book, published by the Commercial Press, Shanghai, from 1936 to 1945; China Handbook, 1937-1945, published by the Macmillan Company, New York. After World War II, the title of China Handbook was continuously used but has now been changed to China Yearbook, published in Taipei, Taiwan.

Early periodicals used for reference include Chinese Repository (Canton, monthly, May 1832-December 1851); North China Herald (weekly edition of the North China Daily News; Shanghai, 1850-1941); Chinese Social and Political Science Review (Peking, quarterly, 1916-1941). Among the current ones, The China Quarterly (London) contains many valuable articles on Communist China. The Journal of Asian Studies is especially useful for its "Bibliography of Asian Studies," published in September annually.

Reference is also made to magazines and newspapers published in Taiwan and the mainland. The Central Daily News, Tso Kuo I Chou (weekly), and Free China Weekly (in English) have airmail editions. For Peking's official views, see Renmin Ribao (Jen-min Jih-pao or People's

Daily), Hongqi (Hung-ch'i or Red Flag, formerly semi-
monthly, monthly since 1965), Peking Review (weekly, in
English; successor to People's China and China Digest),
and also daily news released in English by Hsinhua News
Agency (NCNA). Among the publications by the American
Consulate-General in Hongkong, Current Background, Survey of China Mainland Press, and Extracts from China Mainland Publications are frequently consulted for developments
on China's mainland.

INDEX OF TREATIES

This Index comprises chiefly treaties under different designations. It also contains bipartite and multipartite contracts, as well as Chinese and foreign official acts, such as laws and decrees, diplomatic correspondence, and official statements, which are concerned with China's foreign relations. For convenience, these documents are classified into four categories in the following order: (1) bilateral treaties and other engagements between China and other powers, (2) multilateral treaties and other engagements of which China is a party, (3) treaties and other engagements between other powers concerning China, and (4) Chinese and foreign official acts concerning their mutual relations. Among the treaties, the following are of unique nature: (a) imposed by foreign powers but rejected by China, (b) concluded by foreign powers with regional authorities of China, and (c) adhered to by one government of China but denounced by the other during the period of civil war. Under category (1), countries are classified according to alphabetical order; entries in all categories are arranged chronologically. For listings other than the above, reference should be made to the Subject Index.

I. BILATERAL TREATIES AND OTHER ENGAGEMENTS BETWEEN CHINA AND OTHER POWERS

Afghanistan
3/2/1944   Treaty of Friendship. 382,n.108,n.109
8/26/1960   Treaty of Friendship and Mutual Non-aggression. 359
11/22/1963   Boundary Treaty. 359;382,n.111

Austria (also Austria-Hungary)
9/2/1869   Treaty of Peking (with Austria-Hungary). 41,n.89; 275,n.3

plementation of the Geneva Agreements. 414-
415,n.34

II. MULTILATERAL TREATIES AND OTHER ENGAGEMENTS OF
WHICH CHINA IS A PARTY

1869   Rules Governing the Mixed Court in Shanghai.
                  113,115;133,n.37,n.44
7/6/1895   Contract with France and Russia (Franco-Russian
                  Syndicate) for the Chinese 4% Gold Loan of
                  1895. 123
3/23/1896   Agreement with Germany (Deutsche-Asiatische
                  Bank) and Great Britain (Hongkong and Shang-
                  hai Banking Corp.) for the Chinese Imperial
                  Government 5% Sterling Loan of 1896. 123
3/1/1898   Agreement with Germany (Deutsch-Asiatische
                  Bank) and Great Britain (Hongkong and Shang-
                  hai Banking Corp.) for the Chinese Imperial
                  Government 4.5% Gold Loan of 1898. 123
1/16/1901   Joint Note Sent by the Allied Powers to China. 74
9/7/1901   Final Protocol for the Settlement of Disturbances
                  of 1900.   53;55;74;84;98, n.78;98, n.79, n.80;
                  108;110;129, n.19;138, n.90;146;167, n.5;219;
                  266;312;322;324
6/14/1902   Protocol regarding Apportionment of the Boxer
                  Indemnity. 138,n.90
1902-1904   Tariff Agreements relating to the Revised Import
                  Tariff of 1902 (signed with 15 powers on 8/29/
                  1902; 3/28/1903; 3/23,30/1904; 11/11/1904).
                  111
6/13/1904   Protocol regarding Legation Quarter at Peking. 74
1907   Hague Convention on Opening Hostilities. 291,n.133
1/13/1908   Agreement with Germany (Deutsch-Asiatische
                  Bank) and Great Britain (Chinese Central Rail-
                  way, Ltd.) for the Chinese Imperial Govern-
                  ment 5% Tientsin-Pukou Railway Loan.   118
10/8/1908   Agreement with France (Banque de l'Indo-Chine)
                  and Great Britain (Hongkong and Shanghai
                  Banking Corp.) for a Loan of £5,000,000 to the
                  Board of Posts and Communications.   117
4/15/1911   Agreement with France (Banque de l'Indo-Chine),
                  Germany (Deutsch-Asiatische Bank), Great
                  Britain (Hongkong and Shanghai Banking Corp.),
                  and the United States (American Group), for

III. TREATIES AND OTHER ENGAGEMENTS BETWEEN OTHER POWERS CONCERNING CHINA

IV. CHINESE AND FOREIGN OFFICIAL ACTS CONCERNING THEIR MUTUAL RELATIONS

6/7/1906   Japanese Imperial Ordinance Sanctioning Organization of South Manchuria Railway Company. 121

8/1/1906   Japanese Government Order regarding South Manchuria Railway Company. 135,n.77,n.78

3/18/1913   Statement of the United States Government in regard to the Support requested by the American Banking Group. 124;138,n.93

7/25/1919   Karakhan Declaration (Declaration of Soviet policy, signed by Karakhan to the Chinese People and to the Governments of North and South China). 203;219,220;224;239,n.4.n.8;273

8/2/1919   Statement of Japanese Minister for Foreign Affairs on the Shantung Question. 181,n.100

8/6/1919   Statement of President Wilson on the Shantung Question. 181,n.100

9/27/1920   Karakhan Declaration (second one). 220

1/27/1927   Statement by the Department of State concerning United States Policy in China. 233

4/3/1948   China Aid Act of the United States. 299;327,n.14

6/27/1950   Statement of President Truman concerning Formosa (Taiwan). 311

9/5/1951   Statement of John Foster Dulles, Special Representative of the United States President, at San Francisco, concerning China. 310;336, n.115

January 1955   Joint Resolution of United States Congress, Authorizing the President to Employ American Armed Forces to Defend Taiwan and the Pescadores (Penghu). 347

SUBJECT INDEX

(For treaties and other documents concerning China's foreign relations, see the Index of Treaties and Other Documents.)

Tai, Tse, 172,n.34

Taiping Rebellion (Revolution), 24; 26; 45; 107; 128,n.1; 151; 152; 173,n.41,n.42,n.43

Ever Victorious Army, 152

Taiwan (Formosa), 5; 10; 45; 46; 47; 58,n.24; 169,n.16; 269; 274; 303; 309; 310; 311; 313; 319; 335,n.99, n.100; 346; 347; 348-349; 361; 369, n.11, n.16; 370,n.20, n.21; 390; 393; 397; 405; 408; 409; 420,n.80; 425,n.115

Formosa Incident, 196,n.16

Formosa Strait, 311; 345; 347; 393

Republic of, 46

Taiwanese, 408; 409; 425,n. 115

Takaaki, Kato, 175,n.62

Takahira, Kogoro, 76

Taku Forts, 25; 26; 52; 53; 54; 65,n.75; 84

Talai Railway, 284,n.93

Talifu, 28

Tanaka, Giichi, 258

T'ang Dynasty, 2; 43

T'ai-tsung, Emperor, 12,n.4

Tangshan, 105,n.118

Tannu-Tuva, 355,n.379,n.81

Tao-Ching Railway, 119

Taokow-Chinghua Railway, 119

Taonanfu, 136,n.78; 137,n.84

Taonanfu-Anganshi Railway, 136,n.78

Taonanfu-Jehol Railway, 137,n. 84

Taotai, 107; 114

Tariff, Chinese, 54; 107; 110; 111; 123; 130,n.24; 192; 202; 203; 211,n.40; 250; 281,n.69

autonomy, 9; 193; 203; 204; 252; 254; 255; 282,n.73

customs duties, 56,n.9; 86; 110; 253

restrictions, 9; 100-111; 249; 250; 255

revision, 28, 111

rules, 110; 128,n.2

Tariff, Chinese (continued)

uniform, 8; 20; 21; 22; 107; 110; 111; 160

Tariff Conference at Peking, 254; 281,n.69; 282,n.71

Tashichiao-Yingkow Railway, 121

Teheran Conference, 269

Thailand, 12,n.1; 131,n.25; 395; 396; 399; 400; 401; 416, n. 41; 419,n.71,n.72; 421,n. 82; 422,n.95; 423,n.98,n.99;

Thiers, 148

Third International, The, 224; 226; 228,n.22

Tibet, 8; 59,n.37; 75; 77-80; 313; 316-319; 337,n.119; 339,n.144; 341,n.158; 358; 363; 385,n.141; 392; 396; 417,n.47

Autonomous Region of, 317; 339,n.142; 362

British Mission of Exploration, 29; 77-80

Dalai Lama, 318; 339,n.140

Inner Tibet, 79

Outer Tibet, 79

Tien-shan region, 354

Tientsin, 72; 73; 105,n.118; 169, n.13; 322; 323

Tientsin-Pukow Railway, 118

Tinghai, 20

Tito, Marshal, 35; 350; 374

Togo, 411,n.6

Tokyo, 183,n.113

Trans-Siberian Railway, 76

Transit duty, Chinese, 101,n. 100

Treaty,

designations of, 8

reciprocal provisions of, 8; 99,n.89; 249; 254; 282,n.73; 299

revision of (Chinese), 23; 25; 54; 250; 251; 252; 253; 256; 279,n.45

Tributary system, Chinese, 1; 2; 12,n.1; 47; 59,n.36; 357